I0188010

Subordinated Ethics

VERITAS
Series Introduction

"... the truth will set you free" (John 8:32)

In much contemporary discourse, Pilate's question has been taken to mark the absolute boundary of human thought. Beyond this boundary, it is often suggested, is an intellectual hinterland into which we must not venture. This terrain is an agnosticism of thought: because truth cannot be possessed, it must not be spoken. Thus, it is argued that the defenders of "truth" in our day are often traffickers in ideology, merchants of counterfeits, or anti-liberal. They are, because it is somewhat taken for granted that Nietzsche's word is final: truth is the domain of tyranny.

Is this indeed the case, or might another vision of truth offer itself? The ancient Greeks named the love of wisdom as *philia*, or friendship. The one who would become wise, they argued, would be a "friend of truth." For both philosophy and theology might be conceived as schools in the friendship of truth, as a kind of relation. For like friendship, truth is as much discovered as it is made. If truth is then so elusive, if its domain is *terra incognita*, perhaps this is because it arrives to us—unannounced—as gift, as a person, and not some thing.

The aim of the Veritas book series is to publish incisive and original current scholarly work that inhabits "the between" and "the beyond" of theology and philosophy. These volumes will all share a common aspiration to transcend the institutional divorce in which these two disciplines often find themselves, and to engage questions of pressing concern to both philosophers and theologians in such a way as to reinvigorate both disciplines with a kind of interdisciplinary desire, often so absent in contemporary academe. In a word, these volumes represent collective efforts in the befriending of truth, doing so beyond the simulacra of pretend tolerance, the violent, yet insipid reasoning of liberalism that asks with Pilate, "What is truth?"—expecting a consensus of non-commitment; one that encourages the commodification of the mind, now sedated by the civil service of career, ministered by the frightened patrons of position.

The series will therefore consist of two "wings": (1) original monographs; and (2) essay collections on a range of topics in theology and philosophy. The latter will principally be the products of the annual conferences of the Centre of Theology and Philosophy (www.theologyphilosophycentre .co.uk).

Conor Cunningham and Eric Austin Lee, *Series editors*

Not available from Cascade

Deane-Peter Baker	*Tayloring Reformed Epistemology: The Challenge to Christian Belief.* Volume 1
P. Candler & C. Cunningham (eds.)	*Belief and Metaphysics.* Volume 2
Marcus Pound	*Theology, Psychoanalysis, and Trauma.* Volume 4
Espen Dahl	*Phenomenology and the Holy.* Volume 5
C. Cunningham et al. (eds.)	*Grandeur of Reason: Religion, Tradition, and Universalism.* Volume 6
A. Pabst & A. Paddison (eds.)	*The Pope and Jesus of Nazareth: Christ, Scripture, and the Church.* Volume 7
J. P. Moreland	*Recalcitrant Imago Dei: Human Persons and the Failure of Naturalism.* Volume 8

Available from Cascade Books

[Nathan Kerr	*Christ, History, and Apocalyptic: The Politics of Christian Mission.* Volume 3][1]
Anthony D. Baker	*Diagonal Advance: Perfection in Christian Theology.* Volume 9
D. C. Schindler	*The Perfection of Freedom: Schiller, Schelling, and Hegel between the Ancients and the Moderns.* Volume 10
Rustin Brian	*Covering Up Luther: How Barth's Christology Challenged the Deus Absconditus that Haunts Modernity.* Volume 11
Timothy Stanley	*Protestant Metaphysics After Karl Barth and Martin Heidegger.* Volume 12
Christopher Ben Simpson	*The Truth Is the Way: Kierkegaard's Theologia Viatorum.* Volume 13
Richard H. Bell	*Wagner's Parsifal: An Appreciation in the Light of His Theological Journey.* Volume 14
Antonio Lopez	*Gift and the Unity of Being.* Volume 15
Toyohiko Kagawa	*Cosmic Purpose.* Translated and introduced by Thomas John Hastings. Volume 16
Nigel Zimmerman	*Facing the Other: John Paul II, Levinas, and the Body.* Volume 17
Conor Sweeney	*Sacramental Presence after Heidegger: Onto-theology, Sacraments, and the Mother's Smile.* Volume 18
John Behr et al. (eds.)	*The Role of Death in Life: A Multidisciplinary Examination of the Relation between Life and Death.* Volume 19

---

1. Note: Nathan Kerr, *Christ, History, and Apocalyptic,* although volume 3 of the original SCM Veritas series is available from Cascade as part of the Theopolitical Visions series.

Subordinated Ethics

Natural Law and Moral Miscellany
in Aquinas and Dostoyevsky

CAITLIN SMITH GILSON

Foreword by ERIC AUSTIN LEE

CASCADE *Books* · Eugene, Oregon

SUBORDINATED ETHICS
Natural Law and Moral Miscellany in Aquinas and Dostoyevsky

Veritas 38

Copyright © 2020 Caitlin Smith Gilson. All rights reserved. Except for brief quotations in critical publications or reviews, no part of this book may be reproduced in any manner without prior written permission from the publisher. Write: Permissions, Wipf and Stock Publishers, 199 W. 8th Ave., Suite 3, Eugene, OR 97401.

Cascade Books
An Imprint of Wipf and Stock Publishers
199 W. 8th Ave., Suite 3
Eugene, OR 97401

www.wipfandstock.com

ISBN: 978-1-53268-640-5

Cataloguing-in-Publication data:

Names: Smith Gilson, Caitlin, author. | Lee, Eric Austin, foreword.
Title: Subordinated ethics : natural law and moral miscellany in Aquinas and Dostoyevsky / Caitlin Smith Gilson ; foreword by Eric Austin Lee.
Description: Eugene, OR : Cascade Books, 2020 | Series: Veritas 38 | Includes bibliographical references and index.

Subjects: LCSH: Ethics. | Natural law. | Thomas—Aquinas Saint—1225?–1274. | Dostoyevsky, Fyodor, 1821–1881. | Law and ethics.
Classification: BJ1012 .S57 2020 (print) | BJ1012 .S57 (ebook)

For Our Daisi,

You were and are everything that's right about this world: endlessly gentle, unknowingly beautiful, with a wit that could make one find that ethereally silly part in the soul which may well be the only needful thing in this world. Alternatively, that same wit, always and equally spirit, would return you to the ground with a wisdom older than any single age. So, my dear eternal child, I think you know better than most that your death is everything wrong with the world, and because of this, we are lost without you. We cannot of our own power make it right, just as we cannot make the rain fall and the grass grow, and yet we need these things to live and to love. Nor can we be the ocean waves at play and the mountains at dusk, as you were little one. You were these things! We will forever breathe the earth and breathe you, now the elegy of the birdsong at morning's break. Please help me to love as best as I can, and thus to love as you loved; and to laugh as best as I can, and thus to laugh as you laughed. Perhaps then you may bring us up into that joy that incarnates every worthy moment in this life and the next, and return us to soft pastures underfoot.

—Love Always,

Your Aunt Caitlin

There's a famous freak rock near us,
A black savage skull of a thing on the moor.
Monks built a chapel there and one wall stands
Facing the sea still, high on the schorl mass.
Gales from both coasts have struck the pinnacle
A thousand times, and shaken this church door
Which we approached under fragrant leafage
Up the lane from a July-scorched stile ...
Something remains impregnable, holds evidence
Without a technique of defence.

—Jack Clemo, "In Roche Church"

Contents

Foreword

"Entering the Chase":
The Effortless Drama of Natural Law's *longior via*

IT IS ALL TOO easy to enshrine discussions of natural law within current political accounts of ultimately facile and pithy attempts at moralistic obedience. The political false dilemmas of any given decade in this sense are as reactionary as they are legion. If we agree with one Catholic saint invoking another that the natural law is nothing else but "the light of understanding infused in us by God, whereby we understand what must be done and what must be avoided" to the extent that this light was even given to us as a law upon our hearts at our very creation,[1] then surely we know what propositional, mental, and obediential boxes to check. It is an odd predicament we find ourselves in when we can in one sense be wholly "right" by one light yet in our prescriptive anger we can snuff out that same light of understanding in an unattractive false certitude which cuts to the quick in premature reduction. We do ourselves and others no favors if while we claim that we see in a glass darkly we further darken our vision with varieties of unnecessary moralistic fallibilism and thus offer a blind path for others.[2]

The path forward is not easy, to be sure, so we could offer instead that the drama of existence is an essentially difficult one. There is a deep truth to affirm along with Socrates (who affirms an ancient proverb) that all that is beautiful is difficult.[3] Again, we must be careful, for while it is true to say that God is love, the obverse that all love is God is not a

---

1. *Veritatis Splendor*, §40, quoting Thomas Aquinas, "Prologus: Opuscula Theo-logica," II, no. 1129, p. 245; Cf. Thomas Aquinas, *ST* II-II, 91, 2.

2. See Aquinas, *ST* I-II, 48, 3.

3. Plato, *Hippias Major*, 304e8.

theological truth, lest we endanger ourselves toward pantheistic platitudes; likewise, all that is difficult may not be beautiful, and a struggle
for its own sake may lend itself more toward a merely pagan virtue that
is ultimately closer to classical or Enlightenment *agon* than may be truly
beautiful, true, or good. Accordingly, we seem to harbor an implicit mis-
trust of that which is effortless because we do not want to accept that
which is a gift.[4] Natural law must be fought for, indeed, it could be argued
that we must defend it for its own sake because tradition must of itself
resist all change and maintain continuity to stem the tide of an over-eager
progressivism.

   In one sense this sounds like an upright and righteous charge, but in
and of itself it is a fallibilist posture that demands that natural law has to
always incur the hard work of the theologian, philosopher, or pastor that
still finds itself within another modern dilemma of technocracy versus
populism: virtue is found within the learnèd "virtuous," and the rest of
us simple folk have the option of blind deference or the *ressentiment* of
rejection. The gospel is hidden from the learned and wise, and revealed
to the simple, the child-like;[5] this is true, but does this yet lead us to conclude that the head no longer requires feet or vice versa?[6] If we keep with
this Pauline metaphor for a moment, insisting that we can work out our
part in the hard work alone of our position, the "true" is only won at the
expense of the good, and what's more, at the expense of the other. On
the contrary, Josef Pieper highlights this problematic when he notes that
for Aquinas, "The essence of virtue consists in the good rather than in
the difficult." That is, "Not everything that is more difficult is necessarily
more meritorious; it must be more difficult in such a way that it is at the
same time good in yet a higher way."[7] Along with Aquinas, Pieper dares
to suggest against our modern proclivity toward the self-meritorious difficulty of work that "the sublime achievements of moral goodness are
characterized by effortlessness—because it is of their essence to spring
from love."[8] Yet once more, "effortlessness" is not the goal either, in the
same way that difficulty for its own sake is not the goal, for the end is that
which is good for its own sake, a life lived in love of God and neighbor.

4. See Pieper, *Leisure: The Basis of Culture*, 35–36.

5. Luke 10:21.

6. Cf. 1 Cor 12:21.

7. Pieper, *Leisure*, 33–34, citing Aquinas, *ST* II-II, 123, 12, ad. 2 and *ST* II-II, 27,
8, ad. 2.

8. Pieper, *Leisure*, 34.

If neither difficulty nor effortlessness for their own sakes are the goal, but may both be very real descriptions of the experience of living out a life lived within an obedience to the natural law, Gilson recommends something different than prescription and something otherwise than reactionary steadfastness. *Subordinated Ethics* is not a detailed treatise on the specifics of natural law theory nor a set of recipes for how one "enacts" the natural law within a series of steps to follow, cultural attitudes to mimic, nor particular "stances" to take—although, of course, many ethical ways of life naturally follow within a path taken along this route, and that is precisely her point: the natural law is that which first and foremost is itself not first, but second, for it itself *follows* the eternal law.

Following along such a path begins here by way of an acknowledgement in the form of a response. Gilson, who often has St. Thomas as her guide, proposes here a longer way that "ends its journey in seeing what was there to begin with and what initiated its pilgrimage: the non-mediated presence of *To Be*. The journey itself is a *response* to the non-mediated mystery of being."[9] Here, as in her previous work, Gilson explores the nature of the *longior via* ("longer way") by attending to a metaphysics of causality that finds its "resolution" in God. To understand the path of the *longior via* it is important to acknowledge that this road is not purely immediate grasping of cause and effect, but the truth of this way is discovered along a road that realizes our creaturely place in the order of things. Again, this path is not simply a pronouncement of affirming that God is the ultimate cause because we somehow have direct access to God as the first cause.[10] As Gilson says elsewhere, "The longer way is a twofold process: we begin in effects and arrive at first causes *only* because we already understand the nature of effects to be effects *of*. We possess or partake in causal meaning as original to our being. Causative efficacy is identical with our own intentionality and our originary otherness. We possess not the knowledge but the ground of knowledge which is, in its way of the uncreated."[11] Along with Aquinas, Gilson affirms our creaturely, existential situation of always already being *in via*, on the way, where we find

9. C. Gilson, *Immediacy and Meaning*, xii, emphasis in original.

10. Aquinas calls this particular misstep an error of the Platonists. See *Commentary on the Metaphysics of Aristotle*, X, 3.1964.

11. C. Gilson, *Immediacy and Meaning*, 180, emphasis hers. *Commentary on the Metaphysics of Aristotle*, X, 3.1964. Thomas also notes that Plato errors in a similar way in conflating the order of knowledge with the separable forms (*ST*, I, 84, 1).

ourselves within a world of effects, and where we ourselves are an "effect" born out of our own otherness within creation. Making the next step to acknowledging the causality is what Aquinas calls a "resolution" within being from the sensible to the intellectual of the divine science.[12] Hence, in this way, the first becomes that which for us is the last: for it is only natural to proceed "from the sensible to the intelligible, from the effects to the causes, and from that which is later to the first."[13] This "reversal" from that which is last in the order of things to the first uncaused cause requires a metaphysical judgment that Gilson calls a necessity to stop, or *ananke stenai*: "The *ananke stenai* is the originating stop in the order of explanation and in Being."[14] Without such a judgment the spectre of an infinite (or as she calls it, "indefinite") regress would paradoxically limit our ability to see things as they truly are. In every exploration of the various five ways of Thomas, Gilson shows us that one must at some point recognize that all the things of the world, within the spectrum of their miscellany, point back to that which is first—this very recognition is itself the judgment which enacts the "resolution" where we find ourselves within the viatoric chase of our creaturely existence toward the infinite.

Gilson's proposal to "enter the chase," therefore, is discerned and lived as an achievement over a lifetime of living through the stuff of life, a life that has its place not among the angels in an immediate vision[15] but experienced in a "catching up" within the distance between God and man as existence itself. "This distance is the longer way, the way that allows finitude to be a 'vehicle' of transcendence. Through it there is always something more and Other, something not yet said and done, and thinking must indeed 'catch up' to Being."[16] Natural law, then, is not something to prescriptively secure[17] but is received within the analogical distance of living within the embrace of eternal law's inscription in our hearts.

---

12. See Aquinas, *In Boethii De trinitate*, q. 6, a. 1, co. 22. For a helpful summary of the details in Aquinas, see Aertsen, "Method and Metaphysics."

13. Aquinas, *In I Sent.*, 17, 1, 4. Translation Aertsen's.

14. C. Gilson, *Metaphysical Presuppositions*, 172. See especially chapter 4.

15. Aquinas, *ST* I, 65, 2, ad. 1: "Man was not intended to secure his ultimate perfection at once, like the angel. Hence a longer way was assigned to man than to the angel for securing beatitude."

16. C. Gilson, *Metaphysical Presuppositions*, 125.

17. See chapter 3, especially the section "Ten Principles in Search of an Author: Tradition, Virtues, Limits."

Woven throughout, Gilson also attends to Dostoyevsky's *The Idiot*, a work which she puts in conversation with Thomas's five ways that may at first appear tangential but draws us to the heart of things. Like her previous excursions,[18] here she brings in the literary and poetic to enlighten this notion of being "on the way" but here with a focus (along with Thomas Aquinas) on originary *praxis* by way of counterpoint. That is, Dostoyevsky's Myshkin exemplifies a longing to return to our origins, that longing to be reconnected with that "first" which we only discover "last." What both Thomas and Prince Myshkin illuminate is that our attitude and even, one might say, our metaphysical comportment need be reconfigured by the *act* of playfulness in order to return to our originary *praxis*. Our original practice as children is something we forget: our awe before existence, our desire to have an experience "again" (like that of a child's playful exuberance), our original ability to see the light of dawn where everything is again new. Whether we like it or not, we are entrenched within life's miscellany, and while we can all too easily romanticize the "messiness of life," Gilson, like these authors and literary characters with whom she is in conversation, takes us to an emphasis on that which is present, a present presence here in all its immediacy.

To rightly see the joy of these realities requires not merely philosophical and theological acumen but a simplicity of heart. That is not to say, however, that these two need be opposed. The effortlessness spoken of above can indeed be learned by way of habit, of the action of our intellect which engages in the child-like play that is the very essence of such a simplicity. One of the many joys of being a parent[19] is that paradoxical endurance of learning again to have the heart of a child. Learning to return to our own originary *praxis* is done amidst an encounter with an other, a presence that calls us again and again to not only start over, but to become that which is itself good.[20] Lest we further confuse ourselves, one cannot simply abide by a prescription to "be child-like" either, because it is itself a practice to inhabit, a suggestion to live within the risk of an embodied, soul-entrenched immediacy within a world that claims it is the

18. C. Gilson, *Immediacy and Meaning*.

19. I mean this in the broadest sense possible, whether biological, foster, adoptive, as well as the pastors, deacons, priests, nuns, and the consecrated laity who are our fathers and mothers in that their own simplicity is to watch over us in prayer.

20. Cf. the section "Socrates as a Stand-In for the Good," in Schindler, *Plato's Critique*, 179–88.

most "grown up" thing to not have children for any number of excuses which purport to be "rational."

In reading this book by Gilson, I commend the reader to understand that it is written with—and should be read with—a deep allergy to all that is reactionary. That which is reactionary leads to moralistic prescription for it is not the basis of a generative, originary presence. That which resounds most truly in our soul is never the self-imposition of the ego but an openness to the otherness which is our existence made resplendent by the otherness of an infinite, Triune God in Whom we find our very being. Gilson's exhortation to this originary presence and to our originary practice can only be rediscovered as a *following* of the natural law that participates in the eternal law, eschewing imposition of both the conservative prescription as much as it so very much otherwise than the progressivist piety that is self-defined, in turn, by its reaction to this moralism. The path is as immediate as it is risked in the longer metaphysical and theological paths she recommends we travel by returning once again to Thomas's five ways. One can simply read the five ways or be inspired by Dostoyevsky's *Idiot* without inhabiting them; Kierkegaard's Johannes Climacus can see and write endlessly about what is on the other side of the "leap" without in fact taking that leap. Just because we fail over and over again when we do enter the chase should not be a fly in the ointment, but a spur for our souls.

> [T]he Church takes place and grows constantly in the hearts of people and in the living reality of environments and social situations. It does this in encounter with the living presence of Jesus Christ, in the existential self-enrichment of the certainty of this encounter, and in experiencing His real capacity to save the human being in all his drama and mundaneness.[21]

Eric Austin Lee

Eastertide 2019

---

21. Savorana, *Life of Luigi Giussani*, 637, citing Giussani's article "La certezza della fede e la cultura Cristiana" ["The Certainty of Christian Faith and Culture"], appearing in the October 29, 1982 issue of *L'Osservatore Romano* (translated by Sullivan and Bacich).

Preface

Stating the Problem of Ethical Enactment

> Knowing that a man is not justified by the works of the law,
> but by the faith of Jesus Christ, even we have believed in Jesus
> Christ, that we might be justified by the faith of Christ, and not
> by the works of the law: for by the works of the law shall no flesh
> be justified.
>
> —Galatians 2:16

THE MORAL LIFE CANNOT be left un-advocated—without a technique
of defence—and yet it lies about stifled by the professor and the
politician, the pedagogue and the propagandist; rigid and contrived
when it should *have* and *give* life.[1] It is an odd predicament—and perhaps
the predicament of our day, but I suspect otherwise—to find oneself
understanding those who relish revolt as much as languishing in its
consequences. And yet, can that desire to break free and put the tradition
into tension be solely a negative aspect of ethical meaning, can it be
solely the sensuous weapon of the progressive? How then is the reality
of a chaste anarchism[2] actually critical to the invocation of natural law?

---

1. We are bombarded by the ravages of societal manufacturing; quite simply the
Good can no longer compete with the spectral imprimatur of progressivism. Charles
Péguy, over a century ago, knew too well the progressivist attitude. Cf. Péguy, *Notre
Patrie*, 55: "Some people want to insult and abuse the army, because it is a good line
these days. . . . In fact, at all political demonstrations it is a required theme. If you do
not to take that line you do not look sufficiently progressive . . . and it will never be
known what acts of cowardice have been motivated by the fear of looking insufficiently
progressive."

2. Cf. C. Gilson, *Political Dialogue*.

If the ethical life in its modern and post-modern context is beautiful at all, it increasingly appears discovered in nostalgia, but nostalgia can only function as a propaedeutic to a good will when one does not seek merely to remake what once was. The temptation to nostalgia is forgivable but not without consequences. The world is the moving image of the eternal and yet always *novitas mundi*. If we concoct an ethics nostalgic for what it cannot relive, we live and abide by a frustrated end. Within that which cannot complete itself, the beautiful will flee, replaced by the bitter, or ridiculous, or revolutionary. And yet a nostalgia, not in competition with the futural, but intersecting in Presence, has more to offer ethics than a merely frustrated incompletion. When we let it place us in our failing it can instill in us repentance in the face of the finite form and a rediscovery of what has been lost in a new and renewed form.

How is there to be an ethic rebuilt in a godless world, which has violated foundational meaning, and if it needs to be rebuilt, does this demonstrate a failure on the part of the originary ethic? Does it mean that the authentic moral life must constantly be in a phoenix state, born to die? Or is there some other more primal identification whereby the ethic is *naturally* a failing; not a failure as such but an *in*-failing, that it cannot hold its own because it is not built to withstand, but instead to be subordinated? One with no technique of defence but courageous surrender; an ethic, which takes heed from Wittgenstein: "ethics, if it is anything, must be supernatural and our words will only express facts as a teacup will only hold a teacup full of water."[3] By subordinated, we mean an ethic that recognizes, when it places its natural law template upon experience, that an aspect of the natural law itself is obscured. The translation from immutable imbedded law to changeable and conditional law should not be managed with some worldly political facticity as the movement from that which is not in our power, the eternal law, to that which tempts us with the confluence of power, the human law. This odd straddling of the natural law between the two, as the revelation of the former and the foundation for the latter, reveals the natural law in the light of a certain playfulness—a quality of appearance and disappearance compatible with the alethiological emphasis of truth as un-veiling.[4] The natural law does not have an in-itself objectival quality: it is either the face of the

3. Wittgenstein, *Lectures on Ethics*, 9–10.

4. Cf. Heidegger, "Existential Structure of the Authentic Potentiality-for-Being which is Attested in the Conscience," §295–301. See also Plato's "Seventh Letter" in *Complete Works*, 344.

eternal law or the hidden bones beneath the flesh of the human law. It moves without capture. When it is caught it is more often than not the convention or *nomos* placed on the world, and yet it must be something more and other in order for those *nomoi* to be. This is the language game of tradition as enduring, and yet neither static nor uninformative. It also shows us that what is more apparent is actually the lesser, and yet, because the lesser, the human law is in our hands, and we press it into service as an imposition, as a leading position rather than as a struggling to catch-up to its source in-Being.[5] If the immutable and always preceding eternal law is understood *as* the natural law through our rational participation in it, and if this participation then creates the human law as mutable, then without our ability to take hold of the situation—to pause in the eternal and see it for what it is—we have moved from that which precedes and cannot fail to that which follows and fails in the blink of an eye. And so the awkwardness and danger of human action: we act *from* eternity when we act *in* time, with all the dangers and temptations implicit in that action. And yet, what else is there to do, even in spite of the postmodernist interdict on eternity in favor of the progressivist ideological political correctness which has ridiculed and exiled the natural public orthodoxy which, whatever its limitations, maintains the relation between human action and non-temporal implication and foundation. We have created an artifice structure in danger of becoming artificial, susceptible to a protracted and often intentional infidelity to the eternal. The eternal reveals itself in the natural, the natural in the human, and in one sense nothing is lost because that which is eternal cannot be stripped of Being, but the revelation on our side points to a failing, that our grasping of this eternality must be done through a blindness, that we only see the immutable through the mutable, through a glass darkly, the always preceding order through the shambolic malleability of the effects. If we do not recognize this failing, then we live by a non-subordinated ethics where the natural law takes on the mode of prescriptive imposition identical with the human law, pressed to lead rather than to follow. Or it is lost altogether. But ethics must find its true subordination in the reality of our exteriorized

5. See *ST* I-II, 97, 1, ad. 1: "The natural law is a participation of the eternal law, as stated above (I-II:92:2), and therefore endures without change, owing to the unchangeableness and perfection of the Divine Reason, the Author of nature. But the reason of man is changeable and imperfect: wherefore his law is subject to change. Moreover, the natural law contains certain universal precepts, which are everlasting: whereas human law contains certain particular precepts, according to various emergencies."

existence,[6] whereby the natural law occurs as connaturally "promulgated by the very fact that God instilled it into man's mind so as to be known by him naturally."[7] Any other subordination is false and is actually a form of in-subordination. But still there are times when the true subordinated ethic takes on the character of the chaste anarchist, an ethics of insubordination precisely because it will not surrender to anything other than its naturally supernatural ordering. And this is martyrdom.

Perhaps in response to our fallen and falling world, or perhaps because our personal and collective fear finds it easier to abide by a rule than to be the lived invocation of its intelligibility, ethical rules were placed at the forefront of human ordination, dilemma, and action. Ethics is pressed into a service it cannot fulfill. It is laden with the terrifying responsibility to lead, even and especially if the ethical system claims to adhere to divine meaning. The more rabidly defended, the more this adherence appears in name only. Ethics becomes the frontispiece of divine meaning, the way *into* the divine so that all theological understanding is malformed in a way not entirely dissimilar to Kant:[8] rendering God little more than a moral imperative, so much so that the whole theological drama can be read like one of Aesop's fables.[9] What is understood of

6. Cf. *ST* I, 75–76.

7. *ST* I-II, 90, 4, ad. 1.

8. For a prime example of the non-subordinated ethics see David Walsh's landmark work *The Modern Philosophical Revolution*, most particularly his chapter "Kant's 'Copernican Revolution' as Existential," 27–75. See also Péguy, *Man and Saints*, 57: "Kantianism has clean hands because it has no hands."

9. The deleterious results of a non-subordinated ethic can be seen most acutely in the debates over life. What is lost is the fact that all ethical questions must be subordinated to the Presence as spiritual, both as creative and incommunicable. When abortion was sequestered as solely and primarily an ethical and legal problem, the arguments for life were immeasurably weakened. Such advocacy functioned on a mis-remembering of metaphysical foundation that, even if acknowledged, was acknowledged in an artificial and strained manner. Abortion utilizes metaphysical and natural theology vis-à-vis a pernicious gnostic strain of reference to God, but one aimed more so at deviation and bypass. The questions over life bogged down into biological, scientific, and legal statutes which, again, can only pay lip-service to Christ. By beginning the argument for life in the natural impossibly divorced from the supernatural, the ethical realm is improperly emancipated from its subordination to the spiritual and metaphysical dimensions which illuminate the universalizing particularity of the God-Man. This diminished form of ethics is then pressed to argue for a totality of meaning which it cannot possess. Pro-life advocacy seeks an eerily similar Hegelian program to absolutize its points precisely because it had deviated from the only absolute which can be concrete, particular, and creative: the only mystery to invoke clarity.

ethics, and what is affectively impressed upon us, is an ethics disengaged from any otherness, and held only and openly within and by itself. Ethical action has taken on the language and imprimatur of the conscience symbol—a self-enclosed ideational dictum—and in doing so has evacuated the primitive and the mystical, the mysterious and the super-sensual which once gave rise to moral order, when the sacred knew its ground *because* it was in play. If ethics is to *guide* us along the way, it cannot *lead*, either as *politburo* or even as public orthodoxy.[10] It cannot be smugly symbolic but must be by way of signage, of directionality, of the open realization that ethical meaning is *en route*, pointing the way *because* it is *on* the way, as only sign, not symbol, can point to the sacramental terminus. *Description must precede prescription.* The courtesies of dogma and tradition are the road signs and guideposts along the *longior via*, not themselves the termini.

An ethics that is *in*-failing (but not a failure) adheres to a different rhythm/*metron*; it resides as signage *because* it wholly depends upon the sacral for its enactment. The little things of the world are too beautiful to be "true" and yet they exist, so that their beauty is and must be the truth. The world is too fallen to possess such beauty, and yet the world is the place where that beauty is made known, so that beauty abides by a truth *other* than the world in order to be the *bearer* of the world. That truth is beyond but never leaves the world as the way in which true transcendence reconfigures a soul in longing, to be "more human than any human was ever likely to be."[11] A subordinated ethics lives by that riddle, by the beauty not of the world *in order to be* the bearer of the world, by the truth that condemns in order to save. It is the ethics of surrender and endurance, of paradox and seeming contradiction, of the anarchism born only of the ardent desire for true order and life-giving *entelechy*. It is the incommunicable uniqueness of each human soul in communion with its transcendental mystery, and in union with other incommunicable souls.[12] What indeed is art but the attempt to capture the beauty of this

---

Of course, the pro-abortion lobby had and has no use for the divine imperative, having supplanted it with its own Hegelian criterion of absolute self-right over the other. For a stunning and incisive anthropo-theological accounting of this "art" of misremembering, see O'Regan, *Anatomy of Misremembering*.

10. See Wilhelmsen and Kendall, "Cicero and the Politics of the Public Orthodoxy," 25–59; Kendall, *Conservative Affirmation*, 50–76.

11. Chesterton, *Everlasting Man*, 126.

12. See Maritain, *Range of Reason*, 70: "The intellect may already have the idea of

temporal passing moment in relation to its mysterious transcendental a-temporality? What are tears for if not the recognition of its uncapturable but utterly human relation? Even—perhaps especially—the *polis* cannot escape this without escaping its essence, meaning, and beauty.

Ethical meaning can persist only by a loving suppression, as being shaped and filtered by the spiritual and the exotically primitive. It requires that it be born, not of or in isolation, but in the connatural non-mediated un-reflective love of play and ecstasy which knows no loss. It is this formation which prepares us for all other formations, all of which lead to our own anticipation of forgetfulness. This is the beyond-reason recognition of that-which-is-fated and that-which-is-free as the prime compatibility prefiguring all human action. This emphasis on the formation of the non-reflective love is crucial to any subsequent ethical reflection. The danger of a non-subordinated ethic, which mimics the truth but cannot carry it, is that it is consistently disseminated by an intelligence which has begun in reflection, in the awareness of ego and concept, which must merge and inhabit and then dictate to existence its meaning.[13] It begins

---

God and it may not yet have it. The non-conceptual knowledge which I am describing takes place independently of any use possibly made or not made of the idea of God, and independently of the actualization of any explicit and conscious knowledge of man's true last End. In other words, the will, hiddenly, secretly, obscurely moving (when no extrinsic factor stops or deviates the process) down to the term of the immanent dialectic of the first act of freedom, goes beyond the immediate object of conscious and explicit knowledge (the moral good as such); and it carries with itself, down to that beyond, the intellect, which at this point no longer enjoys the use of its regular instruments, and, as a result, is only actualized below the threshold of reflective consciousness, in a night without concept and without utterable knowledge. The conformity of the intellect with this transcendent object: the Separate Good (attainable only by means of analogy) is then effected by the will, the rectitude of which is, in the practical order, the measure of the truth of the intellect. God is thus naturally known, without any conscious judgment, in and by the impulse of the will striving toward the Separate Good, whose existence is implicitly involved in the practical value acknowledged to the moral good. No speculative knowledge of God is achieved. This is a purely practical cognition of God, produced in and by the movement of the appetite toward the moral good precisely considered as good. The metaphysical content with which it is pregnant is not grasped as a metaphysical content, it is not released. It is a purely practical, nonconceptual and non-conscious knowledge of God, which can co-exist with a theoretical ignorance of God."

13. Cf. C. Gilson, *Immediacy and Meaning*. See also Pope Francis, "Gaudete et Exsultate," §49: "Those who yield to this pelagian or semi-pelagian mindset, even though they speak warmly of God's grace, 'ultimately trust only in their own powers and feel superior to others because they observe certain rules or remain intransigently faithful to a particular Catholic style.' When some of them tell the weak that all things can be

in the type of reflection whereby the mind must make a bridge to the world, a bridge it can never complete without remaking the world in the image and likeness of the ego.[14] Thinking of itself as aware of itself and its responsibilities, it may reject those who dictate to existence its meaning, but then dictates to existence its alternative forms of meaning, placing itself in the same trap, the same ideological *cul-de-sac*. If ethics is resolutely a *praxis*, it cannot begin or end in a political *theoria*. This *praxis* summons existence to prepare the prerequisites for a consecrated sensibility, a mythic entrenchment of the soul in existence. When a genuine subordinated ethic takes on genuine reflection, it sees not from a conceptually abstractive or theoretical ground but from how the soul is the form of the body.[15] It sees with the eye which knows itself as sight because it is in and of the world, and would be blind without it. Thus, to prepare for this *praxis* requires an enactment which is not preparation in the reflective theoretic sense, but abidance in the non-reflective love of Being, which those who anticipate their own forgetfulness can remember in the child at play. This exteriorizing *praxis* lives by a reclamation and inculcation of un-reflective living, of living so awash in the acts of mercy, ritual, familial bond, that it knows nothing but play and imagination. And here both Rousseau and Hobbes might agree. This is the resurrection of the affective intelligence from the materialisms and psychologisms which reduce the soul to the appetite, and/or mistake the ego for its own appetite as the meaning of the appetitive power.

If *praxis* is what it is only in act, and seeks the seamless act of the good without hesitation, then how it begins, how it is formed, takes on a different but not opposing path to the theoretical and contemplative life. In fact, if we understand that the intellect must guide the will, then the intellect has a place of primacy in that it situates the distance needed to distinguish the *desire* for the good from what is *actually* good. By that same token, the intellect leads only because it is first guided, first sparked by desire—so much so that the fulfillment of the intellect and will leads to

---

accomplished with God's grace, deep down they tend to give the idea that all things are possible by the human will, as if it were something pure, perfect, all-powerful, to which grace is then added. They fail to realize that 'not everyone can do everything,' and that in this life human weaknesses are not healed completely and once for all by grace. In every case, as Saint Augustine taught, 'God commands you to do what you can and to ask for what you cannot, and indeed to pray to him humbly: Grant what you command, and command what you will.'"

14. Cf. É. Gilson, *Unity of Philosophical Experience*, 193.

15. Cf. *ST* I, 76, 1, *resp.*

something far closer to the true appetitive depth in the blinding clarity of love. For no knowledge of God, even speculative knowledge of the highest order, satisfies us,[16] because it entails the distance or the estrangement from the full with-ness of lover and beloved. If the intellect is to guide the will, it must itself be guided by a primal appetitive *praxis* which has set the stage for genuine reflection. Why else does Aristotle open his *Metaphysics* with that shocking antithesis to common sense: all men by nature desire (stretch forth/yearn) to understand.[17] What triggers this non-predatory erotic lust? This originary *praxis* has so immersed the body and soul in the communion with Being, that when the dark night does come, when the dryness and the anticipation of our forgetfulness replaces our non-reflective love with vicarious innocence, reflection returns to a source that is not reflection, that is not the ego enclosed on itself, attempting to build a bridge from *idea* to reality, but to the source which genuinely triggers the intellect to lead and which provides its hearth and home—in that mystery which sentiment craves but cannot name: the *non*-teleological end.[18] Practice does indeed make perfect.

This journey into the gainful loss of the subordinated ethic will seek the voice of *the other*, both in its non-reflective love as foundational to any genuine ethic, and in its anticipation of forgetfulness, which is the recognition of what is lost and what is always in-failing. As such, we will find ourselves traversing the theological, philosophical, poetic, and literary registers in an effort to illuminate the voice of *the other*, not in the form of the ego but in the form of itself. This will be a dialogue between two seemingly contradictory voices: that of Dostoyevsky's holy idiot Prince Myshkin[19]—who is neither Christ nor an *alter Christus*—and St. Thomas's Five Ways. Myshkin's voice is the language of presence, the attempt at reconciliation in a world of disintegrating images, and it is in recoil from the methodical awareness which demonstration and proof place upon the task of living justly. This voice will guide our conceptual unpacking of the Five Ways, no longer one of abstractive certainty but of a certitude which plays to and for the connatural ground of un-reflective

16. Cf. SCG III, 39.

17. *Met.* 980a.

18. Cf. Heidegger, *Ponderings*, §138: "Where does the human being stand?—In organized lived experience as the lived experience of organization—and this position is to be understood as a total state which determines contemporary humanity *prior to* and beyond any political attitude."

19. Cf. Dostoyevsky, *Idiot*.

love. We will approach "proof" in the strangest sense of the word: one unafraid of the fact that our conviction requires we be *en route*, that the certitude gained is never final, and could never situate us in the truth, even and especially when it provides the truth to secure the path. It is providing instead the admission into our gainful loss, into a subordinated ethics which enacts truth in us as movement, as doing, as seamless unity so in-tune that it forsakes us and even lets us doubt. The truth gained is the very movement of how *praxis* should manifest, giving us passage-way into Being rather than replacing that viatoric entrenchment. It is the truer certitude born not of a strained attempt to read the world, but from the otherness which reads its nature within us. For all play, every game, has its rules as part of, and essential to, the game. They are not imposed *upon* the game but flow *from* the playful game itself.

From the dialogue between Dostoyevsky's *The Idiot* and St. Thomas's Five Ways, we will seek to uncover how that-which-is-fated and that-which-is-free are one and the same in the subordinated ethics. What is understood as the theological apocalyptic[20] will find its companion ethic in this essential subordination. The Holy Idiot and the Dumb Ox have much in common. It is one thing to be Anselm's fool who can mouth the words but cannot think the thought, and quite another to be Dostoyevsky's idiot, the dumb ox who can only speak the *to be* of what *is*. Speaking in the mythic language of creation, and the entanglement of virtue and vice, will also assist in setting the stage to view this non-reflective love, this incarnational animal, in its supernatural naturalness. The tension be-tween those inhabited by the divine, and who thus live by a subordinated ethic, and those in whom the divine has faded, thereby causing ethics to lead and form abstractively the political and social orders, will then be brought to light. And here we will see how the *traditional problem of eth-ics is the ethical problem of tradition*, the lived-world in courteous transit through death to the non-reflective foundation of life.

Throughout, we will be tasked with setting out the image and ac-tion of the un-reflective or pre-reflective lover who lives by a subordi-nated ethic. This is the ethical soul who can bear the burden of reflection because such a soul is in contact with the foundation which precedes thought and is in harmony with Being *as* doing.[21] We must be careful

20. Cf. O'Regan, *Theology and the Spaces Apocalyptic*.

21. See Halliwell, *Aristotle's* Poetics, 42–108. Aristostle, in his discussion of aes-thetics, defends *techne* as necessarily preceding so as to ground aesthetic reflection so much so that while in *NE* 1139b we find a careful separation of *episteme* and *techne*

here, because the eidetic distance needed to illuminate such a figure awash in true self-presence, in the underlying co-naturalness of Being, has the danger of missing the point of such a figure. One can describe and easily admire, or admire and then dismiss, the effects of such a figure—as one sees, smiles and then bypasses the holy idiot. This bypassing becomes a ready-made option because the originary root of such a figure lays fallow, missing the stunning presence which reveals the un-reflective lover as the only truly reasonable being. To do so, we endeavor to recover a series of quiet, behind-our-backs transformations which set the stage for our political, social, ethical and thus interior lives. We will revisit non-reflexive love through how play becomes *mythos*, and imagination becomes consecration. Thus, affective intelligence transformed through *mythos* and consecration subordinates both the intellect and the will, and in doing so lives at the highest order of our animal nature in an enshrined unknowing immortality capable of grounding ethics not in reflection but in the ground of reflection, in Being as divine-bearing, a pre-thematic *theotokos*. The effort is to show how building up the animal—the affective intelligence—in us cultivates the true *ratio* because it is capable of situating within us a will that binds itself to the spiritual and to the living. By having a will that lives by a subordinated ethic, surrendered to the holy embodiment of love in ritual and familial accord, the intellect can then guide the will without beginning in the false sight of the ego, and only then will the fatal and free be in unison, where

> Truth predicts the eclipse of truth, and in that eclipse it condemns man.[22]

This odd foundation which lives by being bypassed, which emphasizes the idiocy of Being,[23] could be mistaken as the safe ground for an

---

this is deepened by their union in the following: *Pr. An.* 46a 22; *Met.* 981a1-b9, *NE* 1097a 4-8, *Rhet.* 1355b 32, 1362b 26, 1392a 25. The doing/making/originating is more primal than the artistic gaze, giving rise to the gaze. If we are all "gaze" and have no primal wellspring of non-reflexive union, then our ethical as well as our aesthetic ventures are forms of gnostic egoism. When the gaze repeatedly dissociates from its primal contact with presence, it first forgets its source, then demands the source be its own self-enclosed architectonic. Whether one "has" a faith-based ethical structure within this form of disintegrating image is of little improvement. For in doing so, the natural law being defended is prescriptively reduced to a perspective which *as* perspective is unable truly to compete for primacy except through force.

22. Jack Clemo, "On the Death of Karl Barth," in Davie, *New Oxford Book of Christian Verse*, 291.

23. Cf. Desmond, *Ethics and the Between*, 170–76.

anti-ethics, or more precisely an ethics where all is "forgiven" only because there is nothing any longer to forgive. The saintly are meek but not vulgarly tolerant, and the fine line which allows one to go the distance in love of the other is only present because loss *is* present, because forgiveness *is* needed, because transcendence has been displaced by ignorance. We seek to articulate not a weak ethic, as companion to a so-called weak theology,[24] but an ethical engagement which endures because it receives its strength from its incarnated subordination as viatoric and unfailingly guided by that originary affectivity. This is an ethics which can truly judge because it never relinquishes its status as secondary, as participant in Being-as-such; an ethics that can truly forgive because it lives within the beat of Being which alone can truly judge in its unity of fate and freedom. The beauty and terror of existence are not entitatively outside the participant, but sweep him up into the moving image of eternity, enabling him to judge authentically, living out the position which may rise above change but never above time. As such, this is an ethics of the Furies as much as it is of the Eumenides: the beauty beyond but not contrary to the world as the bearer of the world, even and especially in its failing, is experienced not *by* the judge but *as* the judge. The subordinated ethics must judge because, not only does it seek love, it is the enactment of love. It is an ethics experienced acutely in the repulsion from the lie, the unrelenting repulsion from the world which seeks to render the falsehood true, and it will not dismiss that experiential repulsion as if it is contrary to the go-the-distance love needed to judge and to save.[25] If it were to dismiss what repels, having confused love and mercy with pandemic acceptance, it would disengage itself from the very subordination which gives all things life and reminds us that when we act in time we act from eternity. The experience of repulsion, not unlike the experience of joy, reveals our secondary status. Being repelled shows that we are not leading nor merely following but are reacting to a ground which precedes

24. For a solid rationale for the interior intelligibility of this weakened theology, see Franco Crespi, "Absence of Foundation and Social Project," in Vattimo and Rovatti, *Weak Thought*, 253–68.

25. Plato's famous *maieutic* method is such a subordination. It refuses to place into the lead one who is not ready and only leads—as in the case of the Stranger—when subordinated to the Good which invests the soul with the embodiment of "teacher". The genuine teacher is lover, synonymous with the natural forgetfulness of the ego which occurs when awed by the ordered newness of Being. Only in this form of forgetfulness does one gain what is lost—the self in its truer manifestation as beautifully *in* and reverently *not of* the world.

thought so as to inform it. We are neither leading in an ideologically enclosed manner nor following in a non-noetic indifference. Instead, we are in-formed so as to be formed through our always preceding contact with Being. In repulsion, we are being informed of a displacement of Being in our search for Being. Neither leading nor following represents the originary ethics, for both equate ethical meaning with prescriptive rule which overlooks the phenomenological harmony in which things are attuned to existence. Far too quickly our uneasy repulsion is put aside or quantified as a sociological apparatus reacting to social norms rather than as *mystique* incarnated in a *politique*. But this reduction occurs because, again, ethics loses union with that *ab origine* affectivity. If the natural law is to reveal its ever-deepening intelligibility as the shepherd of man, it is in how it reveals joy and repulsion, the former in its startlingly universal-into-particular communion of all things, placing the super-sensuous into the sensuous, and the latter, in the aching alienation of a world amiss, not at a distance but at such proximal nearness, so that the failings of one are the failings of all. If the natural law cannot somatically invoke the innocence and the fallenness of our natures, it becomes simply prescription and nothing more. And if it does invoke such experiential movements, it does so as *movements*, where each is informed of the ethical dimension of being-in-the-world *because* ethics is in failing, in trust to its secondary status.

If the secondary status is to be taken seriously, then the true political animal is far closer to the peasant than to the politician. The politician is not to be discarded nor his role lessened. But, for him to function properly, he must be aware of the dangerous territory, the *polemos*, of stepping out of the fertile ground of connatural communion where it would be better, thus truer-to-ethics, to remain. In one real sense, the politician must exile himself from the garden of daily affairs in order to defend the order of daily affairs. But, because the intelligibility of daily affairs is only genuinely revealed to us non-reflexively, if the politician stays too long in thought, he defends a perverted image. This is the paradox of political life. To think of the political life is, in a damning sense, to fall away from it. And yet, of course, we need to fall away as much as we need to return. Societies are built—but slowly rotting away[26]—on their successive

---

26. Cf. Voegelin, "Republic," in *Order and History*, 3:126. Voegelin likens Plato's understanding of democracy to a slow, comfortable, and often pleasurable rot, but one which must exhaust its own so-called aesthetic, revealing its abyss of depravation, red in tooth and claw.

powers to stray, to fall away. But how do we return?[27] How do we defend what can only be enacted by familial into-the-earth entanglement? The much quoted and as often misunderstood "all men by nature desire to know" must be extrapolated in its relation to wonder. Aristotle is clearly seeking a somatic knowledge, one where phenomenologically the form is invested in matter, and thus where knowledge is never disengaged from Being as prime revealer.[28] This knowledge is triggered by the naturalness of harmonious desire, not by the type of unsubordinated desire which exaggerates a defective human condition. It is knowledge *as* wonder. All men *by nature* overflow in participatory wonder, a wonder which naturally inoculates the participant against selfishness. Such political animals rarely, if ever, begin in the "I," in the ego. They know themselves the proper way, non-reflexively, too busy to invoke the "I," too full of love of the little things of the dappled earth. Wonder is the unifying principle aligning our being with the natural law as natural signage. The political animal is a being of wonder, his desire to know is never malformed by an ego which exists as a disservice to wonder, historically causing us to fall into knowledge.[29] The difficulty: the politician more often than not exiles himself from wonder *in order to* defend the so-called ethical and social norms which are *connaturally* produced in wonder. How then can the natural law survive authentically if it pressed into a region alien to its very efficacy? If the natural law arises *only* in wonder, what happens to the natural law and its participants when wonder ceases and eidetic egoity takes hold?[30] The true political animal is too busy *being* engaged

27. Cf. C. Gilson, "Christian Polis: *Noli Me Tangere*," 241–70.

28. Cf. DA 430a 20–25: "Actual knowledge is identical with its object: in the individual, potential knowledge is in time prior to actual knowledge, but in the universe as a whole it is not prior even in time. Mind is not at one time knowing and at another not. When mind is set free from its present conditions it appears as just what it is and nothing more: this alone is immortal and eternal (we do not, however, remember its former activity because, while mind in this sense is impassible, mind as passive is destructible), and without it nothing thinks."

29. See Shestov, *Kierkegaard and the Existential Philosophy*, 1–28.

30. One here is reminded of the Hindu teaching on the Four Yugas or Four Age Cycle, i.e., *Satya, Treta, Dvapara, Kali*. See Gonzalez-Reimann, *Mahabharata and the Yugas*. In *Satya* one has that prelapsarian harmony, where breath, movement, and action are in perfect connatural karmic unity. What has/will become the cosmogonic in *Kali Yuga* was perfectly moving in seamless unreflexive innocence. Only the soul in reflection, estranged and tethered to the self which can only fear its own death, sees the fear, lives out the disharmony. In *Treta*, we begin to see the estrangement. No longer is the man aligned to the divine by a non-reflexive fully incarnational immediacy but

by wonder.[31] How then does the prescriptive recover what it has lost, how

---

by the spectatorial step-back so essential in knowledge. This is also paradoxically the age of heroes. The presence of the divine is most certainly still desired but can only be seen through the heroic, the larger than life. The desire thus for the hero reveals that the world is falling away from a perfected form. This is the same knowledge that often seeks wisdom but just as often tramples on it underfoot. This is where knowledge aligns itself with death; where it constructs the phantom self. The transition from our *unknowing* co-naturalness to our *knowing* courtship is a form of mediation which has already stripped the immediate *of its immediacy*, where ethical engagement has squandered its secondary status in favour of unsubordinated prescriptions. We then speak of that immediacy, but the speaking itself conveys reflection and our estrangement. Here the gods as less potent must entice our nearness, their presence has dwindled that now we must see, so to speak, to believe. In that third Yuga (Dvapara), this may be the golden age for man—a humanism of ideals, resources, intellectual insights—because, paradoxically, the divine has lessened considerably. In many ways, it's a golden age built on shifting sands. It's the ascent which prepares the most visceral of falls. We've constructed a pseudo-permanence which blinds us into seeing its impermanence. Only the "mad," the one who has not made this ascent, understands how foolish it is for our natures to seek independence from the dust and clay; the earth itself is our brutal and gentle grace. We are in the final Yuga, where suffering is most intense, where the bull legs will be cut down to one as the moral karmic order is dramatically lessened. *Kali Yuga* is that prime antagonizing force undoing Vishnu at every turn. This is an apocalyptic age in the Christian sense. And yet, there is Salvation to be gained within all of these ages. Kali Yuga reveals itself in and through a heart-aching pandemic spiritual malaise—that out of all the ages, this one is the most entrenched in the necessity to suffer, to be pressed into relentless work, into the yoke of necessity. Transcending suffering in this period can only come about by entering the suffering so fully that the suffering can no longer claim you as its own. This suffering is of a visceral intensity and it seems as if this period, *Kali Yuga*, is where one is most apt to find the means to overcome suffering. But can one become so lost that they freely become unfree? Have we lost something along the way, in *Sutya Yuga*, that immemorial immediacy, which alone can lift us above the suffering? Does the Kali Yuga period, most apt to suffer, have the tools to overcome it? Or are they most apt to suffer *because* they have squandered or hidden or forgotten where to find those tools? This is why the battle between Kalki (Vishnu's final avatar) is described in apocalyptic language.

31. See Chesterton, *St. Thomas Aquinas*, 19: "St. Thomas takes the view that the souls of all the ordinary hard-working and simple-minded people are quite as important as the souls of thinkers and truth-seekers; and he asks how all these people are possibly to find time for the amount of reasoning that is needed to find truth . . . [this] shows both a respect for scientific enquiry and a strong sympathy with the average man. His argument for Revelation is not an argument against Reason; but it is an argument for Revelation. The conclusion he draws from it is that men must receive the highest moral truths in a miraculous manner; or most men would not receive them at all. His arguments are rational and natural; but his own deduction is all for the supernatural; and, as is common in the case of his argument, it is not easy to find any deduction except his own deduction. And when we come to that, we find it is something as simple as St. Francis himself could desire; the message from heaven; the

does the statesman defend without losing his ability to return?

Double Intentionality

> To know is primarily and principally to seize within the self a
> non-self which in its turn is capable of seizing and embracing
> the self: it is to live with the life of another. To know means
> principally and first of all to accept and embrace within oneself
> the other who is just as capable of accepting and embracing; it
> means to live the life of the other living thing . . . [The Intellect]
> is essentially acquisitive of reality and not merely a process of
> forging propositions.[32]

Intentionality in its primal truth overcomes knowledge reduced to
a copy theory or to a relativism of differing labels, while profiling human
persons as the privileged beings who alone extract the meaning of Being
as such, and that, in a way, the weight of Being resides in them alone.
Otherness is as implicit in knowledge and ethics as it is explicit in love.

To say that the weight of Being resides in persons alone can only
be understood when liberated from the deficient views of the soul as
closed up in matter, as if body and soul are bifurcated into two accidentally related substances. Or, alternatively, one argues that the soul is the
form of the body but, by neglecting the profound implications of such
a statement, inchoately reflects a divided nature and an artificial union.
The soul is *already* outside itself, it lives a radically exteriorized existence,
so much so that what primarily constitutes our own nature is also the
site of our own surpassing of self. What we own the least are our own
selves, precisely because the soul in its innermost reality is existentially
dependent on Being for its existence, and this is manifested most acutely
in the act of knowledge.[33] In knowledge, the human soul reveals itself to
be the alterity of the divine, becoming, in a way, all things. Because we are

---

story that is told out of the sky; the fairytale that is really true."

32. Rousselot, *Intellectualism of St. Thomas*, 8–13. See also Eckhart, "Sermon 34:
When Our Work Becomes a Spiritual Work Working in the World," in *Breakthrough*,
483: "Listen then to this wonder! How wonderful it is to be both outside and inside, to
seize and to be seized, to see and at the same time to be what is seen, to hold and to be
held—*that* is the goal where the spirit remains at rest, united with our dear eternity."

33. Cf. DA 430b–431a: "The cognizing agent must be potentially one contrary, and
contain the other. But if there is anything which has no contrary, it is self-cognizant,
actual and separately existent . . . Knowledge when actively operative is identical with
its object."

not separately existent, we must arrive at ourselves by becoming identical with otherness.[34]

The self is thus permanence in transit. It is what distinguishes each in his own transcendent dignity, and this distinction is *permanently* unstripped. Yet, the *what*-it-is of what is unstripped is always in transition; the self is an actuating permanence, the moving image of eternity. Because the soul is united to the body, where each is the realization of the other's perfection, a dual unity, we act in and out of time. As moving image, the intentional-self acts towards eternity while already being in union with the eternal which alone enables the self to act towards what-it-is in its nature.

We see our pre-cognitive acting from eternity when we act in time in our most originary access to the natural law. The Greek roots of *synderesis* call to mind vigil, watchfulness, preservation, and safeguarding. It is a non-mediated intuitive inclination towards the eternal good, which issues the effect of conscience and self-knowing. Even the most interior form of self-knowing, self-awareness, is a place where the self *surpasses* itself in order to be itself! Intentionality is inherent in all interior and exterior human acts. *Synderesis* is thus a pre-conscience, the immediate union with the eternal good which precedes and helps to issue conscience.[35] *Synderesis* is not reduced to a capacity which can be geared towards good or evil—it is an unstripped and non-acquired habit or innate ability, a pre-cognitive union always unified with the eternal law. Yet its dignity straddles the meaning of *habitus* in a way that reflects our nature as on the *confinium* between time and eternity.[36] If not capacity, it is described by Saint Thomas as a *habitus*, the un-erring ability to read the principles of moral action.[37] But this must be distinguished

---

34. Moral arguments which advocate "it's my body, my right" in, for example, abortion, envision a fallacious sense of self-sufficiency that exists neither in practice nor in the act of knowledge itself. It is simply nowhere to be found, and the very heart of intentionality attests to this moral truth. Human beings realize themselves only in ontological dependency.

35. Cf. DV XVI, 1, ad. 9: "*Synderesis* does not denote higher or lower reason, but something that refers commonly to both. For in the very habit of the universal principles of law there are contained certain things which pertain to the eternal norms of conduct, such as, that God must be obeyed, and there are some that pertain to lower norms, such as, that we must live according to reason."

36. SCG II, 80–81.

37. *ST* I, 79, 12, *resp.*: "*Synderesis* is not a power but a habit; though some held that it is a power higher than reason; while others [Cf. Alexander of Hales, Sum. Theol. II,

from habit in the Augustinian sense, which can be overwhelmed by the appetite. This is instead what Saint Thomas calls the "habit of first principles." *Synderesis* is the cause that helps to issue the effect of our acts of judgment or conscience. How does *synderesis* reflect that the human soul acts from the eternal while acting in time? *Synderesis* as *non-mediated* is an un-erring union with the eternal law, a union made possible because the human soul is itself aeviternal. And because our aeviternity is acted out through embodiment, time, and change, *synderesis* when cognized is thus the principle of the act of conscience, transformed into reflexive self-knowing. When conscience is actualized, this is the self-same participation and illumination of the natural law. Astonishingly, within the very structure of human nature itself, there is a pre-cognitive union with the eternal law, which issues the effect—conscience or self-knowing, which, as reflexive, is the knowing participation in the natural law. If the natural law is our participation in the eternal law, then *synderesis* is the pre-conscience or the pre-self-knowledge of our eternal union with the eternal law, while our reflexive self-knowing or conscience is the temporal participation in the natural law:

> Although an act does not always remain in itself, yet it always remains in its cause, which is power and habit. Now all the habits by which conscience is formed, although many, nevertheless have their efficacy from one first habit, the habit of first principles, which is called *synderesis*. And for this special reason, this habit is sometimes called conscience, as we have said above.[38]

73] said that it is reason itself, not as reason, but as a nature. In order to make this clear we must observe that, as we have said above (Article 8), man's act of reasoning, since it is a kind of movement, proceeds from the understanding of certain things—namely, those which are naturally known without any investigation on the part of reason, as from an immovable principle—and ends also at the understanding, inasmuch as by means of those principles naturally known, we judge of those things which we have discovered by reasoning. Now it is clear that, as the speculative reason argues about speculative things, so that practical reason argues about practical things. Therefore, we must have, bestowed on us by nature, not only speculative principles, but also practical principles. Now the first speculative principles bestowed on us by nature do not belong to a special power, but to a special habit, which is called 'the understanding of principles,' as the Philosopher explains (Ethic. vi, 6). Wherefore the first practical principles, bestowed on us by nature, do not belong to a special power, but to a special natural habit, which we call *synderesis*. Whence *synderesis* is said to incite to good, and to murmur at evil, inasmuch as through first principles we proceed to discover, and judge of what we have discovered. It is therefore clear that *synderesis* is not a power, but a natural habit."

38. *ST* I, 79, 13, ad. 3.

The human person stands on the horizon between time and eternity, the lowest of spiritual substances and the highest of corporeal creatures.[39] It is this unique nature that begins to radicalize the meaning and power of the intentional act whereby the soul *is*, in a way, all things. If this is our nature, then we share the unique privilege of actions specific to incorporeal and corporeal designation. We act from eternity when we act in time.[40] As Saint Thomas remarks in Question 2 of the *Summa Theologica*, incorporeal substances are not in space and thus, if not in space, they are not in time. To take up space—for there to be expansion and the appearance of presence—is to take up time. Space is the temporalization of presence, for in space we mark off the chronological happening of what is raised before us. In Question 76, we are reminded that the human intellect is not only incorporeal but a substance, which means that it is subsistent. This is why the objector asks how this soul, if not a body, can

39. Cf. SCG II, 68: "Dionysius says: Divine wisdom has joined the ends of the higher to the beginnings of the lower. Thus in the genus of bodies we find the human body, composed of elements equally tempered, attaining to the lowest member of the class above it, that is, to the human soul, which holds the lowest rank in the class of subsistent intelligences. Hence the human soul is said to be on the horizon and boundary line [*Confinium/aeviternity*] between things corporeal and incorporeal, inasmuch as it is an incorporeal substance and at the same time the form of a body." SCG III, 61: The human person, by virtue of his intellectual soul stands on the borderline, the horizon or *confinium* between eternity and time. St. Thomas stresses this point throughout his works emphasizing that the soul is shown to hold the last place among intellectual things. See SCG II, 80–81; SCG II, 80; DV X, 8 resp. See also Pseudo-Aristotle, *Book of Causes* §22: "Indeed, the being that is after eternity and beyond time is Soul, because it is on the horizon of eternity from below and beyond time."; §84: "And indeed, Intelligence encompasses the things it produces, both Nature and the horizon of Nature, namely, the Soul, for it is above Nature." See also É. Gilson, *History of Christian Philosophy*, 235–37.

40. Cf. Maritain, *Degrees of Knowledge*, 192: "The philosopher knows that bodies have absolute dimensions, that there are in the world absolute motions, an absolute time, simultaneities which are absolute for events divided as far as may be in space: absolute signifies here entirely determined in itself, independently of any observer: the knowledge of what these are, the discernments of these absolute dimensions, movements, simultaneities (at a distance), time, by the aid of our means of observation and measurement, the philosopher renounces, voluntarily conceding that it is not possible. It is sufficient for him that they can be discerned by pure minds, which know without observing from a given point of space and time. The physicist makes a like renunciation, and with good reason. But for him, who does not philosophize and who is concerned with what he can measure and to the extent that he can measure it, the existence of these absolutes does not count and in their place he knows and handles only relative entities reconstructed by means of measurable determinations: *entia rationis cum fundametito in re*."

affect the body.[41] How can the soul "touch" the body; between the mover and the moved there must be this touch or contact which requires embodiment. Saint Thomas responds by identifying two forms of contact: quantity and power. The former requires that contact be bodily, material, corporeal; the latter invokes the subsistent, indeed a-temporal nature of the soul. What then are we to understand about the unified nature of the human person as body and soul, if the body is in time, always exteriorizing its presence in and to the world, while its moving principle, the soul, is, in a way, in and yet *not* in time? The soul is *in* time if we accept that not only its power is to be the mover of the body, but its perfection is found in an exteriorized existence, perfected by its unity with the body. And yet, strangely enough, to be the moving principle of the specifically human person, who is free, who is an intellectual substance, requires that its movement is not reducible to time and to the causal determinisms of being that do not rise above change. The soul must act from eternity when it acts in time and if the soul and body are a dual unity, then man himself is connaturally in and *not* in time in every intentional action. That latter aspect is often overlooked and, in turn, its dramatic implications are bypassed.[42] Our task is to recover that eternal action within an existential grounding, not divorced from it.

In a way we act from the same incorporeality, the same eternity or aeviternity,[43] as the angels, but realize this activity in manifestly different ways. The angels act from eternity, identical to their incorporeal intellectual substance existentially dependent on God. That is why each angel is its own species. Human persons act from eternity as united to their incorporeal intellectual substance which, as the form of the body, protracts that eternity into the moving image of their own selves. This is why embodied existence, as existentially dependent on God, is our individuating principle and why human beings are of the same species. Eternity under the mode of an incorporeal aeviternity befits the angelic nature. This is why a total immediate eternal damnation befits the fallen angels and eternal totalizing elevation is fitting for the thrones and dominions. Eternity

41. See the objectors in ST I, 76, 5.

42. Cf. Pegis, *Thomistic Notion of Man*, 14: "Like other thinkers of their age, William of Saint-Thierry and Godfrey of Saint-Victor . . . had great difficulty in understanding how a simple and immaterial soul was present to the body and yet not in a spatial way. But this problem, which is at least as old as Plotinus and St. Augustine, not to mention Nemesius, is witness to the metaphysical innocence of the twelfth century."

43. *ST* I, 10, 6, ad. 2.

under the mode of an embodied aeviternity befits human nature. But for human beings, a longer way was assigned. This longer way is the moving image of eternity discovered in the experience of time. We are able to be the moving image of eternity because our aeviternal nature directs us to one aeviternity by which all—man and angels—are measured, thereby reaffirming that we act from eternity when we act in time.[44]

This longer way is what places us squarely in the midst of the miscellany of life, in the realm of the immediately existing otherness of life, society, love, and death. And it is this that subordinates our ethical enactment

44. Cf. *ST* I, 10, 6, *resp*: "A twofold opinion exists on this subject. Some say there is only one aeviternity; others that there are many aeviternities. Which of these is true, may be considered from the cause why time is one; for we can rise from corporeal things to the knowledge of spiritual things. Now some say that there is only one time for temporal things, forasmuch as one number exists for all things numbered; as time is a number, according to the Philosopher (Phys. iv). This, however, is not a sufficient reason; because time is not a number abstracted from the thing numbered, but existing in the thing numbered; otherwise it would not be continuous; for ten ells of cloth are continuous not by reason of the number, but by reason of the thing numbered. Now number as it exists in the thing numbered, is not the same for all; but it is different for different things. Hence, others assert that the unity of eternity as the principle of all duration is the cause of the unity of time. Thus, all durations are one in that view, in the light of their principle, but are many in the light of the diversity of things receiving duration from the influx of the first principle. On the other hand, others assign primary matter as the cause why time is one; as it is the first subject of movement, the measure of which is time. Neither of these reasons, however, is sufficient; forasmuch as things which are one in principle, or in subject, especially if distant, are not one absolutely, but accidentally. Therefore the true reason why time is one, is to be found in the oneness of the first movement by which, since it is most simple, all other movements are measured. Therefore time is referred to that movement, not only as a measure is to the thing measured, but also as accident is to subject; and thus receives unity from it. Whereas to other movements it is compared only as the measure is to the thing measured. Hence it is not multiplied by their multitude, because by one separate measure many things can be measured. This being established, we must observe that a twofold opinion existed concerning spiritual substances. Some said that all proceeded from God in a certain equality, as Origen said (Peri Archon. i); or at least many of them, as some others thought. Others said that all spiritual substances proceeded from God in a certain degree and order; and Dionysius (Coel. Hier. x) seems to have thought so, when he said that among spiritual substances there are the first, the middle and the last; even in one order of angels. Now according to the first opinion, it must be said that there are many aeviternities as there are many aeviternal things of first degree. But according to the second opinion, it would be necessary to say that there is one aeviternity only; because since each thing is measured by the most simple element of its genus, it must be that the existence of all aeviternal things should be measured by the existence of the first aeviternal thing, which is all the more simple the nearer it is to the first. Wherefore because the second opinion is truer, as will be shown later (I:47:2) we concede at present that there is only one aeviternity."

to the non-prescriptive, and, therefore, non-ideological natural law, as we shall see. Ideology seeks to overcome, indeed eliminate, the unsought particulars that actually constitute the meaning of time, life, and history. In the name of an absolute abstraction, all otherness is destroyed, rendering null and void the very context of ethical action—and all in the name of a contextual historical relativism.[45]

The phenomenological experience of time that permeates all experience *is* the experience of human nature as aeviternal, and communal human nature as historical. Time does not exist outside of human nature. Animals may affectively experience change, but they do not experience time or historicity. Time is the unity which occurs when a being resides on the horizon between eternity and time, where the soul acts from eternity in order to raise its own being into freedom above change and succession. Historical being demands the impossible: the human person is the totalizing unity of the embodied *as* the spiritual, while still pointing to the spiritual which the embodied craves; the temporal is realized *as* the eternal while pointing to the eternal which it lacks and needs in order to fulfill itself. If we do not merely take up some "space" between time and eternity but are the beings whose natures reside on the *confinium* itself, then our temporalizing actions must reveal our eternity *as* history, history which itself points to the eternal which it desires *as other*. We see this in the union of spouses and of parents to their children who are others-as-other, but yet seek to be that other contemporaneously. These unions exceed knowledge, while at the same time seeking out knowledge to express and complete themselves. As we act from eternity when we act in time, time itself alone reveals to us that we act from the eternal. And *how* we realize this temporalizing revelation of the eternal is through an incarnated intentionality whereby I know and love myself *only* by being the other who in turn is capable of being the other who *I am*. When Adrienne von Speyr remarked that the I who receives the sacrament is not the I who I think I am,[46] we see the dramatic newness of souls that are *in* and yet *not-in* time. To another intentional agent I reveal the other that I have taken in and become. What I have become is the other—that agent's self. Thus, what the agent takes *in*, when knowing his self, is the unity of the illumination of my own I who reveals the agent's self. This illumination is twofold, each *in* and *for* the other. This dualizing unity reflects that

---

45. Cf. Voegelin, *Science, Politics, Gnosticism.*

46. Cf. von Speyr, *Cross.*

knowledge is, in a way, all things. More still, when I first reveal to the
intentional agent his or her own self, I do so only because *the soul knows
itself only in the face of Otherness,* because the other has revealed my own
self as illuminating his or her self in me. The only origin of this infinitiz-
ing mutual dependency would be that each acts from eternity when acting in time. With Levinas, who recognizes how our pre-cognitive union
in the eternal places us, in a way, closer to the infinite than to the finite:

> The sense of the human is not to be measured by presence, not
> even by self-presence. The meaning of proximity exceeds the
> limits of ontology, of the human essence, and of the world. It
> signifies by way of transcendence and the relationship-to-God-
> in-me (*l'a-Dieu-en-moi*) which is the putting of myself into
> question. The face signifies in the fact of summoning, *of sum-
> moning me*—in its nudity or its destitution, in everything that
> is precarious in questioning, in all the hazards of mortality—to
> the unresolved alternative between Being and Nothingness, a
> questioning which, ipso facto, *summons me.* The infinite in its
> absolute difference withholds itself from presence in me; the In-
> finite does not come to meet me in a contemporaneousness like
> that in which *noesis* and *noema* meet simultaneously together,
> nor in the way in which the interlocutors responding to one
> another may meet. The Infinite is not indifferent to me. It is in
> calling me to other men that transcendence concerns me. In this
> unique intrigue of transcendence, the non-absence of the Infi-
> nite is neither presence, nor re-presentation. Instead, the idea of
> the infinite is to be found in my responsibility for the Other.[47]

With Pegis:

> Merely to juxtapose the spiritual and material within man, by
> simply relating soul and body to one another as form to mat-
> ter, was not enough since it left the internal unity of man unex-
> plained. Like the world of Aristotle, he still remained a two-part
> anomaly; he had no integrity and there was no meaning to the
> role of organic matter within his nature—unless that meaning

47. Levinas, "Beyond Intentionality," in *Levinas Reader*, 5. See Walsh on Levinas
in *Modern Philosophical Revolution*, 311: "Love is love only when it loves an other as
an other, not just as an other self. The Child is that unmerited event by which an other
is 'more exactly, me, but not myself.' Transcendence has reached its goal when it has
endangered, beyond its own finality, the finality of the transcendence of an other. I can
love myself in the child but never as myself; it is always as other that the child is loved."
As such, the lines in *Galatians* are deeply suggestive of the intentional union we seek
to elucidate. See Gal. 3:28 (KJV): "There is neither Jew nor Greek, there is neither bond
nor free, there is neither male nor female: for ye are all one in Christ Jesus."

were no more than the perpetuation of the anomaly itself. What
was needed was nothing less than the total inclusion of the
material within the spiritual in man's nature, so that what the
human body contributed as an organic and material instrument
was already present within the soul *in a spiritual form and as a
spiritual exigency.*[48]

Fallen time—that time inextricably aligned to the experience of death—
often obscures the eternal at the heart of all temporal experience. In fallen
time, we tend to see time as something existing outside the primordial
experience of our existential comportment. In a word, we conflate time
with change. There is order, structure, beauty to the world whether we see
it or not. But when it is seen and experienced, this is the temporalizing
action of existence.

> Time is the substance I am made of. Time is a river which sweeps
> me along, but I am the river; it is a tiger which destroys me, but
> I am the tiger; it is a fire which consumes me, but I am the fire.[49]

In a way, time is relative as related to consciousness as consciousness *of*.
If nothing is conscious of time, then there is no time to be *had*. To *have*
time is to be making, wasting, fleeing, or recovering time. We have falsely
bifurcated body and soul, and time and eternity: these are hallmarks of
fallen time. The repercussion of such divisions is most pernicious in the
knowing union of two beings capable of intentionality, and, as we shall
see, in the moral ordering of political society.

The human soul has the capacity to become the other as other in
knowledge and to know the real thing itself. What happens if the other
that I seek to know in itself is not an object enclosed in matter, but another self who acts from eternity when acting in time, and who becomes
the other as other in his or her own act of knowledge? Am I becoming
the other of myself when I take on the other self who has become me in
otherness? Does the other take on his own self which I have taken on
when I became all things and became the other as other? And in this
dualizing intentionality, are acts of knowledge without end, or rather,
never completed, because to be a knower requires that the soul act from
eternity when acting in time?

> Time presents itself as the solitary instant, as the consciousness
> of solitude . . . If being is conscious of itself only in the present

48. Pegis, *Thomistic Notion of Man,* 51.
49. Borges, "New Refutation on Time," in *Labyrinths,* 234.

instant, how could we not realize that the present instant is the sole domain in which reality is experienced? If we were eventually to eliminate our being we should still have to start from ourselves to prove being . . . If our heart were large enough to love life in all its detail, we would see that every instant is at once a giver and a plunderer, and that a young or tragic novelty—always sudden—never ceases to illustrate the essential discontinuity of time.[50]

What do we know when we know the other which is capable of knowing us? Must all knowing of the intentional other demand an infinitization, whereby all termini are revealed to be intermediaries? In this dualizing intentionality, we are required to re-visit, re-know what we have already grasped and yet already exceeded us each time it is grasped. Is this what is meant by Plato when he describes human beings as the moving image of eternity?[51]

Is there a double intentionality that we have lost when we exiled time from eternity through sin, vice and the other falls into knowledge? Is there the capacity for either a heightening or a diminution of the integral reality of selves each time we revisit knowing the other as other? Have we reduced intentionality to an act which cannot transform the human person because it reduces the human dimension to an entitative form of sensory intentionality? What happens when we bypass the radical truth that the human person is transformation-in-act:

> The notion of intentionality cannot be reduced to a connection with an object. In other words, taste is always taste of something, and similarly thought and other intentional acts must have their corresponding objects. This way of presenting intentionality

50. Bachelard, *Intuition of the Instant*, 6–8.

51. *Timaeus*, 37d. Cf. Kierkegaard, *Concept of Anxiety*, §IV 358–59: "'The moment' is a figurative expression, and therefore it is not easy to deal with. However, it is a beautiful word to consider. Nothing is as swift as a blink of the eye, and yet it is commensurable with the content of the eternal . . . Whatever its etymological explanation, ['the sudden'] is related to the category of the invisible, because time and eternity were conceived equally abstractly, because the concept of temporality was lacking, and this again was due to the lack of the concept of spirit. The Latin term is *momentum* (from *movere*), which by derivation expresses the merely vanishing. Thus understood, the moment is not properly an atom of time but an atom of eternity. It is the first reflection of eternity in time, its first attempt, as it were, at stopping time . . . The moment is that ambiguity in which time and eternity touch each other, and with this the concept of *temporality* is posited, whereby time constantly intersects eternity and eternity constantly pervades time. As a result, the above-mentioned division acquires its significance: the present time, the past time, the future time."

has a grain of truth but it is nonetheless reductive since it does not take stock of the most decisive point of the intimate union between knower and known.[52]

Since the other is eternal, no single temporal intentional act can know the other, it becomes a revisiting of that other as self, and turns into a heightening of the other. The reality of such dualizing intentionality is that I *am* truly myself only when I am *always* more in the other, and this alone unveils the earthy transcendence befitting our embodied spirituality.

> But it is important to understand that because of the proper function of the will, and its un-materiality which is certainly not less pure in itself, but less 'separated' from things, and entirely turned towards their concrete state (cp. Sum. theol. i, 82, 3), intentionality here plays an entirely different part. The intentional being of love is not, like the intentional being of knowledge, an esse in virtue of which one (the knower) becomes another (the known), it is an *esse* in virtue of which—an immaterial but wholly different process—the other (the beloved), spiritually present in the one (the lover) by right of weight or impulsion, becomes for him another self.[53]

52. Possenti, *Nihilism and Metaphysics*, 349.

53. Maritain, *Degrees of Knowledge*, 453. The operation of the will within ourselves involves also another procession, that of love, whereby the object loved is in the lover, see *ST* I, 27, 3, *resp.*, and Hegel, *Natural Law*, 104: "There is nothing else but the performance, on the ethical plane, of the tragedy which the Absolute eternally enacts with itself, by eternally giving birth to itself into objectivity, submitting in this objective form to suffering and death, and rising from its ashes into glory. The Divine in its form and objectivity is immediately double-natured, and its life is the absolute unity of these natures. But the movement of the absolute contradiction between these two natures presents itself in the Divine nature (which in this movement has comprehended itself) as courage, whereby the first nature frees itself from the death inherent in the other conflicting nature. Yet through this liberation it gives its own life, since that life *is* only in connection with this other life, any yet just as absolutely is resurrected out of it, since in this death (as the sacrifice of the second nature), death is mastered."

Acknowledgments

I AM ENTIRELY GRATEFUL to Eric Austin Lee for his insightful comments, assiduous review, and patience! Thank you to the community at University of Holy Cross for their support, especially and including the awarding of the Adams Endowed Professorship, which assisted greatly in the completion of this book. In particular, special thanks to Drs. Claudia Champagne, Michael LaBranche, Victoria Dahmes, and David M. "Buck" Landry. I am also most grateful to Mrs. Jane Simoneaux, Mrs. Cindy Self, Ms. Rhonda Aucoin, Ms. Celia Zaeringer, and Ms. Daisi Sue Smith. Thank you to my students at Holy Cross, who make each day an adventure in the classroom!

Abbreviations

Aristotle

De Anima	DA
De Caelo	DC
Metaphysics	Met.
Nichomachean Ethics	NE
Physics	Phys.
Prior Analytics	Pr. An.
Rhetoric	Rhet.

St. Thomas Aquinas

Summa Contra Gentiles:	SCG
Summa Theologiae:	ST
Commentaria in Libros Aristoteles de Caelo et Mundo:	*Comm. De Caelo*
Commentary on the Gospel of St. John:	*Comm. St. John*
In Librum Beati Dionysii de Divinis Nominibus Expositio:	DN
Scriptum Super Sententiis:	*In Sent.*
De Ente et Essentia:	*De Ente*
Quaestiones Disputate de Potentia Dei:	*De Pot.*
De Veritate:	DV

1

Quiet Homes: The Paradox of Freedom

Wherever an altar is found, there civilization exists.[1]

FREEDOM IS AS MUCH an accomplishment as a given,[2] a non-temporal consequence of the intellectual-spiritual nature of human existence in its journey across time. The will follows upon human intentionality whether or not a choice of consequences is involved. We are in a situation at all because we are by nature free. We are in *this* situation as a consequence of our own, and others, freedom, though not at all necessarily as a result of choice. Being-in-a-situation is not the negation of freedom but the necessary prerequisite of freedom.[3] The essence of freedom is identical to the paradoxical essence of human being,[4] located in its natural intentionality: to be-come what I am, I must be-come what I am not: this is a necessity flowing from the radical non-necessity *qua* contingency of

---

1. Maistre, *St Petersburg Dialogues*, 44.

2. *ST* I, 83, 2, ad. 2. And this accomplishment, for Saint Bernard, is only so because of a grace-filled union which enables one to desire the good, fulfilling the will in its activity. See Bernard, *On Grace and Free Choice*, 28: "It is creative grace which gave existence to the will; it is saving grace which giveth it moral success; it is the will itself which bringeth about its own moral failure. Accordingly, free choice maketh us possessed of will; grace maketh us possessed of good will. It is in virtue of free choice that we will, it is in virtue of grace that we will what is good."

3. Cf. Sartre, *Being and Nothingness*, 1–8.

4. Cf. C. Gilson, "Rebellion of the Gladiators," 13–72.

1

my being and action. My essence is not finished, a "done deal," a made thing. It must be achieved. This "must" is the sign and guarantee of my freedom. Freedom is a primordial given, but more a lifelong struggle to accomplish. The long historical failure to distinguish these aspects, without absorbing or reducing the one into the other, leads to the muddle of opposing and equally fatuous theories of freedom, choice, and determinism. We may or may not be "responsible" for our situation. That is not the fundamental point. It is *because*, and only because, we are free that we have—must have—a situation. Cancel the situation and we cancel freedom. Both subjectivism and traditional objectivism fail miserably and utterly in understanding this. Thus, immanence and transcendence are not opposed.[5] The transcendent act is not a merely transitive act.[6] For the ultimate is attained not by corporeal steps but by the movement of the heart.[7] And like a garden, freedom requires nurture, development, pruning, weeding. The given of human nature is a seed, not a fruit. Liberty is a tree: *arbitrio*/arbor: the free act is the rooted act, not, contra Gide,[8] the gratuitous act. Freedom as accomplishment unites body and soul, and ethical, social, political freedom require the careful gardener. In this sense, politics and ethics are "*a posteriori*" while moral sensibility is "*a priori*." Personal-social-political unity requires subordination to an underlying *elan*, towards a pure and purely Other, reversing in some sense and uniting in another sense, Bergson's open and closed societies, for Being is the unitary root of the *elan vital*, of the gardens of society and the mystical soul where *theoria* reveals itself as *praxis*. The free ethical act is not "knowledge" in the sense of being in possession of the prescriptive rulebook; rather is it, to paraphrase Lonergan, freedom *from* the rulebook.[9]

The Predicament of the Natural Law

> For many generations, as long as the divine nature lasted in
> them, they were obedient to the laws, and well-affectioned

5. This reflects the unitive relationship between immanent acts and transitive acts in Aristotle. See Met. IX, 1050a; NE VI, 1140a.

6. Cf. *ST* I, 85; DV, X, 8, ad. 1; X, 11, ad. 10.

7. Cf. Prov 3:5–6 (DRC1752): "Have confidence in the Lord with all thy heart, and lean not upon thy own prudence. In all thy ways think on him, and he will direct thy steps."

8. Cf. Sender, "Freedom and Constraint in Andre Gide," 405–19.

9. Cf. Lonergan, *Collected Works of Bernard Lonergan*.

towards the god, whose seed they were; for they possessed true and in every way great spirits, uniting gentleness with wisdom in the various chances of life, and in their intercourse with one another. They despised everything but virtue, caring little for their present state of life, and thinking lightly of the possession of gold and other property, which seemed only a burden to them; neither were they intoxicated by luxury; nor did wealth deprive them of their self-control; but they were sober, and saw clearly that all these goods are increased by virtue and friendship with one another, whereas by too great regard and respect for them, they are lost and friendship with them. . . . When the divine portion began to fade away, and became diluted too often and too much with the mortal admixture, and the human nature got the upper hand, they then, being unable to bear their fortune, behaved unseemly, and to him who had an eye to see grew visibly debased, for they were losing the fairest of their precious gifts; but to those who had no eye to see the true happiness, they appeared glorious and blessed at the very time when they were full of avarice and unrighteous power.[10]

The ethical life rooted in the natural law envisions a number of things, one of which is happiness, albeit a peculiar faith-demanding sort which must be distinguished from affectivity and pleasure and yet not isolated from them; fulfilled, in fact, by them in love.[11] This love fulfills *because* it abolishes the speculative distance of the intellect.[12] The intellect chastens the will so that the will achieves a martyrological violence, not to itself but to the intellect to which it had first and long-since surrendered. Such happiness invokes submission and rebellion, and the lines between the two are more blurred than one might even imagine. Our abidance by and adherence to the natural law requires us to become the delicate weight in the swinging pendulum between an affective dominance and an over-intellectualization of act-into-*conceptio*, somehow striking an unearthly middle ground—human flourishing.[13] Happiness is triggered by the immediacy of the will but agonically lengthened into a distance by the intellect—into an end to be achieved, a teleological goal—which must turn away from and somehow retain this initial will-based trigger.

10. *Critias*, 120d–121b.

11. See Saint Thomas on whether the contemplative life has nothing to do with the affections, and pertains wholly to the intellect. *ST* II-II, 180, 1.

12. Cf. SCG III, 25–40.

13. Cf. *ST* I-II, 94, 3.

It is precisely this "turning away" which initiates the ethical system, thus inevitably conceiving it as an imposition. In this jarring of orders, everything carries purpose unto glory; all persist with clean lines and harmony raised by the unseemly, uneven and forgotten. Ours is an order offering up its own iniquity, and yet it retains its beauty as neither figmentary nor spectral. [14] By its "imposition" ethics is, from the outset, a preparation for judgment. Because ethical meaning places us in the enactment of time as a participant, a moving finger that writes and then moves on[15] in the order of things, all ethical action seeks the imprimatur of the Other. Even if an ethical system devolves into a progressivist materialist egoism where otherness is affirmed as nothing more than mere ontical validity—as token gratuity or obstacle—all imposition, by being artifice-intelligence, sustains itself because it invokes judiciary vision, requiring something other from the world than the world. Underneath all the falsehoods is the unstripped natural law; its placement lifts us from the world and strips us down; it is a supernatural ratification as much as it is a sacrificial disrobing of our being.

> They must be stripped bare of all those things before they are tried; for they must stand their trial dead. Their judge also must be naked, dead, beholding with very soul the very soul of each immediately upon his death, bereft of all his kin and having left behind on earth all that fine array, to the end that the judgement may be just.[16]

The law is said to be "natural" and yet it opens the door to the meaning of our nature precisely because it must lift us out of our natural connaturality,[17] reclaiming a new nature in order for it to be so enacted.

---

14. Cf. Doctorow, *Reporting the Universe*, 122: "Whitman when he walked the streets of New York loved everything he saw—the multitudes that thrilled him, the industries at work, the ships in the harbor, the clatter of horses and carriages, the crowds in the streets, the flags of celebration. Yet he knew, of course, that the newspaper business from which he made his living relied finally for its success on the skinny shoulders of itinerant newsboys, street urchins who lived on the few cents they made hawking the papers in every corner of the city. Thousands of vagrant children lived in the streets of the city that Whitman loved. Yet his exultant optimism and awe of human achievement was not demeaned; he could carry it all, the whole city, and attend like a nurse to its illnesses but like a lover to its fair face."

15. Khayyam, *Rubaiyat*, §51, 71, 76.

16. *Gorgias*, 523e.

17. Maritain, *Approaches to God*, 111–12: "Nothing is more human than for man to desire naturally things impossible to his nature. It is, indeed, the property of a

We are seeking instead to step back, to reside in the ground *before* the imposition of the natural law becomes identical to the ethical-political structure it guides; before it takes on the character of habit from which, for Saint Thomas, it is distinct:

> A thing may be called a habit in two ways. First, properly and essentially: and thus the natural law is not a habit. For it has been stated above (I-II:90:1 ad 2) that the natural law is something appointed by reason, just as a proposition is a work of reason. Now that which a man does is not the same as that whereby he does it: for he makes a becoming speech by the habit of grammar. Since then a habit is that by which we act, a law cannot be a habit properly and essentially. Secondly, the term habit may be applied to that which we hold by a habit: thus, faith may mean that which we hold by faith. And accordingly, since the precepts of the natural law are sometimes considered by reason actually, while sometimes they are in the reason only habitually, in this way the natural law may be called a habit. Thus, in speculative matters, the indemonstrable principles are not the habit itself whereby we hold those principles, but are the principles the habit of which we possess.[18]

If the natural law in its originary precept can never be "blotted out from the hearts of men"[19] we do much justice to human nature when we speak of it as super-natural, trans-natural, naturally supernatural, in but not *of* the world. Perhaps, still, we are missing something crucial, namely the missing components of ethical meaning. The language of our super-natural nature occurs as a *secondary* action leaving a first order behind; it

---

nature which is not closed up in matter like the nature of physical things, but which is intellectual or infinitized by the spirit. It is the property of a metaphysical nature. Such desires reach for the infinite, because the intellect thirsts for Being and Being is infinite. They are natural, but one may also call them transnatural. [And this desire] . . . Is not a simple velleity, a superadded desire, a desire of super-erogation. It is born in the very depths of the thirst of our intellect for Being; it is a nostalgia so pro-foundly human that all the wisdom and all the folly of man's behavior has in it its most secret reason. And because this desire which asks for what is impossible to nature is a desire of nature in its pro-foundest depths, St. Thomas Aquinas asserts that it cannot issue in an absolute impossibility. It is in no way necessary that it be satisfied, since it asks for what is impossible for nature. But it is necessary that by some means (which is not nature) it be able to be satisfied, since it necessarily emanates from nature."

18. *ST* I, 94, 1, *resp.*

19. *ST* I, 94, 6, *resp.*

is the spiritual framing of ethical imposition, it occurs only *after* the first order of human action, once unified with the world, is hidden.

What occurs *before* brings us to the un-reflexive recognition of Being which grounds metaphysics and, through it, our desire for the good and our aversion to evil, thereby providing the source for all natural law precepts. Saint Thomas speaks of our first encounter in knowledge not as a conceptual undertaking but as the universal apprehension that grounds knowledge and which allows the metaphysical and practical orders to unfold. And while it is a simple, singular universal apprehension, it is by no means a simplistic one. It is this seamless unity of thinking and Being which opens to us our beatitude, and which grounds the very complexity of all theoretical and practical action where thinking and Being more often than not *fail* to align:

> Now a certain order is to be found in those things that are apprehended universally. For that which, before aught else, falls under apprehension, is 'being,' the notion of which is included in all things whatsoever a man apprehends. Wherefore the first indemonstrable principle is that 'the same thing cannot be affirmed and denied at the same time,' which is based on the notion of 'being' and 'not-being:' and on this principle all others are based, as is stated in Metaph. iv, text. 9. Now as 'being' is the first thing that falls under the apprehension simply, so 'good' is the first thing that falls under the apprehension of the practical reason, which is directed to action: since every agent acts for an end under the aspect of good. Consequently, the first principle of practical reason is one founded on the notion of good, viz. that 'good is that which all things seek after.' Hence this is the first precept of law, that 'good is to be done and pursued, and evil is to be avoided.' All other precepts of the natural law are based upon this: so that whatever the practical reason naturally apprehends as man's good (or evil) belongs to the precepts of the natural law as something to be done or avoided.[20]

The language of our natural super-nature is used to justify—and not wholly inauthentically—the turn away from the immediacy of the will; it is the judicial placing of the dams which hold back affective immediacy until it can be rerouted and managed by distance, spectatorship, and virtue training.[21] These are the courtesies of tradition, education, and

---

20. *ST* I-II, 94, 2, *resp.*

21. But this "holding back" is done only so that it can deliver the sweetness of contemplation wholly mingled with the active life. See Saint Thomas's response as to

prescription, the rules of the game of which we spoke, and of which we will have cause to speak again in greater detail. But what then was there *before* all was held back and suspended? If it be natural—and thus *good*—mustn't that non-reflexive love be foundational for the ethic? Our supernatural ordination finds its meaning by being born from our ethical predicament, the oddness of a natural law which imposes order upon nature, while refusing to call that placement alien. The natural law is as much a frail and exotic artifice—for no state of nature is natural—while claiming to be the prime substance of our innermost being. We can see this odd stance in the way in which all acts of virtue are prescribed by the natural law, finding their indelible image in its precepts. Yet when many virtuous acts are considered in themselves, the lineage to the natural law appears hidden; nature does not first incline the virtuous act but instead requires the enactment of reason. Our supernatural ordination attests more to our glaring estrangement from nature than to our proximity. With Saint Thomas:

> For it has been stated that to the natural law belongs everything to which a man is inclined according to his nature. Now each thing is inclined naturally to an operation that is suitable to it according to its form: thus fire is inclined to give heat. Wherefore, since the rational soul is the proper form of man, there is in every man a natural inclination to act according to reason: and this is to act according to virtue. Consequently, considered thus, all acts of virtue are prescribed by the natural law: since each one's reason naturally dictates to him to act virtuously. But if we speak of virtuous acts, considered in themselves, i.e. in their proper species, thus not all virtuous acts are prescribed by the natural law: for many things are done virtuously, to which nature does not incline at first; but which, through the inquiry of reason, have been found by men to be conducive to well-living.[22]

Our ethical ordination is not able to fulfill our natural supernaturality without first reuniting and rediscovering its meaning *before* the natural law appeared identical with ethical prescription, as

whether a religious order devoted to the contemplative life is superior to one devoted instead to the active life. While the former is superior it is only so when it embodies the non-mediated into-the-world nearness of the latter. The sweetness of contemplative perfection occurs when one returns from contemplation so as to be its irradiating presence. *ST* II-II, 188, 6, *resp*: "Better to illuminate than merely to shine to deliver to others contemplated truths than merely to contemplate."

22. *ST* I-II 94, 3, *resp*.

something *other* than seamless unity and action. While those essential descriptions ("naturally supernatural," "trans-natural" that "manifesting in your life the image of God impressed on your rational nature"[23]) cast the necessary gravity within the realms of metaphysics, epistemology, and theological discourse, their relevance within their own origin in the ethical life appears strained and unproductive. The natural law carries with it more than a whiff of Nietzschean irony. The overemphasis on ethics as an imposition fails to address the nature we seek to save and illuminate, becoming one of abandoning an unclear first-order nature in favor of a finality which cannot be clarified. And how could it clarify our end if it cannot dwell on and in our origin?[24] If this supernatural end is said to be the fulfillment of our nature rather than its antithesis, then the natural law must have a meaning before it becomes prescription.[25] The natural law remains an obscure end-to-be-perceived, and cannot become an eschatological and living realm, without that placement illuminating our first-order nature, our non-reflexive love—our timeliness *because*

---

23. *Catholic Encyclopedia*, 9:77.

24. For Saint Augustine, the eternal law is imprinted on all men and when we act on the eternal law this is the enactment or realization of the natural law. Cf. *ST* I-II, 93, 2, *resp*: "A thing may be known in two ways: first, in itself; secondly, in its effect, wherein some likeness of that thing is found: thus, someone not seeing the sun in its substance, may know it by its rays. So then no one can know the eternal law, as it is in itself, except the blessed who see God in His Essence. But every rational creature knows it in its reflection, greater or less. For every knowledge of truth is a kind of reflection and participation of the eternal law, which is the unchangeable truth, as Augustine says (De Vera Relig. xxxi). Now all men know the truth to a certain extent, at least as to the common principles of the natural law: and as to the others, they partake of the knowledge of truth, some more, some less; and in this respect are more or less cognizant of the eternal law."

25. Dr. Herbert Hartmann speaks to this on the question of Saint Thomas on Prudence and the Natural Law. "St. Thomas and Prudence," 87: "Saint Thomas' entire ethical teaching can, in a sense, be seen as an extended meditation upon the scriptural text: 'God made man from the beginning, and left him in the hand of his own counsel.' The fact that Aquinas was a Christian theologian did not lead him to denigrate the human virtue of prudence. For Aquinas, to err or misunderstand the creature and his proper excellence is to error or misunderstand the Creator. In short, a denigration of the powers of the rational creature, man, eventually would lead to a denigration of God's power in nature. Therefore, Saint Thomas has no interest in degrading the human wisdom of prudence for the sake of elevating his praise of God's power. Instead, his self-appointed task is to understand the nature of things as they are (and consequently man's own place in the order of the universe) so that man, 'who by faith is led to God as his last end,' does not through ignorance of the truth lead himself astray."

imprinted by the eternal law[26]—rather than suppressing it by way of a systematic over-intellectualizing of action into *theoria*. The natural law should be the signpost for freedom, it should widen the scope of mystery rather than diminish it. The Vienna Circle's Moritz Schlick surprisingly endorses such a view in a remarkable passage:

> The concept of *duty*, which so many philosophers place at the center of their ethics, presupposes the concept of purpose; to obey the commands of duty means nothing else but to stand under the dominion of purposes . . . Let us recall Schiller's remark, that the principle of play as the true vocation of man will attain its deepest significance if we apply it to the seriousness of duty and destiny. What does this mean? It was Schiller who rebelled against the doctrine of Kant, whereby, of course, the moral is primarily to be found where man acts by conquering himself. For in Kant's view an action is moral only when it springs from reverence for the law of duty as its sole motive; and since in the actual man conflicting inclinations are always present, moral action means a struggle against one's own inclination, it means laborious work. Schiller was utterly and entirely right, for this account of the good is infinitely remote from the meaning that everyone is otherwise naturally accustomed to associate with the word. We do not call *him* the best man, who is obliged unceasingly to resist his own impulses and is constantly at war with his own desires; we say this, rather, of the man whose inclinations are kindly and benevolent from the start, so that he simply does not fall into doubt and self-conflict. The man who struggles with and conquers himself is perhaps the type of the *great* man but not of the *good* one . . . There is the deepest wisdom in the biblical injunction: 'unless ye become as little children.'[27]

---

26. Cf. *ST* I-II, 93, 5, *resp*: "Now just as man, by such pronouncement, impresses a kind of inward principle of action on the man that is subject to him, so God imprints on the whole of nature the principles of its proper actions. And so, in this way, God is said to command the whole of nature, according to Psalm 148:6: 'He hath made a decree, and it shall not pass away.' And thus, all actions and movements of the whole of nature are subject to the eternal law. Consequently, irrational creatures are subject to the eternal law, through being moved by Divine providence; but not, as rational creatures are, through understanding the Divine commandment."

27. Schlick, *Philosophical Papers*, 125.

The Predicament of the Five Ways

If a genuine and efficacious ethics requires an accessible and meaningful natural law, this very natural law itself requires the existence of a divine and eternal Being. And thus the demonstration of God's existence takes center stage in order to understand eternal action. Because of his faith, and not in spite of it, Saint Thomas, like Anselm, believes it absolutely critical that he demonstrate the existence of God. God is not the cause of some aspect of man or of some ideas and not others. He has caused everything that is real and existing in the world. The notion of *creatio ex nihilo* means that God is the universal cause and that all things in the world are the effects of God; the only thing we own outright is our own nothingness.[28] He knows that in the natural world effects necessarily demonstrate the *existence* of their cause.[29] Herein lies the predicament of Saint Thomas in his demonstrations for the existence of God: the faith that God created out of nothing has asserted that God is the universal cause. There can be no other primal cause for existence than God. Man and world are *all* effects of God as Cause. The faith is telling him that reason should be able to demonstrate beyond a reasonable doubt the existence of God because the God of the faith is the *only* universal cause of all that is in nature, and that in the natural order of things, effects necessarily point toward the existence of their cause.

The demonstrations for God are not logical or scientific proofs. Precisely because God's essence is unknown to us,[30] we cannot demonstrate Him by intellectual empirical description alone but must work within the relationship between the connatural immediacy of the will and the speculative distance of the intellect. The demonstrations are thus properly called ways or *viae*, meaning they are *pointing towards* what is needed, beyond any reasonable doubt, to be our primal and ultimate cause. What they are pointing toward is the *mystery* of God, a Being unlike any other

28. Cf. Maritain, *God and the Permission of Evil*, 10: "In the order of Being and reality, God is the primal causation and thus the interior intelligibility of the known thing. This means that, for example, "in the line of the good, God is the first and transcendent cause of our liberty and our free decisions, so that the free act is wholly from God as first cause and wholly from us as second cause; because there is not a fibril of Being which escapes the causality of God. Our liberty has the initiative of our acts, but this is a second initiative; it is God who has the first initiative . . . in the line of good: all that which God knows in created existence, He knows because He causes it."

29. *ST* I, 2, 1, *resp.*

30. Cf. *ST* I, 2, *resp*; DN I, 3, 77; In Sent. VIII, 1,1.

Being in the world, a Being that was not caused but always existed, that is eternal, perfect, unchanging, infinite, all-good, all-knowing, all-powerful. Thus, what exactly *can* we demonstrate of this being when such attributes so surpass our limited powers as temporal, limited in knowledge and power? How can we get from the finite to the infinite?[31]

The predicament of Saint Thomas is as such: The faith urges reason that it must be able to demonstrate something of God beyond a reasonable doubt because effects necessarily demonstrate the existence of their cause. To say that this does not apply to God and man would imply that the truths of reason are not compatible with the truths of faith, and this is a dangerous precedent that Saint Thomas would never advocate. But at the same time, Saint Thomas knows that whatever he demonstrates of God *cannot* violate the effulgent mystery and plenitude of God. Saint Thomas's demonstrations must demonstrate God beyond a reasonable doubt in order to respect the relationship between cause and effect, and at the same time demonstrate God in such a way not only that the demonstrations do not violate the mystery of God which is accessed only by the faith or, in the end, in the beatific vision of God, but actually opens the invitation to the mystery. The language of the reflexive intellect and the non-reflexive originary *praxis* of the will must both be at play in the demonstrations. Without the balance of the two, the Five Ways will fall either into reducing God to a cheap empirical certitude, or not going far enough to show that there is no other way to understand our complex existential situation but to affirm this efficacious supernatural origin.

31. See McDermott's prefatory comments in *Summa Theologiae: A Concise Edition*, xxxi–xxxii: "Negations are, so to speak, the shadows cast in our language by the affirmations we would like to make: God's simpleness, for example, his lack of parts, is a shadow thrown onto our expectation of what perfection is—richness of complexity—by God's all-embracing concentration of perfection in one entity, a perfection that sums every variety of created perfection that imitates it. In similar ways, Thomas will show that God is-and-isn't in space: not existing in space as himself located, but present as the active doing of all spatial location and locatedness; and even more mysteriously, that God is-and-isn't in time: not himself measured by time but present in all temporal measuring and measuredness. The principle appealed to throughout is the same principle that led to God's existence in the first place: God exists as the doing of all being, the existence that acts in all existence, an existence in the world's existing but not of it, no thing, but not therefore nothing."

God as Self-Evident? The Pedagogy of Suggestion

> Verily, it is a blessing and not a blasphemy when I teach: Over all things stand the heaven Accident, the heaven Innocence, the heaven Chance, the heaven Prankishness. 'By Chance'—that is the most ancient nobility of the world, and this I restored to all things: I delivered them from their bondage under Purpose. This freedom and heavenly cheer I have placed over all things like an azure bell when I taught that over them and through them no 'eternal will' wills. This prankish folly I have put in the place of that will when I taught: 'In everything one thing is impossible: rationality.' A little reason, to be sure, a seed of wisdom scattered from star to starthis heaven is mixed in with all things: for folly's sake, wisdom is mixed in with all things. A little wisdom is possible indeed; this blessed certainty I found in all things: that they would rather dance on the feet of chance.[32]

The rules of the language game of the divine are neither self-evident nor *a priori* nor even synthetic *a priori*—but they are naturally indubitable. The problem is that reflection *on* the natural separates us *from* the natural, creating the distance that requires what it should not require—demonstration! And it is this that puts God into the dock, and reveals Myshkin to be the enigma of simplicity that he is or, what Santayana calls, in referring to Nietzsche, the geniality of imbecility.[33]

Saint Thomas opens his Five Ways with a proposed rejection of the self-evident existence of God. We must ask ourselves why this clarity of vision, this type of certitude, must be dismissed from the outset? This is Aquinas's opening salvo, and it carries the tone and approach for the unfolding of his arguments, a tone and approach which are to lead us to the door of the divine and claim a groundwork unlike any other type of proof precisely because it is not "proof." Rather is it a *way*, a signpost pointing, beyond any reasonable doubt, to that *difference as such* at the heart of Being. And yet, Thomas's *difference as such*, this beyond reasonable doubt *mystery* which serves as foundation for all empirical truths, even as it resides beyond them, carries its own presential self-evidence, a communion with un-reflexive love. Saint Thomas does not merely reject the self-evident existence of God, but points to a different

---

32. Nietzsche, *Thus Spoke Zarathustra*, 166.
33. Santayana, *Egotism*, 135.

order of self-evidence with first principles[34] which retains the crucial importance of that strange clarity, that self-evident communion with Being so clear and real that it is unquestionably present. This presence is there for Dostoyevsky's Prince Myshkin, not as a thing to be aspired to or studied or even religiously sustained as a promise[35] but simply a presence to which the bodily soul is united:

> Myshkin is different from others because, as an Idiot and an epileptic who is at the same time an exceptionally clever man, he has much closer and less obscure relationships with the Unconscious. He has had rare instants of intuitive perception, occasional seconds of transcendent exaltation. For a lightning moment he has felt the all-being, the all-feeling, the all-suffering, the all-understanding. He has known all that is in the world. There lies the kernel of his magical being. He has not studied, and is not endowed with, mystical wisdom, he has not even aspired to it. He has simply experienced the thing itself. He has not merely had occasional significant thoughts and ideas. He has literally, once and more than once, stood on the magic borderland where everything is affirmed, where not only the remotest thought is true, but also the contrary of such thought.[36]

Now what occurs in *ST* I, 2, 1 is not so much a rejection of the principles of self-evidence as it is a relocation of their placement, not in that second order where natural law is identical with its necessarily prescriptive role in the *polis*, but in that first order which is clear to those who, like Myshkin, live one in being with a bodily soul. It is therefore not a question of dismissing that certitude as without foundation or basis, but showing that something does indeed change when man acts only

34. Cf. *ST* I, 2, 1.

35. Cf. Pegis, "Aquinas and the Natural Law," 5: "The Christian man, who knows by faith that God has made that hope of human nature into a promise and a reality, can understand the mystery of human destiny with greater depth, but as the end for philosophy as for reason the vision of the perfect good remains a hope—not indeed a hope without substance, since it is discovered and expressed within a world of divine providence. What could—and even would—come to man, if he but opened himself to it, for a God who was pure love? Let us say, then, that a philosophical ethics ends in human hope sustained by a mystery, whereas religious ethics begins with a covenant and is sustained by a promise." This lecture was referred to by Leo Strauss in his University of Chicago, 1965 winter quarter class "Introduction to Political Philosophy: Aristotle," sessions 10–16. He purportedly noted that he had never understood Thomism in such a manner, and found the talk profound.

36. Hesse, "Dostoevsky's *The Idiot*," 203–4.

by reflection and places the natural law, as necessary imposition, upon his being. When he interrogatively uncovers his naturally supernatural status, he affirms and yet by that very act loses that very status! By being eidetically circumscribed as a "state" or "status," that supernatural appellation betokens more alienation than union, a not-*of*-the-world recognition which has the tendency to veer into the unnatural or to bypass the natural as a merely uninformative starting point, losing the forest for the trees, losing the actual *to be* of the what *is* in the mediated flux of *what* is. The divine multiplication of intermediaries invites the soul to reflection but also tempts the soul to put the emphasis on the wrong syllables of existence, forfeiting immediacy to distance. And yet this is the *longer way* and must be efficacious. The self-evidence of God is too easy an answer, and existence, while a gift, is not easy. It is unease in essence. It is ill at ease without being dis-eased. And while God is not self-evident, He is ineluctable.

That first order clarity is obscured *because* we have turned reflexive, claiming our naturally supernatural state in the second order of prescription and imposition, thereby becoming identical with our own imposition. This movement is not unnatural; it is the essential movement which reveals the natural law to be our rational participation in the eternal law.[37] But all movements receive their meaning from their efficient and final causation, from their *arche* and *telos*. The *telos* is gathered by way of the intellect which creates distance-as-separation and places us as spectator; but the *arche*, which had originally ignited our desire for the *telos*, is gained not by *conceptio* or *theoria* but by an originary *praxis*. It is one with the bodily and simple soul which lives *before* aspiration so that aspiration may occur, which *precedes* contemplation so that that dwelling can be inhabited. It is the play before work which allows the work to be creative in the realm of sanctification.[38] It is the first order of

37. Cf. *ST* I-II, 91, 2, *resp.*

38. Cf. Moritz Schlick, "On the Meaning of Life," in Hanfling, *Life and Meaning: A Philosophical Reader*, 60–73, esp. 64: "There is, however, no irreconcilable opposition between play in the philosophical sense and work in the economic meaning of the term. Play, as we see it, is any activity which takes place entirely for its own sake, independently of its effects and consequences. There is nothing to stop these effects from being of a useful or valuable kind. If they are, so much the better; the action still remains play, since it already bears its own value within itself . . . Play too, in other words, can be creative; its outcome can coincide with that of work . . . And that is also true in the end of those actions which engender neither science or art, but the day's necessities, and which are seemingly altogether devoid of spirit. The tilling of the

our being before existence is reordered[39] in terms of a judiciary futurity in which essences are determined, decisions made, and responsibilities assumed, "for the sake of" realm in which every end is incremental and temporally futural, for the sake of the objective to be attained. Now in some sense this seems an inversion of the distinction between practical and theoretical, where *praxis* is the realm of the for-the-sake-of while *theoria* is the realm of the in-itself. Only when a soul has lived *before* futurity can it access within itself the natural law in a way which recognizes the law's necessary imposition, but moves beyond it as only the child, saint, martyr, or idiot can.[40] If our ethical life is to hold both the *in* and the *not-of* the world without surrendering the former in favor of the latter, this requires we become like children, or like the lilies.

> Youth, in fact, is not just a time of growing, learning, ripening and incompleteness, but primarily a time of play, of doing for its own sake, and hence a true bearer of the meaning of life. Anyone denying this, and regarding youth as a mere introduction and prelude to real life, commits the same error that beclouded the mediaeval view of human existence: he shifts life's center of gravity forwards, into the future. Just as the majority of religions, discontented with earthly life, are wont to transfer the meaning of existence out of this life and into a hereafter, so man in general is inclined always to regard every state, since none of them is wholly perfect, as a mere preparation for a more perfect one.[41]

---

fields, the weaving of fabrics, the cobbling of shoes, can all become play, and may take on the character of artistic acts. Nor is it even so uncommon for a man to take so much pleasure in such activities, that he forgets the purpose of them. Every true craftsman can experience in his own case this transformation of the means into an end-in-itself, which can take place with almost any activity, and which makes the product into a work of art . . . The individual would lead an existence, as in the profound and beautiful saying of the Bible, like the life of the lilies of the field."

39. See Saint Thomas on whether there was faith in angels and in man in their original states. *ST* II-II, 5, 1, ad. 1: "Their contemplation was higher than ours, and by means of it, they drew nearer to God than we do and so could in a clear way know more things about divine actions and mysteries than we can. For this reason, there was not in them a faith by which God is sought as being absent, in the way that He is sought by us. For He was more present to them by the light of wisdom than He is to us, even though He was not present to them as He is to the blessed through the light of glory."

40. Cf. Unamuno, *Our Lord Don Quixote.*

41. Schlick, "On the Meaning of Life," 68.

"The Kingdom of Heaven belongs to children"[42] not because the child at play is weak, pacified by all things to the point of impotence, as is the danger of Prince Myshkin, who reminds one of Christ but more of what Christ is not. Hesse speaks of the similarity between Christ and Myshkin as both sharing a morbid fear of entanglement with the erotic vicissitudes of incarnated being,[43] but this is not what is meant by the child to whom Christ offers the kingdom of heaven. The child at play is Christ-like because she alone is able to sustain existence as it *is*, in itself, incarnated in the present where *praxis* truly originates. When the natural law moves from the first order of un-reflexive love to the second order, the recognition of our naturally supernatural state, it is in danger of losing the lesson of Presence, downgrading the mystery of the bodily soul and obfuscating the self-evidence of the child-like first order. This imposition often engulfs *praxis* in the futural, stripping it of its interior non-temporality which a genuine affectivity provides. It demands that practical actions have the *same* vision as the intellect, as if its outcomes, choices, and actions need to be guided by advantage gained or lost, as if happiness resides only by what is won or surrendered. It replaces origins with ends. It does seem that I am inverting a classic distinction in terms of the temporal framework customarily attached to *praxis* and *theoria*. Historically, *praxis—as for the sake of something else—*is naturally aligned with the futural and *theoria* is the in-itself non-futural play which distinguishes itself as the good-for-itself." The justification could be made that while classically, *praxis* embodies the futural, it does so when aligned with the intellect as if it is a handmaiden to *theoria*. Praxis adjectivally attaches to the intellect and thus embodies a futurity, but often a vacant and perspectival one where the intellect seeks its next advantage or foothold in time. We seek the originary praxis which grounds the intellect in its own pre-cognitive union with Being. But this union can be seen in practical action, in the into-the-world cyclical repetition of the day's events in which the pattern outwardly and by the dissection of the intellect reveals a futural movement but inwardly within our primal affectivity provides a harmony with the ebb and flow, the unveiling and veiling of

---

42. Matt 19:14 (VOICE).

43. Cf. Hesse, "Dostoevsky's *The Idiot*," 199: "Only one trait in Myshkin's character, but an important one, appears to me as Christlike. I allude to his timid, morbid purity. The secret fear of sex and of procreation is a trait which must be reckoned with in the message of Christ for it plays a distinct part in his world mission. Even the superficial portrait of Jesus by Renan does not entirely overlook this feature."

Being. Only when *praxis* is allowed both its outward futurity recognized by the intellect and its inward immediacy enacted by affectivity can it be genuinely meaningful. The degeneration of *praxis* into *homo faber* is a prime example of *praxis* sequestered to its outward view managed by the intellect. God is found among the pots and pans but only when *praxis* carries this two-fold harmony.

It is difficult to distinguish how the will, guided by the intellect, cannot take on the intellect's futurity, even in its recollection, and when it does this, the ethical life is commoditized, becoming a store shelf of products to be achieved.[44] The futurity proper to the planning intellect lengthens the will's immediacy, stretches it as it does with hope, denoting "a movement or a stretching forth of the appetite towards an arduous good."[45] But this stretching requires connection and stability to its origin, for without it it would be carried along as anticipating some point of finality beyond itself, all the while losing its fortitude and endurance, terminating in *ennui*. It stretches in a deeper way *because* it retains the immediacy of all-being.[46] It is the *union* of Martha and Mary.[47]

44. We seek here the distinct non-mediated temporal presence, particular to the will, the region in beings where grace transforms desire into self-giving, evoking a co-naissance intimacy with Being, one which paradoxically prepares the intellect to guide the will. Cf. Nichols, *Word Has Been Abroad*, xv.

45. *ST* II-II, 17, 3, *resp.*

46. Cf. *Critias*, 109b–c: "In the days of old the gods had the whole earth distributed among them by allotment. There was no quarrelling; for you cannot rightly suppose that the gods did not know what was proper for each of them to have, or, knowing this, that they would seek to procure for themselves by contention that which more properly belonged to others. They all of them by just apportionment obtained what they wanted, and peopled their own districts; and when they had peopled them they tended us, their nurslings and possessions, as shepherds tend their flocks, excepting only that they did not use blows or bodily force, as shepherds do, but governed us like pilots from the stern of the vessel, which is an easy way of guiding animals, holding our souls by the rudder of persuasion according to their own pleasure;—thus did they guide all mortal creatures."

47. Cf. Eckhart, "Sermon 34," in *Breakthrough*, 478: "Three things caused Mary to sit at our Lord's feet. The first was that God's goodness had embraced her soul. The second was a great, unspeakable longing: she yearned without knowing what it was she yearned after, and she desired without knowing what she desired! The third was the sweet consolation and bliss she derived from the eternal words that came from Christ's mouth. Three things also caused Martha to run about and serve her dear Christ. The first was a maturity of age and a depth of her being, which was thoroughly trained to the most external matters. For this reason, she believed that no one was so well suited for activity as herself. The second was a wise prudence that knew how to achieve external acts to the highest degree that love demands. The third was the high dignity of

The Realism of Remembered Things[48]

If *praxis* becomes futural, both the practical and intellectual realms are undermined. The intellect loses its source of contemplation in the longing not to reside in longing itself but in the presence of *to be*. It loses the ability for recollection to be a re-collection of being one with the Other as embodied bodily soul. The practical, when carried along, having surrendered its stretching forth, then creates an ethics where the futural is identical with the progressive and where the exotic artifice of the city state becomes fully alien. The imposition of the natural law no longer has the *in* which makes the "not-of" a relation to the natural rather than its antithesis, rendering the exotic flower of political life an artificial flower where *toujours la politesse* is easily transformed into a "you will do this" political correctness that often even contradicts and overrules the healthy public orthodoxy of common things.[49]

> Now different gods had their allotments in different places which they set in order. Hephaestus and Athene, who were brother and sister, and sprang from the same father, having a common nature, and being united also in the love of philosophy and art, both obtained as their common portion this land, which was naturally adapted for wisdom and virtue; and there they implanted brave children of the soil, and put into their minds the order of government; their names are preserved, but their actions have disappeared by reason of the destruction of those who received the tradition, and the lapse of ages. For when there were any survivors, as I have already said, they were men who dwelt in the mountains; and they were ignorant of the art of writing, and had heard only the names of the chiefs of the land, but very little about their actions. The names they were willing enough to give to their children; but the virtues and the laws of their predecessors, they knew only by obscure traditions; and as they themselves and their children lacked for many generations the necessaries of life, they directed their attention to the supply of their wants, and of them they conversed, to the neglect of events that had happened in times long past; for mythology and

---

her dear guest. The masters of the spiritual life say that God is ready for every person's spiritual and physical satisfaction to the utmost degree that the person desires. We can clearly distinguish with respect to God's dear friends how God satisfies our spiritual nature while, on the other hand, he also provides satisfaction for our physical nature."

48. Cf. Ortega y Gasset, *Meditations on Quixote*, 85.

49. Cf. Voegelin, "On Hegel: A Study of Sorcery," in *Published Essays, 1966–1985*.

the enquiry into antiquity are first introduced into cities when they begin to have leisure, and when they see that the necessaries of life have already been provided, but not before. And this is reason why the names of the ancients have been preserved to us and not their actions.

And it is here that the fateful disjunction, recognized throughout all history and all religion, comes to its explanatory place on center stage: the distinction between the human *nature* and the human *condition*. Perhaps all human beings *by nature* desire to understand—but certainly not *by condition* as we shall see. Most would rather live on in the cave of illusion.[50] Yes, by *nature* we all yearn to ascend. How can we live in a world wherein nature is divorced from condition, where only the idiot and the child see the self-evidence of the divine? The objector states:

> It seems that the existence of God is self-evident. Now those things are said to be self-evident to us the knowledge of which is naturally implanted in us, as we can see in regard to first principles. But as Damascene says (De Fide Orth. i, 1,3), 'the knowledge of God is naturally implanted in all.' Therefore, the existence of God is self-evident.[51]

Saint Thomas knows like Plato that what was "implanted in the brave children of the soil" was obscured by the lapse of time, by tradition, and by the very enactment of our supernatural natures. The demonstrations are not for those who already have God by non-eidetic pre-possession. They are unnecessary for those standing "dreaming on the verge of strife, magnificently unprepared for the long littleness of life,"[52] who are unaware that it is idiotic to carry all of one's possessions in a small satchel and to wear gaiters and a coat ill-suited for the damp Russian thaw:

> The owner of the hooded cloak was a young man, also twenty-six or twenty-seven years old, somewhat above the average in height, with very fair thick hair, with sunken cheeks and a thin, pointed, almost white beard. His eyes were large, blue and intent; there was something calm, though somber, in their expression, something full of that strange look by which some can surmise epilepsy in a person at first glance. The young man's face was otherwise pleasing, delicate and lean, though colorless, and at

---

50. Strauss, *On Tyranny*, 22–132.

51. *ST* I, 2, 1, obj. 1.

52. Cf. Cornford, "Youth," in *Poems*, 15.

this moment even blue with cold. From his hands dangled a meager bundle tied up in an old, faded raw-silk kerchief, which, it seemed, contained the entirety of his traveling effects. He wore thick-soled boots and spats—it was all very un-Russian.[53]

Prince Lev Nikolaevich Myshkin is introduced to us, having left Switzerland, a recovering epileptic patient surrounded by snow which is bright and pure, little children whom he loves, and nature dappled by green and quiet. His benefactor, Pavlishtchev, who once had a child like him, found Myshkin years ago and took compassion on the dumb creature. But after four years in Switzerland, Pavlishtchev had died and Myshkin is sent unprepared into the world of exodus on business which will bring him all the troubles of navigating the impositions of the natural law—money, social entanglements, pity, love, confusion, and death. Everything in *The Idiot* is exodus and each sub-story mirrors others throughout. Myshkin begins his journey on a third-class train face to face with Parfyon Rogozhin, the very man who, because of their shared agony—their all-consuming entanglement with Nastassya Filippovna, another *alter Christus*—will return him to Switzerland, to his epilepsy, but deliver him lost.

In one of the third-class carriages, right by the window, two passengers had, from early dawn, been sitting facing one another—both were young people, both traveled light, both were unfashionably dressed, both had rather remarkable faces, and both expressed, at last, a desire to start a conversation. If they had both known, one about the other, in what way they were especially remarkable in that moment, they would naturally have wondered that chance had so strangely placed them face to face in a third-class carriage of the Warsaw–Petersburg train. One of them was a short man about twenty-seven, with almost black curly hair and small but fiery gray eyes. His nose was broad and flat, his cheekbones high; his thin lips continually curved into a sort of insolent, mocking and even malicious smile; but the high and well-shaped forehead redeemed the ignoble lines of the lower part of the face. What was particularly striking about the young man's face was its deathly pallor, which lent him an exhausted look in spite of his fairly sturdy build, and at the same time something passionate to the point of suffering, which did not harmonize with his insolent and coarse smile and his sharp and self-satisfied gaze. He was warmly dressed in a full, black,

53. Dostoyevsky, *Idiot*, 4.

sheepskin-lined overcoat, and had not felt the cold at night, while his neighbor had been forced to endure all the pleasures of a damp Russian November night, for which he was evidently unprepared.[54]

If post-fall man were to return to Eden and look up into the skies with those before the fall, he would neither see nor hear nor breathe what was loved by the latter. No matter where post-fall man resides, inside or outside the gates, he is in exodus, always somewhere east of Eden. Myshkin will return to Switzerland unable to survive exodus. Roghozin throughout never denies this even when he completes his end, and the one each loves, Nastassya, understands the impossible balance between the two. These two faces on a train, one an unknowing holy innocent and the other always in exodus but in a *knowing* exodus—differentiating him from the rest—both communicate what is and is not Christ. *The Idiot* is a meditation on the return to the place preceding exodus, as exile in a world deconstructed from any enduring narrative. This meditation illuminates what comes *before*, mostly by mocking our originary *praxis* but never without longing for its return. Every movement of the story finds a companion movement or sub-story, but no companion is a bedfellow, none can bring the other meaning, all fall into futility. It is a story of competing fatalisms and of what a soul must be in order to survive and love its fate, thereby making fate the highest form of freedom.[55]

Saint Thomas's demonstrations are for those racing towards their fate, cast into exodus and living only, if at all, by the prescriptive imposition of the natural law. It is not a demonstration for those who

---

54. Dostoyevsky, *Idiot*, 4.

55. Cf. See Jocasta's foreshadowing remarks. Sophocles, "Oedipus the King," in *Three Theban Plays*, §1070–72: "What should a man fear? It's all chance, chance rules our lives. Not a man on earth can see a day ahead, groping through the dark. Better to live at random, best we can." See also Milton, *Paradise Lost*, 658–61: "The reason'd high of providence, foreknowledge, will and fate, fixt fate, free will, foreknowledge absolute, and found no end, in wand'ring mazes lost." Cf. Hegel, *Natural Law*, 105: "Tragedy consists in this, that ethical nature segregates its inorganic nature (in order not to become entangled in it), as a fate, and places it outside itself: and by acknowledging this fate in the struggle against it, ethical nature is reconciled with the Divine being as the unity of both. To continue this metaphor, *Comedy*, on the other hand, will generally come down on the side of absence of fate. Either it falls within absolute vitality, and thus presents only shadows of clashes (or mock battles with a fabricated fate and fictitious enemies) or else it falls within non-life and therefore presents only shadows of self-determination and absoluteness; the former is the old, or Divine, comedy, the latter the modern comedy."

abide by what *is* but for those enmeshed in futurity by condition. It is a language game of seeing what is there to be seen, but which is rarely seen at all: the divine *presence*. Like the characters in *The Idiot*, these are *The Ways*, given to those who have forgotten by condition the un-reflexive love, so that futurity cannot be liberation but only the fatal flaw, the *hamartia* which casts a long shadow:

> Things are now as they are;
> they will be fulfilled in what is fated;
> neither burnt sacrifice nor libation
> of offerings without fire
> will soothe intense anger away.[56]

With the exceptions of Roghozin and Nastassya who race towards it in knowledge, every other character attempts "to avoid the unavoidable fatalism—the inevitable inevitability of narrative."[57] Only Myshkin for a time is freed from the need for demonstration, from the need to accept that God is not self-evident. As a demonstration catering to the fatal soul, to those retired to the secondary act of the natural law and its futurity, the demonstrations provide a reminding certainty of God's presence, and a certainty of their own dispossession within the mystery.

The Five Ways demonstrate God because they show that the stretching forth of the will requires union, and requires it to return to what has been forgotten when it first claimed its own im-positional supernaturality. When this imposition occurs, that imprint of the eternal law is then understood to us in a "general and confused way."[58] We are *in* but not *of* the world by way of alienation and the weight lies in that "not-of" without reference to the *in* union with the world. How we are "not-of" the world cannot be illuminated until we recover what places us *in*. Our placement in the world is not accidental and thus it too must offer something more than a mere starting block to our supernatural status, left behind as we ascend and aspire to our nature, where at best we become coaches but not players, little gods but no longer "divine playthings."[59]

56. Aeschylus, "Agamemnon," *Oresteia*, §67–71.

57. Young, *Dostoevsky's* The Idiot, 149.

58. *ST* I, 2, 1, ad. 1.

59. Cf. *Laws* 644d; 803b–c: "I assert that what is serious should be treated seriously, and what is not serious should not, and that by nature god is worthy of a complete blessed seriousness, but that what is human, as we said earlier, has been devised as a certain plaything of god, and that this is really the best thing about it. Every man and

For all those aspirations and ascensions are the makings of missing the mark. Only the idiot does not commit Oedipus's error in believing that because "nothing can make me other than I am," that this amounts to knowing what and who you are, as if reflection constitutes the soul:

Let the storm burst, my fixed resolve still holds,
To learn my lineage, be it ne'er so low.
It may be she with all a woman's pride
Thinks scorn of my base parentage. But I
Who rank myself as Fortune's favorite child,
The giver of good gifts, shall not be shamed.
She is my mother and the changing moons
My brethren, and with them I wax and wane.
Thus sprung why should I fear to trace my birth?
Nothing can make me other than I am. [60]

Saint Anselm's Thicket of Perfection: That Which Rises Up against Death

For how great is that light from which shines every truth that gives light to the rational mind? How great is that truth in which is everything that is true, and outside which is only nothingness and the false? How boundless is the truth which sees at one glance whatsoever has been made, and by whom, and through whom, and how it has been made from nothing? What purity,

woman should spend life in this way, playing the most beautiful games." Cf. Rahner, *Man at Play*, 40: "Surely only a man whose foundation is in the reality of God can thus call life on earth a game and a shadow-play? For only such a man as this, only to a man who truly believes that this world has proceeded out of the fullness of God's creative being, is it given to say 'Nay' along with his 'Yea', and to say it without demur or hesitation. In other words, only such a man can accept and lovingly embrace the world—which includes himself—as God's handiwork, and, at the same time, toss it aside as a child would toss a toy of which it had wearied, in order then to soar upward into the 'blessed seriousness' which is God alone. Only thus does gay melancholy become possible and justified, the mood which must always govern the Christian, the true *Homo Ludens*, as he follows his middle road. Love for the world and rejection of the world—both of these must draw him and he must at one and the same moment be ready to fold that world in his embrace and to turn his back upon it."

60. Sophocles, "Oedipus the King," in *Three Theban Plays*, §1077-86.

what certainty, what splendor where it is? Assuredly more than
a creature can conceive.[61]

The Dumb Ox recognizes the delicate position of the Five Ways:
he must demonstrate God beyond a reasonable doubt but must also
demonstrate the mystery, the incommunicability, the dramatic difference-
as-such, which can be viewed by the secondary ethic but can only be
accessed by our originary *praxis*, the childhood of a bodily soul. And to
do this, the *Ways* must primarily invoke the longer way of the natural
law as imposition, and then leave open the door to the immediacy of the
Anselmian logic of perfection. Saint Thomas must turn away from the
self-evidence of God so as to return to it in its proper place.

For Anselm, the idea of the perfect Being is the perfect idea.
Whatever else the argument may or may not demonstrate, it does
demonstrate that I cannot think of God without thinking of him as
existing, if I am thinking of him as *quo maius*. And once I think of him
as that than which nothing greater can be thought, thus recognizing the
commensurate/incommensurate relation, I am also thinking of him as
greater than anything that can be thought. This is a paradox but not a
contradiction. But how does he get here? By taking the idea from and
within the faith, not by discovering it in the warehouse of his mind nor
by demonstrating it step-by-step. We do not mean a mere natural faith,
or a rational assent to a cloaked and hidden God. This is a faith of the
dramatis personae—of God and man. It is faith thoroughly supernatural
and dependent on God because his pure *To Be* is not ideational, but lives
in the cosmic naturalness of the actions of the noble soul. Here we have
natural law as religious promise, as divine covenant:[62]

> Ah, blessed they, who pass through life's journey unstained, who
> follow the law of the Lord! Ah, blessed they, who cherish his
> decrees, make him the whole quest of their hearts! Afar from
> wrong-doing, thy sure paths they tread. Above all else it binds
> us, the charge thou hast given us to keep. Ah, how shall my steps
> be surely guided to keep faith with thy covenant? Attentive to
> all thy commandments, I go my way undismayed. A true heart's
> worship thou shalt have, thy just awards prompting me. All shall
> be done thy laws demand, so thou wilt not forsake me utterly.[63]

61. See "Monologium," XIV, in Anselm, *Proslogium, Monologium, Cur Deus Homo.*
62. Pegis, "Aquinas and the Natural Law," 5.
63. Ps 119.

The bifurcated view of nature and grace wreaks its havoc on the language of the natural and supernatural, and this can be seen in how faith is witnessed and enacted in the soul's relationship of will and intellect.[64] If faith is not achieved by the intellect's powers alone, if there is no amount of rational climbing that can help us arrive at the *non-sequitur* of the Incarnation, then the view of the intellectual ascent to God is only partially competent to reveal to us the vision of the faithful. If faith—even and especially in its absence and dryness—must carry a witness-like[65] quality to it, it is because the originary *praxis* which works itself into the soul of the saint or the martyr transmits what is incommunicable.

Is God self-evident? The question is framed in terms of intellectual assent, and the answer, within that vein, must be a resounding No. But because God's essence and existence *are* identical, Saint Thomas presents the genuine non-mediated connectivity between God's creative *To Be* and man's active responsiveness to that immediacy:

> God is in all things; not, indeed, as part of their essence, nor as an accident, but as an agent is present to that upon which it works. For an agent must be joined to that wherein it acts immediately and touch it by its power; hence it is proved in Phys. vii that the thing moved and the mover must be joined together. Now since God is very being by His own essence, created being must be His proper effect; as to ignite is the proper effect of fire. Now God causes this effect in things not only when they first begin to be, but as long as they are preserved in being; as light is caused in the air by the sun as long as the air remains illuminated. Therefore as long as a thing has being, God must be present to it, according to its mode of being. But being is innermost in each thing and most fundamentally inherent in all things since it is formal in respect of everything found in a thing, as was shown above (Question 7, Article 1). Hence it must be that God is in all things, and innermostly.[66]

For the intellect, God is not self-evident, for to be so would undermine the freedom and integrity of the creature and of God. But in order to ground that freedom and the *longer way* of the intellect's assent, God must be present according to our mode of being—to our *desire* to know. God

64. Cf. *ST* I-II, 94, 6, ad. 2. On whether the natural law can be abolished from the heart of man. "Although grace is more efficacious than nature, yet nature is more essential to man, and therefore more enduring."

65. Cf. Balthasar, *Christian Witness*, 18; see also Berry, "Tested in Fire," 145–70.

66. *ST* I, 8, 1, *resp.*

must be present—immediately and connaturally self-evident—in the bodily immediacy of the soul as exteriorized existence. If man is already outside himself in order to know himself and the world, he is already, by that dual intentionality, in the self-evidence of God by presence of the will. This is a non-demonstrable—because *pre-* and *non*-intellectual— starting point for the intellect to guide the will towards what it desires. And how could the will desire God if it does not "know" God? Moreover, the will does not act by "knowing" but by acting, and thus it must have an acting immediacy or self-evidence of God for it to desire God. Again, how can the intellect guide the will to its desire, if neither the intellect nor the will is in possession of what it desires?[67] God is in no way self-evident to the intellect, for this would be the sort of proto-occasionalism of select medieval thinkers,[68] which diminishes the ontological dimension of God and of our personal freedom. It would render the will a vacuole having no role or reference point in its relationship with the intellect.

Saint Thomas's rejection of the argument for self-evidence resides solely on the question of the intellect, but it leaves open the door for a different order of self-evidence, one absolutely necessary for the grounding of his metaphysics of *To Be*. If there is no form for connatural self-evidence, then the possibility of God as innermost in all things would be impossible. God would be idea but not Being. Let us change the question. If the question was "Is Being self-evident?" what would Saint Thomas's answer be? It would certainly be "yes." The existence of God is not self-evident to us though it is, in itself, self-evident. If we knew God's essence as existence, as identical, then God's existence would be self-evident:

> [The] proposition, 'God exists,' of itself is self-evident, for the predicate is the same as the subject, because God is His own existence as will be hereafter shown (I:3:4). Now because we do not know the essence of God, the proposition is not self-evident to us; but needs to be demonstrated by things that are more

---

67. This is why Plato places such a unique and privileged status on the nature of wonder. See *Theaet.* 155d: "I see, my dear Theaetetus, that Theodorus had a true insight into your nature when he said that you were a philosopher, for wonder is the feeling of a philosopher, and philosophy begins in wonder. He was not a bad genealogist who said that Iris (the messenger of heaven) is the child of Thaumas (wonder)."

68. Cf. É. Gilson, "Medieval Experiment," Part 1 of *The Unity of Philosophical Experience*.

known to us, though less known in their nature—namely, by effects.[69]

Once you have identified God's essence with His *To Be*, then Anselm is right and God cannot *not* exist, the richest idea cannot be the poorest, the most meaningful cannot be the emptiest.[70] If I already knew that God *is* Being, his existence would be self-evident. But God as Being is not self-evident to the intellect.[71] While on the horizon between time and eternity, and sharing an immediacy of vision with the angel, we understand, for the most part, by composition and division, especially when the essence is not common to all[72] and knowledge of first causes must proceed by effects:

> As in the intellect, when reasoning, the conclusion is compared with the principle, so in the intellect composing and dividing, the predicate is compared with the subject. For if our intellect were to see at once the truth of the conclusion in the principle, it would never understand by discursion and reasoning. In like manner, if the intellect in apprehending the quiddity of the subject were at once to have knowledge of all that can be attributed to, or removed from, the subject, it would never understand by composing and dividing, but only by understanding the essence. Thus, it is evident that for the self-same reason our intellect understands by discursion, and by composing and dividing, namely, that in the first apprehension of anything newly apprehended it does not at once grasp all that is virtually contained in it. And this comes from the weakness of the intellectual light within us, as has been said (Article 3). Hence, since the intellectual light is perfect in the angel, for he is

---

69. *ST* I, 2, 1, *resp.*

70. Cf. *ST* I, 3, 4, *resp*: "If the existence of a thing differs from its essence, this existence must be caused either by some exterior agent or by its essential principles. Now it is impossible for a thing's existence to be caused by its essential constituent principles, for nothing can be the sufficient cause of its own existence, if its existence is caused. Therefore that thing, whose existence differs from its essence, must have its existence caused by another. But this cannot be true of God; because we call God the first efficient cause. Therefore, it is impossible that in God His existence should differ from His essence."

71. Cf. *ST* I, 3, *pr.*: "Having recognized that something exists, we still have to investigate the way in which it exists, so that we may come to understand what it is that exists. But we cannot know what God is, only what he is not. We must therefore consider the ways in which God does not exist rather than the ways in which he does."

72. *ST* I, 2, 1, *resp.*

a pure and most clear mirror, as Dionysius says (Div. Nom. iv), it follows that as the angel does not understand by reasoning, so neither does he by composing and dividing.[73]

The intellect achieves this unifying and distinguishing *because* it works from and within the basis of Being, from an avenue of connatural self-evidence not immediately granted to the speculative intellect. By their nature as *speculative*, the intellectual powers work counter to that bodily immediacy, but never in contradiction to it; it is, again, the basis for those powers. How can one seek God if God is not in a way present; how can we know we are lost without knowing where we should be; how can composition and division be achieved without a ground already present from which unity and distinction proceed? This non-mediated, un-reflexive self-evidence resides identical to the proper good of the will while at the same time remaining at an essential distance from the intellect, reflective of our stance within the *confinium* of time and eternity. The will's non-futural being-towards, saturated presence which desires the good, desires it because it is present. When reflected upon by the domain of the intellect, reflection necessarily obscures that self-evidence because it cannot be reduced to an eidetic vision. The will's non-futurity is the un-observed essence of the intellectual life, as follows:

1. It is the time when we are *in* the unmeasured—as God is the unmeasured measurer.[74] We do not anticipate beyond the present, we are *in* and *of* the beauty and play of life.

In this sense, childhood should not be mere preparation for adulthood, as if the meaning of the child is bound up as a point of progress in the unfolding of maturation. If preparation, it is only because it should give the adult something other than the long littleness of life; it should provide a glimpse into that non-futurity where one is not reducible to the age or the time. This is Tolstoy's green stick[75] and Sebastian in *Brideshead Revisited*:

73. *ST* I, 58, 4, *resp.*

74. *ST* I, 2, 2, *resp.*

75. Tolstoy dictated to N. N. Gusev, his personal secretary, that he wanted to be buried at Yasnaya Polyana and his reasoning is ever timely. See "Tolstoy's Grave": "'There should be no ceremonies while burying my body; a wooden coffin and let anybody who will be willing to take it to the Old Zakaz forest, to the place of the little green stick, by the ravine.' Tolstoy heard the legend about the little green stick from his most beloved eldest brother Nikolai when a child. When Nikolai was 12 years old, he once told his family about a great secret. If it could be revealed, nobody would die any more, there would be no wars or illnesses, and all the people would become ant

I should like to bury something precious in every place where I've been happy and then, when I was old and ugly and miserable, I could come back and dig it up and remember.[76]

2. The non-futural basis of the will in its non-reflexive union with Being is the true transcendence, closer to God, the true foundation for our *athanatizein*, our immortality.

Transcendence is over-intellectualized, so that the desire triggering transcendence is seen but passed over as the intellect seeks to manage that desire in an organized cognitive longing. This management is not wrong, but it will frustrate itself, not only because no earthly action can complete our happiness[77] but also because one has not exhaustively joined with the clay and substance of the earth which truly brings us to the threshold of all our needs and desires, all our memories of joy and tragedy.

> The Franciscan Nun tells young Joan
> What those that are carnal lack, as we know, is being pure.
> But what we ought to know is that those that are pure lack being carnal.
> The angels are certainly pure, but they aren't the least bit carnal.
> They have no idea what it is to have a body, *to be* a body.
> They have no idea what it is to be a poor creature.
> A carnal creature.
> A body kneaded from the clay of the earth.
> The carnal earth.
> They don't understand this mysterious bond, this created bond,
> Infinitely mysterious,
> Between the soul and the body.
> This my child is what the angels do not understand.
> I mean to say, that this is what they haven't experienced.
> What it is to have this body; to have this bond with this body; to be this body,
> To have this bond with the earth, with this earth, to be this earth, clay and dust, ash and the mud of the earth,

brothers. To make it happen, one just needed to find a little green stick, buried on the edge of the ravine in Old Zakaz, as the secret was written on it. Playing the game of 'ant brothers,' the Tolstoy children settled under arm-chairs covered with shawls; sitting there and snuggling up together (like ants in their little home), they felt how good it was to be together 'under the same roof,' because they loved each other. And they dreamed of the ant brotherhood for all the people. As an old man, Tolstoy wrote: 'It was so very good, and I am grateful to God that I could play like that. We called it a game, though anything in the world is a game except that.'"

76. Waugh, *Brideshead Revisited*, 25.

77. Cf. Pieper, *Happiness and Contemplation*, 20–32.

The very body of Jesus.[78]

3. This primary form of saturated transcendence prepares us for the secondary transcendence, the transcendence of the intellect guiding the will, which is patterned after death, which speaks of desire, need, and loss in an often poignantly inarticulable vision of the unchanging meaning of change, a being-towards-death that is not merely a matter of tick-tock time elapse, but of a mode of temporality as inarticulable vision of the past as present, and the present as more than the "now," a present as presence.

If God is the saturated presence, the will in its non-futurity abides by God as Presence. We are the Other which is also presence to God's Presence. The heart-aching immortality of the intellect is that its actions are always reducible to the mumbo jumbo of one's age, because every desire, every futural need is confined and delimited by time.[79] Without the will's non-futural basis, the intellect's anticipatory futurity will actualize itself on a nihilatory basis, it will build its house on sand rather than rock.[80]

---

78. Péguy, *Portal of the Mystery of Hope*, 45–46; cf. Péguy, *Basic Verities*, 275–77:
Blessed are those who died for carnal earth.
Provided it was in a just war.
Blessed are those who died for a plot of ground.
Blessed are those who died a solemn death.
Blessed are those who died in great battles.
Stretched out on the ground in the face of God.
…
Blessed are those who died for their carnal cities.
For they are the body of the City of God.
Blessed are those who died for their hearth and their fire,
And the lowly honors of their father's house.
For such is the image and such the beginning
…
Blessed are those who died in this crushing down,
In the accomplishment of this earthly vow.
…
Blessed are those who died, for they have returned
Into primeval clay and primeval earth.
Blessed are those who died in a just war.
Blessed is the wheat that is ripe and the wheat that is gathered in sheaves.

79. Cf. Chesterton, *Catholic Church and Conversion*, 113: "The Catholic Church is the only thing which saves a man from the degrading slavery of being a child of his age."

80. Cf. Matt 7:24.

4. A transcendence which does not pass over the non-futural resides
   in the ground which can survive the freedom that is a fatalism—in
   and through it, the remembrance of things past remains as past and
   present, as the fatal and the freeing.

The will achieves its futurity only in union with the intellect, and
the intellect achieves its placement or presence only in union with the
will. The intellect and will are distinct but never separated, as if one could
ever act in isolation from the other. Nevertheless, their distinction calls
to mind a need to distinguish further their powers so that identification
of the one does not disintegrate into the other.

The will's desire is seen precisely because the intellect's speculative
powers elongate that desire, making it visible. But the intellect's ability to
see itself as a spectator, to see itself distinct from the sweeping tide of time,
requires the non-futural immediacy of desire that places us in Presence.
Only with the will can the spectator be *in* but not *of* the world, where that
"in-ness" is of such immersive power that it calls forth the fact that we
are not *of* the world. We are not *of* the world, but not because we reside
in stoic indifference. To the contrary, we are not *of* the world because we
are granted access into it in such a way that we are closer to its Being than
anything else. And because of this, we cannot doubt *that* there is truth,
that there is meaning, *that* there is goodness, but *what* exactly they are in
their fulfillment, in a way in which our eyes can take-in, is unclear, and
even open to foolish denial, thus vindicating both Anselm and Aquinas.
We cannot take-in, in vision, the source of the vision as source of the
sight of the vision. The will lays in union with the existential ground
of existence which is not knowledge but the ground of the possibility
of knowledge. *What* exactly unveils that ground, in its meaning, is by
that same token unknown to us. God is both "known" or enacted by
the will and unknown by the intellect, or known by the intellect only
by dispossession. The intellect must turn to a ground greater than itself
and, as it does, it cannot put into vision a source of which it is *already*
pre-possessed in order to turn. There are no shortcuts or innate ideas, for
this pre-possession cannot be reduced to an innate idea; it is instead the
ingrained non-ideational activity of the divine which allows the freedom
of ideas to persist.[81] But nevertheless, the capacity to turn towards what

---

81. Cf. *ST* I, 2, 1, ad. 1. See also Burrell, *Knowing the Unknowable God: Ibn Sina,
Maimonides, Aquinas*, 46–47: "The best way I know to put this is to remind ourselves
that simpleness is not an attribute of God, properly speaking, so much as a 'formal

the intellect cannot place within its speculative grasp points to a natural power or capacity of the soul that is aligned with that non-ideational self-evidence.[82] This *whatness* requires reflexive action which prompts the *longer way*, which achieves much knowledge, but cannot achieve completed happiness—for no act of the speculative reason can fulfill our desire for God.[83] But reflexive action knows its kinship with the non-reflexive as foundation for its turn. Reflexive action seeks a homecoming which requires the distinctive powers of the intellect and will to become something other—an *athanatizein*—in the way which Plato envisioned but which placed him in his own *aporia*: it is not enough to know the good, one must be the good, for true knowing is being.[84] The confused and general way in which we grasp the certitude of first principles is a kind of self-evidence that cannot be clarified until the completion of the

---

feature' of divinity. That is, we do not include 'simpleness' in that list of terms we wish to attribute to God—classically, 'living', 'wise', 'willing'. It is rather that simpleness defines the manner in which such properties might be attributed to God. When we say God is simple, we are speaking not about God directly but about God's ontological constitution; just as when we say that Eloise is composite, we are not predicating anything about her in any of the nine recognizable ways of Aristotle. So it would be putting the cart well before the horse to think of simpleness as a constituent property of God whose very "*existence is a necessary condition of* [God's] *existence*" [Alvin Plantinga]. 'Formal properties' are not so much said of a subject, as they are reflected in a subject's very mode of existing, and govern the way in which anything whatsoever might be said of that subject."

82. Saint Thomas's remarks on obediental potency as the divine inflictive benefaction raising us beyond our own powers requires that within us there is a natural openness to be raised. This natural openness is housed not in the intellect but in the intellect's trigger mechanism, desire, in its most profound sense, as potency. What is described in obediential potency can be understood as reflecting the meaning of the will in its non-reflexive originary praxis. Cf. DV, XXIX, 3, answers to three difficulties: "The capacity of a creature is predicated on the potency of reception which it has. Now the potency of a creature to receive is of two kinds. One is natural; and this can be entirely fulfilled, because it extends only to natural perfections. The other is obediential potency, inasmuch as it can receive something from God; and such a capacity cannot be filled, because whatever God does with a creature, it still remains in potency to receive from God. Now a measure which increases when goodness increases is determined by the amount of perfection received rather than by that of the capacity to receive."

83. Cf. SCG III, 26–40. Saint Thomas unveils a litany of options as to what human felicity does not consist in.

84. *Theaet.* 176b1. NE, 1177b33; 1179a22–30; Met., 1072B14–26.

demonstrations, and until it is understood that God's essence and existence are identical.[85]

> Nothing is more seductive for man than his freedom of conscience, but nothing is a greater cause of suffering. And behold, instead of giving a firm foundation for setting the conscience of man at rest for ever, Thou didst choose all that is exceptional, vague and enigmatic; Thou didst choose what was utterly beyond the strength of men.[86]

One can take the Anselmian *"fides quaerens intellectum"* as a metaphysical injunction. As long as a thing "has" being, God must be present to it according to its mode of being. Thus, in one sense, man reflects on the otherness of Being in the way in which a face sees itself in the otherness of a mirror, and realizes its own nature as an I only in communion with the Other. The Other is the mirror by which we reflexively know ourselves as knowers and then know ourselves as other. But because the I and the Other "have" Being and therefore "have" God innermost in us, and because man is a reflexive being, something odd is present in him as the preparatory condition to his reflexivity or peculiar mode of being. We recognize we are reflecting or mediating what cannot be mediated, because to see ourselves we must have the Other in total view as distinct and objectively quantifiable. But Being refuses this level of entitative disengagement both on the part of the I and on the part of the Other. And thus we remain mysteries even to ourselves.

The faith proclaims God to be Being itself (the "I am Who Am" of Exodus[87]). Anselm has already identified God with his own Being and as Being itself, and since one cannot deny Being, one cannot deny God. Put

---

85. God is not self-evident in our condition; but self-evident in our nature. This is the difference between natural law as imposition when reflecting our condition and as a connaturality in our nature. The difficulty of clarifying the meaning of *traditio* as a set of enduring truths wholly irreducible to a Humean irrational sentiment yet, at the same time, not easily open to verification, is realized in the language of natural law's simultaneous self-evidence and refusal to unveil its mystery. Russell Kirk's famous Ten Principles, perhaps, when read within this light, give them a whole new vantage by which to approach the relationship between tradition, conservatism, and the natural law. For the original six principles see Kirk, *Conservative Mind*. For their communion expansion see Kirk, *Politics of Prudence*.

86. Dostoyevsky, *Brothers Karamazov*, 268.

87. Cf. Armand Maurer, "Gilson's Use of History in Philosophy," in Russman, *Thomistic Papers V*, 25–47. See also É. Gilson, *Spirit of Thomism; Reason and Revelation; God and Philosophy*.

another way: if God exists; and if God is his own essence; and if his own essence is *To Be*—then God is Being itself, and one would indeed be a fool to deny it. The issue, therefore, is less one of inferring existence from the concept as if the proposition "God exists" is a necessary proposition, but more the unpacking of what is proposed to thought about God as a necessary Being. The problem for Anselm is that he both uses and does not use the full Platonic sense of Idea. His characterization of God in some way parallels Plato's *Agathon*: it is both everything and beyond everything. It is both a starting point and a notion, more the former than the latter.[88] The idea of God is not an innate idea for Anselm: it is found in and by faith and is "demonstrated" by the epistemological concept of fittingness within the larger metaphysical structure of participation and the *analogia entis*. So that the idea of God is not "self-evident," and Anselm is not inferring existence from essence, and least of all is the idea of God as that-than-which-nothing-greater-can-be-thought a "clear and distinct idea" in any modern sense. It is closer to Saint Thomas's fourth way than might at first be noticed.[89] Saint Thomas's rejection of the existence of God as self-evident must be taken as a cautionary tale and not a rejection of our underlying immediacy as such. The demonstrations for the existence of God are directed towards those who must recover what lay hidden as foundational for the first principles. This is why his Five Ways get us, beyond a reasonable doubt, to God but also place us squarely *within* the mystery and incommunicability of the divine. Saint Thomas paradoxically rejects self-evidence on grounds not incompatible with Anselm's own defense of self evidence—namely, the unavoidability of supernatural meaning particularly when beings naturally lead to Being-as-such. Any self-evidence reducible to the intellect would, for Saint Thomas, destroy the truth that God is not merely the highest in the ladder of beings but of a different order altogether, a Being whose demonstration must also demonstrate his mystery, refusing reflection in order to be its *grundsatz*:

> God is greater than all we can say, greater than all that we can know; and not merely does he transcend our language and our knowledge, but he is beyond the comprehension of every mind

---

88. Cf. Pegis, "St. Anselm and the Argument in the Proslogion," 228–67.
89. Cf. Hartshorne, *Anselm's Discovery*.

whatsoever, even of angelic minds, and beyond the being of every substance.[90]

Thomas's rejection of self-evidence seeks to protect the truer recovery of our connatural self-evidence, that the *arche* is the *telos* not only in the metaphysical but also in the epistemological registers: we seek what we already possess, we are dispossessed of what we never possessed. This is why Saint Thomas argues that we can demonstrate God's existence—*that* this difference-as-such exists, but *what* exactly that Being *is* cannot be reducible to the mind. This *"that"* which is being demonstrated is first triggered by the undeniability of first principles which place us interrogatively within the Five Ways.

> The name *qui est* ['He who is'] expresses 'Being' [esse] as absolute and not determined through any addition; and Damascene says, therefore, that it does not signify what God is but as it were an infinite ocean of substance which is without determination. When therefore we proceed towards God by the way of remotion, we first deny of him anything corporeal; and then we even deny of him anything intellectual, according as these are found in creatures, such as 'goodness' and 'wisdom'; and then there remains in our minds only the notion that he is, and nothing more: wherefore he exists in a certain confusion for us. Lastly, however, we remove from him even 'being' itself as it is found in creatures; and then he remains in a kind of show of ignorance, by which ignorance, in so far as it pertains to this life, we are best united to God, as Dionysius says, and this is the cloud in which God is said to dwell.[91]

Saint Anselm may take a shortcut in the ontological argument but his footing is not wrong; he never weighted the argument in a *conceptio* alien to the world of Being. This can be seen in all aspects of Anselm's life, particularly in how friendship was understood as a mutual intensity and interiorization of the other in order to be the self. In his letters to Gandulf, his greatest friend and fellow monk at Bec Abbey, Anselm unveils a bodily *affectus* as true transcendent, one that overwhelmingly opposes the disembodied, anti-affective Cartesian rationality of *res cogitans*. This affectivity invokes *dulcedo*, the sweetness of being, as its guiding principle:[92]

90. DN I, 3, 77. See also O'Rourke, *Pseudo-Dionysius and Aquinas*, 49.

91. In Sent. VIII, 1, 1. See also O'Rourke, *Pseudo-Dionysius and Aquinas*, 58.

92. Moss, "Friendship: St. Anselm, *Theoria* and the Convolution of Sense," in

> You have my consciousness always with you. If you are silent,
> I know that you love me; when I am silent, you know that I
> love you. You are conscious that I do not doubt you and I give
> witness to you that you are sure of me. We are then conscious of
> each other's consciousness.[93]

This type of affectivity as non-reflexive basis for all subsequent intellectual reflections is essential to understanding the Anselmian logic of perfection in its proper place; not as a polar opposite to Saint Thomas, but as a different facet of the same unified meaning. Saints Anselm and Thomas Aquinas recognize the purposiveness of the will's own union with the self-evidence of Being. If there *is* goodness, if meaning, truth and thus beings are self-evident—what then fulfills and orders them? Is it a natural or super-natural cause? If the existence or *thatness* of goodness, truth and beauty cannot be denied, *what* kind of causation is its source principle?: this is the inevitable question. Saint Thomas's distinction therefore relies on the strange self-evidence to the will and the emphatic non-self-evidence to the intellect. The *Ways* unite certitude and mystery so that each reflects the other, both embodying the self-evidence of the unified will-in-Being and the intellect which must take the *longer way*. These demonstrations stand for those who have no faith, but their subtlety invites one into the faith. When Saint Thomas gets us to the door of the divine, he does not arrive at an impersonal entity with little or no potential for relationality, but at a being whose fecundity of Goodness is identical with His Being.[94] This powerful union returns us again to the

---

Milbank, *Radical Orthodoxy*, 127–42, esp. 132.

93. Moss, "Friendship," 132.

94. Cf. Clarke, *Explorations in Metaphysics*, 48–49: "Not only does every being tend, by the inner dynamism of its act of existence, to overflow into action, but this action is both a self-manifestation and a self-communication, a self-sharing, of the being's own inner ontological perfection with others. This natural tendency to self-giving is a revelation of the natural fecundity or "generosity" rooted in the very nature of being itself. We are immediately reminded of the ancient Platonic tradition—well known to St. Thomas—of the 'self-diffusiveness of the Good' (*bonum est diffusivum sui*, as the Latins put it). What St. Thomas has done is to incorporate this whole rich tradition of the fecundity of the Good into his own philosophy of being, turning this self-diffusiveness, which the Platonic tradition identified as proper to what they considered the ultimate ground of reality, the Good, into a property of being itself, of which the good now becomes one inseparable aspect (or transcendental property). Whereas in Platonism, and especially Neoplatonism, being itself is only a lesser dimension of the Good, for St. Thomas the good is a derivative property of existential being itself, expressing more explicitly the primal dynamism of self-expansiveness and

fact that Saint Thomas demonstrates God beyond a reasonable doubt, and yet *what* it is that is beyond any doubt is mystery itself. This is the very mystery which, when the intellect engages it as Other, realizes that its reflection requires it be prepossessed in a non-reflexive way, in the affective basis of the Good. Saint Thomas never departs from his Pseudo-Dionysian heritage:

> The cause of all things, through an excess of goodness, loves all things, produces all things, perfects all things, contains and turns all things towards himself; divine love is good through the goodness of the Good. Indeed, love itself which produces the goodness of beings, pre-subsisting super-abundantly in the Good, did not allow itself to remain unproductive but moved itself to produce in the super-abundant generation of all.[95]

Ex divina pulchritudine esse omnium derivatur.[96]

Through a glass darkly we recognize the first principles through our connatural pre-possession, but our intellect cannot grasp that un-measured essence in its startling effulgence.[97] We can only recognize that our pre-possession cannot be rooted in a natural power, where essence is distinct from existence. Moreover, whatever steps ground our trajectory to the divine cannot be passed over as if rungs of a ladder on the great chain of Being.[98] This non-reflexive pre-possession speaks more to our ethical life than anything else because it is a union of the will with Being. What we lay out in the demonstrations for the existence of God will also provide a renewed accounting of the meaning of the natural law, not merely as imposition but as the fundamental unity with Being as Personal, because it is our originary and connatural relation of Being as the Good.

---

self-giving inherent in the very nature of being as act of existence. The primacy always lies with existence for St. Thomas. Nothing can be good unless it first actually is; and from the very fact that it is, it naturally follows that it is good, since the act of existence is the root of all perfection in any domain, 'the actuality of all acts, and the perfection of all perfections.'"

95. Pseudo-Dionysius, "Celestial Hierarchy," IV, 10, 159.

96. DN IV, 5.

97. *ST* I, 2, *resp.*; DN I, 3, 77; In Sent. VIII, 1, 1.

98. Cf. Lovejoy, *Great Chain of Being.*

2

New Beginnings: The Place of the Subordinated Ethics

Flood my soul with your spirit and life. Penetrate and possess my whole being
so utterly that all my life may only be a radiance of Yours.[1]

Truly, I say to you, unless you turn and become like children, you will never
enter the kingdom of heaven.[2]

H OW THEN DO WE invoke our access to that subordinated ethics when
it appears to require a kind of death in order even to be seen? It
requires a reversal of our stance as lover, of our way of envisioning the

---

1. "The Prayer Radiating Christ" attributed to Bl. Henry Cardinal Newman. See
"Jesus the Light of the Soul" in Newman, *Meditations and Devotions*, 365: "Stay with
me, and then I shall begin to shine as Thou shinest: so to shine as to be a light to others.
The light, O Jesus, will be all from Thee. None of it will be mine. No merit to me. It
will be Thou who shinest through me upon others. O let me thus praise Thee, in the
way which Thou dost love best, by shining on all those around me. Give light to them
as well as to me; light them with me, through me. Teach me to show forth Thy praise,
Thy truth, Thy will. Make me preach Thee without preaching—not by words, but by
my example and by the catching force, the sympathetic influence, of what I do—by my
visible resemblance to Thy saints, and the evident fullness of the love which my heart
bears to Thee."

2. Matt 18:3 (ESV).

natural law as imposition, to become the beloved to see this incarnating law as liberation. As Saint Thomas knew and even Anselm suspected: no intermediated demonstration can illuminate the self-evidence of God. The divine's effulgent self-evidence precedes demonstration in a non-discursive immediacy and/or follows upon it in a sort of "now I see what was always there to be seen" dawning moment. "My mind in the flash of a trembling glance came to absolute Being—That Which Is."[3] The disciples were witnesses not from their own eyes but through Christ's eyes: Christ breathed on them and they were one in vision.[4] If our originary *praxis*, this un-reflexive love, is the ground needed so that our secondary ethics has a foundation, then the teacher does not teach by disseminating material but by providing the step-back in order to encounter what precedes.[5] And this is the deeper meaning both of *maieutics and anamnesis*: the true teacher is no propagandist in search of intellectual/political disciples but a disciple of truth. Ethics cannot lead, it must abide by its subordination to the Presence, living not as a failed attempt to liken itself to the intellect, but by in-failing—failing (and knowingly so) to catch up to the beauty and the terror of existence. But we do not, for the most part, live by that originary *praxis*, rather we hand over the will to the intellect in a way in which we also relinquish the unique temporal mode of the will; or we hand the intellect over to the will as self-absorbed ego seeking only its own vanity. And while the intellect must guide the will, it must guide it *because* the will is distinct and will not surrender its immemorial entrenchment to

3. Augustine, *Confessions*, VII, 17, 23.

4. Cf. John 20:19–21: "On the evening of that first day of the week, when the disciples were together, with the doors locked for fear of the Jewish leaders, Jesus came and stood among them and said, 'Peace be with you!' After he said this, he showed them his hands and side. The disciples were overjoyed when they saw the Lord. Again, Jesus said, 'Peace be with you! As the Father has sent me, I am sending you.' And with that he breathed on them and said, 'Receive the Holy Spirit. If you forgive anyone's sins, their sins are forgiven; if you do not forgive them, they are not forgiven.'"

5. Cf. Kierkegaard, *Works of Love*, 314: "The true lover, who could not for any price find it in his heart to let the beloved girl feel his superiority, brings her the truth in such a way that she does not notice that he is the teacher; he lures it out of her, puts it upon her lips and hears her say it, not himself, or he draws truth forward and hides himself. Is it humiliating then, to learn the truth this way? And so it is of the vanquished, of whom we speak here. Expression of grief over the past, remorse over this wrong, petition for forgiveness—in a certain sense the lover receives all this, but he immediately lays it all aside in holy abhorrence, as one lays aside that which is not his: that is, he intimates that it is not due him; he places it all in a higher category, gives it to God as the one to whom it is due. This is the way love always conducts itself."

the gaze of the conceptual or to the emptied content of the futural.[6]

In order to see what only death can allow us to see, not with our own eyes which construct concepts and distance, we let the image lay bare. Here is one such image: there is a man, an elderly caretaker of the British cemetery in Corfu.[7] The cemetery is not far from the seafront center of Corfu and a few steps from the Platia Theotoki or San Rocco square. One takes the same road to the prison as to the cemetery. This man's father had taken care of the graves before him and his father before. He was well into his eighties but looked more childlike in expression. Work was hard but it was play. It was the same thing every day, tending nature which never relents, never lays down its shovel. Sun and rain, heat and dirt were always on schedule and only death regularly came, regardless of the seasons. The difficulty of years of hard labor did not undermine the fact that for this caretaker it was play, the serious and holy play which Plato knew.[8] Play lived within and through the work, becoming indistinguishable from it, together making something more of his nature than merely "naturally supernatural";[9] he became so in union with nature that to others he exceeded nature, he appeared a survivor of its cosmogonic fatalism. But for him this language of survival would be alien, a foreign tongue:

> Because children have abounding vitality, because they are in spirit fierce and free, therefore they want things repeated and unchanged. They always say, 'Do it again'; and the grown-up person does it again until he is nearly dead. For grown-up people are not strong enough to exult in monotony. But perhaps God is strong enough to exult in monotony. It is possible that God says every morning, 'Do it again' to the sun; and every evening, 'Do it again' to the moon. It may not be automatic necessity that makes

6. Cf. C. Gilson, "St. Thomas and the Paradox of Mediation and Intentionality," 17–94.

7. See the story of elderly caretaker George Psailas, "Corfu's Constant Cemetery Gardener."

8. Cf. Plato, *Resp.* 604c: "Nothing in mortal life is worthy of great concern." See also Ardley, "Role of Play in the Philosophy of Plato," 226–44.

9. Cf. Plato, *Symp.* 212a: "Or don't you realize, that here alone it will be possible for him, on seeing the beautiful by that by which it is visible, to give birth not to phantom images of virtue, because he is touching on that which is not a phantom, but to true virtue, because he is touching on the truth; and once he gives birth to true virtue and raises it, it is open to him to become dear to the gods, and if it is open to any other human being, for him to become immortal [to put on immortality]?" For this putting on immortality and clothing oneself in the imperishable, see 1 Cor 15:53.

all daisies alike; it may be that God makes every daisy separately, but has never got tired of making them. It may be that He has the eternal appetite of infancy; for we have sinned and grown old, and our Father is younger than we.[10]

The little man so cared for the graves with an incarnate gentleness, creating a beautiful garden with shade and sunlight, that people over time came to look at it. This man, now closer to his own death, had cared for the dead since he was a little boy. One can imagine him as a child running exuberantly through the graves on his way to the town, but running—when he remembered or was chided by his father and grandfather—with a caution as to avoid any disrespect. He received a medal from the British Order of the Realm as an honor for his care of the British expats. He kept it in his pocket proud of it; child proud—never tired of that symbolic kindness which to others is usually given out of a passing generosity, a generosity which, fearing death, seeks immortality, from the monument to the trinket. The old man's final act is to show us his own grave, set in Arcadia, in a tranquil corner of the cemetery which would give him the vantage to see and continue to care for the rest of the graves after he died. He had tended his own portion of his garden and his name was on the headstone and flowers strewn with grace, growing in order, but a wild order, a mindfulness that nature is always victor.

> As death, when we come to consider it closely, is the true goal of our existence, I have formed during the last few years such close relationships with this best and truest friend of mankind that death's image is not only no longer terrifying to me, but is indeed very soothing and consoling, and I thank my God for graciously granting me the opportunity...of learning that death is the key which unlocks the door to our true happiness. I never lie down at night without reflecting that—young as I am—I may not live to see another day. Yet no one of all my acquaintances could say that in company I am morose or disgruntled.[11]

10. Chesterton, *Collected Works*, 60.

11. Wolfgang Amadeus Mozart's letter to his father, the composer Leopold Mozart, 4th of April 1787 in Steptoe, *Mozart-Da Ponte Operas*, 84. See also Shakespeare's "King John," III.iv.93–99, in *Complete Works*: "Grief fills the room up of my absent child, lies in his bed, walks up and down with me, puts on his pretty looks, repeats his words, remembers me of all his gracious parts, stuffs out his vacant garments with his form; then, have I reason to be fond of grief?"

In another story, there is a monk living high in the mountains of Greece. He shares his company with numerous other monks who walk the halls of the monastery carved into the façade of a cliff and who pray in the chapel painted over a thousand years prior. This monk casts his eyes upward to the very heights of the chapel. There is painted an order of hierarchy within the dome, residing highest the face of the Pantokrator, next to him Our Lady Theotokos and below surrounding him the apostles and the saints. But we look around and see no other monks, the hallways groan in their echoes, woken periodically from long silence by the same single steps. Our monk comes to show us his companions and we follow him from room to room expecting the next room to be full of life, to find this mythic population, but there are none that we find. The monk takes us out into an open-air hallway, a lookout over the mountains, from there a bell tower up ahead. We curve around the parapet and then, tucked inside, we find a little room and at the other end, an ossuary. The skulls of his brothers are cleaned and placed in honor. The desert image is a garden image:

Lady of silences
Calm and distressed
Torn and most whole
Rose of memory
Rose of forgetfulness
Exhausted and life-giving
Worried reposeful
The single Rose
Is now the Garden
Where all loves end
Terminate torment
Of love unsatisfied
The greater torment
Of love satisfied
End of the endless
Journey to no end
Conclusion of all that
Is inconclusible
Speech without word and
Word of no speech
Grace to the Mother
For the Garden
Where all love ends.[12]

12. Eliot, "Ash Wednesday," in *Collected Poems, 1909–1962*, 87–88.

Hidden in Plain Sight

Prince Myshkin displays to us another image of the subordinated ethic, an execution through the eyes of the executed. Throughout the novel we are confronted a number of times with different iterations of it for, again, every movement of the story has a companion reflection.[13] After his train ride into St. Petersburg, he waits in the drawing room of the Yepanchin household for distant relatives with whom he seeks to connect. He speaks out of custom to the attendant who is at first ill-disposed but then utterly gracious and accommodating. Myshkin relays to him the image of death when it cannot be avoided, when hope is utterly extinguished. It is the despairing, resigned agony of the guillotine[14] where that last bat-squeak of possibility, no matter how threadbare, has been irrevocably abolished. What is being transmitted cannot be expressed.[15] It is more and other than the hopelessness of war, it is a despair so pure and final that it has lost even the object of hope which initially triggered the despair, the

13. There are a number of examples of companion narratives. To name a few: If Myshkin is an alter Christus, we find other avenues for it in Rogozhin and especially Nastassya, the mad heroine, whose madness exposes the failings of Myshkin's holy idiocy; the execution scenes by firing squad are retold with companion stories of the guillotine on more than one occasion, one of which Myshkin asks—oddly enough— the middle Yepanchin daughter, Adelaida, to paint; unable to take-in or reconcile the bloodied gangrenous Christ by the painter Holbein at Rogozhin's house with the redemptive Christ of the Resurrection, and yet Myshkin admits he dreams about the execution of a convict who, unlike Christ, is not born to die; Myshkin's compassion for the homeless and scorned Swiss consumptive, Mary, is seen again in the scornful and dying Hippolyte who cannot bring himself to suicide; the Swiss children who once taunted Mary but then became like children again, Myshkin searches for the child in all his new companions in Russia, seeing it as the source of their friendship and their true nature; and for all those who claim Myshkin is an idiot but then on their own, as if in a confessional, admit the contrary, we find ourselves confronted with his descent into true idiocy with the death of Nastassya at the end of the novel. Many of these scenarios will return throughout the book.

14. In 1873 Dostoyevsky wrote in his diary of his own similar experience of waiting for execution in the Fortress of Saints Peter and Paul; he is reprieved moments before the firing squad at Semyonovsky Square. Cf. Shestov, *Dostoevsky, Tolstoy, and Nietzsche*, 156.

15. Cf. Republic, 439e–440a: "I once heard something that I trust. Leontius, the son of Aglaion, was going up from the Piraeus under the outside of the North Wall when he noticed corpses lying by the public executioner. He desired to look, but at the same time was disgusted and made himself turn away; and for a while he struggled and covered his face. But finally overpowered by the desire, he opened his eyes wide, ran towards the corpses and said: 'Look, you damned wretches, take your fill of the fair sight.'"

object which allows us to understand and encounter, from the outside, its meaning. As the fortress is being overrun, as certain death is upon the person, hope finds a way to persist because the sentence has not been cast down. Those who remain have not been dragged to the public spectacle of the guillotine; the phantasmic hope of a door which leads to a secret garden always lives in the soul. But Myshkin is presenting us with the alternative, the garden as desert:

> 'Yes—I saw an execution in France—at Lyons. Schneider took me over with him to see it. 'What, did they hang the fellow?' 'No, they cut off people's heads in France.' 'What did the fellow do?—yell?' 'Oh no—it's the work of an instant. They put a man inside a frame and a sort of broad knife falls by machinery— they call the thing a guillotine—it falls with fearful force and weight—the head springs off so quickly that you can't wink your eye in between. But all the preparations are so dreadful. When they announce the sentence, you know, and prepare the criminal and tie his hands, and cart him off to the scaffold—that's the fearful part of the business. The people all crowd round—even women—though they don't at all approve of women looking on.'[16]

Dostoyevsky cannot shake the image of a man before death, the moments in which time appears at its threshold,[17] for they alone are able to renounce the chronological and the biological. He relays another story, of Countess du Barry during the French Revolution, faced with the inevitability of death, begging her executioner for just "one more moment."[18] With the Countess, it is all too much to be forcibly returned

16. Dostoyevsky, *Idiot*, 21–22.

17. We can see this in Dostoyevsky's *The Gambler* and *The House of the Dead*. Cf. Bakhtin, *Dostoevsky's Poetics*, 172: "Both the life of convicts and the life of gamblers— for all their differences in content—are equally 'life taken out of life' (that is, taken out of common, ordinary life) . . . And the time of penal servitude and the time of gambling are—for all their profound differences—an identical type of time, similar to the 'final moments of consciousness' before execution or suicide, similar in general to the time of crisis. All this is time on the threshold, and not biological time, experienced in the interior spaces of life far from the threshold."

18. Dostoyevsky, *Idiot*, 197: "The way she died was that, after such honors, this former ruling lady was dragged guiltless to the guillotine by the executioner Samson, for the amusement of the Parisian fishwives, and she was so frightened that she didn't understand what was happening to her. She saw that he was bending her neck down under the knife and kicking her from being—with the rest all laughing—and she began to cry out: '*Encore un moment, monsieur le bourreau, encore un moment!*' Which means: 'Wait one more little minute mister boorow, just one!'"

to that Presence which does not dissipate into the ontological avoidance found in anticipation and diversion. The homecoming into the Presence which is now irrevocably linked to death is no longer connatural or inviting, but has sized one up. There are no pretenses, flirtations, actions which can stretch time wherein the ego might still appear as the dominant architect.

> The criminal was a fine intelligent fearless man; Le Gros was his name; and I may tell you—believe it or not, as you like— that when that man stepped upon the scaffold he cried, he did indeed,—he was as white as a bit of paper. Isn't it a dreadful idea that he should have cried—cried! Whoever heard of a grown man crying from fear—not a child, but a man who never had cried before—a grown man of forty-five years. Imagine what must have been going on in that man's mind at such a moment; what dreadful convulsions his whole spirit must have endured; it is an outrage on the soul that's what it is. Because it is said 'thou shalt not kill,' is he to be killed because he murdered someone else? No, it is not right, it's an impossible theory. I assure you, I saw the sight a month ago and it's dancing before my eyes to this moment. I dream of it, often. 'Well, at all events it is a good thing that there's no pain when the poor fellow's head flies off,' he remarked. 'Do you know, though,' cried the prince warmly, 'you made that remark now, and everyone says the same thing, and the machine is designed with the purpose of avoiding pain, this guillotine I mean; but a thought came into my head then: what if it be a bad plan after all? You may laugh at my idea, perhaps—but I could not help its occurring to me all the same. Now with the rack and tortures and so on—you suffer terrible pain of course; but then your torture is bodily pain only (although no doubt you have plenty of that) until you die. But here I should imagine the most terrible part of the whole punishment is, not the bodily pain at all—but the certain knowledge that in an hour,—then in ten minutes, then in half a minute, then now—this very instant—your soul must quit your body and that you will no longer be a man—and that this is certain, certain! That's the point—the certainty of it. Just that instant when you place your head on the block and hear the iron grate over your head—then—that quarter of a second is the most awful of all.[19]

19. Dostoyevsky, *Idiot*, 22–23.

This story is being told to a servant at the Yepanchin household. Myshkin, having only arrived in St. Petersburg, seeks out Lizaveta Proko-fyevna Yepanchin,[20] a princess, a Myshkin by birth and a distant relative of the Prince. Myshkin had written her while still convalescing in Swit-zerland but had received no reply. Having arrived in St. Petersburg with only his satchel, and neither plans nor ambitions, he seeks from her the potential for familial bond, and proceeds to the Yepanchin household in hope that his unanswered letter was only an oversight. At the same time his seeking is not intelligibilized by a need to define himself. He seeks and yet never quite connects in a way in which his personality or view of life is restricted by the politics, conventions, idiosyncrasies of one or a number of souls intruding on another. This is not to say that Myshkin is aloof or unkind but, quite the opposite, his connection is too ethereal, too strange for those who inhabit his world, and yet it undresses and unnerves them, gives them often the inclination for salvation and self-knowledge, but one which cannot find substance and folds into its inevitable fatalism.

> One might say that Myshkin is not able to enter life completely, cannot become completely embodied, cannot accept any defini-tiveness in life that would limit a personality. He remains, as it were, on a tangent to life's circle. It is as if he lacks the necessary *flesh of life* that would permit him to occupy a specific place in time (thereby crowding others out of that place), and therefore he remains on a tangent to life. But precisely for that reason is he able to 'penetrate' through the life flesh of other people and reach their deepest 'I'.[21]

Myshkin may be an image of salvific love but he cannot impart it. He has the sensation of Christ but not Christ's permeation. Dostoyevsky's Myshkin is a man of-and-in-love but a bloodless love which irreconcilably differentiates him from Christ. He seeks love, but in such a way as if all love can return to its originary *praxis* replicating the form it had in the

20. Lizaveta is an indominable character, led by a fierce, erratic but always good-natured will even when she comes across brusque or uneven. On more than one occa-sion, Myshkin lovingly likens her to a child. This does not sour her to him but to the contrary it leaves her vulnerable, she considers this vulnerability a weakness and her reaction to it oscillates between invitation and hostile sarcasm. She immediately finds herself bonded and caring more for the Prince's well-being than she'd prefer. Lizaveta is the wife of kindly Ivan Fyodorovitch Yepanchin who, at the beginning of the novel, has his own lustful yearning for Nastassya, which amounts to nothing, out of a combina-tion of decency, timing and hesitancy to break social mores.

21. Bakhtin, *Dostoevsky's Poetics*, 173.

beginning. The *telos* may be the *arche*, but for us exiles it is not often in the same form. The homecoming is often alienation, it is more often mouthed in the words of the Countess begging her executioner for another moment that cannot offer a different form of meaning. Much rarer is the homecoming, the garden of our ecstasy where our Monk is found walking with the dead as if they are seated beside him in their bodily souls. Myshkin either has the experience but misses the meaning, or has the meaning but misses the experience, but he never has them both. And yet, he knows this trapping, he knows that he holds the experience at the inestimable cost of missing the meaning, only to hold the meaning at the graver cost of missing the experience. It is why he is preoccupied with the moments before death, recoils at Holbein's Christ figure,[22] and it is the underlying tragedy of Dostoyevsky's own Don Quixote of disintegrating images.[23]

22. Dostoyevsky, *Idiot*, 218. See also Sheck, "Dostoyevsky's Empathy": "Frail, epileptic, and defying building regulations, in the Basel Museum he dragged a chair in front of Holbein's Dead Christ, and then—to his wife's horror—climbed up on it so he could stand face to face with the brutalized, blue-green corpse with open eyes and rigid, open mouth, this executed man on the verge of decomposing. He would place this corpse in his new novel, The Idiot."

23. Cf. Dostoyevsky, *Idiot*, 22–23: "This is not my own fantastical opinion—many people have thought the same; but I feel it so deeply that I'll tell you what I think. I believe that to execute a man for murder is to punish him immeasurably more dreadfully than is equivalent to his crime. A murder by sentence is far more dreadful than a murder committed by a criminal. The man who is attacked by robbers at night, in a dark wood, or anywhere, undoubtedly hopes and hopes that he may yet escape until the very moment of his death. There are plenty of instances of a man running away, or imploring for mercy—at all events hoping on in some degree—even after his throat was cut. But in the case of an execution, that last hope—having which it is so immeasurably less dreadful to die,—is taken away from the wretch and *certainty* substituted in its place! There is his sentence, and with it that terrible certainty that he cannot possibly escape death—which, I consider, must be the most dreadful anguish in the world. You may place a soldier before a cannon's mouth in battle, and fire upon him—and he will still hope. But read to that same soldier his death-sentence, and he will either go mad or burst into tears. Who dares to say that any man can suffer this without going mad? No, no! it is an abuse, a shame, it is unnecessary—why should such a thing exist? Doubtless there may be men who have been sentenced, who have suffered this mental anguish for a while and then have been reprieved; perhaps such men may have been able to relate their feelings afterwards. Our Lord Christ spoke of this anguish and dread. No! no! no! No man should be treated so, no man, no man!"

God Hidden and Self-Evident

> Then in our philosophic dream we may accompany great
> naturalists and subtle logicians through unending windings;
> the eye may range over prospects discursive or intensely
> concentrated; we may summon spirits and work magic; but
> the Will in us will never swerve from its first animal direction,
> from blind craving or idle play. In these reaches we shall find
> the peripatetic Aristotle, the reasoning Parmenides, the Stoics,
> Spinoza, and Hegel: all naturalists and historians in their
> ultimate allegiance, and never more so than when they raise
> pure intelligibles or sheer substance or infinite existence into a
> supreme idol. They may call it God, but it is still fact or truth
> that they are worshipping, not excellence. Or, weary of that
> pursuit, we may turn down other paths, less stately and trodden,
> but more fragrant, where the poets walk. At the end, not far
> distant (since repentance follows close upon love) we may find
> some saint in his hermitage or some cynic in his den, or perhaps
> Epicurus in his little walled garden. Here every alley will be
> blind, with no thoroughfare. We must turn back into the maze,
> or stay with these solitaries forever.[24]

Having isolated the necessary language needed to enter into Saint
Thomas's Five Ways, we realize that we are being wound up, refused entry
into our originary concordance with Being, only to prepare us to return
to it when ready to withstand whatever homecoming it has in store for
us. Not only is there that *exitus-reditus* framework structure throughout
the entirety of the Summa,[25] but it is placed within individual questions,
laying the groundwork for our onto-theological homecoming.[26] God is

---

24. Santayana, *Realms of Being*, 774–75.

25. Cf. Chenu, "Le Plan de la Somme Theologique de S. Thomas," 93–107; Chenu, *Introduction a L'Etude de S. Thomas d' Aquinas*.

26. This *exitus-reditus* structure is not as much an overt chronological happening but an unveiling that is more weighted in individual arguments which lay out implications for how one reads and interprets the Summa as a whole. Thus, some of the criticisms of attempting a specific unpacking of Chenu's accounting of this structure have caused some controversy. Cf. Velde, *Aquinas on God*, 12–14; Heide, *Timeless Truth*, 72–80. I contest that the integrity of such a structure cannot be sourced in seeing if and whether every article succinctly follows that structure, but how the ontological groundwork in the demonstrations, the epistemological nature and will of man, are each calling forth an *exitus-reditus* structure for their fulfillment and are thus further perfected by the articles specifically dealing with the Revelatory aspects of the faith.

not self-evident, not because he doesn't pervade all things as inescapable within the quest for meaning, but because this bodily soul of ours is only itself in the face of the other,[27] which requires synthesis and separation in order to recall prior communion. The whole grammar of freedom and divine-likeness is placed within this strange cyclical trajectory.

We now turn our attention from God's odd self-evidence and Saint Thomas's cautionary tale, to the second article in question 2 on whether God is even demonstrable. Saint Thomas has willingly placed himself in the thicket of non-being; having denied that we know God's essence, the Dumb Ox has denied the middle term by which normal demonstrations must find their center of gravitas.[28] This is the radicality of Saint Thomas's existential philo-logos: his rejection of the self-evidence of the existence of God is done to preserve—not silence—the truer form of immediacy, while his subsequent defense of God's demonstrability is done to silence—so as to preserve—that same immediacy. The first principles are muted, holding the place in the demonstrations as a generalized awareness of perfection and hierarchy without delving into the necessary implications of such awareness. This silencing of the striking role of first principles[29] is done to carve out the *longer way* of beings, which always

---

27. Cf. *ST* I, 84–85.

28. Cf. McCabe, *Faith Within Reason*, 96. In his *Faith Within Reason*, Herbert McCabe describes Thomas's actions as "the most agnostic theologian in the Western Christian tradition—not agnostic in the sense of doubting whether God exists, but agnostic in the sense of being quite clear and certain that God is a *mystery* beyond any understanding we can have."

29. Cf. Ugobi-Onyemere, *Knowledge of the First Principles*, 159: "[The knowledge of first principles] is not entirely an inexpressible mystery or a mere anthology of materialized concepts. It is, so to say, a conceivable reality that hangs on the existential act which defies representation but is accessible to the human mind's understanding. Existence is available to us not merely by way of experience but also through any judgment of existence about being in actuality. There exists, also, an act of judgment that is beyond the classical definition of judgment, the judgment of existence that something 'is' . . . all knowledge is both essential and existential. Being comes first and remains there as being; it does not give way to something else. In effect, all our representations are accompanied by being. It is not just enough to say being; it is such that we are hemmed in and by being. A thing as seen from afar is 'a being,' at a closer range is a being, and at very proximate quarters remains 'a being,' the only change is the successive determination of that being. Subsequently, where there is no actual existent being to respond to the knowledge of being, there is no knowledge in that presupposition, hence, as Aquinas suggests, being is not just the initial and original object of the intellectual knowledge; it is the cognition into which every other knowledge resolves."

and inescapably proceeds along the way of those first principles, but is only revealed to do so in their *reditus*, their return. Self-evidence in its profoundest sense is never left behind, it is the *way* in which we see, and because it is the way *through* which we understand, it must paradoxically be re-discovered:

> That which the intellect first conceives as, in a way, the most evident, and to which it reduces all its concepts, is being. Consequently, all the other conceptions of the intellect are had by additions to being. But nothing can be added to being as though it were something not included in being—in the way that a difference is added to a genus or an accident to a subject— for every reality is essentially a being.[30]

For the Dumb Ox, the process of discovery means that, at the same time, God is not self-evident to the intellect; that Being does not reduce itself into concept in order to be seen; that it never gives itself away,[31] becoming something other. If Being became reflexive, the very ground of our reflexivity would cease to be. We understand that God is his own existence, that existence and essence are identical in God as Being itself. This aniconic *To Be* is innermost in things, because it is the eye through which we see the appearances of Being. Yet to be knowing beings freely responsive to Being itself, we must be able to respond to Being which does not give itself away, becoming something other and visibly eidetic. The impossibility of knowledge is its very essence: we must respond to Being which is not an object of knowledge but the ground of the possibility of knowledge. Being enables our response and as such provides nothing separate or distinct or left over to which to respond. Being is not simply presence, it is the Presence which cannot merely be present. Our act of responding-to-Being places us in the originary *praxis* of our connatural self-evidence of God, but the response itself is held suspended because Being does not give itself away. This suspense banishes any so-called self-evidence. As such, the soul must be outside itself to know itself, becoming the substitute for Being's suspended response; the soul puts itself in place of Being. But Being never loses its place and as such when our soul becomes the response *to* Being, we respond *with* and *in* Being. And this is what it means for the soul to become the other *as other*, while remaining itself, in knowledge. We are, by Being-itself, placed on

30. DV I, 1, *resp.*
31. É. Gilson, *Being and Some Philosophers*, 205–10.

the threshold of our own response, our natures elongated and open. We may fool ourselves into reducing knowledge to the ontical or material, but these reductions cannot circumvent even the clumsiest uttering of first principles. As such we are placed back in Being by the fact that we respond to Being by being responsive through Being: that which is the All appears simultaneously as Nothing. In this prime respect Being is self-evident but God is not. Our actions are both fated and free.

We can see these paradoxes unfold in the relationship between Truth and Being. Is it tautologous to call Being true? Saint Thomas says no.[32] In the *De Veritate*, our Angelic Doctor speaks at the threshold of contradiction but remains firmly in the region of mystery:

> The true is a state of being even though it does not add any reality to being or express any special mode of existence. It is rather something that is generally found in every being, although it is not expressed by the word being. Consequently, it is not a state that corrupts, limits, or contracts . . . There is a conceptual difference between the true and being since there is something in the notion of the true that is not in the concept of the existing—not in such a way, however, that there is something in the concept of being which is not in the concept of the true. They do not differ essentially nor are they distinguished from one another by opposing differences.[33]

What can be added to Being if no reality or addition can be added to Being? When we designate being as a substance, for instance, we make no "addition" to the being it was exercising prior to the designation: it is not now doing or being something it was not doing or being before, as if we were attributing to the being that which it was not already; nor yet is the designation a mere conceptual appellation, circular and uninformative. No reality is added to being; no difference is attributed. But rather "substance" simply expresses, as Aquinas says, a special manner of existing, namely, as a being in itself, a subsistent, an ontological independent. Thus, we are disengaging, without either prescinding or hypostasizing, the way of being in which the being is, the kind of being exercised by a particular being within an order of beings, which very order is itself participating in the hegemonic order of Being first and

---

32. Cf. DV I, 1, *answers to contrary difficulties* 1: "The reason why it is not tautological to call a being true is that something is expressed by the word true that is not expressed by the word being, and not that the two differ in reality."

33. DV I, 1, *answers to difficulties* 4, 6.

encompassingly present to the mind. Thus does Being still and always contain all and everything. We never remove ourselves, our concepts, language, and reflections from Being, and least of all in metaphysics. But we do delineate Being's configurations, and this within our very language, concepts, reflections, and ideas, all of which must be resoluble in Being. Being never hands itself over in technical self-evidence, but because it initiates a response it is already present and evident-in-Being. The waters forever change, but the river . . .

The proposition "God exists" appears neither as an analytic statement—where the definition of the subject is irreducibly related to the definition of the predicate—nor as a synthetic statement. If Saint Thomas is so drastic as to withhold the middle term of meaning and judgment, he has relinquished not only any analytic claims of proof but may also have isolated himself from other natural avenues of demonstration. In the empirical order, the subject and predicate may have no absolute definitional relation; relations often occur by happenstance—the cat on the mat, Thomas in Monte Cassino—and not of an essential necessity, hence proof requires a sensible or empirical judgment to affirm its truth value. If God's existence does not fit into the category of an analytic statement, neither does it fit neatly into an empirical one. Should God's presence be demonstrated in existence, must it be because the subject, God, is not necessarily related to the predicate, existence; is it because this relation occurs by happenstance and is inessential? Both points are clearly absurd and yet both point us back to the problem of a quick forfeiting of self-evidence when attempting to understand *how* God is demonstrable, and how that demonstrability must distinguish itself from synthetic empirical judgment. The problem lies in the fact that God is not *in* existence as Thomas is *in* existence, but is instead identical with and exceeding existence. God, in a way, must be self-evident, which Saint Thomas has paradoxically both denied and supported when he affirmed that God's essence remains incommunicable to us.

Let us turn to the *responsio* in article 1 where the nature of self-evidence is described as if it were one of Wittgenstein's language games.[34] Self-evidence is organized in the following manner:

34. For Wittgenstein, "God exists" is not a statement of fact but neither is it an empty statement. "God exists" is not an expression about a thing as if it is among a penumbra of things in the world; it is not a descriptive statement compatible with how natural objects are described in the natural world. It could never be a claim about an entity; more than anything else it is not an empirical statement. "God exists" may be

1. *Self-evident in itself and to us*: "the whole is greater than any one of its parts"; "a line segment is a line linking two points." These statements are self-evident; in each, the definition of the predicate and subject are mutually related.

The reality shared by beings who do not exist in their own right but are existentially dependent on another for their existence places us within the same noetic architectonic. It is this communion which allows us to grasp, by the intellect, self-evident truths. We are "caused causes" whether by generation, corruption, birth and death, and potentiality underlies every form of our actuality,[35] opening the door to the questions of possibility and necessity.[36] There is a dramatic difference between the potentiality delimited by matter and form, which is not necessarily creational, and the overwhelming of that language through possibility and necessity. Creaturely possibility moves us from form and matter to the question of essence and existence, and is unabashedly creational in nature and execution.[37] If we do our best to think as Aristotelians, there is but one act of *To-Be*—formal or essential—which negotiates meaning and reality throughout existence. This identification, while attempting to court the question of existence through a material identification, is unable to be existential in nature. As non-creational, this articulation of existence must be essentialist in understanding; existence cannot have a real role to play other than being the material covering for the form or essence. How could matter truly affect, change, add, strengthen or limit Being *qua* Essence if essences are eternal and impervious to generation

non-empirical but it is not empty, it hits at an underlying "system of reference." Cf. Wittgenstein, *Culture and Value*, 64: "It strikes me that a religious belief could only be something like a passionate commitment to a system of reference. Hence, although it's a belief, it's really a way of living, or a way of assessing life. It's passionately seizing hold of this interpretation." Cf. Leo Tolstoy, "My Confession," in Hanfling, *Life and Meaning*, 9–19, esp. 19: "Faith is the power of life. If a man lives, he believes in something. If he did not believe that he ought to live for some purpose, he would not live. If he does not see and understand the phantasm of the finite, he believes in that finite; if understands the phantasm of the finite, he must believe in the infinite. Without faith one cannot live."

35. See Saint Thomas's Five Ways, most particularly demonstrations 1 and 2, on the questions of motion and efficient causation.

36. See demonstration 3, the cosmological Argument, where a preliminary understanding of gift and grace is being elucidated.

37. Cf. "Matter and Form in Relation to Nature and Grace" in C. Gilson, *Political Dialogue*, 53–65.

and decay?[38] The hypostatic union is a necessary explanation to address the *aporia* which confronts all existence not yet opened to the dramatic and revelatory reality of *creatio ex nihilo*. But when the principles of the hypostatic union are actually dissected, the yawning chasm, the font of unknowability springs forth. There is no way matter can truly alter and inhabit the form within its definitional limitations. If it could, form would cease to be form. And yet, Aristotle is not wrong, we have a world where we understand the things themselves, *this* tree, and then proceed to understand its essence.[39] What is strange about the progression of the demonstrations is that Saint Thomas begins with two demonstrations—movement and efficient causation—which could be subsumed within the non-creational template of matter and form,[40] but which then explode

38. Cf. É. Gilson, *Being and Some Philosophers*, 49–50: "I should like to know, Aristotle, whether you really mean that there are certain forms of which individual beings partake and from which they derive their names: that men, for instance, are men because they partake of the form and essence of man."

"Yes, Socrates, that is what I mean."

"Then each individual partakes of the whole of the essence or else of part of the essence. Can there be any other mode of participation?"

"There cannot be."

"Then do you think that the whole essence is one, and yet being one, is in each one of the things?"

"Why not, Socrates?"

"Because, one and the same thing will then at one and the same time exist as a whole in many separate individuals, and will therefore be in a state of separation from itself!"

"Nay, Socrates, it is not so. Essences are not Ideas; they do not subsist in themselves but only in particular things, and this is why, although we conceive them as one, they can be predicated of many."

"I like your way, Aristotle, of locating 'one' in many places at once; but did you not say that essence is that whereby individual beings are?"

"Yes, Socrates, I did."

"Then, my lad, I wish you could tell me how it may be that beings are through sharing in an essence, which itself is not!"

39. It is through Saint Thomas's existential metaphysics that essence receives a more proper companion, one which can more justly ground individuality, personhood, virtue and vice, a companion which can include matter but is not reducible to it. Only in the repercussions of *creatio ex nihilo* will existence have a real role to play. Whether that dependency is immaterial, material or a confluence of the two, our creaturely dependency on God's uncreated To Be—a dependency which is primary and filters all our acts—can truly affect the form without it being one of altering or changing. Only when existence has a real role to play does our nature move from a formal and therefore non-individual species identification to a personal one.

40. Cf. Pegis, *Thomistic Notion of Man*.

in the third demonstration with the question of existence itself. This is a subtle but no less dramatic alteration which requires, indeed demands, that the language of matter, form, actuality, and potentiality be resolved in a dramatically different type of Being—Personal Creational Being— which will alter their very meanings. Actuality and potentiality as set out in the first two demonstrations have one meaning, and after the linchpin of the *third way*, acquire a whole new order of meaning. These caused causes no longer have a material causation and a formal in-itself eternality. Instead, that eternality is under question and its meaning now changed.[41] No being is eternal but God, which means the eternality ascribed to all creaturely forms or essences cannot be a true eternality but only a participated eternity. All beings, as we shall later discuss, are possible beings, beings that do not have to be. The language of matter and form is deepened into existence and essence, as the roles of actuality and potentiality enter the domain of necessary and possible beings.

Something peculiar has just transpired without our notice. Things which are self-evident belong to the order where essences are common to all; where essences do not exist in their own right, because God alone exists in His right.[42] We are beings of two unified but genuinely distinct acts: essence and existence; essentially "eternal" but existentially dependent on God for that eternality. This paradox requires an utter unity between creaturely essence and existence, but is nevertheless a real distinction. For Saint Thomas, essence and existence are irreducibly distinct and yet an essential unity. These two acts of To-Be are distinct, their distinction allows them to be a unity. They are not one in the sense that one collapses into the other. In the case of human existence, they are one unity, each a distinct act of existence. Essence and existence are distinct because, if existence collapses into essence, we have just essences/species and no individuals. And if there were only existents with no essence, which is not possible at all—there would be nothing at all. Essence and existence are a unity in man because without essence there would be nothing persisting, nothing to be able to identify ourselves as individuals within the order of mankind, with all the meaning and possibilities within this universal sense of mankind. We are given our existence by God; each is given his or her own to-be. God creates out of nothing the existence of each individual person, He did not indiscriminately put souls into

41. See Saint Thomas on aeviternity, *ST* I, 10.
42. *ST* I, 3.

bodies, as Thomas affirms they were created conjointly with the specific existentiality designated to each person as the unity of body and soul. [43] God intended and freely created each of us. This means: existence has primacy over essence, not in a Sartrean manner but in a metaphysics not stultified by an ideational essentialism. We are first and primarily created by God personally as individual. Our existence is the prerequisite to understanding essence. Therefore, we relate to everything, especially and including the universals filtered, understood, and fulfilled through that personhood/individuality. We understand the universal in a personal way. By that same token, truly to recognize the extent that each of us is "this" individual requires that each partakes in the form or substance of mankind, otherwise our individuality is meaningless. We are individuals only within the universal order of mankind. Without having a persisting universal identity of "mankind," there cannot be an individual "man." Unity and incommunicable individuality bound in-dissolvable, each in the other. Diversity presupposes identity.

God's essence and existence are identical not because they fold into an essentialist identification such as a prime mover, but identical so that he is the entheotic Being in and through which all creatures act. We are peculiar creatures capable of freedom *and* reflexive action. If we come to realize by our own natural powers that we do not exist in our own right, then by that same token we see that the *things which are self-evident share that same existential status*. We claim God is not self-evident because— rightly so—his Essence as Existence is not merely different from ours but the Difference-as-such. Yet, again, to know we do not exist in our own right necessitates a fidelity or union to the Being who does, so that we can identify and differentiate our natures. When Saint Thomas makes the move from demonstrations 1 and 2, which can resolve themselves in a non-creational order, only to revolutionize them through the pre-thematic creational apparatus of demonstration 3, he is again playing a most serious game with us. Our existence has gone from a form of non-material eternality (but an eternity nevertheless) to one which suspends our eternity in the power of Otherness.

Here is the game in play: If the question were, again, is Being self-evident? the answer would be yes. But the question is framed in terms of whether God's existence is self-evident, and the answer is no. But God is Being itself; an essence identical with his existence, as we soon find

---

43. Cf. *ST* I, 90, 4.

out in the question directly following the demonstrations.[44] Being is self-evident, God is not, but God is identical with Being. Yes; no; yes; and no. Perhaps Saint Thomas sought to distinguish the *proposition* from the reality. In reality, God is self-evident but the proposition or judgment needed to ascertain God's self-evidence is not itself self-evident. In this aspect of the game, the intellect knows itself only in the face of reality but also fails to mirror reality, for it is never the same as reality, precisely because the quest of thinking is to be the same as Being.[45] This proposition, confined to the intellect, cannot grasp what is self-evident in reality but self-evident only to those actions which are unified to Being and do not function by the spectatorship of composition and division. The game continues: beings which are self-evident to God *and* to us are those which, before us and like us, do not exist in their own right; their essence structure is delimited by their dependency on otherness for their existence. This dependency, by circumscribing their being, allows us a full vision of their essence. This is the necessary foundation for both analytic and self-evident knowledge. But God is not self-evident to us; as his own existence, nothing existentially delimits his essence. Still, God must also, in a way uneasy and unmanaged, be self-evident to us. He is the foundation for the knowledge of our existential dependency and thus for the acquisition of the self-evident truths of the natural world. If we understand that things are aspects *of* a source, we must be connaturally unified to that source: the *of* linguistically requires that identification.

Alea iacta est! Being is self-evident, God is Not. But God is identical with Being. What is self-evident is common to our essences, those existences which do not exist in their own right. But as reflexive beings, to know ourselves requires we know our essence which is not bound up in us but in the otherness of God's Being, which alone exists in its own right and whose essence is not self-evident to us. Prior to the *knowledge* of particular, empirical and also self-evident truths of the natural world, we must know ourselves as knowers, which requires knowing our essence. But our essence is as much unknown to us as known because it lives both in and beyond us. If we are to know anything of the natural world, our turn as knowers necessitates that the God who houses our essence through our existential dependency on him must be self-evident in some manner for us to act as knowers, and at the same time his Essence must

44. Cf. *ST* I, 3.

45. Cf. C. Gilson, *Metaphysical Presuppositions*, xi–xiv.

be an incommunicable mystery so as to require our freedom, striking and elongating the very act of knowledge.

2. *Self-evident in itself though not to us*: "God exists" is self-evident to God (thus in itself), though not to us.[46]

We do not know the essence of God and yet we can describe participations in that essence. These are the famous degrees of being and knowledge.[47] This of course begs the question: how can we describe something of which we do not possess the middle term? Even if we substitute the effects for the middle term, the difficulty is still not avoided. How can we know we are inserting the effects of God in place of his essence if we are not in some way already pre-possessed of his essence as middle-term? Saint Thomas argues we are demonstrating the *existence* of God and not his essence and yet, in the following question,[48] we learn that God's existence and essence are identical. Thus, if we are demonstrating *that* this Being must *be*, this existential "thatness" is already speaking to some very real degree to God's quiddity. Thus, Saint Thomas's rejection of God's self-evidence, on the basis that we do not know God's essence, is more a suspension of our access into that self-evidence. For it is true that God is not self-evident. We don't know God's essence, not because it is obscured and far-off but because we are wholly of the fabric of his self-evident non-mediacy. He already is the eye through which we see. We are too near to know of this self-evidence by spectatorship and can only know it through divine assertion. Just as we see the very nose on our faces *only reflexively* through the mirror, we are too near God as his immediate effect to see him except reflexively through his effects. And yet, when *seen* reflexively, the divine self-evidence must be presupposed as prior, indeed *a priori* but only after the fact! But if God as Being does not need to add anything to existence to impart itself as the True, the Good, and the Beautiful (for these things "do not differ essentially nor are they distinguished from one another by opposing differences"[49]), then God's

46. Saint Thomas also has a potential third category, "Self-evident but only to the learned." He uses the example of knowledge of spiritual substances not being in space. Such knowledge would be self-evident to those who understand the nature of an incorporeal and aeviternal being.

47. Cf. Lovejoy, *Great Chain of Being*; Maritain, *Degrees of Knowledge*.

48. Cf. *ST* I, 3, 4.

49. DV I, 1 *answers to difficulties* 6.

revelation to us is revelatory in the truest sense of the word: revealing what we are-in-and-of.

3. *Because God is not self-evident to us, His existence must be demonstrated by things more known to us, namely his effects: man, the world, experience, etc.*

Here Saint Thomas has set out the apparatus for the unfolding intelligibility of the *Quinque Viæ*. The language of "effects-to-cause" is almost legalistic in nature, not unlike a courtroom, and indeed the stakes are high. Saint Thomas is attempting to arrive at that truth beyond a reasonable doubt in keeping with the causal intelligibility of the natural world and the injunction of the faith. Effects necessarily point to their cause, and if all natural effects have God as first efficient cause, then God's existence must be manifestly demonstrated, quelling doubt and ambiguity. But the process of effects-to-cause also has another key point: this structure enables him to protect the mystery of Gozd, and can be seen as an expressly ontological form of the *via negativa*. By ensuring that we cannot approach God's essence head on, that we cannot gaze at or grasp what is too near to be self-evident to the intellect, Saint Thomas's route to God must be by way of To Be's causal effects.[50] This *longer way* illuminates the negative dialectic each time it asserts that a different order of intelligibility must exist in order for the natural order to exist. Defined by its delimited and dependent *quiddity*, the natural order gives us all the empirical evidence needed to show us that, beyond a reasonable doubt, empirical evidence could neither ground nor existentially suffice to maintain existence. *Empirical* evidence *empirically* tells us that it requires something other than an *empirically* bounded nature as first cause; the very parameters which constitute an empirical being require it be an intermediary being, always requiring something other in order to be. Thus what is empirical-as-secondary points beyond itself to something refusing empirical reduction. It is precisely our blindness in the face of God's existence which is demonstrated in each of the Five Ways. It is this blindness which is the pointing towards a *difference as such* needed to ground those things we *can* see, touch, hear, sense, and cognize. The fact that we can sense or cognize something in its entirety, as if enshrined by the intellect, shows us that the thing itself is circumscribed

---

50. But again, even to go by way of effects requires some form of knowledge—perhaps not by the intellect—of the cause, for how can one unite parts without some prior sense of their unity?

by a dependency on something other than itself for its existence. These enshrined or empirical things cannot be the true *causa efficiens* nor can they of their own power invoke their own finality. Their finality is bound up in a true *causa efficiens* by which each natural thing, especially natural efficient causes, are shown to be intermediary causes.[51] Saint Thomas will attempt to argue from effect to cause, from our experience/knowledge of the natural world to our non-knowledge of God and, in the process, speak about God in knowledge. Our Dumb Ox is, again, straddling that odd tension of the simultaneous self-evidence and the hiddenness of God. We speak about what we do not know and we arrive at a truth beyond a reasonable doubt only because we must know what we do not know when we speak the truth about it.

> Now when the Creator had framed the soul according to his will, he formed within her the corporeal universe, and brought the two together, and united them centre to centre. The soul, interfused everywhere from the centre to the circumference of heaven, of which also she is the external envelopment, herself turning in herself, began a divine beginning of never ceasing and rational life enduring throughout all time. The body of heaven is visible, but the soul is invisible, and partakes of reason and harmony, and being made by the best of intellectual and everlasting natures, is the best of things created.[52]

The Subordinated Ethics:
Responding to the Self-Evidence as Mystery

Thomas's subterranean articulation of self-evidence-as-mystery places us squarely within the subordinated ethics. A delicate balance is needed to differentiate a genuinely subordinated ethics from its false alternatives, and to show how certain acts of a chaste anarchism or an enduring non-subordination are still forms of a genuine ethics in-failing. This is an ethics which:

1. maintains its following of God, cloaked and veiled, when all the temptations seek to place it in the lead, to become insubordinate-as-worldly. This placement in the lead is commonly enacted in both

---

51. Cf. *ST* I, 2, 3, *resp.*
52. *Tim.* 36d–37a.

Christian and non-Christian ethical alternatives and both are detrimental to the connatural exhortation of the natural law;

2. finds its meaning in the connatural, the primitive, and the serious play of the sacred. The world of fact is seen as secondary to the world of sacral meaning; facts are not unreal or unimportant but they have their place in the subordination as the products of world-views. Facts may guide reason but they do not constitute it. A subordinated ethics redeems the non-rational, supra-rational and even irrational, because its enactment of ethical meaning is not *firstly* rooted in a weighing of the facts, which is often a partitioning of the good of the soul from itself, but instead of the Good, Beautiful and True as fashioned into our cosmogonic experience.

3. is witnessed as a form of fortitude and endurance—joyfully serious. The ethics of the naturally supernatural is natural by nature but not by condition. We live for the most part by condition, not by nature—the Good is, as Plato cautioned, the last thing ever seen and only with great effort.[53] Unlike the alternatives, both Christian and secular, which fail to subordinate their ethical meaning within the play of God's self-evidence as mystery, this is the true ethic which can form the soul to endure the alien and the hostile, and can persist without any seeming sustenance. By being subordinated to this sanctifying play, it holds the power of the natural law *before* it codifies as prescription. It thus understands something truer than our conceptual recognition of the natural law, it achieves participation in it, having taken the sustenance of Being-with God, within; where natural law is not a shortcut substitute for actual engagement *in situ* along the *longior via*.[54]

4. is equally un-subordinated, having no master but the chase, its fidelity to a God so certain we cannot turn away, so mysterious that to turn away one would lose him, lose one's footing in the chase. This subordination illuminates our ethic as one which differentiates love from mindless tolerance, the uniqueness of the person from the vulgar homogeneity of ideational diversity. This is an ethics that, because it will never place itself in the lead, will never surrender

53. Plato, *Resp.* 517b.

54. *ST* I, 62, 5, ad. 1: "Man was not intended to secure his ultimate perfection at once, like the angel. Hence a longer way was assigned to man than to the angel for securing beatitude."

itself to anything else that does. It is the ethics of Achilles and of
Christ.

This subordinated ethics follows and remains following God as revelatory and aniconic, even when all the temptations seek to place it in the
lead. This is an ethics which is bound to the divine *To Be*, not as a static
figure but as the *mysterium tremendum*, so real it cannot be denied.[55]
Ethics must place its language and movement in the natural-supernatural
movement of being-in-the world. And because this truer self-evidence is
the mystery, it is an ethics which inoculates itself against the temptation
to make God like man by viewing the natural law as identical with its
prescriptions placed on existence:

> The codification of the natural law is not the law itself, which is
> simply man's nature understood as the wheel of the barque of
> humanity. We become keenly aware of this when we remember
> that the remote origins of natural law were not judicial as such
> but rather ontological. Natural law, before its articulation at the
> hands of the Stoics, was thought to be the perfection or full flow-
> ering of human nature which thus followed upon a 'law' written
> into the symphony of being.[56]

In *The City of God,* Saint Augustine cautions those who take the natural
law as if it is an unbreakable rule for observable phenomena; in such
a way God is effectively nothing more than a more powerful regent,[57]
reduced to His prescriptions. Man therefore is man only insofar as he
conforms to those prescriptions, not becoming *godlike* but becoming an
inverse replica, a petty bureaucrat of existence.

> There is, then, another phenomenon at present open to their
> observation, and which, in my opinion, ought to be sufficient to
> convince them that, though they have observed and ascertained

---

55. For an intensely moving meditation on the often overlooked mystery of
the Christian aesthetic, see Hart, *Beauty of the Infinite*, 15: "The Christian infinite,
though, is 'ethical' only because it is first 'aesthetic;' it opens up being and beings—to
knowledge or love—only within the free orderings of its beauty, inviting a desire that
is moral only because it is *not* disinterested. For Christian thought there lies between
idolatry and the ethical abolition of *all* images the icon, which redeems and liberates
the visible, and of which the exemplar is the incarnate Word: an infinite that shows
itself in finite form without ceasing to be infinite—indeed, revealing its infinity most
perfectly thereby."

56. Wilhelmsen, "Natural Law, Religion," 146.

57. Cf. Saint Augustine, *City of God*, XXI.

some natural law, they ought not on that account to prescribe to God, as if He could not change and turn it into something very different from what they have observed. The land of Sodom was not always as it now is; but once it had the appearance of other lands, and enjoyed equal if not richer fertility; for, in the divine narrative, it was compared to the paradise of God. But after it was touched [by fire] from heaven, as even pagan history testifies, and as is now witnessed by those who visit the spot, it became unnaturally and horribly sooty in appearance; and its apples, under a deceitful appearance of ripeness, contain ashes within. Here is a thing which was of one kind, and is of another. You see how its nature was converted by the wonderful trans-mutation wrought by the Creator of all natures into so very dis-gusting a diversity, an alteration which after so long a time took place, and after so long a time still continues. As therefore it was not impossible to God to create such natures as He pleased, so it is not impossible to Him to change these natures of His own creation into whatever He pleases.[58]

Augustine is not falling into a nearly Occamite divine command theory, but is instead withholding from the static views of God which actually unleashed such kinds of theory. Once the natural law becomes identical with its prescriptive force, then the relation of man to God is reductively changed.[59] God causes the Good because it *Is* the Good, precisely because He *Is* the Good.[60] This Goodness plays on the language of certitude and

58. Saint Augustine, *City of God* XXI, viii.

59. See David Solomon's pithy remarks in "The Complexities of Natural Law," 42: "A few years ago I appeared on 'Firing Line' with my Notre Dame colleagues Gerhardt Niemeyer and Ralph McInerny for a discussion of natural law. My memory of that oc-casion is vivid: our attempt to discuss the possibilities for the theory of natural law in the contemporary intellectual climate was frustrated throughout by the way we seemed to be talking about three different subjects. Father Niemeyer approached the topic of natural law as if it essentially concerned moral objectivity, and, from his point of view, Kant was as much a defender of the theory of natural law as Suarez; McInerny and I quibbled about how much of the specifically Thomist project can still be defended; and William F. Buckley, the host of the program, was primarily concerned about whether a natural law argument could be mounted to show that the progressive income tax was unjust. In short, we spent most of the program simply talking past one another."

60. Cf. ST I, 6 *resp*: "God alone is good essentially. For everything is called good according to its perfection. Now perfection of a thing is threefold: first, according to the constitution of its own being; secondly, in respect of any accidents being added as necessary for its perfect operation; thirdly, perfection consists in the attaining to something else as the end. Thus, for instance, the first perfection of fire consists in its existence, which it has through its own substantial form; its secondary perfection

mystery not as polar opposites but as mutual illuminators. The natural law as our participation in the Good is both a directive to an order, a structure or way of being, but also an indicator that this order, structure or way reinforces our open nature or *deiformitas*.[61] Because the Good is God himself, ethics subordinates itself to this chase: it is firmly implanted in that which is certain for our knowledge and action but, at the same time, a profound chasing of that certainty, because the Good identical with God's *To Be* never reduces itself to the objectival or ontical horizon. The Good of the natural law does not cast itself into the region of idea that we can separate or combine as if it is a finish line one seeks to cross. We separate and combine, not because this is the essence of the natural law, but only one of its effects and more often than not an accidental one. Once the natural law becomes nothing more than a litany of impositions, a code of moral rectitude, it has lost its subordinated *entelechy*. This occurred both in and outside the Christian views of morality.[62]

> Before the physical union in animal nature, which leads to death, and before the legal union in the social-moral order, which does not save one from death, there ought to be the union with God, which leads to immortality because it does not merely limit the mortal life of nature by the law of humans, but regenerates it by the eternal and imperishable power of grace. This third element—the first in the true order—with

consists in heat, lightness and dryness, and the like; its third perfection is to rest in its own place. This triple perfection belongs to no creature by its own essence; it belongs to God only, in Whom alone essence is existence; in Whom there are no accidents; since whatever belongs to others accidentally belongs to Him essentially; as, to be powerful, wise and the like, as appears from what is stated above (I:3:6); and He is not directed to anything else as to an end, but is Himself the last end of all things. Hence it is manifest that God alone has every kind of perfection by His own essence; therefore, He Himself alone is good essentially."

61. Cf. *ST* I, 12, 6, *resp.*

62. See Jeffrey Stout's analysis of moral codes having any reference to ontological meaning. His criticism is a result of natural law already reduced to a prescriptive view and thus metaphysics takes on the diminished role of justifying such rules. Jeffrey Stout, "Truth, Natural Law, and Ethical Theory," in George, *Natural Law Theory: Contemporary Essays*, 71–104, esp. 89: "I am objecting . . . to the idea that we need a theory of moral truth in a sense that transcends the result of both descriptive anthropology and ordinary moral deliberation. Descriptive anthropology tells us how the term "true" functions in moral discourse. Ordinary moral deliberation tells us which moral sentences we have good reason to deem true in *media res*. I see neither the need for more than this nor the likelihood that trying for more will end outside the Serbonian bog."

the demands inherent in it, is wholly *natural* to a human in his entirety, as a being partaking in the supreme divine principle and forming a link between it and the world. But the two lower elements—animal nature and social law—likewise natural in their proper place, become *unnatural* when they are taken apart from what is higher and relied upon in place of it.[63]

It must be observed that the end of human law is different from the end of Divine law. For the end of human law is the temporal tranquility of the state, which end law effects by directing external actions, as regards those evils which might disturb the peaceful condition of the state. On the other hand, the end of the Divine law is to bring man to that end which is everlasting happiness.[64]

There is also a necessary distinction to be made between the language of God's commandments and the reductive prescriptive force invoked in the name of the natural law and/or God. The commandment invokes a signpost along the way of Being, a guide to survive and excel on the way of life. The commandment gives the means to fortify the soul, and its prohibitions as warnings are directed towards the health of the soul as naturally supernatural. They are a divine courtesy, parental advice rather than judicial *fiat*. The prescriptive force by which the natural law is often reductively exposed and encountered mirrors commands but without its intelligibility or its courtesy. Genuine command is accomplished in a world as guidance along the way, but the prescriptive version of command is no longer guiding *along* the way because the command has become identical *with* the way. The *polis* is artificial in that the achievement of leisure requires our artefactual separation from the cosmogonic sway. This artifice state—like all things in the fallen world—is both natural

63. Solovyov, *Meaning of Love*, 80. For a work which deftly illuminates the historical underpinnings and creative encounters between Hans Urs von Balthasar and the renewal of Christian theology in the West, and Eastern Orthodox spirituality, see Martin, *Hans Urs von Balthasar*, 53: "The purpose of the reduplication of beautiful natural forms in art is, according to Soloviev, not a repetition of nature, but rather an extension of the gradual embodiment of spirit begun in the natural world, but unable to be completed in biological forms. For Soloviev, the teleological (anthropological) end of these natural processes is that the human being as a conscious agent of this universal process can achieve an 'ideal goal—a complete, mutual permeation and liberated solidarity of the spiritual and the material, the ideal and the real, the subjective and the objective.'"

64. *ST* I-II, 98, 1, *resp.*

and yet, when left to its own devices, an almost inevitably malignant Leviathan. The naturalness of the fallen world is a naturally falling into disarray, for nature is no longer prelapsarian. It takes a Herculean effort to remain faithful to the invocation of the natural, and it takes our communion with the supernatural to maintain that fidelity, a communion which was severed *because* of our fallenness. The *polis* is a circuit breaker of sorts. It is reflective of the fact that we are on the horizon between time and eternity both in our pre-fall and post-fall states; it is an effort to remain harmonious with the specifically unique nature accorded to us, and yet this harmony comes always at a price. To be faithful to our natural state constantly in a deleterious flirtation with both the cosmogonic and our own fallenness, the *polis* seeks either the static or the moving: tradition *because* traditional or progress *because* changing and thus different from the so-called *status quo*. The Husserlian phenomenological bracket lives on in its most vibrant inevitability in the *polis*, where conservatism often seeks a frozen-in-time nostalgia or liberalism demands a mechanical and corrosive progression heralded by progress and absolute rights. Both are brackets placed on the unwieldy supernatural natural law, and neither can invoke it in its proper manner. Seeking to manage the nature it cannot completely envision (nor should it) the *polis* is often in danger of recreating—indeed recasting as it dismisses—nature to its own specifications. The prescriptive force of this *polis* may look like a biblical command but it is the image cast in the carnival mirror. There is no longer a command seeking to guide one on the way of life, for this presupposes nature as naturally united to each participant as it habitually inculcates and delineates the true good of moral choice. And when there is no sense of the ethical as the breath of the eternal, progress as the dismantling of prescriptive rules becomes its substitute and surrogate for that endurance.[65] Dietrich von Hildebrand sees the most deleterious results of the

65. In the religious field one see this parallel. For a frightfully prophetic accounting of the intellectual morass of twentieth-century progressivism, see former Harvard president (1869–1909), C. W. Eliot's address to students of Harvard Summer-School of theology (July 22nd, 1909). There he outlines the proto religious humanism that has infected academia. It can be found in Duffy, "President Eliot Among the Prophets," 722–23: "Religion is not fixed, but fluent, and it changes from century to century. The progress in the nineteenth century far outstripped that of similar periods, it is faith to assume that progress of the twentieth century will bring about what I call the new religion. The new religion will not be based upon authority, either spiritual or temporal. As a rule, the older Christian churches have relied on authority. But there is now a tendency toward liberty and progress and, among educated men, this feeling is irresistible. In the new religion there will be no personification of natural objects;

prescription over and against the mystery of the Other, in the existential and epidemic denigration of sex which so characterizes and captivates leftist ideology:

> The one who desecrates the mystery of sex by seeing in it a harmless satisfaction of a bodily instinct, who approaches the world having extinguished the light of morality, moves in a dull, falsified world without depth, without thrill, without grandeur. His world is the magnified office of a psychoanalyst. He is not tragic; rather, he is immersed in hopeless boredom because it is the moral light, the great tension of good and evil, which elevates and widens human life beyond the frontiers of our earthly existence. As Kierkegaard said, 'The ethical is the very breath of the eternal.'[66]

These carnivalistic commands subsume the nature they seek to replace, for it is easier to replace nature with a false utopia than to deal with its sway, where certitude is always aligned with mystery. The ideological prescription becomes the nature, or the nature becomes homogenized by the prescription so that the command does not guide but rather dictates the meaning of action. This is wholly opposed to the true nature of natural law, whose commands are invoked so as to guide us in the midst of our fallen condition but not suppress the in-and-beyond nature which imparts our true supernatural accord. What is understood as a will-based ethics is the result of a suppression of the will's proper natural law foundation in its pre-reflexive immediacy. When the intellect's guidance of the will renders the will to be homogenously aligned with the intellect's futurity, the intellect loses its own proper futural vision. It loses what our originary *praxis* offers—immediacy with the Other that cannot be

---

there will be no deification of remarkable human beings . . . In primitive times sacrifice was the root of religion; even the Hebrews were propitiated by human sacrifices. The Christian Church has substituted for that the burning of incense. It will be of immense advantage if the religion of the twentieth century shall get rid of these things, for they give the wrong conception of God. A new thought of God will be its characteristic. The twentieth century religion accepts literally Saint Paul's statement: 'In Him we live and have our being.' This new religion will be thoroughly monotheistic. God will be so immanent that no intermediary will be needed. For every man God will be a multiplication of infinities. A humane and worthy idea of God then will be the central thought of the new religion. This religion rejects the idea that man is an alien or a fallen being who is hopelessly wicked. It finds such beliefs inconsistent with a worthy idea of God. Man has always attributed to man a spirit associated with but independent of the body. This spirit is the most effective part of every human being."

66. Hildebrand, *Man, Woman*, 97.

reduced into eidetic consciousness. Thus, no longer a futurity built on the aniconic nearness of Being, the intellect's futurity has no choice but to find that futurity within its own broken nature, discovering it in an unfolding ideological and gnostic solipsism. A will-based ethics is neither properly of the will nor of the intellect, but the malformation of both. But how it is malformed is often misunderstood by those committing that same perversion. Either futurity is surrendered at the cost of an anything-goes antinomianism utterly at odds with the immediacy it claims to possess ("living in the now") or that futurity is falsely drafted into consciousness, becoming the different variations of the world spirit (left- and right-wing Hegelianisms). A will-based ethics is no different from an intellectualized one; they are identical departures from Being. Shestov, highly critical of a rationalized ethics, sets out the chain of rationality which freezes ethics within the vein of a systematized *theoria*:

> Spinoza wrote in the *Ethics* that daily experience shows us that successes (good) and failures (bad) are distributed equally among the just and the impious. Hegel, of course, was completely in accord with Spinoza in this matter. In his *Philosophy of Religion* he affirms that a miracle, as a breaking of the natural relationships of things, would be violence against the spirit. Hegel shows himself in this case even more Spinozist than Spinoza himself. Spinoza appeals to daily experience which convinces him that successes and failures are distributed indifferently among the good and the wicked. This knowledge, like all empirical knowledge, is still not the highest, true knowledge (the *tertium genus cognitionis, cognitio intuitiva*) that philosophy seeks. Hegel does not in any way appeal to experience; what he knows, he knows before all experiences. He does not need 'experience.' He, like Spinoza, needs *tertium genus cognitionis*, and he is not content with the simple fact but finds for it a foundation in the very structure of being. If misfortune struck only the impious and if the just alone knew success, this would be a miracle; but a miracle is violence against the spirit. Consequently, since the spirit does not tolerate violence, virtue—to employ the language of Socrates—is one thing and knowledge is another.[67]

The subordinated ethics cannot persist in a *polis*—even if bonded to a religious allegiance—oriented only by prescription over and against ordination. This is not to say that the natural law does not naturally

---

67. Shestov, *Athens and Jerusalem*, 130. See also van Goubergen, "Shestov's Conception of Ethics," 223–29.

bond to its Christian flourishing, quite the contrary. It naturally bonds because the figure of the cross is its *arche* and *telos*, because the genuine commands are signposts along the way of Being, and we seek not Being in-general but Being as personal, as the prime responder to our actions.

It is critical to distinguish the proper Christian *entelechy* within and in the midst of a subordinated ethics versus a prescriptive ethics which has placed itself in a leading position by summoning a vacant, ghastly and gnostic apparatus. The former leads to Christ *because* it was pre-possessed in Christ in a non-reflexive originary *praxis*, whereas the latter decimates that originary *praxis* in favor of a *praxis* indistinguishable from *theoria*, where moral judgment is nothing other than the execution of the idea. In this vein, morality is nothing other than the obligation to fulfill a command without any reference to the larger illumination of our connaturality which elicits that command *before* it is even knowledge. It is this sense of the command residing in us *before* it rises to knowledge which deepens the meanings of obligation, duty, and act, and without it these things find themselves grounded in an artificial tautology where nature is identical with command, but where Being invested in all things has nothing to do with that prime identity. And because Being has nothing to do with that identity, the ethics relinquishes any subordination and becomes an outpouring of the ego. Prescriptive Christianity is unsubordinated and grounded in the circular *theoria* of an ego-driven imposition of truth; this is not the opposite of secularism but its bedfellow. Obligation and duty beholden to these vacancies require a shortsighted vision of Being which makes "men without chests"[68] and cannot effectively transmit the supernaturality of the natural law. But obligation and duty, springing from an originary *praxis*, understands command before it rises to knowledge so that the success of its actions does not rise and fall within the cycle of its own origins but in the origins of the Other as Person:

> Natural law theory was made to work within Western Christendom because it was lifted into something infinitely larger than itself, the Christian vision of existence. Natural law became that part of the Divine Law which God has apportioned to men. Acquiring legitimacy and legality because it acquired personality, natural law also acquired loyalty, not precisely because it was natural but because its source was supernatural. No Christian seeking the origins of his decision to act like a man,

68. Lewis, *Abolition of Man*, 25–26.

to act decently in a moment of crisis and when passing through the darkness of severe temptation, could do better than appeal to that Pauline text which states that by our sufferings we 'fill up what is lacking in the sufferings of Christ.' A philosopher's God could not have oiled the machinery of the classical spirit: it took the Christian God on the Cross to do so.[69]

More grave were the attempts to reconnect a teleological and ontological foundation to a natural law already reduced to those accidental effects. In name only was the metaphysics foundational; instead it had to be at the service of the moral order as justifier, thereby perverting how the moral life should be accessed. God, for Descartes, was nothing more than an explanatory template, used to connect what do not need connection— the mind and the world. And metaphysics pressed into service to justify a natural law reduced to prescriptions upon or against the human condition—and God as reduced to orderer—is a form of "objectivism" far closer to the Cartesian debacle than one would like to imagine. Often we ignore the implications of God's essence *as* existence, responding only to his creativeness, but in doing so form our understanding of that creational power as if God were merely a super-man; as if God's existence were but a mode of his essence. We must respond not only to God's creativeness but to his uncreatedness. To be Creator, as Saint Thomas sees it, and for the world to be creational, requires that the difference between God as Pure Act (pure *uncreated* Being) and God as Creator be continually respected in the Creator, so much so that all of creation is therefore shot through with a continuous gratuity.[70] Our nature-as-respondent to that Pure Act actually responds not only to God's creativity but to his un-created Act. If we view God as Creator only, we are in danger of seeing creation as mechanistic and God's power pantheistically identified with the world. These misguided efforts have reduced the *To-Be* of God to a mechanistic Creator who imparts his creative power either arbitrarily or necessarily:

> But it ought to be remembered that the law promulgated in fear by a spirit of slavery is one thing, and that given sweetly and gently by the spirit of liberty is another. Those who are sons are not obliged to submit to the first, but they are always under the rule of the second.[71]

69. Wilhelmsen, "Natural Law, Religion," 148.

70. Cf. *ST* I, 3, 8, *resp.*

71. Bernard of Clairvaux, *Some Letters*, 200.

The natural law is *onto-logical* because it is wrapped up in the *Being-Word* of God and of the chase which must take place on the ground of participated nature as sacral. It is not metaphysical simply because one can strain to make connections to a veiled and more often than not secular teleological end.

> Classical natural law theory as well as its cause, classical virtue, received at the hands of St. Augustine in the *Civitas Dei* what was probably the most severe criticism ever levelled against it by a representative of Christian orthodoxy and a Doctor of the Church. Augustine's criticism of classical virtue, the end of natural law theory, can be concentrated in the following complaint: you Greeks have built a good motor but you have no oil to make it run! Human perfection and order are goals of natural law but in no sense do they supply sufficient personal motivation. We cannot say that men will be good because goodness is beautiful: evil things are often beautiful as well. We cannot say that magnanimity will do the job because the supposed largeness of the philosopher who does not wish the applause of others turns out to be the most crippling and corrupting kind of egotism after all: he may not want the applause of others but he wants to please himself. This kind of Stoic virtue is intolerable to real men who ultimately do good in the world in order that they might make some person or persons happy.[72]

The prescriptive reality of the natural law may be what is most visible, but this is not because it is essential to the law. This judiciary apparatus arises out of our condition, not from our nature—it is a conditional necessity because we are too weak to chase God and subordinate ourselves to *To Be's* revelatory hiddenness, so infirmed are we by sin or by the Golden Mean of Mediocrity. The natural law is a strange reality only for those eyes ready to see it. It is made for our nature and not our condition. For the most part, we see only vestiges of it in the imposed character of human laws, which are a form of accidental intelligibility. At best, these enclosed commands prepare our condition to rediscover its nature, but at worst continually conflate the prescriptive with the natural.[73] Because God *Is* the Good, the natural law not only lays down a prescriptive intelligibility; it also, at the same time, abolishes that same prescription for those prepared to be *of* the law. This is why the saint can live outside the

72. Wilhelmsen, "Natural Law, Religion," 147–48.

73. Plato, *Laws* 10, gives a strikingly direct linking of the meta-theological foundations not only of ethics but of politics.

gates of the City: he has subordinated all to God's cosmic chase. And it is also why the saintly is often the martyrological, having refused subordination to anything else.

> Listen to me, you islands; hear this, you distant nations: Before I was born the Lord called me; from my mother's womb he has spoken my name. He made my mouth like a sharpened sword, in the shadow of his hand he hid me; he made me into a polished arrow and concealed me in his quiver. He said to me, "You are my servant, Israel, in whom I will display my splendor." But I said, "I have labored in vain; I have spent my strength for nothing at all. Yet what is due me is in the Lord's hand, and my reward is with my God."[74]

This is a God Whom we cannot grasp and know, Whose essence eludes our capture, and yet it is in and through his Being that we must enact our ethical lives. Our chase *sources* our ethics, for it is our relationship with God which is the realization of the natural law. This is the key to the natural law, understanding that relation and seeing it in the midst of our sacred subordination. When reduced to its prescriptive effects, God is reduced to governor, boss, or an impersonal gnostic historical idea that one must follow. But in these circumstances the natural law, while always present in Being, is also obscured onto-noetically because the presence of the natural law is triggered only in our enactment of the relation with God. This is the prime freedom and responsibility of the natural law, not merely to follow commands but to actualize the law by entering the chase. The relation is not won by anything other than the movements of the lover-beloved, where the lover is the beloved and the beloved is the lover.

The natural law is grounded in certain and enduring principles, but ones which do not shut us off from the immanentization of the transcendent or the transcendence of the immanent. When God is all too mysterious so that he is unapproachable, then ethics takes on a self-imposed artificial template. It may speak or announce the natural law but has failed to enact it in lived-experience. If God's mystery is viewed as unrelatability, then we either produce an anything-goes ethical antinomianism or attempt to overcome such a stance by proffering our own form of self-evidence—in the name of God. In doing the latter, we enact an ethics which leads, which forgets its subordination. And while such a Christian ethics is an alternative to the various post-Hegelian

---

74. Isa 49:1–6 (NIV).

egoisms that populate modernity, it is itself another form of egoistic aseity.[75] If the mystery is forfeited in favor of the certitude, as if the mystery is not an identification of God's self-evidence, then the certitude curls in on itself and becomes one of fact over and against meaning.[76]

The Idiot as Guide: Play and the Ethics In-Failing

> Reality is by no means as substantial as it may seem, and personal existence, like all existence, is surrounded by and suspended over the powerful and perilous void, from which at any instant the monstrous may rise to embrace us. To such natures revolution, catastrophe, *Untergang* are not distant possibilities, but an integral part of existence. It is easy to reply that such feelings are typical of the emotional crises....but it is also possible that they express something completely 'normal,' the truth. The sense of the uncertainty of existence is just as well-founded as that of its opposite, that of the certainty of existence. Only the two forms of experience together contain the whole truth. These vague sensations so difficult to express and still more difficult to interpret receive their clear significance from revelation, which warns us that all is certainly not well with the world; that on the contrary, human nature is profoundly disordered; that its seeming health and stability are questionable precisely because they conceal that disorder.[77]

The metaphysical foundations for an ethics in-failing are not primarily justifications for actions and decisions, let alone for comfort and consolation. When we attempt to give a metaphysical foundation to moral action, we simultaneously defend and undercut the true ontological purposiveness at root in ethical action. Before any justifications can be made, we must examine why justifications even need to be made. They are made because we are either too much *in* the world or too much *not of* the world; our position on the horizon or *confinium* has been abandoned in either case. Our contact with the natural-supernaturality of the

75. Maritain seeks to differentiate a genuine Christian ethics discoverable in the connaturality of Being and fulfilled in Christ from those that hold Christ as a manifestation of the ego, over and against our originary praxis. See Maritain, *Moral Philosophy*, 79. See also Desmond, *Hegel's God*.

76. Balthasar addresses whether Christianity is nothing more than the consistent practice of humanism. See Balthasar, *Who Is a Christian?*, 47–48.

77. Guardini, *Meditations Before Mass*, 173–74.

natural law which enacts our relation with God and our self-knowledge is obfuscated. Rather, the metaphysical foundation is arrived at *before* the articulation of an ethical structure but is arrived at *through* ethical action by way of our originary *praxis*.[78] And this is the essence of play.

How then is this metaphysical foundation rediscovered? Our originary *praxis* illuminates it through pure contact with the playfulness of our beings. Our playfulness is our closest belonging to God: we were not his necessary labor but a free creation, and our *imago dei* is revealed in our own act of play as our higher purposiveness. If pure *To Be* refuses to be reduced to a concept, and if this is the foundation for moral decision, the proper vision of this ontological groundwork is not a legalized ledger of prescriptive and prohibitive actions. The vision of Being is communicated only through that visionless act of Being-at-play preceding and permeating man at play.

> It (Being) plays because it plays. The 'because' withers away in the play; the play is without 'why.' It plays for the while that it plays, there remains only play: the highest and the deepest. But this 'only' is the all, the one, the unique.[79]

The play that precedes the reflexive "why" is carried within us, and it is the truer metaphysical basis for ethical decision. The "rules" of the game follow the originary playfulness as implications for better play. Rules do not impede the game, they give life to it. But rules are in the service of the game and not its essence. They are not arrived at by straining to find a rationale for one's action as nobler than the next, truer than the next, but only in the growing of the bodily soul in accord with the play of Being. This play sensualizes the primitive, mystical and exotic within the mind and heart and concretizes donative love into the destiny of all deliberation.

> Nothing is private. The more intimate and personal an expression of love, the more public it is in the kingdom of God; the more everyone can lay claim to it. Not only the floor of heaven is made of transparent crystal, but all the walls too. Everyone has entry into the house in Nazareth, to the heart of the Virgin; even

78. Cf. Balthasar, *Glory of the Lord*, 5:369: "Nature is implicitly understood as the mutual reciprocity and indwelling of subject and object: All that is in the subject is in the object and something more besides; all that is in the object is in the subject and something more besides."

79. Heidegger, *Principle of Reason*, §188.

people with grubby shoes and ragged clothes for whose odour
the last image you'd choose would be the scent of lilies.[80]

Only a soul made to withstand the monotony of fact over meaning, because it has bathed in the personal existence which exceeds factum, can
be the connection between the ethical and the ontological. Only a soul in
play understands the Good not as a mere end to be achieved but as the
Kingship of the Spirit, as the dance and the festival.

> A coming-to-be and a passing away, a building up and tearing
> down, without any moral glossing, in innocence that is forever
> equal—in this world it belongs only to the play of artists and
> children. And as the child and the artist plays, so too plays the
> ever living fire, it builds up and tears down, in innocence—such
> is the game that the aeon (life, time) plays with itself.[81]

This visionless vision requires we retreat into the ground of immediacy
preceding *theoria* and which enables vision to have its context. We have
forgotten that the city-state, all communities and the family begin in
play, in the formation of rituals which derive their meaning only in and
from the play. Their meaning is no mere social contract but resides in a
personal nature from the outset. Natural law requires us to understand
nature. Not the doldrum nature of a subject/object divide which, in reality, leaves both poles unattended.[82] Natural law as our participation in the
eternal law, a law so near to personal *To Be* that it cannot be reduced into
our vision, plays with us so that we play with nature. Our play places us
in the nearness of God and then expels us in our difference:

> Creation is God's play, a play of his groundless and inscrutable
> wisdom. It is the realm in which God displays his glory . . .

80. Balthasar, *Who Is a Christian?*, 120–21.

81. Nietzsche, *Tragic Age*, 62. That was Nietzsche's take on the following Heracli-
tean fragment: "Time (*aion*) is a child playing a game of draughts. The kingship is in
the hands of a child." That translation is to be found in Caputo, *Mystical Element in
Heidegger's Thought*, 82. Also see Heraclitus, *Presocratics Reader*, §B52: "A lifetime is a
child playing, playing checkers; the kingdom belongs to a child."

82. Cf. *Republic* 604b–c: "The law, I suppose, declares that it is best to keep quiet
as far as possible in calamity and not to chafe and repine, because we cannot know
what is really good and evil in such things and it advantages us nothing to take them
hard, and nothing in mortal life is worthy of great concern, and our grieving checks
the very thing we need to come to our aid as quickly as possible in such case. See also
Laws 803b: "Human affairs are not worth taking seriously: the misfortune is that we
have to take them seriously."

> When we say that the creative God is playing, we are talking
> about a playing that differs from that of man. The creative God
> plays with his own possibilities and creates out of nothing that
> which pleases him. When man is playing he is himself at stake
> in the game and he is also being played with.[83]

This play so involves the entirety of civilizational meaning that the act
of ritual can, in a way, stand the universe on edge or set it moving once
more. While there is a cosmic indifference to nature, and nothing stops
the threat of time from being fulfilled, from it leaving all ravaged by the
exquisite commonality of the dust, nature presents us also with our own
difference as such. Nature's indifference is a prelude to the way it plays
with us, it demands we make nature, that we set the rules by which we
survive a world that refuses to pause in the eternal. Natural law is our
play in the divine which requires it play in us—as the always-preceding
cause[84]—in order to allow us to know of our participation. Our play
reenacts the divine movement in us because we cannot know, envision, or
circumscribe that originary play. Our own play conveys our participation
in the divine and it conveys it without separation from the act of play.
Those who see nature as determinism fail to see that the fatal cycle of
nature is equally one of play, that in its inevitability is the wellspring of
our freedom, the enactment of our movement in God. Just as play gives
experience to meaning, religious ritual gives meaning to experience, and
between the two, man resides as both its originator and its recipient. This
does justice both to Nietzsche's serious play[85] as well as to Shakespeare's
seven ages.[86]

83. Moltmann, *Theology of Play*, 17–18.

84. For an analysis of God as the always-preceding cause see C. Gilson, "Efficacious Prayer, Suffering, and Self-Presence," 153–264.

85. Nietzsche, *Essential Nietzsche*, §94: "The maturity of man—that means, to have reacquired the seriousness that one has as a child at play."

86. Cf. Shakespeare's "As You Like It," II.vii.40–68, in *Complete Works*: "All the world's a stage, and all the men and women merely players; they have their exits and their entrances, and one man in his time plays many parts, his acts being seven ages. At first, the infant, mewling and puking in the nurse's arms. Then the whining schoolboy, with his satchel and shining morning face, creeping like snail unwillingly to school. And then the lover, sighing like furnace, with a woeful ballad made to his mistress' eyebrow. Then a soldier, full of strange oaths and bearded like the pard, jealous in honor, sudden and quick in quarrel, seeking the bubble reputation even in the cannon's mouth. And then the justice, in fair round belly with good capon lined, with eyes severe and beard of formal cut, full of wise saws and modern instances and so he plays his part. The sixth age shifts into the lean and slippered pantaloon, with spectacles

Natural law as something specifically human involved the recognition of the human spirit by itself and hence the recognition that man alone in the universe can affirm or deny his own nature. This awesome freedom, often frustrated by fate and fortune and by the inscrutability of chance, in a terrible sense involves the whole order of nature: man when he affirms himself, affirms the whole and when he denies himself he denies the whole. Thus it was that St. Thomas could hold that suicide is a sin against the community of existence; that Chesterton could write that were the trees capable of knowledge they would shed their leaves and wither into hideous stumps when insulted by the same cosmic blasphemy.[87]

The gaze upon nature reveals our play in hindsight. It reveals that nature speaks to us differently, that by sending us away from our con-naturality in order to reflect on it, it has first played with us so that we can play with it. Nature exiles us so that we make nature in the various forms of play: the family, the community, the city-state. Nature is soul, sight, and person for it is through these things that we achieve our soul and sight and personhood. Speaking more to what is not necessary than to what is, our nature as play combines the tragic and transcendent. We play with the glory befitting the undying, and all which surrounds and supports that play enlivens this mystical immortality. What violates the sacred nature of the play is "wrong;" what enhances it is "right." "Wrong" and "right" in accord with what? With the nature of man as sacred play, and *this* is natural law. This is the sacred play which precedes the secondary ethics of prescription and direction. Factical perspective is seen as secondary to the world of sacral meaning; facts are neither unreal nor unimportant but in play they do not exceed their place. They have their proper subordination as the products of worldviews, guiding reason but not constituting it. Play lays down the facts not because they are not already present but because they are expressions of how the play will proceed. In the highest form of play, sacral meaning is identical with the world of facts, the factical *is* the transcendent. Only when ethics loses its subordination as divine plaything do facts appear at odds with the sacred. Facts opposed to the sacral persist because we have accepted our fallen

---

on nose and pouch on side; his youthful hose, well saved, a world too wide for his shrunk shank, and his big manly voice, turning again toward childish treble, pipes and whistles in his sound. Last scene of all, that ends this strange eventful history, is second childishness and mere oblivion, sans teeth, sans eyes, sans taste, sans everything."

87. Wilhelmsen, "Natural Law, Religion," 146–47.

state and gaze upon the sacral as a good to be perceived rather than a realm to be lived in. We vacate Beauty, the backdrop of Being. With Pope Benedict XVI echoing Balthasar:

> One may speak of a *via pulchritudinis*, a path of beauty which is at the same time an artistic and aesthetic journey, a journey of faith, of theological enquiry. The theologian Hans Urs von Balthasar begins his great work entitled The Glory of the Lord— a Theological Aesthetics with these telling observations: 'Beauty is the word with which we shall begin. Beauty is the last word that the thinking intellect dares to speak, because it simply forms a halo, an untouchable crown around the double constellation of the true and the good and their inseparable relation to one another.' He then adds: 'Beauty is the disinterested one, without which the ancient world refused to understand itself, a word which both imperceptibly and yet unmistakably has bid farewell to our new world, a world of interests, leaving it to its own avarice and sadness. It is no longer loved or fostered even by religion.' And he concludes: 'We can be sure that whoever sneers at her name as if she were the ornament of a bourgeois past—whether he admits it or not—can no longer pray and soon will no longer be able to love.' The way of beauty leads us, then, to grasp the Whole in the fragment, the Infinite in the finite, God in the history of humanity. Simone Weil wrote in this regard: 'In all that awakens within us the pure and authentic sentiment of beauty, there, truly, is the presence of God. There is a kind of incarnation of God in the world, of which beauty is the sign. Beauty is the experimental proof that incarnation is possible. For this reason all art of the first order is, by its nature, religious.'[88]

In this modern reductive view, the world of facts must be managed, and an impositional ethics controls the world of *nomos* and custom. But when the soul is built in play, the fact is natural to the play as the play guides the fact and the fact guides the play, for God plays with us as we play in God's play. In this realm, ethics has its true metaphysical basis: this is not one of a straining attempt to connect the ethical to the teleological, but of understanding the human person in play as the metaphysical transmission of ethical truth. No ethical truth can be understood by pointing to an impersonal metaphysical foundation, as if ethics can function by some form of muted identity and difference.

---

88. Benedict XVI, "Meeting with Artists."

Ethics is personal in its ordination and must find its foundation in the person. Most ethical systems fall upon this in haphazard ways. Some refuse the metaphysics in favor of the person but then reduce the system to a cyclical egoism.[89] Others attempt to combat that anti-metaphysical system with an impersonal metaphysics which strains to connect personal deliberation to an indifferent nature, entering into the absurdity of attempting to explain the greater by the lesser. This chain dominates Spinoza and then Hegel.[90]

The personal is needed and the metaphysical dimension as ground-work is essential, but the personal must *be* the metaphysical and the metaphysical the personal. And because the *To Be* which grounds actions refuses to be reduced to an eidetic vision, the transmission of this meta-physical personhood must be our being in play. Play is our union with nature, not as a "why" or a "how" but in the radical freedom of being one in-Being.

> To play is to yield oneself to a kind of magic, to enact to oneself the absolute other, to pre-empt the future, to give the lie to the inconvenient world of fact. In play earthly realities become, of a sudden, things of the transient moment, presently left behind, then disposed of and buried in the past; the mind is prepared to accept the unimagined and incredible, to enter a world where different laws apply, to be relieved of all the weights that bear down, to be free, kingly, unfettered and divine. Man at play is reaching out ... for that superlative ease, in which even the body, freed from its earthly burden, moves to the effortless measures of a heavenly dance.[91]

89. Cf. Maritain, *Moral Philosophy*, 81: "Later, with Kant, and particularly with Hegel, in their desire to construct an ethics capable of integrating all values, and the most vital ones, recognized by the common consciousness, the philosophers were to engage in an enterprise of absorption and substitution of vastly more profound signifi-cance, in which philosophy would explicitly assume the whole burden which theology regarded as its own, and finally, in the name of the God of history, would take charge of the destinies and salvation of the human race."

90. Cf. Shestov, *Athens and Jerusalem*, 131: "How useful the knowledge of this doctrine is for the conduct of life ... First, inasmuch as it teaches us to act solely ac-cording to the decree of God, and to be participants in the divine nature, and so much the more, as we perform more perfect actions and more and more understand God ... This doctrine then ... teaches us wherein our highest happiness or beatitude consists, namely, solely in the knowledge of God. Secondly, inasmuch as it teaches us how we ought to conduct ourselves with regard to the gifts of fortune or things that are not in our power ... namely, to await and endure both faces of fortune with equanimity."

91. Rahner, *Man at Play*, 65–66; see also 1–2: "Run home to thy house and there

The Heavenly Dance of Mysticism

When our Prince Myshkin is finally introduced to Madame Yepanchin and her three daughters, Adelaida, Alexandra, and Agayla, the introductions weave from formality to a naïve or unworldly candor. Having been asked about his first impressions leaving Russia to convalesce in Switzerland for epileptic fits, Myshkin speaks of recovering from an unbearable estrangement, a cruel foreignness by the unremarkable and the sweet braying of a donkey:

> What impressed me terribly was how *foreign* everything was. I understood this. This foreignness was killing me. I completely recovered from this depression, as I recall, one night when I reached Switzerland and was in Basel, when I was awakened by the braying of a donkey in the marketplace. The donkey made a great impression on me and for some reason pleased me intensely, and at the same time everything seemed to clear up in my head. . . . From that time I developed a great fondness for donkeys; it is even a kind of special affection. I began to ask questions about them, because I had never really seen them before, and I was immediately convinced that it is the most useful of animals, hardworking, strong, patient, cheap, and long-suffering. And suddenly through this donkey all Switzerland became pleasing to me, so that my former feeling of sadness passed completely.[92]

Our Prince is not intended to be of this world. Dostoyevsky sought to put to life a truly human person, one in whom the conflicting perfections of Christ were not cast aside as impossible, but unknowingly communicated in a man too good and too beautiful, because truly good and truly beautiful in all actions. An unassuming, intimate, and breathing Truth animated Myshkin's body before knowledge could corrupt it. Dostoyevsky is attempting to sketch the movements of an *alter Christus* and yet every *alter Christus* knows the literal preposterousness of the

---

withdraw thyself, play and do what thou hast a mind." Also Sir 32:10–13 (CEBA): "Lightning comes before thunder, and good favor walks in front of a modest person. Rise up to leave in time, and don't be the last person out; go back to your own home, and don't miss your work the next day. Enjoy yourself there, and do what you please, but don't sin with arrogant words. More than this, bless the one who made you and who lets you drink freely from his good bounty."

92. Dostoyevsky, *Idiot*, 57–58.

claim.[93] Such a figure is wholly *in* but not *of* the world, and the within-ness is a relentless, a hands-in-dirt entirety. And the *not-of* requires that this muck of existence be simultaneously transfigured and transformed into the shocking white snow of redemptive innocence and sanctification. Dostoyevsky's prince has the unblemished soul, but his entrance into the existential sludge is withheld so as to maintain that brightness, that unknowing communication of the good. He carries the true subordinated ethics in-failing, and solely by virtue of carrying it he subordinates himself to nothing false, he has no master idol, no politics of diversion and disenchantment. But neither does he seek to recover this in-failing that he possesses. Myshkin does not fight to save his own soul, and this is essential to the *alter Christus*. Saving does not necessarily mean preservation but it does mean entering into the reflexive realm where the heart and soul come to terms with their own unworthiness and their desire to be worthy in love. In that sense, Myshkin's seamless white robe is not whitened by the blood of the Lamb even though he is of the Lamb.[94] We have a Christ-like figure as much as we have a figure unlike Christ, unable to survive the carnal *as* incarnate, instead surviving it vicariously and ephemerally:

> At the center of the novel stands the carnivalistically ambivalent figure of the 'Idiot,' Prince Myshkin. This person, in a special and *higher sense*, does not occupy any *position* in life that might define his behavior and limit his *pure humanness*. From the point of view of life's ordinary logic, the entire behavior and all the experience of Prince Myshkin appear incongruous and eccentric in the extreme. Such, for example, is his brotherly love for his rival, a person who made an attempt on his life and who becomes the murderer of the woman he loves; this brotherly love toward Rogozhin in fact reaches its peak immediately after the murder of Nastassya Filippovna and fills Myshkin's 'final

93. And yet, while utterly impossible, the *alter Christus* is the integral human-into-divine activity that enables generationally the keys of the kingdom to be passed down. See Chesterton, *Saint Francis of Assisi*, 108–9: "If Saint Francis was like Christ, Christ was to that extent like Saint Francis. And my present point is that it is really very enlightening to realise that Christ was like Saint Francis. What I mean is this; that if men find certain riddles and hard sayings in the story of Galilee, and if they find the answers to those riddles in the story of Assisi, it really does show that a secret has been handed down in one religious tradition and no other. It shows that the casket that was locked in Palestine can be unlocked in Umbria; for the Church is the keeper of the keys."

94. Cf. Debout, *My Sins of Omission*, 68–69.

moments of consciousness' (before he falls into complete idiocy.) The final scene of *The Idiot*—the last meeting of Myshkin and Rogozhin beside Nastassya Fillipovna's corpse—is one of the most striking in all of Dostoevsky's art.[95]

Our study of Myshkin carries with it all the heartache and risk of the true subordinated ethics: a) all men *by nature* desire to be good, desire to know the Good, but not *by condition*, and b) the Good, pre-possessed in us, is the last thing ever seen, and then experienced and loved only with great effort. This pre-prescriptive ethical life is enticement before it is known for what it is and, when it is understood, becomes a warning for the stranger on the outside looking in. That all desire the Good is equally rephrased as: no one desires the Good, only the so-called good he can impose by his will.[96] And yet these surrogate goods which seek to destroy the Good carry a lineage to it, because each points, in varying ways, to our prepossession in the play of Being. What passes as the common-sense social decorum shows us that what fails in the *polis* of our condition is more often what endures as the Good by nature.

During his first meeting with the Yepanchin ladies, Myshkin spoke of the waterfall to which he would listen when he had gained enough strength to come near, where it bubbled and thrashed the water below. There, he would dream of the horizon line where earth and sky meld into each other and believe the greatest of mysteries are to be discovered walking along that line. Myshkin imagined lives more turbulent than he could ever conceive, calling to mind the frenetic visceral throng of Naples and then even conceive that one with such mysteries internalized could have a "tremendous life in prison too."[97] Each finds him odd and yet each is transfixed by his lack of convention, his ambitionless candor which disarms and secures the other. This oddness is used to dismiss

---

95. Bakhtin, *Dostoevsky's Poetics*, 173.

96. Cf. Plato, *Gorg.* 519e: "But in the name of friendship, my good fellow, tell me if you do not think it unreasonable for a man, while professing to have made another good, to blame him for being wicked in spite of having been made good by him and still being so"; Plato, *Gorg.* 482a: "If you want to silence me, silence philosophy, who is my love, for she is always telling me what I am now telling you, my friend; neither is she capricious like my other love . . . She is the teacher at whose words you are now wondering, and you have heard her yourself. Her you must refute, and either show, as I was saying, that to do injustice and to escape punishment is to the worst of all evils; or, if you leave her word unrefuted, by the dog the god of Egypt, I declare, O Callicles, that Callicles will never be at one with himself, but that his whole life will be a discord."

97. Dostoyevsky, *Idiot*, 60.

him as an idiot, a term that is proffered—often to his face—and retracted
on countless occasions throughout the book. And yet this idiot endears
himself to the Yepanchin household in the way that time has no bearing
on the transmission of meaning; he has eternalized the moment and made
himself theirs through a presence liberated from the time which merely
passes for pleasantry, all the while achieving this through innocuous
pleasantry. It is reminiscent of a moment which helped Dostoyevsky
survive imprisonment in Siberia:

> When he was nine, Dostoyevsky's family bought a small coun-
> try house in Darovoe. It was there that one day a peasant man,
> Marei, reached out and gently stroked the boy's face. In prison,
> Dostoyevsky later said, 'the memory came back to me and
> helped me survive.'[98]

Even though the Yepanchin women meet Prince Myshkin only once
before the chaos with Nastassya drives him away from St. Petersburg for
a half a year and without any contact initiated by Myshkin, Madame
Yepanchin finds herself in cycles of worry and agitation over lack of
news. She has become begrudgingly maternal over him, and her own
and the womens' lives are immensely changed by that afternoon. It is
during this first encounter that he speaks again of the moments before
execution—even suggesting such a painting would be an appropriate
subject for young Adelaida[99]—and also relays in story his love of
children.[100] These two images back-to-back are jarring and yet naturally
slide into one another, comprising the potency of our tragic figure as
truly *viatoric*. Prince Myshkin's reflections are often more telling than his
actions; in them we see the presence of the Christ figure as one in which
contradiction is the mode of union, where Christ is too bright to be seen,
and yet he condescended to infant flesh so as to welcome the little things
which get passed over; where the world is too ugly, too violent to welcome

98. Sheck, "Dostoyevsky's Empathy."

99. Cf. Dostoyevsky, *Idiot*, 67: "'Draw the scaffold so that only the top step of the
ladder comes in clearly. The criminal must be just stepping on to it, his face as white
as note-paper. The priest is holding the cross to his blue lips, and the criminal kisses it,
and knows and sees and understands everything. The cross and the head—there's your
picture; the priest and the executioner, with his two assistants, and a few heads and
eyes below. Those might come in as subordinate accessories—a sort of mist. There's a
picture for you.' The prince paused, and looked around."

100. Myshkin also speaks of Madame Yepanchin as an absolute child, an expression
of his highest form of love and admiration.

salvation and too beautiful not to be made for it. In his stories laid bare, we can see the perplexity of the Christ figure and the agonic impossibility and yearning necessity of the *alter Christus*:

> If I say 'Suppose the Divine did really walk and talk upon the earth, what should we be likely to think of it?' I think we should see in such a being exactly the perplexities that we see in the central figure of the Gospels: I think he would seem to us extreme and violent; because he would see some further development in virtue which would be for us untried. I think he would seem to us to contradict himself; because, looking down on life like a map, he would see a connection between things which to us are disconnected. I think, however, that he would always ring true to our own sense of right, but ring (so to speak) too loud and too clear. He would be too good but never too bad for us: 'Be ye perfect.' I think there would be, in the nature of things, some tragic collision between him and the humanity he had created, culminating in something that would be at once a crime and an expiation. I think he would be blamed as a hard prophet for dragging down the haughty, and blamed also as a weak sentimentalist for loving the things that cling in corners, children or beggars. I think, in short, that he would give us a sensation that he was turning all our standards upside down, and yet also a sensation that he had undeniably put them the right way up.[101]

Myshkin, again, speaks of the moments before execution. This meditation is somehow injected into the pleasantry of his first meeting and woven into the conversation in such a way that all who listen not only cannot turn away from the story but process it as if it is a vibrant but natural course for conversation, as if it naturally sprung from the backdrop and will recede back into it. Each enters the eternalizing moment and, as without a glance of difference, returns to the idle chatter which precedes and follows it, and yet each is changed, for again only one meeting made each of them worry for Myshkin as if he was a long-time dear friend.

> At last he began to mount the steps; his legs were tied, so that he had to take very small steps. The priest, who seemed to be a wise man, had stopped talking now, and only held the cross for the wretched fellow to kiss. At the foot of the ladder he had been pale enough; but when he set foot on the scaffold at the top, his face suddenly became the colour of paper, positively like white notepaper. His legs must have become suddenly feeble

101. Chesterton, "Jesus or Christ," 757.

and helpless, and he felt a choking in his throat—you know the sudden feeling one has in moments of terrible fear, when one does not lose one's wits, but is absolutely powerless to move? If some dreadful thing were suddenly to happen; if a house were just about to fall on one;—don't you know how one would long to sit down and shut one's eyes and wait, and wait? Well, when this terrible feeling came over him, the priest quickly pressed the cross to his lips, without a word—a little silver cross it was—and he kept on pressing it to the man's lips every second. And whenever the cross touched his lips, the eyes would open for a moment, and the legs moved once, and he kissed the cross greedily, hurriedly—just as though he were anxious to catch hold of something in case of its being useful to him afterwards, though he could hardly have had any connected religious thoughts at the time. And so up to the very block.[102]

This image is given to us directly before we are to hear of his time in Switzerland with the village children who once mocked and threw stones at him but who became for him the source of all his joys. Myshkin speaks of children as the true font of wisdom where the soul finds its healing.[103] The child understands more, sees more, precisely because the Good is not an object but Being-as-such in play.

I have often been struck by the fact that parents know their children so little. They should not conceal so much from them. How well even little children understand that their parents conceal things from them, because they consider them too young to understand! Children are capable of giving advice in the most important matters. How can one deceive these dear little birds, when they look at one so sweetly and confidingly? I call them birds because there is nothing in the world better than birds![104]

The juxtaposition of these two images, the execution and the child, is the very language of the *alter Christus* at both poles of his being. The child does not need to earn the good or to carry it, he or she has not yet become the baggage, stone or yoke, either in the sense of a virtue ethics or in the Kantian sense of duty. Unreflexive love is not naïve but the font of magnanimity; the joy which chastens all crucibles into a thing of grace. The Good is the last thing ever seen and only with great effort, but when it is

102. Dostoyevsky, *Idiot*, 65.
103. Dostoyevsky, *Idiot*, 69.
104. Dostoyevsky, *Idiot*, 69.

seen it is seen *again* for the *first* time. It can only be recognized because it is already experienced in play, and it is seen for the first time, because the originary *praxis* is not a seeing but a being-with.

> The love of the creature for the creature is thus a natural ana-
> logue of the most obvious sort for the supernatural mystical
> experience. Bergson, in his lectures at the College de France,
> liked to refer to this sentence: 'I have suffered enough for my
> friend really to know him;' and he would also invoke the inti-
> mate knowledge which a mother has of her child. If the child, he
> said, stirs in its cradle, she wakes up, whereas the discharge of a
> cannon might perhaps not even half waken her.[105]

It is seen for the first time, for example, in the eternalizing moment before death. The figure awaiting execution can hear his breath compete with his heart, see the age spots on the hands of his executioner, hear the clacking on the steps as loud as bombs skirting overhead. This life *right before* dying has senses so sharp they become confused with one another, where, for example, the smell of the blood is tactile and sticky. The moment is indeed eternalized, perhaps because the human condition has not enough distraction to suppress the human nature; or nature itself in terror of death repeals both itself and its condition, leaving only the primitive and ritual soul alone. Now it is the stranger viewing, in freeze-frame, the dancing of Being rather than being the child at play within the dance. Christ unites what was once lost: he is both the child as the body of un-reflexive love and, because he alone was born to die, the stranger who can pause in the midst of the dance to take in the inevitability that he freely places upon himself. With both together he moves freely unto death. Free and fatal as one: this is the soul of the *alter Christus*.

> There is one point that cannot be forgotten, round which
> everything else dances and turns about; and because of this
> point he cannot faint, and this lasts until the very final quarter
> of a second, when the wretched neck is on the block and the
> victim listens and waits and *knows*—that's the point, he *knows*
> that he is just *now* about to die, and listens for the rasp of the
> iron over his head. If I lay there, I should certainly listen for that
> grating sound, and hear it, too! There would probably be but the
> tenth part of an instant left to hear it in, but one would certainly
> hear it. And imagine, some people declare that when the head
> flies off it is *conscious* of having flown off! Just imagine what a

105. Maritain, *Ransoming the Time*, 267.

thing to realize! Fancy if consciousness were to last for even five seconds![106]

While the executed recedes from a world of certainties to imagine as remarkable what is unremarkable within his surroundings; to know the world through its own dominance and not another's, the child has not yet exiled the world from himself. The child's imagination does not invent from a world of certainties, but is living out the gentle coax of the cosmogonic, the wave that invites rather than terrorizes. There is no template of ready-made meanings by and through which play occurs. This may be placed upon the child to explain, guide, or categorize play, but on the contrary what actually occurs in play is the exteriorization of the soul in the world which is the soul itself. The child in play is entering his own soul and the good he achieves is the good of his own soul as free.

Play carries the truest form of ethics because it acts in the way in which ethics must be invested in the soul as a pre-conceptual, indeed non-conceptual, loving of the Good, not as object, not as *other* in the ontical sense, but as *other* whereby the soul is in a way all things, pre-reflexively united to the dance of Being. It is this foundation alone which can prepare us for the secondary ethics of static prescription and the attendant succubae which prey on our condition-against-nature, and the many so-called shortcuts to the good. Father Zossima who, in the *Brothers Karamazov*, is perhaps more than all of Dostoyevsky's creations nuanced into life as the *alter Christus*, understood the critical metaphysics of this foundation. The will cannot act like knowledge, if knowledge is to guide the will; the intellect needs something *different* from itself to guide, otherwise what exactly is it guiding if it guides only by suppression or conformity? And if the intellect guides that originary in-the-world communion, then through that interchange, the will wrestles from the intellect its greatest good: to abide in the mystery with an intellect not isolated in spirit but one that is concretized, reified, by a soulful body that will not and cannot separate the good of itself from the good of being. This is Father Zossima's preaching of love, a love that is born in child's play, and it is what Myshkin evokes as a single vision in his reflections on the execution and on the child:

> Brothers, have no fear of men's sin. Love a man even in his sin,
> for that is the semblance of Divine Love and is the highest love
> on earth. Love all God's creation, the whole and every grain of

---

106. Dostoyevsky, *Idiot*, 65.

sand in it. Love every leaf, every ray of God's light. Love the animals, love the plants, love everything. If you love everything, you
will perceive the divine mystery in things. Once you perceive it,
you will begin to comprehend it better every day. And you will
come at last to love the whole world with an all-embracing love.
Love the animals: God has given them the rudiments of thought
and joy untroubled. Do not trouble it, don't harass them, don't
deprive them of their happiness, don't work against God's intent.
Man, do not pride yourself on superiority to the animals; they
are without sin, and you, with your greatness, defile the earth by
your appearance on it, and leave the traces of your foulness after
you—alas, it is true of almost every one of us! Love children especially, for they too are sinless like the angels; they live to soften
and purify our hearts and, as it were, to guide us. Woe to him
who offends a child! Father Anfim taught me to love children.
The kind, silent man used often on our wanderings to spend
the farthings given us on sweets and cakes for the children. He
could not pass by a child without emotion. That's the nature of
the man.[107]

The life and death of the consumptive, Marie, a village outcast
loved only by the children and given a piteous form of love by Myshkin,
is particularly important. It is in this story that the whole of Myshkin's
fate is laid bare and through it we can see the subordinated ethics in its
presence and absence. Marie, a frail, pale young woman, hit the lottery
of unfortunate circumstances: consumptive, fatherless, an invalid mother
who soon shuns her daughter while simultaneously accepting her
continued care. Her mother ran a small shop out of her house, selling
tobacco, soap, and other goods. But the income did not support the family
and so Marie, ill herself, went from house to house supporting them with
various labors, sweeping yards, feeding livestock, scrubbing floors, all
for menial sums only to return home to bathe her mother and tend her
needs. Marie possesses what Belloc described as the creative endurance
needed for that dark business of life.[108] In times, before and after her exile

107. Dostoyevsky, *Brothers Karamazov*, 318–19.

108. Cf. Belloc, *Silence of the Sea*, 270–71: "Fortitude is the virtue of the menaced,
of the beleaguered. It is the converse to and the opposite of aggressive flamboyant
courage, yet it is the greater of the two though often it lacks action. Fortitude wears
armour and wears a sword. It stands ready rather than thrusts forward. It demands no
supplement; it is nourished not from without but from within. It is replenished of its
own substance. Sometimes fortitude will earn fame, but not often. Always, however,
it will earn reward. Fortitude is primarily endurance: that character which we need

from the village, the townsfolk would find her singing. Surprised and
with a mocking dismay, they could not accept that she, who had nothing
and was nothing, would be capable of any form of play. They sought to
excise and eradicate whatever form of endurance remained:

> A French commercial traveler seduced her and took her away,
> and a week later deserted her and went off on the sly. She made
> her way home begging, all mud-stained and in rags, with her
> shoes coming to pieces. She was a week walking back, having
> spent the nights in the fields and caught a fearful cold. Her feet
> were covered with sores, her hands were chapped and swollen.
> She wasn't pretty before, though; only her eyes were gentle, kind
> and innocent . . . In those days, people were still kind to her,
> but when she came back broken down and ill, no one had any
> sympathy for her. How cruel people are in that way! What hard
> ideas they have about such things! Her mother, to begin with,
> received her with anger and contempt: 'You have disgraced me!'
> She was the first to abandon her to shame. As soon as they heard
> in the village that Marie had come home, everyone went to have
> a look at her, and almost all the village assembled in the old
> woman's cottage—old men, children, women, girls, everyone—
> an eager, hurrying crowd. Marie was lying on the ground at the
> old woman's feet, hungry and in rags, and she was weeping.
> When they all ran in, she hid her face in her disheveled hair and
> lay face downward on the floor. They all stared at her, as though
> she were a reptile.[109]

After Marie returns to the village, she is increasingly exiled from the
town, with her own mother's goading approval. Not only does this pride-
ful infection reside with the strong of the town and the aged, it proceeds
to infect the children who began to tease and throw dirt at her. Ashamed
of herself and in her same dirty clothes, she was permitted into her family house only to care for her mother, bandaging her inflamed legs after
bathing them in hot water. Hungry and turned out to the cold each night,
she returned each day to care for her mother until her death two months
later. By the time of her mother's death, Marie's dirtied clothing—the
same apparel she wore to beg her way home, had turned to rags and her

---

the most in the dark business of life. But if fortitude be endurance, it is also creative
endurance, and at the same time it involves some memory of better times and some
expectation of their return. It involves, therefore, fidelity and hope; and, without these
two, fortitude would be of little use: but above all fortitude is endurance."

109. Dostoyevsky, *Idiot*, 70–71.

shoes had since been reduced to bare soles. She found a home only in the sense of location, cessation and peace out in the fields herding the cows. The cowherd after a while stopped shooing her away, noticing her usefulness with his livestock. Once in a while he would leave out bread and cheese for her, considering it a form of enormous charity.

> When the mother died the pastor saw fit to hold Marie up to public shame in church. Marie stood behind the coffin in her rags and wept. A large crowd had gathered to watch her weeping and walking behind the coffin; and then the pastor—who was a young man whose ambition was to become a great preacher—pointed to Marie and addressed them: 'Here is who caused the death of this respectable woman (which was not true, because she had been ill for two years). Here stands before you not daring to look up because she has been marked by the finger of God. There she stands barefoot and in rags, a warning to those who lose their virtue! Who is she? Her own daughter!' And so on, in the same manner. And just imagine, this vileness pleased almost everyone; but just then an extraordinary thing happened. The children took her part because by this time the children were already on my side and had begun to love Marie.[110]

Before the children broke from the influence of an ethics in the image and likeness of condition and convention, and returned to the non-reflexive union in play, they would tease and taunt both Prince Myshkin and Marie. But Myshkin, through his childlike kindness, with no ambition or scheme to coerce the good, brought them home. From afar, Myshkin would witness the increasing isolation of Marie from the town, seeing her become in the eyes of the other, a curious animal, an unfortunate oddity, one which must cause respectable eyes to avert in the streets. The young men when drunk would sometimes forget their hurling insults and throw instead farthings which she'd collect, spitting up blood, and then retreat to her field with the cows. At that time Myshkin had no real source of income, living off the kindness of his benefactor who was paying for his treatments in Switzerland. Having watched the sad affair and desiring to ease her suffering, Myshkin sold his only valuable possession, a diamond pin, to a peddler for a fraction of its value.

> I tried for a long time to meet Marie alone; finally we met at a hedge outside the village, on a small path leading up the mountain, behind a tree. There I gave her the eight francs and told

110. Dostoyevsky, Idiot, 72.

her take good care of them because I would have no more; and then I kissed her and told her not to think I had evil intentions, and that I kissed her not because I was in love with her but because I felt very sorry for her, and that from the very beginning I had not thought her guilty but only very unhappy. I wanted very much to comfort her then and assure her that she should not consider herself beneath everyone, but she didn't seem to understand.[111]

At the moment, Myshkin clasping her hands and about to kiss them, the children caught sight of the pair, the two oddities of the village— the consumptive and the epileptic—and began to tease, throwing mud and insults at them. Prince Myshkin even fought with them as Marie, coughing and wheezing, failed to catch her breath from the intrusion. Then, as if by magic or a vicarious grace, our Prince wears the children down into their natural innocence before the gaze of the other becomes an objective form of egoism. Over the next weeks he talks to them while they tease him. He speaks of Marie's sad lot and of the pitiful situation life has hurled upon her. For some time, they continued to tease, soon they listened momentarily only to run away, then they listened for lengthier periods in silence,[112] no longer running away but walking with heads bowed, and finally with great interest they began to feel affection towards Marie. The children began to greet her in the streets, bowing with courtesy when no one else cast more than a dismissive glance. They brought her food and bits of clothing and over time their gifts would be simply the play of love—to run up to her with nothing more than an embrace and a *"Je vous aime, Marie!"* and Marie would flow with tears and smiles. The children would return to Myshkin flushed with joy and tell him of their deeds and ask him to tell them stories and he would oblige and then would play with them for hours in the hills and forest, unaware of time.

The soul of the child is not to be made in the image and likeness of the parent, in any idealized goal, or in any form of futurity. It is the

111. Dostoyevsky, *Idiot*, 72.

112. This is Marian silence of the child's heart. See Lynch, *Woman Wrapped in Silence*, 6: "And when the hour had come that was to move the long days onward to Bethlehem until a faint cry should break across our air that hand not heard such cry before, weighted with ungarnered potencies, high portent unreleased, and tremulous with mercies still unsaid, a moment paused above a quiet place, and found, just this, a woman wrapped in silence, and the seed of silence was her heart that tried to give all that it held to give, and ever more."

sacred time when we are in the unmeasured—as God is the unmeasured. Because children do not anticipate beyond the present, they activate our originary *praxis* in the beauty and play of life. Nietzsche knew that no super or everlasting man was made from a soul forfeiting its play and condemned to climb the ladder of ontical presences-at-hand.

> I have a question for you alone, my brother: like a sounding lead, I cast this question into your soul that I might know how deep it is. You are young and wish for a child and marriage. But I ask you: Are you a man entitled to wish for a child? Are you the victorious one, the self-conqueror, the commander of your senses, the master of your virtues? This I ask you. Or is it the animal and need that speak out of your wish? Or loneliness? Or lack of peace with yourself? Let your victory and your freedom long for a child. You shall build living monuments to your victory and your liberation. You shall build over and beyond yourself, but first you must be built yourself, perpendicular in body and soul. You shall not only reproduce yourself, but produce something higher. May the garden of marriage help you in that! You shall create a higher body, a first movement, a self-propelled wheel—you shall create a creator.[113]

Thus, the raising of the child is a perilous affair, where the parent must be a commander of the senses, unflinching in the face of the cosmogonic, too full of the Good to see it separate from himself. And that is the key: too full of the Good to see it as separate from the soul. This is not a mere conscious fullness, and never an imposed or inflated one. It is a soulful body so woven into the fabric of Being that it fulfills and nourishes the primal truth that the soul *is in a way all things.* The soul is firstly all things not by intellect which knows by composition and division,[114] but by the non-futurity of the will. When Nietzsche and Heidegger loathe the Christological metaphysical move, they would not be wrong if that move did place all of existence in the gaze of the futural. If it did, it would render itself unworthy of commitment. The bastion of non-futurity, essential to the true child, prepares one for the secondary ethics of prescription, permission and prohibition. If that preparation is deep enough within the dance of Being, then the secondary ethics never takes over. The subordinated ethics lives and the good that the secondary ethics prescribes is already held *as natural,* without need of deliberation

113. Nietzsche, *Thus Spoke Zarathustra,* 69–70.
114. *ST* I, 85, 5, *resp.*

in the one who acts by *first* nature. If the non-futural is obscured by the dismissal of play, then ethics has no basis but *theoria* (or, worse, ideology) and the systematization of acts enchained around an *idea* of the Good, an *idea* of God, an *idea* of the self which can neither glimpse nor escape its vacuous solipsism. All ideologies begin this way. An ethics which has the *idea* of the good but never the good itself does not have the Good. Only a subordinated ethic which refuses all worldly masters, most especially the intellect seeking to make the will in its image, can invoke the Good.

In contact with the Prince's own playful immediacy—both tragic and transcendent—the children recover their *first* nature, their originary *praxis*. These little birds held Myshkin's and Marie's love as a purity in need of their fortification and would play the go-between, speaking to one of the other's love and then back again. When Myshkin met Marie near the waterfall or her herding of the cows, often only briefly, the children would stand at a distance as sentry. Their joy was unknowingly vicarious, and because it was not their own happiness it became all their own in the purest form of time. This is the time dictated not by a perception all too aware that it is outside the game, but the *aeviternity* realized for those who live by nature and not by condition. It is often spoken of as a pause or a cessation, but only by those who have sensed this time and have already lost it. This is the time as moving image of eternity for those seamlessly moving in the eternal. They are in a time without generation or decay but moving in the bodily splendor of the cosmogonic. This is the time of play, the sacred play which gives experience to meaning in the timeless region where meaning receives the breath of life:

> They would come to me in the evenings, there sometimes in secret, I think my love for Marie was an immense pleasure for them. I did not tell them I didn't love Marie—I mean that I was not in love with her but only felt very sorry for her; I saw they wanted it to be as they imagined it among themselves; so I said nothing and pretended that they had guessed right. And how delicate and tender their little hearts were! For one thing it seemed impossible to them that their good Leon should so love Marie when Marie was so badly dressed and without shoes. Well, would you believe it? They managed to get her shoes, stockings, and linen and even a dress of some sort. How they did it, I don't know. The whole crowd of them worked at it together. When I

questioned them they only laughed merrily, and the little girls clapped their hands and kissed me.[115]

When the funeral for Marie did happen and the young ambitious preacher launched into his moral panegyric, the children, having returned to play and having loved Marie, became angry with him. The villagers blamed the Prince for corrupting their children but the little ones would not lose sight of themselves again. They were one in being with the dance from play to death, from the gentleness of the cosmogonic ardor to its underbelly heaving with terrifying indifference. And they loved Marie, and she them, with all the freedom and fatalism which unites the child at play and the heart in us all awaiting the executioner. Only an ethics rising from the ashes of such a ground can withstand the crushing totality that all freedoms are *in-failing*, that they lead to the fatal as all death is swallowed into the freedom of being a divine plaything.[116]

> I assure you that because of them [Marie] died almost happy. Because of them she forgot her deep misery; it was as if she had been pardoned by them, because to the very end she considered herself guilty of great wrongdoing. Like little birds, they beat against her window every morning and called to her, 'Nous t'aimons, Marie.' She died very soon. I thought she would live much longer. On the eve of her death I dropped by her house at sunset. I think she recognized me, and I pressed her hand for the last time; how dry it was! Then suddenly the next morning they came and told me that Marie had died. The children could not be restrained: they decked the coffin with flowers and placed a garland on her head. In the church the pastor did not hold the dead girl up to shame, and there were few at the funeral anyway, only a few who had stopped out of curiosity, but when the moment came to carry the coffin the children all rushed forward to carry it themselves. Since they could not carry it alone, they helped carry it, and they ran behind the coffin and they all wept. From that time on Marie's grave has always been tended by the

115. Dostoyevsky, *Idiot*, 74.

116. Cf. "Dies Irae," from the pre-Vatican II Requiem Mass, attributed to Thomas of Celano (*dc.* 1250): "Low I kneel, with heart's submission, see, like ashes, my contrition, help me in my last condition. Ah! that day of tears and mourning, from the dust of earth returning man for judgement must prepare him, spare, O God, in mercy spare him. Lord, all-pitying, Jesus blest, grant them Thine eternal rest. Amen." See Schaff, *Christ in Song*, 372.

children; they cover it with flowers every year and planted roses around it.[117]

What Myshkin does achieve, unknowingly close to an *alter Christus* state, is a hurtling towards the heavy fatalism with all the freedom that play alone can bring. In this regard Dostoyevsky's references to Don Quixote ring true.[118] Myshkin has never been led by facts and thus the good he desires is not a product, an entity, a thing that can be possessed even if described as "divine" or "transcendent." The Good is instead utterly natural in and through him so that it never takes on an objectival quality as a result of his condition infirming and overcoming nature. When the good is seen as an object to be attained, something essential is already lost and one can be sure the ethics is far more prescriptive, even if subjectivist/relativist, than originary. The Prince has been spared such an ethics and, because of this, his soul grew to the rhythm of the unremarkable-as-remarkable and to the sensation of meaning as identical with experience:

> You know, I don't understand how it's possible to pass by a tree and not be happy to see it. To talk with a man and not be happy that you love him! Oh, I only don't know how to say it . . . but there are so many things at every step that are so beautiful, that even the most confused person finds beautiful. Look at a child,

---

117. Dostoyevsky, *Idiot*, 75–76.

118. January 13, 1868, in a letter from Geneva, Dostoyevsky confided to his favorite young niece, Sophia Ivanova, how immensely difficult it was to realize his idea for a new novel. He wrote, "The main idea of the novel is to present a positively beautiful man. This is the most difficult subject in the world, especially as it is now. All writers, not just ours, but European writers, too, have always failed whenever they attempted a portrait of the positively beautiful. Because the task is so infinite. The beautiful is an ideal, but both our ideal and that of civilized Europe are still far from being shaped. There is only one positively beautiful person in the world, Christ, and the phenomenon of this limitlessly, infinitely beautiful person is an infinite miracle in itself. (The whole Gospel according to John is about that: for him the whole miracle is only in the incarnation, in the manifestation of the beautiful.) But I am going too far. I'd only mention that of all the beautiful individuals in Christian literature, one stands out as the most perfect, Don Quixote. But he is beautiful only because he is ridiculous. Dickens' Mr. Pickwick (who is, as a creative idea, infinitely weaker than Don Quixote but still gigantic) is also ridiculous but that is all he has to captivate us. Wherever compassion toward the ridiculed and ingenious beauty is presented, the reader's sympathy is aroused. The mystery of humor lies in this excitation of compassion." This letter appeared in Dostoyevsky, *Polnoe Sobranie Sochinenii*, 251. See also Loseff, "Dostoevsky & 'Don Quixote.'"

look at God's sunrise, look at the grass growing, look into the eyes that are looking at you and love you.[119]

Is It Peter Who Is Approaching?

Incarnatus est, home of Being's consciousness.[120]

Every good thing given and every perfect gift is from above, coming down from the Father of lights, with whom there is no variation or shifting shadow.[121]

Even were it perpetual day on the surface of the earth, we humans do not escape the equivocal. The 'too muchness' of light would as much blind us as sight us—and perhaps we have to be blinded to be sighted—something must remain reserved or we die. The everyday can become strange and mysterious again— like the face of a beloved familiar, long known and not known, granted to us but too often taken for granted. Reawakening to our dwelling on the surface means being faced with a mystery: at the extremity of our determinate knowing, and perhaps our mortal condition. One thinks of Orpheus and Eurydice: coming to the surface of the earth out of Hades, to turn back, the too direct look, even out of love, brings about vanishing and loss.[122]

We have experienced the intimate strangeness of Aquinas's denial of self-evidence only to protect its truer incarnation, a longer way grounded on and feeding from a given immediacy of Being. If God were simply like us—beings-in but not *Ens* itself, not the *in* itself—then he would simply fail to reach the threshold of self-evidence. But because God is too near for us to take-in within our vision, we must reside on the borderline of Being[123] where something must be withheld, veiled, and reserved. Saint Thomas's categorical rejection of self-evidence does not reduce God to a figure in time, a self-enclosed essence structure, a creaturely being who fails to live up to self-evidence. As Existence, God cannot be missed, overlooked, or avoided even if in the rational act we mostly achieve a

---

119. Dostoyevsky, *Idiot*, 533.

120. F. Gilson, "And Dwelt Among Us."

121. Jas 1:17 (NASB).

122. Desmond, *Intimate Strangeness of Being*, 184.

123. Cf. SCG III, 61; DV X, 8, *resp.*

blindness towards him. This blindness never precedes but always follows from our own visionless vision, our unity with the uncreated through our bodily enactment of the Good. Within the mortal entanglement of condition and nature, reason is far more oriented to grasp what is last in the order of Being than what is first, but what is last must always follow and never lead. The last is not indicative of our highest nature but of what we possess by dispossession. Aquinas's rejection is founded upon the fact that God is the *only* Being Who is uncreated. God's essence as identical with his existence requires, in a way visionless but primordially self-evident, the unmistakable presence of God in all things. God is not self-evident by reason but for our reason to come to God beyond its own finite powers necessitates that our limited being enjoy an intimacy with his uncreated *Ens*, a pre-reflexive enactment more readily held in the life of our originary *praxis*. This reserving or withholding in order to see God is magnified in the incarnation. The Christ child is cloaked in the limits of flesh and blood, hidden in a finite vessel in order for us to approach him.[124] For if he revealed himself in the uncreated we would, like Orpheus, be unable to withstand within our creational vision what is too direct and too near to us. The unfolding meta-logic of the *Quinque Viae* places the Angelic Doctor within an onto-theological truth no mere metaphysics of identity can grasp. The gap, the non-sequitur, the gratuity of existence must be acknowledged not only as an explanation of religious meaning, but of the role of a personal and creative God. The gratuity must reside within the cosmogonic as a foundational companion to the soul at play whose freedom always dances with the fatal. The aspect in existence that does not add up is identical with the God Who freely creates out of nothing, which means that our identification of God is always present and always broken, always intruding and overthrowing our recollection of that intrusion, always in the way as background, context, *mise-en-scène*, seemingly irrelevant passerby. God's identification in us is the only form of identity which renders us incapable of seeing ourselves with our own eyes. Our identification in God is always preceded by God's identification in us, an identification that hurls us into the originary newness of being

124. Cf. Thomas Aquinas, *Praying in the Presence of Our Lord*, 119: "Godhead here in hiding, whom I do adore, masked by these bare shadows, shape and nothing more, see, Lord, at thy service low lies here a heart lost, all lost in wonder at the God thou art. Seeing, touching, tasting are in thee deceived: how says trusty hearing? that shall be believed; what God's Son has told me, take for truth I do; truth himself speaks truly or there's nothing true." See *Catechism of the Catholic Church*, §1381.

like him, utterly cast out, spanning the abyss and deriving our union with God from the nothingness of vision. This is the gainful loss of the Five Ways which sets out the entirety of Thomas's rarefied metaphysics.

> Objection 1. It seems that the existence of God cannot be demonstrated. For it is an article of faith that God exists. But what is of faith cannot be demonstrated, because a demonstration produces scientific knowledge; whereas faith is of the unseen (Hebrews 11:1). Therefore, it cannot be demonstrated that God exists.[125]

The relationship between reason and faith, what can be grasped by the so-called natural light of reason and what can only be possessed through God's revelatory dispensation, has always caused bloodthirsty controversy. Claims of an overt or subtle fideism or of a rabid rationalism dot the post-scholastic landscape, and have elicited not only a reticence but a pan-refusal to encounter metaphysics beyond a strained Aristotelian categorization of substance, identity, and distinction. It is often easier for the professional metaphysician to think metaphysically by not thinking about Being! If one were to play the game of Being as occurring in the Five Ways, the reason for the distinction between faith and reason is both indelibly real and yet not what it seems. The distinction is there in reason, for no amount of reason can follow the chain of causality and grasp what does not lay within that chain but always precedes it as an imageless difference. The distinction is again alive and present in reason, for our rational act cannot grasp what first allows it to act. The gratuity cannot be added up to and yet it is not an isolated act; instead it is that which makes the attempt to add up possible. Faith is not an artificial template which lands upon existence and changes the canvas of the land, even though in faith everything *is* changed. It is not merely decorative. Faith was always the canvas of the land, for God's gratuity is identical with the fact that this gratuity is never the effect of our actions as if God's actions are bound by potentiality. God's gratuity is always the preceding cause: thus faith in a way precedes reason as grace in a way precedes nature.[126] Faith is the

---

125. *ST* I, 2, 2, *arg.* 1.

126. Cf. C. Gilson, *Political Dialogue*, 59–60: "Existence is the prime gift and no mere explanatory hypothesis or transient it-goes-without-saying gift. Grace precedes nature, not in a chronological procession, but as the prime accompanying *Act* that makes nature efficacious in its temporal becoming. As the intensification of the prime or prevenient gift of existence only grace actually enables man to recognize the sheer gratuity of grace. As the preveniently open and participating being, man recognizes

contact with the aniconic made visible not by our sight but by the eyes of Being. Faith assents to blindness in order to see with the only eyes which can see what grounds sight. There is in us a primordial or pre-possessive form of faith, a contact with the uncreated, driving our reasonable desire to surrender to that which is beyond but not contrary to reason. A pre-possessive faith precedes reason to make reason's call to the revelatory faith a reasonable call. Thus, when the first objector in article 2 seeks to distinguish faith and reason, arguing against the ability of reason to demonstrate God's existence, he rightly holds that faith and reason are distinct but does not see *how* they are distinct.

> The existence of God and other like truths about God, which can be known by natural reason, are not articles of faith, but are preambles to the articles; for faith presupposes natural knowledge, even as grace presupposes nature, and perfection supposes something that can be perfected. Nevertheless, there is nothing to prevent a man, who cannot grasp a proof, accepting, as a matter of faith, something which in itself is capable of being scientifically known and demonstrated.[127]

The existence of God is a preamble to the articles of the faith—a walking-towards what must in a way already be present within our originary *praxis* in order for the soulful body to have its compass and direction. A pre-possessive faith lets reason be dispossessed in order for it to yearn for a seeing possession given by the revelatory faith of the cross.

> My soul is occupied,
> And all my substance in His service;

---

his total neediness for God; he has thus already approached the distinction between nature and grace! This distinction, much like the real distinction, admits no quantifiable division in the act of being. It reveals something all the more important for the spiritual and moral formation of man: a seamlessness shot through with eternity, so as to emphasize man's dependency on God. If there were a seam, a piece to portion off, then the centrality of the salvific presence would be marginalized. There would be an alternate route or end whereby man could "complete" his open nature and in that act deny his open nature! The free possibility of grace's *alethiological* unveiling and intensification of existence infuses all of man's desires. Man, bound up in the *logos*, desires grace more than he desires life, precisely because grace is life itself. Grace fulfills life by transforming it, and man also somehow desires death only because he desires that transformation. We distinguish only to unite. And this is so even within the order of grace as such, actual grace, operative grace, infused grace, efficacious grace, irresistible grace: all presuppose and yet are not reducible to the prevenient, antecedent grace."

127. *ST* I, 2, 2, ad. 1.

> Now I guard no flock,
> Nor have I any other employment:
> My sole occupation is love.
> If, then, on the common land
> I am no longer seen or found,
> You will say that I am lost;
> That, being enamoured,
> I lost myself; and yet was found.[128]

Faith is not an effect of a disposition, feeling, or attitude. Nor is it extraneous. It is life-giving because the transcendentally spiritual is always immanently ontological. Once Saint Thomas rejects God's self-evidence because we cannot grasp in reason God's essence, and later pointing to the Godhead's uncreated essence as identical with existence itself,[129] then the distinction between faith and reason, while real, must be placed on grounds which respect the self-evident yet *demonstrable unavoidability* of the divine. If the Christian God were Plato's divine mind or Aristotle's prime mover (both non-creational, where existence is but a mode of essence) then the line between faith and reason would be an easier partition. The curtain separating beings from Being would announce the cessation of reason and the advent of faith (if one would even need faith). The prime mover is not innermost in Being, is not personal and relational but instead is prime solely in its distinction *as separation, as isolation* and it is why in the *De Anima*, there are eternal things but no personal immortality.[130] In a Thomistic metaphysics, the distinction between faith and reason cannot fall as a line in existence that separates one order from the other. God as innermost in all things provides our transcendence because of that intimate inwardness. His existence, no longer a category of essence, abolishes any ontological partition between reason and faith.

128. See John of the Cross, *Mystical Doctrine*, 146.

129. Cf. *ST* I, 3.

130. Cf. DA 430a: "Actual knowledge is identical with its object: in the individual, potential knowledge is in time prior to actual knowledge, but in the universe as a whole it is not prior even in time. Mind is not at one time knowing and at another not. When mind is set free from its present conditions it appears as just what it is and nothing more: this alone is immortal and eternal *(we do not, however, remember its former activity because, while mind in this sense is impassible, mind as passive is destructible), and without it nothing thinks*" (my emphasis). Also see Owens, "Note on Aristotle, De Anima," 107–18; Gill, "Aristotle's Metaphysics Reconsidered," 223–41; Ross, *Metaphysical Aporia*.

And while ontologically he abolishes the partition between the two, it is resurrected in a different form *because* the partition is abolished, because God is ontologically nearer to ourselves than we are to ourselves.

> The attentiveness of faith presupposes, therefore, the renunciation of self-sufficiency and by the same token the recognition of the Cross. Yet far from annihilating reason, this mortification brings it, by the boldness of a transgression, to the threshold of its true dwelling place.[131]

If there were an ontological partition mirroring the faith-and-reason divide, would faith even be needed? One would have the gratuity of the faith but not its necessity; it would become the capriciousness of the pure nature stance.[132] Finite beings on the so-called side of reason would, by virtue of their non-creational essence, exist in their own right, for no being other than themselves would be innermost in them. For if there were, then the partition would be dissolved. The oddity of the language of faith-and-reason is that it is language proceeding from a creational Being Who, as uncreated, is pan-entheotic and unavoidable. But the expression of this distinction between the two takes on the conceptual characterization of a non-creational world where a partition between

131. Breton, *Word and the Cross*, 14.

132. C. Gilson, *Political Dialogue*, xi–xii: "The idea of 'pure nature' is itself a fatal foundation for any productive metaphysics, any real relatedness between nature and grace, man and state . . . pure nature is also at the heart of global ideological secular thinking which has replaced both theological and philosophical thinking about the nature of society. Absent any real understanding that grace is always indwelling in man's already open nature, pure nature cannot accommodate the presence of revelation in existence and therefore furthers the present political privatization of faith, rendering the Western debate illustratively pointless, a debate in which the only participants allowed are an antinomian multiculturalism or a rabid secularism, both of which share more in origin and intent than even Habermas realizes in his efforts to split the historical differences when, conceptually speaking, there are none . . . More intensely, does *natura pura* also fail to recognize that Christ's entrance into the onto-noetic domain must entail a dramatic intensification of the nature of man? And this can only be genuine if man is not a 'pure' nature with a correspondent pure-as-impure end, but rather an open nature always in-making in the naturally supernatural world. If man had a pure nature with its correspondent end, wouldn't Christ's entrance convert man by way of annihilation rather than by perfection? Would it not be gratuity but capriciousness? For if grace were not in accord with our nature it would not be 'good' for it, for the good is that which is in accord with nature as fulfilling its natural open desire for the good, which it desires and loves even as it confronts the alternative false candidates for its completion. Thus the supernatural is in accord with the natural law of things, even as a gift."

substances is effectively identical with a partition between beings and Being. This renders God idolatrous, in Marion's sense,[133] and then constructs the ill-fated metaphysics of identity scrambling to identify God in its netting, when God precedes and refuses that eidetic capture and devaluation. When the distinction between faith and reason is circumscribed by a latent non-creational identification, then the ethics which follows from it has no proper subordination. While the genuine distinction resides in the overwhelming reality that God's hiddenness is his entrenched Presence, a Presence which abolishes the distinction while simultaneously resurrecting it because of its visionless nearness, the false distinction relies on an outmaneuvering of Being in favor of a rationalization of faith. Faith is placed in brackets, distinct from the world of reason which persists independent of the faith. Any distinction between faith and reason on these grounds impairs both faith and reason and is a self-inflicted rationalism whether it tends more to the faith or more to the reason.

> Dear God, I don't want to have invented my faith to satisfy my weakness. I don't want to have created God to my own image as they're so fond of saying. Please give me the necessary grace, oh Lord, and please don't let it be as hard to get as Kafka made it.[134]

The partitioned view of the distinction between reason and faith may speak of God in the Christian sense but has isolated him ontologically as nothing more than a prime mover evolved into a post-Cartesian clock-winder ordaining the intelligibility of things. But in this case the intelligibility is restricted to the ethical domain, in the actions which are done as an image of God's actions.[135] God conceived without

---

133. Cf. Marion, *God Without Being.*

134. O'Connor, *Prayer Journal*, 16. See also O'Connor, "Fiction Writer and His Country," 31: "I have heard it said that belief in Christian dogma is a hindrance to the writer, but I myself have found nothing further from the truth. Actually, it frees the storyteller to observe. It is not a set of rules which fixes what he sees in the world. It affects his writing primarily by guaranteeing his respect for mystery."; 146: "The Catholic writer, insofar as he has the mind of the Church, will feel life from the standpoint of the central Christian mystery: that it has, for all its horror, been found by God to be worth dying for. But this should enlarge, not narrow, his field of vision."

135. And in doing so we reduce Christ to humanism's mere moral teacher and to what Kierkegaard lamented—a figure *in* history rather than the very cruciform *of* history. The bloodless, abstract prime mover enchained to Christ as reducible moral teacher, deconstructed together by post-modernity's progressivist irreverence. What is missed when Christ is reduced to some form of moralist stoic sage is also

his uncreated creational imprint makes the faith a form of identity used to express his nature rather than his nature overflowing and illuminating the expression of faith. In this false view, the faith circles around this isolated non-creational God, attempting to bring him into a Creator status and into the world by prescription as the only form of identity and divine likeness. Ethics pretends to be aligned and subordinated to God's will but it is only subordinated to itself, to the ethical miasma encircling a God already exiled from the world.[136]

The distinction between our essence and our existence is real, and its enduring reality places us within the hunt for Being as one leading to the cross. If it were merely conceptual we would exist in our own right and the enterprise of creational need would collapse. There would be no transcendence beyond ourselves in order to be ourselves, but only a recollection of our limited form. And yet if the two were truly separate *as isolated*, neither essence nor existence could *be*. Essence without existence is neither essential nor existing, and an existence without essential content simply does not exist. The mystery of the real distinction, a distinction which permeates the charter of our bodily souls, guides us in understanding the relationship between faith and reason. The distinction

---

the astonishing yearning to unite in Christ's image, a unity which actually unveils the truer transformative power of ethical meaning. See correspondence of Dostoyevsky to Madam Fonvizina in Frank, *Dostoyevsky: The Years of Ordeal*, 160: "I will tell you that at such moments one thirsts for faith as 'the parched grass,' and one finds it at last because the truth becomes evident in unhappiness. I will tell you that I am a child of the century, a child of disbelief and doubt. I am that today and will remain so until the grave. How much terrible torture this thirst for faith has cost me even now, which is all the stronger in my soul the more arguments I can find against it. And yet, God sends me sometimes instants when I am completely calm; at those instants I love and I feel loved by others, and it is at these instants that I have shaped for myself a Credo where everything is clear and sacred for me. This Credo is very simple, here it is: to believe that nothing is more beautiful, profound, sympathetic, reasonable, manly, and more perfect than Christ; and I tell myself with a jealous love not only that there is nothing but that there cannot be anything. Even more: if someone proved to me that Christ is outside the truth, and that in reality the truth were outside of Christ, then I would prefer to remain with Christ rather than with the truth."

136. We are by nature communal, the migration of the faith to a solely private affair, as Plato suspected in the *Republic*, advances its decline, a form of somatic forgetfulness, and then it is casually abandoned as irrelevant to life and meaning. And so faith becomes a "very personal thing" as politicians like to say in order to avoid condemning things like abortion as outside the public square. See C. Gilson, "Grand Refusal," 48–58. For an expanded study, see the Appendix: Case in Point: "The Grandest of All Refusals: Abortion's Pogrom against Contingency and the Historical Defection within the Language Game of Choice."

between reason and faith is as real as the distinction between essence and existence, and it refuses to be understood as entitatively separate, and for similar reasons. As none can draw a line within oneself and divide the body from the soul, existence from essence, neither can one cleave faith from reason. Distinctions are to be made, for what is grasped by faith can only be grasped because that which is most interior and beyond us activates our obediential potency.[137] In the life-giving gratuity of the faith, and in utter risk and utter certainty, we go beyond ourselves in order to be ourselves. Only after the fact can reason describe that difference which faith inaugurates. It can describe what has been presented to it by the faith, but before it is presented, reason may yearn for what is unknown. Yet this yearning dilates meaning. Reason yearns for what it does not know only because it is involved in a form of "knowing" that unknown. Reason which guides the will is in contact with the non-rational, pre-reflexive play that is our originary *praxis* in its primordial faith. Again: is this the naturally implanted but "vague" understanding discussed in objection 2 of question 1? Nature will never satisfy us, and this is a truth of Being. This truth is revealed in its highest meaning in the faith and in the desire for the beatific vision, but it is a truth always present in the cosmogonic. Faith is no alien template put upon beings indifferent in yearning, slanting that indifference towards reception and action. It is the always present in being, the true datum of consciousness, which lets reason withhold Being in order to approach Being and to be a reasoning act with vision and grasp. Faith *as* exceeding-Being also overwhelms reason so that reason makes the most reasonable assent and surrender to the faith, to what *is* true. Revelation is not addition, even though everything is magnified by a gratuity such that life without it would be emptied of presence. Everything changes in faith because faith reveals change as consubstantial with Being. It is indeed Peter approaching!

> Further, the essence is the middle term of demonstration. But we cannot know in what God's essence consists, but solely in what it does not consist; as Damascene says (De Fide Orth. i, 4). Therefore, we cannot demonstrate that God exists.[138]

The second objector in article 2 has placed the weight of his objection squarely on the dramatic conclusion of the preceding article. By withholding God's essence from the vision of the intellect, we must

137. Cf. C. Gilson, "Search for a Method," 51–128.
138. *ST* I, 2, 2, arg. 2.

use the effects of God in place of this middle term. But to use these effects requires that their union with God is not understood in a substance-based metaphysics but one in which existence itself is in conversation with God. Here lies the paradoxical manifesto of the *ways*: We are to demonstrate God's existence and not his essence and yet his existence is identical with his essence, which must be withheld from demonstration because it is beyond reason's vision, and yet the existence must be demonstrated by reason beyond a reasonable doubt. We are to demonstrate *that* there must be this difference as such, all the while knowing that *what* this Being *Is* exceeds our vision. Yet this vision, in order to recognize it, is being blinded or exceeded by Being. It is united to a visionless awareness that the Being it is demonstrating in existence must be identical to it. The distinction between reason and faith is seen here: a pre-reflexive faith precedes reason so that reason can announce the existence of God beyond a reasonable doubt, a God compatible with the faith but which does not constitute its fullness. These real distinctions, essence and existence, soul and body, faith and reason, when magnified by the power of Being to be in all things and to refuse to be seen in things, shows us that the human person is stretched beyond both belief and disbelief. This is why the objector[139] argues against any proportion between God and man:

> Further, if the existence of God were demonstrated, this could only be from His effects. But His effects are not proportionate to Him, since He is infinite and His effects are finite; and between the finite and infinite there is no proportion. Therefore, since a cause cannot be demonstrated by an effect not proportionate to it, it seems that the existence of God cannot be demonstrated.[140]

We are creatures who participate in God's uncreatedness. Our creation recedes into what precedes creation; we exist in time and yet before time. Our being abolishes time in order to make the time proper to our *confinium* natures.[141]

139. *ST* I, 2, a2, arg. 3.

140. *ST* I, 2, 2, 3.

141. See William Desmond's cogent comments in Simpson, "Between God and Metaphysics," 357: "The sense of 'being between' is not confined to the human being as an intermediate being, though in the human being it finds something of the acme of its immanence singularization. The deepening of the immanent sense of the between is coupled with the realization that immanence is porous to what exceeds immanent determination. Thus the space of the between is also between immanence and transcendence as other, and in this space the urgent need to think the significance of religion makes itself more and more felt in my work."

When we are asked by Thomas to use God's effects, which especially include ourselves as interrogative natures, in place of the middle term,[142] this is only possible because, so wholly at odds with a substance-based metaphysics, these effects are not merely copies, resemblances, or imitations of the divine which could not point to the divine, but are themselves divine playthings. The lesser cannot of its own power point to the greater without the greater providing the impetus for that directionality. The effects as lesser do not merely point; each unlocks the yearning, the abyss on the brink of an *ad infinitum* where nothing can explain itself except with and by another. Looked at one way, the effects point to God. Looked at through Being, they point because they are pre-possessed in God. How else could that which is lesser, which cannot reveal the essence of God, demonstrate *beyond a reasonable doubt* the existence of God if it were entirely its own self-enclosed substance? When we use effects in place of the middle term it is because these effects, not existing in their own right, point to a Being which does. This uncreated Being has existence not as a mode of essence but where essence is existence. In this way, the effects point *because* they are already saturated with the play of the Godhead. The effects point because they are in a way the middle term while also a true and real substitute in place of God's essence, for reason only proceeds in knowledge by its precognitive dependency upon, but cognitive dispossession from, Being. Saint Thomas can arrive at God beyond a reasonable doubt because in this metaphysics, the effect plays a role fuller than a middle term—as both itself and its substitute, fulfilling and

---

142. Cf. *ST* I, 2 ad. 2: "When the existence of a cause is demonstrated from an effect, this effect takes the place of the definition of the cause in proof of the cause's existence. This is especially the case in regard to God, because, in order to prove the existence of anything, it is necessary to accept as a middle term the meaning of the word, and not its essence, for the question of its essence follows on the question of its existence. Now the names given to God are derived from His effects; consequently, in demonstrating the existence of God from His effects, we may take for the middle term the meaning of the word 'God.'"

exceeding Plato's moving image of eternity.[143] In this form of original on-
tology, the subordinated ethics surrenders to God and to nothing else.[144]

The final objector in article 2 presents us with the reality that
this hidden God must be respected as the difference—*as such*, and to
proceed without some form of hesitation along the causal highway to
God is frivolous and naive. If by cause and effect we can create a seamless
beeline to God, have we not done exactly what Aquinas alleges against
the ontological argument? Have we not created a shortcut to God by
mistaking his nature altogether? What the preceding article has succeeded
in showing us is a God wholly unlike anything else in existence, so much
so that the phrasing "in existence" is misapplied when applied to him. He
is not ontically *in* existence as the apple lays on the ground near the tree
or as the Platonic demiurge[145] works with the materials at hand while
he and they are "in existence." Anything "in existence," no matter how
different, has proportionality by the fact that it resides *within* existence
and shares a unity because of it. One could make the case that because
God *Is* existence as such, the cause and effect should accomplish the task
at hand and arrive at him, but again the language of arrival places God
idolatrously as a figure in-time, in-being, ontically present-at-hand.[146]
We are arriving at something which exceeds proportionality because it is
the total imageless Otherness which makes proportionality possible. It is
this exceeding proportionality which elevates our understanding of God's
entrenched *To Be* as simultaneously beyond-being, irreducibly beyond

143. Cf. *Tim.* 37c–d: "When the father creator saw the creature which he had made
moving and living, the created image of the eternal gods, he rejoiced, and in his joy
determined to make the copy still more like the original; and as this was eternal, he
sought to make the universe eternal, so far as might be. Now the nature of the ideal
being was everlasting, but to bestow this attribute in its fulness upon a creature was
impossible. Wherefore he resolved to have a moving image of eternity, and when he
set in order the heaven, he made this image eternal but moving according to number,
while eternity itself rests in unity; and this image we call time."

144. *ST* I, 2, arg. 3

145. See *Tim.* 29a–37d; 69c.

146. Cf. Heidegger, *Poetry, Language, Thought*, 151–52: "The bridge 'gathers', as a
passage that crosses, before the divinities—whether we explicitly think of, and visibly
give thanks for, their presence, as in the figure of the saint of the bridge, or whether
that divine presence is obstructed or even pushed wholly aside. The bridge gathers
to itself in its own way earth and sky, divinities and mortals . . . The divinities are the
beckoning messengers of the godhead. Out of the hidden sway of the divinities the
god emerges as what he is, which removes him from any comparison with beings that
are present."

creation. This secures the true freedom of our personhood grounded not on a reflection of abstracted Being, generic principles or universal ideas but of a Being more personal, more present and unified than anything ever was. With Balthasar:

> The kingdom of beauty (of the Thomist *esse non subsistens*) is . . . as being, transparent, to the divine *esse subsistens* only comprehensible as *mysterium*, which is, as a hidden primordial ground, radiant glory. The elevation of God over against being, now at last established by Thomas (over against all pantheism), secures at the same time for the concept of glory a place in metaphysics.[147]

This is why our originary ethics is only subordinated to nothing other when it is truly subordinated to God, the God Whose in-existence precedes placement, making all predicament and placement possible. It is God's entrenchment of his uncreatedness as *Ens* itself which allows the temporal to relate to the eternal, the finite to the infinite, the imperfect to the perfect. We recognize our finitude only because we have a primal non-reflexive knowing of the infinite; we understand the passage of time, the moving image of eternity, only because, preceding and refusing reflection, we are pre-possessed in the eternal.[148] Our imperfections ache as imperfect, cast against our non-mediated but non-reflexive contact with the Good. On our side, there is no proportion between man and God, but as seen in the real distinction and in the language of faith and reason, the language of "our side" is not what it seems. Our side was never our own. Because our existence was never ours but ours only by way of being the divine plaything—by being his original Other—it is precisely the lack of proportionality and the implicit knowledge thereof that constitutes the *longior via*. We add up to Being by failing to get to Being, by concession and surrender. The disproportion is, in a very real sense, the demonstration or, at the very minimum, the ground of the demonstration. We can continue *ad infinitum* with all the proportionate things, none of which can lift the veil of oblivion and bring us to the

147. Balthasar, *Glory of the Lord*, 4:375.

148. Cf. W. Chris Hackett, "Soul and 'All Things,'" in Lee and Kimbriel, *Resounding Soul*, 307–29, esp. 314: "For Christianity the finite no longer lies in tragic contrast to the infinite (either swallowed up by its reality or set over-against it in utter alienation), but rather elevates the finite into new proximity to the divine realms, an elevation that is paradoxically expressive of its *now strange finitude*—how to express it?—an ever-greater finitude in being ever-greater than finitude."

threshold of Being, each needing something else for its existence. The proportionate things do not get us to God, they get us to the *need* for God. But that need is only stoked because we have a union which precedes identity, which refuses proportion because it is one uncreated immediacy. In play, proportion is never a question, it is forgotten because the self is abandoned in favor of the dance, the eventfulness of Being-with. In play, there is no proportionality, but not in Sartre's sense where the loss of God condemns man to be free. The gainful loss of proportionality is understood in the way in which saintly freedom comes from an open and infinite structure which guides the growth of the soul. This is a soul which is stretched and protracted to the limits of earthly being, so immersed in its serious play, not in an abstractive way but in the fullness of the appetitive power:

> You never enjoy the world aright, till the Sea itself floweth in your veins, till you are clothed with the heavens, and crowned with the stars: and perceive yourself to be the sole heir of the whole world, and more than so, because men are in it who are every one sole heirs as well as you. Till you can sing and rejoice and delight in God, as misers do in gold, and Kings in sceptres, you never enjoy the world. Till your spirit filleth the whole world, and the stars are your jewels; till you are as familiar with the ways of God in all Ages as with your walk and table: till you are intimately acquainted with that shady nothing out of which the world was made: till you love men so as to desire their happiness, with a thirst equal to the zeal of your own: till you delight in God for being good to all: you never enjoy the world. Till you more feel it than your private estate, and are more present in the hemisphere, considering the glories and the beauties there than in your own house: till you remember how lately you were made, and how wonderful it was when you came into it: and more rejoice in the palace of your glory, than if it had been made but to-day morning.[149]

In *ST* I-II, q. 40, a. 2, the objector makes a case as to why hope should be a cognitive power and not an appetitive one. Hope itself involves a waiting, a spectatorship position, a scanning over the hills for the good which will satisfy and fulfill that hope.[150] Moreover, certainty—certainty

149. Traherne, *Centuries of Meditations*, 20–21.

150. *ST* I-II, 40, 2, arg. 1: "It would seem that hope belongs to the cognitive power. Because hope, seemingly, is a kind of awaiting; for the Apostle says (Romans 8:25): 'If we hope for that which we see not; we wait for it with patience.' But awaiting seems

of the faith—is united to hope, for the unique certitude of the faith is that, unlike empirical certitudes which extinguish or fulfill earthly hopes, our certitude must inflame hope.[151] If certainty and faith belong properly to the cognitive power, then hope as united in mutual intensity must also belong to this power of the soul.[152] Saint Thomas's response places us right within the midst of the originary *praxis* at root in this subordinated ethics, one in which the world cannot be enjoyed unless the sea itself flow in our veins, till our spirit is as large as the world and exceeds it, till our desire for others' happiness is as concrete and living as our own.

> Since hope denotes a certain stretching out of the appetite to- wards good, it evidently belongs to the appetitive power; since movement towards things belongs properly to the appetite: whereas the action of the cognitive power is accomplished not by the movement of the knower towards things, but rather ac- cording as the things known are in the knower. But since the cognitive power moves the appetite, by presenting its object to it, there arise in the appetite various movements according to various aspects of the apprehended object. For the apprehension of good gives rise to one kind of movement in the appetite, while the apprehension of evil gives rise to another: in like manner various movements arise from the apprehension of something present and of something future; of something considered ab- solutely, and of something considered as arduous; of something possible, and of something impossible. And accordingly, hope is a movement of the appetitive power ensuing from the appre- hension of a future good, difficult but possible to obtain; namely, a stretching forth of the appetite to such a good.[153]

to belong to the cognitive power, which we exercise by 'looking out.' Therefore hope belongs to the cognitive power."

151. Cf. *ST* II-II, 17, 3, *resp.* For Saint Thomas, hope in relation to God "denotes a movement or a stretching forth of the appetite towards an arduous good."

152. ST I-II, 40, 2, Obj. 3.

153. ST I-II, 40, 2 resp. Cf. ST II-II, 40, 2, ad 2: "Since hope regards a possible good, there arises in man a twofold movement of hope; for a thing may be possible to him in two ways, viz. by his own power, or by another's. Accordingly when a man hopes to obtain something by his own power, he is not said to wait for it, but simply to hope for it. But, properly speaking, he is said to await that which he hopes to get by another's help as though to await [*exspectare*] implied keeping one's eyes on another [*ex alio spectare*], in so far as the apprehensive power, by going ahead, not only keeps its eye on the good which man intends to get, but also on the thing by whose power he hopes to get it; according to Sirach 51:10, 'I looked for the succor of men.' Wherefore the movement of hope is sometimes called expectation, on account of the preceding inspection of the cognitive power."

Hope, as a stretching out of the appetite towards good, resides properly within the appetitive power. But because the intellect must move the appetite by unveiling the good it desires, then hope both remains within the immediacy of the appetitive power while that same immediacy follows from the futurity *present in the anticipation* of a future good. As a unity, the soul is both possessed of Being and dispossessed of it, waiting for the Good and yet because hope is not a cognitional waiting, the bodily soul is also in the midst of the Good; each aspect of its stretching-forth is a filling-up of Being. In this non-reflexive sense of hope, one is so full of the play of Being that the sea fills our veins and stars crown our heads. It is this immediacy which grounds the intellect's unveiling of a future good to be desired. The intellect then unveils that Good which directs hope to stretch towards that Good which it does not possess. But because immediacy grounds all things, the intellect directs the appetite to proceed not like the intellect, in an abstractive distance, but *hopefully* with the in-the-world play of Being. If the basis of our being is given a chance to take-in the world incarnationally, then both the intellect and the will can find their proper unity, each distinct; but their distinction—like the real distinction—cannot be hemmed down the middle.[154] Together they are a dual unity, a moving image of eternity, moving *because* possessed of the Good but incentivized to move because equally dispossessed of it. Here we see the question of proportion. The will is guided by the intellect to move towards a futural good it does not possess, but the will does not move like the intellect by an abstractive, waiting or spectatorial distance. In a way mysterious and profound it *already* carries with it the ecstatic perfume of the divine. But it carries it in such a way that its life with the intellect will stretch the soul to be greater than the world, to be the heir of the world, so stretched that it needs something other than itself to bring itself back into the Good it possesses, to close that *open nature*, to complete what the world cannot complete. Because God is the uncreated *Ens* which enables my act of being, then there can be no proportionality between man and God in the sense that two finite beings, by fact of their dependency, have proportion. But we are reflexive beings who discover the oddness of our lost immediacy, which must somehow be intact in order for us to act and *to be*. It is precisely our cognitional lack of proportionality—there is no ladder that can be climbed by reason to God—which allows reason to stop the ladder of caused causes, of finite

154. For a profound analysis of this and Przywara's contributions, see Gonzales, *Reimagining the Analogia Entis*.

things which do have proportionality. Each places us in a horizontal or cyclical causality, each giving us the same answer or same admission— needing something Other for its existence. Our contact with God was never idolatrous, where his presence cuts down our freedom, where he is in the position of dictator or even earthly monarch. By having a finite existential proportionality with us, the ruler's sole power is prescriptively to restrict or dilate a finite set of freedoms. But God's uncreated *To Be* ushers in the kind of non-proportionality undreamt of. His immediacy within us, as innermost in Being, placing us beyond our creative powers and in contact with our own uncreated non-mediation, places us so full of God that God does not originate in us by reflection which always limits and restricts its view *in order* to see. In that immediacy we stand both in utter union and in a preceding proportion with God. But this preceding proportion is itself a non-proportionality. It cannot be brought into view by reflection and thus, when reflected by the intellect, we see the lack of proportionality between our creaturely powers and the uncreated *Ens*. This is why in the demonstrations, our tracing of proportional beings, gets us to God only insofar as we must surrender beyond a reasonable doubt to the existence of an *un*named Other at which those things cannot themselves arrive. But our surrender is predicated on the certainty that *if* it *Is* then we *are*; *because* it *Is* we *are*. It is not the death of God and the lack of intelligibility to the world which gives us freedom; that would be our death sentence and a wholesale internment of meaning. It is the divine flowing through our veins and mingled in our breath, so full of the perfume of play, that the sheerly given union never separates so as to be reduced by our vision. Because it never rises to the limits of our vision, our cognitional power has the space or distance to abstract and thus to see God at least by his effects.

> The Apostle says: 'The invisible things of Him are clearly seen, being understood by the things that are made' (Romans 1:20). But this would not be unless the existence of God could be demonstrated through the things that are made; for the first thing we must know of anything is whether it exists.[155]

Being too near for us to see it provides, in that nearness, the distance needed for the intellect to abstract and to arrive at God beyond a reasonable doubt. We stand full of God and fully alone, and the unity of the two constitutes our freedom as utterly open and directive. The

---

155. *ST* I, 2, a2, *sed contra*.

intelligibility of the world which guides our incarnational souls is not prescriptive but imaginative in its deepest sense, in that contact with what is the imageless shady nothing out of which the world was made. For the heart, it is pure freedom in pulsation. Thus, there is proportion between man and God, but not in the way in which finite proportions are understood or in a way in which God's presence limits us. His guidance is the ontological conduit of our freedom. The proportion is won only because the intellectual acquisition of our lack of proportion—no finite being can be the cause of the world, thus no finite being can get us to God—*rediscovers the preceding, non-reflective proportion of our originary praxis*! That is why for Saint Thomas effects will get us beyond any reasonable doubt to God, but the God of which we are certain is the God of nihilation and night, of rational otherness and disproportion.

> From effects not proportionate to the cause no perfect knowl-edge of that cause can be obtained. Yet from every effect the ex-istence of the cause can be clearly demonstrated, and so we can demonstrate the existence of God from His effects; though from them we cannot perfectly know God as He is in His essence.[156]

When we begin with the eyes of reason, it is true that there is no proportion between man and God. And one must heed reason, and reason must guide the will, must place its reserves upon the acquisition of the Good. These demonstrations seek not to demonstrate the idea or concept of God but the recognition beyond any reasonable doubt *that* existence *Is* irreducibly and mysteriously supernatural. The Five Ways are not only an exercise of reason but of reason's union with the will. We are demonstrating something which comes closer to the will's *habitus* and its *praxis* of lived-experience amidst the things that are. We are demonstrating something which moves us beyond conceptual gaze and requires, in the end, a surrender, a pointing-to-something-Other, because reason can go no further. Each demonstration enters an infinite regress through reason, and then finds itself invoking an *ananke stenai*, a necessity to come to a stop, which is a limit and also a conservation of the Good and of our place within the Good. No effect in nature can stop and announce what God *is* because it cannot arrive at the truer union where proportionality is exceeded, overwhelmed and maintained. When the intellect surrenders to the *ananke stenai* it accepts what it, through its union with the will, must prepossess in a non-eidetic manner: the

156. *ST* I, 2, 2, ad. 3.

mysterious self-evidence of God housed ever deeper within the *bona voluntas* of the soul.

> My yesterday has gone, has gone and left me tired,
> And now to-morrow comes and beats upon the door;
> So I have built To-day, the day that I desired,
> Lest joy come not again, lest peace return no more,
> Lest comfort come no more.
> So I have built To-day, a proud and perfect day,
> And I have built the towers of cliffs upon the sands;
> The foxgloves and the gorse I planted on my way;
> The thyme, the velvet thyme, grew up beneath my hands,
> Grew pink beneath my hands.
> So I have built To-day, more precious than a dream;
> And I have painted peace upon the sky above;
> And I have made immense and misty seas, that seem
> More kind to me than life, more fair to me than love—
> More beautiful than love.
> And I have built a house—a house upon the brink
> Of high and twisted cliffs; the sea's low singing fills it;
> And there my Secret Friend abides, and there I think
> I'll hide my heart away before to-morrow kills it—
> A cold to-morrow kills it.
> Yes, I have built To-day, a wall against To-morrow,
> So let To-morrow knock—I shall not be afraid,
> For none shall give me death, and none shall give me sorrow,
> And none shall spoil this darling day that I have made.
> No storm shall stir my sea. No night but mine shall shade
> This day that I have made.[157]

---

157. Benson "Secret Day," 3.

3

Undiscovered Ends: Dostoyevsky and the Imaging of the Natural Law

Then I came to myself. It was long before I clearly comprehended what had happened. I saw before me nothing but the
destruction toward which I was hurrying, which I dreaded,
and I saw no salvation and knew not what I was to do! But on
looking back, I saw a countless multitude of boats engaged in
a ceaseless struggle against the force of the torrent, and then I
remembered all about the shore, the oars, and the course, and
at once I began to row hard up the stream and again toward the
shore. That shore was God, that course was tradition, those oars
were the free will given me to make for the shore to seek union
with the Deity. And thus the vital force was renewed in me, and
I began again to live.[1]

The Two Sources of Metaphysics and Tradition:
Et Volabo et Requiescam

THE GRAVEYARD BELONGS WITHIN the walls of the churchyard and
the churchyard belongs within the walls of the town, and the town,
with all the anticipation of the future, must still be a stretching forth
towards an arduous Good which enshrines and illuminates the nobility

---

1. Tolstoy, *My Confession*, 59.

of the Present, of to-day. The graveyard finds its home in the church, the church in the town and the town understands its meaning only in utter Presence in contemporaneity with death, divinity, custom, and duty. This to-day finds itself in creative and ordered tension with tomorrow, not hurling in a progressive blindness to it. This tension is loving and productive, and captures the true language of the will as a non-mediated saturated presence. If the language of the appetitive and cognitive powers is understood as a stretching towards the futural while never departing from the incarnational immediacy of Being, and if this constitutes the true character of the human person, it must then constitute our proper social-political nature, revealing the very fabric of tradition. No Good is truly transmitted from an abstractive top-down approach. This is clear from the disastrous ideologies which impose an alien and prescriptive template against the human person's naturally supernatural nature.[2]

> Once you admit that the individual is merely a means to serve the ends of the higher entity called society or the nation, most of those features of totalitarian regimes which horrify us follow of necessity. From the collectivist standpoint intolerance and brutal suppression of dissent, the complete disregard of the life and happiness of the individual, are essential and unavoidable consequences of this basic premise, and the collectivist can admit this and at the same time claim that his system is superior to one in which the 'selfish' interests of the individual are allowed to obstruct the full realisation of the ends the community pursues.[3]

Even if the Good being imposed is a conceptual expression of the proper Good, its imposition often fails to communicate its meaning because, *as imposition*, it bypasses the way in which it must be infused and inculcated within the bodily soul. The true ethics *in-failing* does not lead but abides by the dramatic play of Being, a play manifested in that language of will and intellect and one expanded to announce the just social and political compact where human destiny is made or broken. And, not so oddly enough, this *takes time* as *history*.

A true traditionalism carries both the gaze to the futural and the enmeshed Presence of the past, understanding that to forsake one in favor of the other is to forsake both. Thus, it must carry both the proportion

---

2. Cf. Walsh, "Politics of Liberty," 123–46. For a profound discussion of the lost aesthetic and redemptive political order embodied in and by the God-Man, see Walsh, *After Ideology*.

3. Hayek, *Road to Serfdom*, 168.

and exceeding non-proportion between man and God, and it is this balance between the two which becomes a vibrating harmony, a delicate balance, the artifice of the city-state, of the community, of the family. This rare and originary traditionalism never forces the will to act like the intellect, attempting to satisfy itself on a cognitional future, an openness or appetitive vacuity that only the intellect *as intellect* can endure. When the will is pressed into a rabid progressivism, it must find outlets for its sensation of Presence, of the To-day, but because its stretching forth in the Present has been refused in favor of the gaze outward over a plurality of potential futural alternatives, it seeks to give incarnation to substitutes for uncreated *Ens*—whether it be in sex, power, gender, the deformation of the family, or God usurpation. In response, the conservatism we see is often reactionary in nature and has abandoned its roots in the vibration of the collective soul, both stretching forth in futurity but stretching *because* it is filled up with the Presence of the To-day. Fearful of the power of an unleashed futurity, it demands an abidance to the Good but does so by another form of top-down approach. The liberal progressivist replaces divine and societal prescription with its own ideological political correctness, one far more coercive than the public orthodoxy of values it mocks and rejects. The reactionary conservatism on the other hand attempts to implace prohibitive and prescriptive blinders in order to maintain the tradition, condemning it to be misread as uncreative and static. Both these orders are in fact top-down. The progressivist has merely confused the naïve by slanting the order of perspective. That gaze to the outward reaches of possibility, independent of God, morality and an enduring order, is merely misconceiving the top-down from a different angle. Those alternative and competing possibilities receive their orders from the ego neutered of its contact with immediacy and thus its contact with personhood. This is ego pressed to identify itself with a cognitional gaze and now separated from immediacy; it achieves frightfully more than what Hegel sought for the absolute *Weltgeist*.[4] It demands conformity that is not only deontological but profoundly de-humanized. The ego separate

---

4. What is the underlying metaphysics of the Hegelian *Weltgeist* but one where the intellect and the will are lifted out of the very nature which intelligibilizes both their objectival gaze and pre-reflexive presence? The more speculative rendering of moral prescriptions would be defined as such. See Hegel, *Phenomenology of Spirit*, §792: "As conscience, it is no longer this continual alternation of existence being placed in the Self, and *vice versa*; it knows that its *existence* as such is this pure certainty of itself. The objective element into which it puts itself forth, when it acts, is nothing other than the Self's pure knowledge of itself."

from immediacy is an alien ego and its conception of the future good—precisely because in increasing separation—becomes increasingly less an expression of human and divine meaning.[5]

All creativity, drive, newness, difference, excitement, exertion, dynamism live in contact with the uncreated *Ens* Who, because personal, is always relational. This is the God Who, because he exceeds proportion, allows us the freedom to rise up in play beyond proportion, beyond reflection. Without respecting our Presence in the exceeding Other, our futural reflection would lock itself down in a collective aseity. Tradition is thus the conservation of our foothold in the ever-moving relation with God, it is the possession of God as unity and variety and it is the recognition of our dispossession of God as seen in our trust in tradition and the heralding of family as the image and likeness of God. Tradition does not make the Good to be an object to be achieved but the ground to live in. This originary conservatism thus differs from its more common reactionary counterpart because it is Trinitarian in lived-experience rather than mono-theistic by prescription.[6] Once God is invoked by prescription it is little different from invoking science or generalized ideals as the goal or apotheosis of human development—all of which are empty *culs de sac*. The relational God, exceeding proportion in order to give us proportion and structure, sets out the following ethical structure:

5. Hegel, *Phenomenology of Spirit*, §11: "Besides, it is not difficult to see that ours is a birth-time and a period of transition to a new era. Spirit has broken with the world it has hitherto inhabited and imagined, and is of a mind to submerge it in the past, and in the labour of its own transformation. Spirit is indeed never at rest but always engaged in moving forward. But just as the first breath drawn by a child after its long, quiet nourishment breaks the gradualness of merely quantitative growth—there is a qualitative leap, and the child is born—so likewise the Spirit in its formation matures slowly and quietly into its new shape, dissolving bit by bit the structure of its previous world, whose tottering state is only hinted at by isolated symptoms. The frivolity and boredom which unsettle the established order, the vague foreboding of something unknown, these are the heralds of approaching change. The gradual crumbling that left unaltered the face of the whole is cut short by a sunburst which, in one flash, illuminates the features of the new world."

6. In his political theology, Donoso Cortés traces the flowering of the Trinity as the exegesis of the socio-political order. Cf. Donoso Cortés, *Catholicism*, ix: "The Father engenders eternally His own Son, and from Father and Son proceed eternally the Holy Spirit. And the Holy Spirit is God, and the Son is God, and the Father is God, triune in the persons and one in essence . . . their unity engenders eternally the variety in which unity consists . . . because He is One, He is God . . . because He is God, He is perfect; because perfect, most fecund; because most fecund, He is variety; because variety, He is family."

1. one that is both dynamic and stable, where tradition is not at odds with creative endurance but inflames it. This is an ethical structure liberated from the limitations of a post-Humean and Burkean influence which has the tradition at the cost of its intelligibility;

2. which revives metaphysics by a return to the pre-rational union with Being,[7] thus returning to the proper materiality of the ritual, the magical and playful obscured by a materialism which demanded fact over meaning, rendering such facts the arbiter of experience;

3. which can respond to the pseudo-independence of the claim that this lack of proportionality renders God dead *because* unrelatable. Sartre views this broken proportion as liberating the person to act out his finitude without any reference to the infinite. His independence as freedom must suspend and overthrow any attempt at relationality. But in the subordinated ethic, God exceeds proportion but does not sever relation. Any ethical structure overly emphasizing a harmony with God creates the type of rebellion which overthrows that harmony precisely because it is seen as a false and uninformative template placed upon existence. In the subordinated ethics, God's exceeding proportion works from within the interiority of each incarnated soul, within its very incommunicability, to enliven the love of the Good. Proportion and harmony in the Good are achieved not from a top-down approach but from the immediacy of each soul's originary *praxis* to stand in its incommunicability and arrive at a shared Good. What is shared is arrived at not through an extrinsicized prescription but through the immortalizing character of the person. There is a world of difference between a traditionalist public orthodoxy and a secularist political correctness. The former is democratic in its deepest sense, while the latter is corrosively dictatorial in its deepest sense.

In order to seize the opportunity of its original freedom traditionalism must approach the threshold of its enduring obligation to found its principles not on the prescriptive, nor even on the natural and creative

---

7. See Martin Coleman's editorial commentary in. Santayana, *Essential Santayana*, 412: "Moral judgment is based on the natural instinct of the animal. The reason one judges some particular thing good rather than another is not itself moral. Rather it is the result of instinctive tendencies and the material push of nature. Morality is the vigorous, sincere, and non-reflective perception of goods minus any dialectic examination."

as it conforms to man, but on the uncreated creational impetus which transforms man beyond himself as the divine plaything.

> First of all, then, the very way in which the intellectual crea-
> ture was made, according as it is master of its acts, demands
> providential care whereby this creature may provide for itself,
> on its own behalf; while the way in which other things were
> created, things which have no dominion over their acts, shows
> this fact, that they are cared for, not for their own sake, but as
> subordinated to others. That which is moved only by another
> being has the formal character of an instrument, but that which
> acts of itself has the essential character of a principal agent. Now,
> an instrument is not valued for its own sake, but as useful to a
> principal agent. Hence it must be that all the careful work that is
> devoted to instruments is actually done for the sake of the agent,
> as for an end, but what is done for the principal agent, either by
> himself or by another, is for his own sake, because he is the prin-
> cipal agent. Therefore, intellectual creatures are so controlled by
> God, as objects of care for their own sakes; while other creatures
> are subordinated, as it were, to the rational creatures.[8]

If we are to ground tradition in the natural law, it cannot solely be in its appearances as the seeking of an objective good, a direction towards a *telos*, but in its hidden innermost manifestation as a *participation* in the eternal law. The appearances, while natural, the harmony of man and nature, while natural, are the *effects* of the natural law and not the law itself. To ground tradition on the effects, neglectful of its origin, leaves it susceptible to a prescriptive-only understanding of a safe intelligibility.

The tradition as manifestation of the human-and-divine personal *character* is increasingly eroded, for it lacks foundation, or more precise-ly, the proper location for its foundation. It is not a question of choosing sides and pitching tents, rather it is a declaration, stripped of all comforts, and facing the bare truth that traditionalist conservatism must—if it is to be a legitimate expression of the world—come to an authentic ontological foundation and one which speaks not in generalized Aristotelian catego-ries or solely in the language of our fallen condition divorced from our inherent nature, but in a theo-noetic personal ordination, a pre-thematic relational understanding fulfilled in and by the metaphysical relationality of the Trinity. This foundation is neither an anti-metaphysical religious acquiescence or the naïve and overtly reconciliatory metaphysics of a

8. SCG III, 112, 1.

religious based ethics. The former refuses the foundation while the latter refuses to think about its foundation. The ideals of traditionalism cannot be founded on a muted natural law[9] but on a natural law as participation in the eternal law as revelatory, personal, communal, familial, diverse, and unitary. This is the lifeblood of traditionalist thought.

If we contend that conservatism is not a political art form, that it cannot be comprehended, let alone rationally defended, as a *doing* or a *making*, are we not reducing it *a fortiori* to the same deficient self-understanding which spurred the post-modern imagination? Traditionalism is an entrenched political noetic, a knowledge which precedes conception, not in order to eradicate it but to enshrine its ontological foundations generationally. It is a knowing which precedes thinking, a political philosophy more closely aligned with wisdom than with a system of thought. It cannot be described principally as a posture, inclination, feeling, disposition, conviction, attitude, sentiment, point of view, or temperament, all of which are tributaries of an egoistic solipsism which places meaning as originating in consciousness as consciousness, rather than consciousness *of*—of the difference as such. Tradition cannot be described in such terms and still claim to be non-ideological or anti-modern. Why? Because it is just this reduction of knowledge to thought, thought to belief, belief to opinion, and opinion to taste and temperament that characterizes modernity as ideological in its essence as the radical denial of man's ability, philosophical, moral, and political *to know the world as other*. And it is this reduction which obscures the exceeding proportion of divine non-mediated meaning which, together with the *longer way* of knowledge, constitute the intelligibility of the tradition.

The strange truth of tradition is that it cannot function as a political philosophy[10] but invokes a political *theo-logos*. This is because its union with nature is naturally intensified by the revelatory need for nature to unmask human nature. But human nature finds itself stranded and then indignant at the utter indifference of the cosmogonic. Nature is the placement of our being-in-the-world but it remains silent even in its givenness.

9. Cf. David L. Schindler's astonishing work *Ordering Love*, 23: "A purely juridical state implies a reductive view of human conscience and a formalistic notion of natural law. In fact, the juridical state, with its proceduralist public ethics, leads logically to nothing less than what Benedict has termed a 'dictatorship of relativism.'"

10. See Michael Henry's introductory comments in Wilhelmsen, *Christianity and Political Philosophy*, 1: "The advent of political philosophy in a society usually augurs ill for the society itself. Political wisdom drifts into the public forum as do leaves in autumn portending the coming of winter."

We are asked to derive the eternal law from this nature which refuses to release its mystery. It is not without pattern, order, or intelligibility, but the *purpose* of our pattern, order and intelligibility within its own is the question. Human nature seeks out in nature its own face or the face of the Other which can uncover the self. The natural law cannot truly be concretized by the pattern, order, and intelligibility of a faceless nature. The bodily soul seeks the originary *praxis* it had in child's play, when goodness was not a disposition or attitude but the essence of action. As this play is forgotten but never extinguished, it is manifested in the potential for the serious play of the social order. But the possibility of play is precarious and uneven, for we are often seeking to root intelligibility in goals to be achieved, in progress, majority preference and the like. We are never present to the Good but always bartering it down to a commodity. Thus the conservative mind, when it seeks to ground its principles of nature as the invocation of the eternal law, will uncover, if faithful, that this eternal law must unmask the faceless Other, must reveal the personal ordination at root in Being and its play within and by us. Otherwise, we are left stranded as to how nature with its order, patterns, and intelligibility truly correlates with our own—for we are indeed strangers in nature, exiles from the garden. Our nature has been deeply disordered by our fallen condition, and the conservative is understandably tempted to invoke prescription, along with continuity, in order to keep the devil at bay. Play concedes its priority to prescriptive rules, giving the secularists their status as comic book, risk-free rebels. But for the tradition, rules do not impede or overwhelm the game, they order, organize, and give life to the game. These prescriptive rules are in the *service* of play, not a substitute or surrogate for the game. Genuine dependence on the game is not alienation but union. Otherwise it becomes a "chilly loveless thing" as Bernard of Clairvaux said of prayer unwarmed by the divine breath.[11]

In *The Idiot*, we encounter a uniformly beautiful and wretched soul in the embittered childlike consumptive Hippolyte. Every good action is undercut by anger and every spiteful one is mollified by oddly placed kindnesses, potencies of a gentler endurance. Hippolyte's contradictory nature reminds one of Montaigne on the unbearable incongruity of human action:[12] a judge writes the order of execution not only on the

11. Bernard of Clairvaux, "On the Love of God," 60.

12. Cf. Montaigne's "On Experience" in *Complete Essays*, 1237: "We must learn to suffer what we cannot evade. Our life, like the harmony of the world, is compos'd of contrary things, of several notes, sweet and harsh, sharp and flat, spritely and solemn;

same pad of paper, but on the same shared sheet used to compose a love letter to his colleague's wife. On one half, a man is extinguished from existence, buried outside the gates of the city only to remain in the shame of others and then become a generational forgetfulness. On the other half, a man enters into the deceitful frivolity, the fallen play of another form of fatal affair. One wonders, were the two written back to back? Which thought came first? How could one not influence the other, and yet neither seems to follow from the other. We can see this incongruity in Pascal's cutting remarks in the *Provincial Letters* on the monk who kills another for questioning his humility.[13] Our actions place us away from nature and yet are we not just as indifferent, as repetitive and surprising as the cosmogonic, each mercilessly driven by the need to survive? When man fell creation fell,[14] so that nature is not only the font of goodness but also a reflection of our fallenness. If we are to bring out the best of our natures through participation in the natural law, the tradition must recognize that nature must be followed to the point that time is redeemed. A genuine relationship with nature leads either by welcome (child's play) or exile (the cosmogonic) to the sacred. And it leads not by enforcing, but by the conaturalness—that natural subordination—which implants in the soul a mystical yearning for God:

> The natural desire to see the Cause of being *derives* from the natural desire of knowing being; it is a corollary thereof; it is in no way identified therewith. From this it follows that every great metaphysic is indeed pierced by a mystical aspiration, but is not built thereon. By an at least theoretically normal effect, the philosophic contemplation of God indeed implants in the soul a longing which mystical union alone will satisfy. In this sense it aspires to such a union, as a lower thing aspires to a higher, but it does not seek to pass into mystical union by virtue of its specific dynamism and of its own constitutive desire.[15]

---

and the musician who should only affect one of these, what would he be able to do? He must know how to make use of them all, and to mix them; and we, likewise, the goods and evils which are consubstantial with life: our being cannot subsist without this mixture, and the one are no less necessary to it than the other. To attempt to kick against natural necessity is to represent the folly of Ctesiphon, who undertook to kick with his mule."

13. Cf. Pascal, *Provincial Letters*, §52.

14. Cf. Rom 8:20 (NIV).

15. Maritain, *Ransoming the Time*, 261. For a sacred unveiling of this transformative longing, see Ps 63 (NIV):

Hippolyte cannot bear that at such a young age and without having experienced the strengths of manhood, he is to die, left to languish in bed counting the cracks on the wall. Then in a more unbearable turn of events, he actually comes to miss his little walled room with every innumerable winding crack burrowed into his memory somewhere between recitation and prayer. He loathes not only death but what dying has made him become: clinging to the confines of a cell of a room, as if it is a bulwark against the marching orders of biological inevitability. One late summer night on Myshkin's balcony, our Hippolyte reads his Manifesto to a motley group who will mockingly rebuke him and dismiss his promise of suicide. This suicidal declaration is more an effort to place an enduring impression on the world, which he knows will become like a handprint on shifting sands. And yet he is compelled to read. In it, he maneuvers seamlessly between ecstatic depths and craven petulance, and speaks more towards Myshkin's *alter Christus* than Myshkin ever could, and sees what Myshkin could not. One such reflection hits precisely at the question of nature—and of the messy business of the cross, at which

You, God, are my God,
earnestly I seek you;
I thirst for you,
my whole being longs for you,
in a dry and parched land
where there is no water.
I have seen you in the sanctuary
and beheld your power and your glory.
Because your love is better than life,
my lips will glorify you.
I will praise you as long as I live,
and in your name I will lift up my hands.
I will be fully satisfied as with the richest of foods;
with singing lips my mouth will praise you.
On my bed I remember you;
I think of you through the watches of the night.
Because you are my help,
I sing in the shadow of your wings.
I cling to you;
your right hand upholds me.
Those who want to kill me will be destroyed;
they will go down to the depths of the earth.
They will be given over to the sword
and become food for jackals.
But the king will rejoice in God;
all who swear by God will glory in him,
while the mouths of liars will be silenced.

our Prince recoiled.[16] What Hippolyte sees is exactly the predicament of traditionalism as grounded in nature. It cannot be rooted in nature as faceless nor in a vacuous religious template set against or even naïvely related to nature, but must be nature so revelatory as to blind, so at odds with everything seen, heard, and experienced that one can rightly wonder whether this nature has turned everything upside down? Prince Myshkin, in great anguish and confusion, suddenly remembers the Holbein painting in Rogozhin's hall:

> His body on the Cross was subjected to the laws of nature . . . His face dreadfully disfigured by blows, swollen, covered with terrible swollen and bloody bruises, the eyes open, the pupils turned up, the large whites of the eyes bright with a sort of deathly vitreous gleam. But strange to say, when one looks at this corpse of this tortured man, a curious question arises: if just such a corpse (and it certainly must have been like this) was seen by all His disciples, by those who were to become His chief apostles, by the women who had followed Him and stood at the foot of the Cross, by all who believed in Him and adored Him, how could they believe, gazing on such a cadaver as that, that this martyr could be resurrected? . . . one conceives of nature in the form of some huge, implacable, dumb beast, or to be more exact, to be much more exact, though it may seem strange, in the form of some huge machine of the latest design which, deaf and unfeeling, has senselessly seized, crushed, and swallowed up a great and priceless Being, a Being worth all of nature and its laws, all of the earth, which was perhaps created solely for the advent of that Being! That picture expresses that notion of a dark, insolent, and stupidly eternal force to which everything is subject, and it conveys this to us unconsciously. The people surrounding the dead man, none of whom is in the picture, must have felt terrible anguish and dismay on that evening which crushed all their hopes at once and almost their belief. They must have parted in the most awful terror, though each carried away with

16. Cf. Dostoyevsky, *Idiot*, 218: "'But I've long wanted to ask you something, Lev Nikolaich: do you believe in God or not?' Rogozhin suddenly began speaking again, after going several steps. 'How strangely you ask and...stare!' the prince observed. 'But I like looking at that painting,' Rogozhin muttered after a silence, as if again forgetting his question. 'At that painting!' the prince suddenly cried out, under the impression of an unexpected thought. 'At that painting! A man could even lose his faith from that painting!' Lose it he does, Rogozhin suddenly agreed unexpectedly . . . 'What?' the prince suddenly stopped. 'How can you! I was almost joking, and you're so serious! And why did you ask me whether I believe in God?'"

him a tremendous thought which could never be taken away
from him. And if on the eve of the crucifixion the Teacher could
have seen His own image as He would be, would He then have
mounted the Cross and died as He did? . . . For a full hour and a
half after Koyla went away, all this drifted through my mind in
fragments, sometimes even in vivid images, perhaps while I was
actually delirious. Can something appear as an image that has
no image? But I did imagine at times that I saw, in some kind of
strange and impossible form, that infinite power, that deaf, dark,
and speechless being.[17]

And we ask this atheist's stunning question: if the Teacher had seen the
result of the cross—the scourged and pitiful cadaver before him—would
he have mounted the cross? How is it that belief in this pitiful figure arises
from, and is transmitted by, hearts so immeasurably weak? How can they
come to believe such a pitiful figure could be the Savior? And yet they
did. And this is the strange predicament, the true conservation tasked to
the tradition. It must ground its principles in nature, knowing that nature
unveils the mystical experience of social life, of the sacred, but that this
unveiling cannot be coerced by an artificial template.[18]

Tradition can never place itself against nature, or dictate nature, or
shortcut the natural process. It must also be aware that admission into
the cosmogonic is equally an exile, and that nature seethes with condition which cloaks and obscures the natural path. This sacred political
conservatism is not static but the active balancing on this moving image
of eternity, moving not only with the eternal but against it. Conservatism
finds itself in union with a theological life because nature surrenders to
revelatory meaning. But *how* it surrenders is key. While faith and tradition may arrive at the personal God, the path to faith and the path to
tradition follow different courses which must be respected. Faith is the
transmission of what was once incommunicable, the life of the witness.
The witness participates in rediscovering his contact with immediacy,

17. Dostoyevsky, *Idiot*, 407–8.

18. Cf. Gilby, *Principality and Polity*, 138: "The New Law imparted life, and was not
bondage . . . It was concerned not only that we should do virtuous deeds but that we
should do them virtuously, and act not as slaves but as the children and friends of God.
It followed from the constitution of human nature in a condition of grace: that this
was entirely God's bounty and beyond our deserts did not mean that the appropriate
operations were forced or arbitrary. On the contrary, *as we have already noticed*, they
proceed from us naturally and congenially and were directed to ends which met our
abilities raised to the highest power."

his soulful body. Gabriel Marcel, in the midst of the ravages of the First World War, and himself a non-combatant veteran, glimpsed this non-mediated union:

> An intellectualism which claims that I can only rise to the condition of faith if I divorce myself, if only mentally, from my sensible nature, is doomed to find the essential characteristic of the very thing it seeks to apprehend in its purity elude it. This, I believe, is what I glimpsed when I wrote on May 4, 1916 that faith must participate in the nature of sensation, the metaphysical problem being to rediscover both through and beyond thought a new infallibility, a new immediacy.[19]

Faith reveals the witness in the presence of revelatory meaning, not as abstractive but incarnational, liturgical and consecrative. Tradition, on the other hand, is the pre-reflexive communication of our originary *praxis*, it is the inculcation of our non-reflexive love, which eases that transmission of the faith, prepares the witness, so that faith incarnates a communion of soulful bodies rather than soulless bodies.[20]

Faith requires the Word of God which is beyond but not contrary to reason, so much so that the highest act of reason is to surrender to what is most reasonable precisely *because* it exceeds reason.[21] Faith's

19. Marcel, *Creative Fidelity*, 168–69.

20. When the pre-reflexive wisdom of tradition is lost, we have what Dostoyevsky describes in the *Demons*—a plaything for the churlish. See Dostoyevsky, *Demons*, 25–26: "You cannot imagine what sorrow and anger seize one's whole soul when a great idea, which one has long and piously revered, is picked up by some bunglers and dragged into the street, to more fools like themselves, and one suddenly meets it in the flea market, unrecognizable, dirty, askew, absurdly presented, without proportion, without harmony, a toy for stupid children." When the pre-reflexive is lived as a wholly into-the-earth union, then the human person in his natural supernaturalness, is recognized as communal being within a personal divine union. See Tolstaya, *Kaleidoscope*, 110: "Christ came now so that man would learn that the earthy nature of the human spirit can appear in such heavenly radiance, in reality and in the flesh and not just in a dream and in an ideal, and that it is natural and possible."

21. Kierkegaard, *Soul of Kierkegaard*, 172–73: "The majority of men in every generation, even those who, as it is described, devote themselves to thinking (dons and the like), live and die under the impression that life is simply a matter of understanding more and more, and that if it were granted to them to live longer, that life would continue to be one long continuous growth in understanding. How many of them ever experience the maturity of discovering that there comes a critical moment where everything is reversed, after which the point becomes to understand more and more that there is something which cannot be understood . . . To them the divine is simply a rhetorically meaningless hiatic superlative of the human: which explains their

transmission is eased by an incarnational conservatism, not by a defensive one. The latter attempts to act like the transmission of faith but because it is not faith—and it hasn't the power of Revelation—it muddles the process, reducing its own transmission to sentiment, taste, posture and disposition. And by doing so, tradition tars and feathers faith with the same fatal brush. Huizinga, in his landmark *The Waning of the Middle Ages*, clarified the dangerous shortcut to God which makes Him the invocation for the ego's self-enclosed intelligibility. God's self-evidence is the self's own confidence in its own system. Such a dead end, ignoring the exceeding disproportion between man and God, overly harmonized all things, so that faith, reason and the political life must act effectively in the same manner. The will is to act like the intellect, and by the confusion of the two, the intellect becomes a protracted expression of the ego—its accepted posture, attitude, belief—as identical with the so-called Absolute.

> Ideas, being conceived as entities and of importance only by virtue of their relation with the Absolute, easily range themselves as so many fixed stars on the firmament of thought. Once defined, they only lend themselves to classification, subdivision and distinction according to purely deductive norms. Apart from the rules of logic, there is never a corrective at hand to indicate a mistake in the classification, and this causes the mind to be deluded as to the value of its own operations and the certainty of the system.[22]

When this shortcut infects tradition, genuine faith and tradition are bound by the same modernist gag order but placed there by the hands of a reactionary conservatism. Their contributions, wholly reducible to sentiment and posture, are considered to be a private affair ill-suited to the very community for which, in essence, they are properly suited. Convictions, yearnings, and beliefs are simply too weak to uphold philosophical, moral, and political truths. To place or stand such truths on the shoulders of mere belief is a rather graceless gymnastic.

---

satisfaction with the idea of being able to form ever clearer conceptions of it, so that if they only had time, did not have to go to the office or their club or talk to their wives, if they only had time enough they would manage to understand the divine perfectly. Socratic ignorance, but *nota bene* modified by the Christian spirit, is maturity, is intellectually speaking what conversion is morally and religiously, is what it means to become a child again. It is quite literally true that the law is: increasingly profundity in understanding more and more that one cannot understand. And there once again comes in 'being like a child.'"

22. Huizinga, *Waning of the Middle Ages*, 195.

For a conservative to describe himself non-ideologically he must define himself as one who claims as his own, i.e., as essential to the structure of his nature, the capacity to know and to understand truths about the world, himself included. Traditional beliefs follow upon the intellect's understanding of the world, and not conversely. If the understanding followed upon the belief, then conservative political theory as the possibility of a non-ideological knowledge would be vain *even if the belief is in the existence of an absolute, transcendent moral order*. For it is not the *content* of belief that is essential to modernity, it is the *reduction of knowledge to belief* that is paradigmatically ideological. Truth comes to be ideas as functions of the Pure Self: whether these ideas are abstract or concrete, metaphysical or historical, pragmatic, empiricist, positivist, or imaginative, is not the important point. What is important is that the world becomes either a radical beyondness or a sheer immanence equivalent to selfhood. Does it matter which head of the Gorgon we prefer to gaze at? In either instance, the world becomes idea-logos, an artificial template. When a conservative reverses the order of intelligibility and grafts truth onto a belief about and an attitude towards the world—a belief in man's nature and divine moral order—by founding all knowledge on conviction, he creates the prescriptive ethics that cannot withstand the sweeping tide of post-modernism, for it functions in like manner. Each can have the absolute and create a system of harmonious intelligibility reflective of his designated absolute. But because this first in the order of intelligibility rests upon, and thus is reducible to, conviction, it is nothing more than a flimsy bubble easily popped and dismissed in favor of yet another solipsistic competing alternative just as absolute and yet as relative as the next. If Saint Thomas's realist knowledge proceeds from what is relative to—related to—what is absolute, this is because truth is founded upon knowledge and knowledge upon being and being in the genuine relation between the nature of the existence of man and the nature of the existence of the world. When the conservative does not rest his principles on the onto-noetic *ananke stenai*, but grounds that structural intelligibility of the tradition on a belief or posture, he reverses that crucial realist order. At best, he promotes a naïve realism but more often opens the door to an ideationally driven secularity which he cannot combat, having been its progenitor. In the prescriptive order, all are absolutes hurled forth to designate meaning and behavior, but these absolutes, when traced to their artificial origin, return us to their relative and nominal ground in belief and posture. If the tradition is to provide not only the overt ideas of goodness but more critically the fertile soil for the non-reflexive union with the Good, then it must be unabashedly realist. It must find this pre-rational union as it moves within the family, the community, where members relate by way of a common good that is not ideational, not transmitted conceptually but arterially because of a non-mediated contact with nature as *personal* and divine:

> As one man is a part of the household, so a household is a part of the state: and the state is a perfect community, according to book one of the *Politics*. And therefore, as the good of one man is not the last end, but is ordained to the common good; so too the good of one household is ordained to the good of a single state, which is a perfect community.[23]

If we are to take seriously the unique arrangement of the demonstrations, then we see in them the foundation for the natural law as revelatory and thus for a tradition which upholds and dynamically conserves the presence of Being as necessary for an enduring moral order. Saint Thomas rejects the self-evidence of God in order to protect the pre-rational immediacy of the divine permeating all things. *This shows us that the enduring order is not firstly accessed by prescription but by that originary praxis.* When the first principles point us to this non-mediated contact we do see the traditional life where values, belief, opinion, posture are genuinely held. We see bodily sentiment and a natural inclination towards the good and beautiful as relational, indeed playful. This is, again, belief in its proper place as situated in custom and *nomos*. Belief is not leading, not prescribing, but illuminating a *way of being*. But in a defensive conservatism, belief is cut off from its connatural pre-rationality and pressed into conceptual defense. It effectively loses its subordination and is asked to lead where it cannot; it is asked to supply the intelligibility for its belief. That which is pre-rational and non-reflexive is asked to reflect on itself severed from the basis for its union. If it can reflect at all in this situation, it cannot help but become a manifestation of the ego. Non-reflexive belief is cut off from its ontological ground and asked to reflect on itself as if it is the source and justification for its own meaning. It inevitably fails, and the protracted suicide of the West resides in the fact that such forms of belief attempt to persist as is, reducing tradition to nothing more than a litany of prohibitions and dispensations.

23. *ST* I-II, 90, 3, ad.3.

Saint Thomas's caution against self-evidence is equally a caution against ethics entering into a stance which mimics self-evidence. Such foundationless beliefs stripped of their immediacy and lived experience have only the ego as their basis, and attempt to shield that ego in the name of God, a divine moral orderer and the like. But what then is this moral orderer if it is used only to justify belief and if belief is used to justify this order? In this tautology, God's evidence can only be justified by a form of *a priori* self-evidence which needn't rely on the world for its evidence. A reactionary tradition is not a realist tradition. The latter has God too near to be self-evident and so present that evidence can be arrived at beyond a reasonable doubt. The former, on the other hand, has created a shortcut to God in order to justify belief severed from God's ontological comportment with man.

When the Angelic Doctor allows us to enter into the thicket of non-being and question whether demonstration is even possible, he does so in order to set up a structure applicable in the theological, anthropological, philosophical, and especially moral registers. Because God *Is* relation, demonstration must follow the rules of relational engagement. The *longer way* of the Five Ways reflects how the conservative mind engages and defends its truth. The non-reflexive, pre-rational integrity of belief, custom, and ritual are present, inculcating hearts and minds. But these things are the fabric and backdrop of the Being of society and of the noble soul. They are not forced into the foreground but provide the essential conversational props through which meaning is accessed, through which reflection begins the longer way home, arriving at the same origin of belief and custom but in a different way, and that difference is critical. Reflection by its nature means a distance and an estrangement, but not an abandonment, in order to find oneself within the community of the Good. The originary traditionalist reflects on this backdrop *because* he does not stand stoically at odds with it but because the backdrop is united to him. His reflection is able to stand separate without division, and trace the longer way to the intelligibility which illuminates belief and thus enlightens his own being. A moral accounting is thus indelibly an anthropological one so that the Good which is arrived at is not an object out on the horizon but the very Good of the soul. Beyond a reasonable doubt Saint Thomas will arrive at the existence of God, and in the fourth demonstration this God is also the maxim of all good, truth, and beauty. But this maxim was discovered because it resided in and overwhelmed its effects so that each effect pointed towards its source. The moral order only points out our nature because our own nature overflows with entelechy and points to it. This mutual illumination renders belief beyond but not contrary to reason while securing the source of belief as the source of reason. The tradition is thus rationally defended but not reducible to a product of reason.

If custom, belief, ritual, and tradition are the effects of the enduring moral order then every cause must pre-exist in its effects. And if the soul is saturated in the living-communion with tradition and thus the effects are better known than the cause, then one must proceed from effects to cause.

> Demonstration can be made in two ways: One is through the cause, and is called 'a priori,' and this is to argue from what is prior absolutely. The other is through the effect, and is called a demonstration "a posteriori"; this is to argue from what is prior relatively only to us. When an effect is better known to us than its cause, from the effect we proceed to the knowledge of the cause. And from every effect the existence of its proper cause can be demonstrated, so long as its effects are better known to us; because since every effect depends upon its cause, if the effect exists, the cause must pre-exist. Hence the existence of God, in so far as it is not self-evident to us, can be demonstrated from those of His effects which are known to us.[24]

And this is the unmistakable mystery of the common good. Its particular good is indeed relative to an absolute, it is the best possible image and likeness of the Good given time, place, circumstance, finitude, and event. The good in all actions is never merely a beyond-the-horizon commodity, a north star, separate from the actor engaging it. His engagement requires that he is connaturally unified to it in order to desire it. Further, the good truly inhabits and reflects the intimacy of the situation. It is living, active, receptive and relational. When Saint Thomas defends our tracing from effect to cause to arrive at the Absolute, it is not a passing over the effects, because each of them is inhabited by the good and may well be the common good for a particular situation. A particular common good, for example, may be the proper signatory of a community ordered by the human law. This is why Saint Thomas can distinguish how human law and divine law are each ordained for diverse communities without placing them in opposition but addressing how the former is still in the image and likeness of the latter.

24. *ST* I, 2, *resp.*

Now human law is ordained for one kind of community, and the Divine law for another kind. Because human law is ordained for the civil community, implying mutual duties of man and his fellows: and men are ordained to one another by outward acts, whereby men live in communion with one another. This life in common of man with man pertains to justice, whose proper function consists in directing the human community. Wherefore human law makes precepts only about acts of justice; and if it commands acts of other virtues, this is only in so far as they assume the nature of justice, as the Philosopher explains (Ethic. v, 1). But the community for which the Divine law is ordained, is that of men in relation to God, either in this life or in the life to come. And therefore the Divine law proposes precepts about all those matters whereby men are well ordered in their relations to God. Now man is united to God by his reason or mind, in which is God's image. Wherefore the Divine law proposes precepts about all those matters whereby human reason is well ordered. But this is effected by the acts of all the virtues: since the intellectual virtues set in good order the acts of the reason in themselves: while the moral virtues set in good order the acts of the reason in reference to the interior passions and exterior actions. It is therefore evident that the Divine law fittingly proposes precepts about the acts of all the virtues: yet so that certain matters, without which the order of virtue, which is the order of reason, cannot even exist, come under an obligation of precept; while other matters, which pertain to the well-being of perfect virtue, come under an admonition of counsel.[25]

Beatitude is the proper end or purpose of the human person, but is it the proper end or purpose of government?[26] How are the aims of the divine law related to the natural law? The beauty of Saint Thomas's effect-to-cause, relative as related to an absolute, is that the Good is dynamic and unfolds via the *longer way* of human knowing which understands not at once but by an active composition and division.[27] The unity of

25. *ST* I-II, 100, 2, *resp.*

26. Cf. Goyette, "Political Common Good," 133–55.

27. Cf. *ST* I, 85, 5, *resp*: "The human intellect must of necessity understand by composition and division. For since the intellect passes from potentiality to act, it has a likeness to things which are generated, which do not attain to perfection all at once but acquire it by degrees: so likewise the human intellect does not acquire perfect knowledge by the first act of apprehension; but it first apprehends something about its object, such as its quiddity, and this is its first and proper object; and then it understands the properties, accidents, and the various relations of the essence. Thus it necessarily

the non-mediated, pre-reflexive self-evidence of God as innermost in all things, and the reflexive noetic longer way reveal the power of the Good to be both an essential disposition and a desired realm to be lived in. As the human person uncovers the good particular to him, he also uncovers the common good particular to place and time. As this common good is being engaged so is Goodness itself in its ultimacy through the interrogative and lifetime encounter with what truly constitutes our beatitude. In this dramatic tracing of effects to cause, the good is never extrinsicized, which is the temptation of the language of a "common good," as if something has to be forfeited to accomplish a homogeneity or agreement amongst diverse populations. Happiness could never be achieved by what is extraneous, what is imposed, what is known only by potency. The whole of Saint Thomas's work recognizes the true meaning of the common good as one which requires the interiorization of the other and the exteriorization of the person:

> Moreover, the knowledge that one has of a thing, only in a general way and not according to something proper to it, is very imperfect, just like the knowledge one might have of a man when one knows simply that he is moved. For this is the kind of knowledge whereby a thing is known only in potency, since proper attributes are potentially included within common ones. But felicity is a perfect operation, and man's highest good ought to be based on what is actual and not simply on what is potential, for potency perfected by act has the essential character of the good. Therefore, the aforementioned knowledge is not enough for our felicity.[28]

The conversion of the soul, often painful, when rediscovering one's nature obscured by a fallen condition, is not the same as the language of forfeiture—as if the good has to be something neutral, broad, and ideational. The only Good which can truly encompass all is one which has the power

---

compares one thing with another by composition or division; and from one composition and division it proceeds to another, which is the process of reasoning. But the angelic and the Divine intellect, like all incorruptible things, have their perfection at once from the beginning. Hence the angelic and the Divine intellect have the entire knowledge of a thing at once and perfectly; and hence also in knowing the quiddity of a thing they know at once whatever we can know by composition, division, and reasoning. Therefore, the human intellect knows by composition, division and reasoning. But the Divine intellect and the angelic intellect know, indeed, composition, division, and reasoning, not by the process itself, but by understanding the simple essence."

28. SCG III, 38, 6.

to strike at the interiority of each soul and that is only possible with an understanding of a good infused in each effect, overflowing each one in its panentheistic directionality so that goods are diverse and yet always unified by hierarchical meaning.

> [Aristotle] says that the city is a perfect community; and this he proves from this, since every association among all men is ordered to something necessary for life, that community will be perfect which is ordered to this, that man have sufficiently whatever is necessary for life. Such a community is the city [*civitas*]. For it is of the nature of the city that in it should be found everything sufficient for human life ... for it is originally made for living, namely, that men might find sufficiently that from which they might be able to live; but from its existence it comes about that men not only live but that they live well insofar as by the laws of the city human life is ordered to the virtues.[29]

This is the power of the distinguishable understandings of human, natural and divine law, their unity and their difference, and it is at root in the conservative mind and its defense of locality. The family, the church, the town, the state and the country must never be subsumed into one undifferentiated governmental identity, for this identification resides in an extraneous and susceptibly ideological rendering, where only prescription can enforce the sought-after intelligibility as uniformity. The artificial template, being too weak to account for the incommunicability of each soul[30] which constitutes the true common good, receives its strength by

29. Thomas Aquinas, *Aristotle's Politics*, 1, lect. 1, n. 23.

30. For Boethius's accounting of the human soul, see Baker, *Fundamentals of Catholicism,* 103: "A person is the individual, incommunicable substance of a rational nature." See also *ST* I, 13, 9, *resp*: "But the singular, from the fact that it is singular, is divided off from all others. Hence every name imposed to signify any singular thing is incommunicable both in reality and idea; for the plurality of this individual thing cannot be; nor can it be conceived in idea. Hence no name signifying any individual thing is properly communicable to many, but only by way of similitude; as for instance a person can be called 'Achilles' metaphorically, forasmuch as he may possess something of the properties of Achilles, such as strength. On the other hand, forms which are individualized not by any 'suppositum,' but by and of themselves, as being subsisting forms, if understood as they are in themselves, could not be communicable either in reality or in idea; but only perhaps by way of similitude, as was said of individuals. Forasmuch as we are unable to understand simple self-subsisting forms as they really are, we understand them as compound things having forms in matter; therefore, as was said in the first article, we give them concrete names signifying a nature existing in some 'suppositum.' Hence, so far as concerns images, the same rules apply to names we impose to signify the nature of compound things as to names given to us to signify simple subsisting natures."

vitiating the ritual, tradition and customs where our pre-reflexive moral life grows. Saint Thomas's effect-to-cause in the Five Ways is a guiding voice to the protection of the unfolding of the good in the decentralized society as alone the intelligible and hierarchical manifestation of the common good.[31]

All is guided towards happiness which is universal and unfailingly intimate. The locality of the family, the Church, the township distinct in their relation to the State and Country each provides, in differing manifestations, the well-fare of the person, body and soul. Government provides the tools of self-sufficiency and thus the potential for leisure necessary for the cultivation of our pre-reflexive originary *praxis*, often a *habitus* discoverable in family and faith. Each instantiation of the good, whether it be local or national, is in contact with the Good—some more perfectly than others—which refuses to be reduced to concept. And because of this refusal, the possession of the good is both pre-possessed in the incommunicability of each soul and grows with our character within the common good.

> The capacity for presence . . . grows with the capacity for recollection. Over and above all agreement on the plane of the perceptible, of words and actions spiritual union takes place only through what is most personal in us and, it has been said, 'through all that is most incommunicable,' for there is no real communion in what is externally communicated.[32]

This entrenched Goodness always returning to the person reveals it to be a personal Good and a personal Orderer. And thus, by a different path than faith, the goods of the moral order naturally move to the divine, not as idea, nor even as revelation, but as the source of relation and the

---

31. Cf. Eliot, *Christianity and Culture*, 162–63: "In a society so graded as to have several levels of culture, and several levels of power and authority, the politician might at least be restrained, in his use of language, by his respect for the judgment, and fear of the ridicule, of a smaller and more critical public, among which was maintained some standard of prose style. If it were also a decentralised society, a society in which local cultures continued to flourish, and in which the majority of problems were local problems on which local populations could form an opinion from their own experience and from conversation with their neighbours, political utterances might also tend to manifest greater clarity and be susceptible of fewer variations of interpretation. A local speech on a local issue is likely to be more intelligible than one addressed to a whole nation, and we observe that the greatest muster of ambiguities and obscure generalities is usually to be found in speeches which are addressed to the whole world."

32. Lubac, *Catholicism*, 345.

very substance of the heart and mind. This "capacity for presence" is the overlooked primitive mystique of the soul, a contact with Being, before it becomes reflection, so that reflection gazes both on the Other and on itself. True "capacity for recollection" abides by an enduring "capacity for presence." The sight of otherness, while distinct from the recollective presence, is also inseparable from it; the good and happiness of the bodily soul is inseparable from its reflection upon the order of things. This is the truth of tradition: it secures the timeliness needed to acquire the sight of the Good. And so tradition is a "handing over" without being a betrayal, and a "handing down" without becoming a hand-me-down![33] We follow these effects, each overflowing with the mystery of beatitude to their Cause and find that they have unveiled the person-in-reflection amongst the community of persons-in-reflection. As effect-to-cause unfolds person in persons, they illuminate the always preceding capacity for presence, the incarnational tradition, the common good.

> The *Summa Contra Gentes*, begun in 1259, reached its third book two or three years later. This was a defence of the traditional doctrine of a particular Providence against the inroads of the Averroist doctrine of a single World-Mind which dealt only with broad effects. It showed that God was not remote and uncaring. His causality did not leave secondary causes to work out the details; his knowledge entered into every minute particular. A reference occurs to the collective good of the community as being more godlike, *divinus*, than any particular good, that is, it better represents God's goodness. But the burden of the discourse was to show that the individual was more important than the race. Human persons were not utilities, pawns in a game, but ends in their own right, responsible agents who could consort with God and share his mind. The very argument that a part is subordinate to the whole was bent to prove the supremacy of the person, for a personal mind could possess all being and so, as a

---

33. Christ both hands over the tradition and is handed over by the traitor, Judas Iscariot. The first Mass on Maundy Thursday, the origins of our tradition, had a traitor priest in its midst. We must bear the weight of this when confronting the horrendous scandals of the church. Through these things, we are reminded of the delicate balance a living tradition must enact in order to distinguish itself from its false substitutes. There is more than a linguistic heritage linking tradition (*traditum*) and traitor (*traditorum*). If tradition is a delivering and a handing down, what is being handed over—as Christ was handed over by Judas—may instead be a traitorship.

microcosm, as such was no longer a subservient component but itself an open and generous whole.[34]

Dostoyevsky's Polyphony:
From the Un-Common Good to Double Thoughts

[I am] a myth that I am making of myself day by day . . . and my task is to make a myth, to make myself a myth. The end of life is to make oneself a soul.[35]

The actual five demonstrations have not yet been addressed in a systematic fashion; we have instead focused on the preceding articles of question 2—the structural scaffold necessary to engage and appreciate the Ways. Before we turn our attention to the Five Ways themselves, we shall return to our idiot prince, our holy fool, whose own passing thoughts on the double intentions of the soul—a simultaneous inclination towards good and evil—reflect the mystery of the uncommon good and the revelatory balance tradition must invoke in order to be genuine. *The Idiot*, like much of Dostoyevsky's work, is captured in polyphonic[36] textures: competing voices, ideas which break up any overriding context. New conversations intrude on meaning only to recast the narrative and return meaning to its home for the first time. Rather than fate seen as a *teleological* force with a direct narrative, Dostoyevsky's multifaceted exegesis presents fate in its truer manifestation as disruptive, surprising, sought after, and the most intimate companion of freedom. For let us not forget that human freedom is bound to its own inescapable fallenness and to the entelechy of its nature and its redemption. None of these can be managed, coerced, or outwitted, nor do they proceed by a distinguishable temporal sequence. They are distinct realities yet wholly inseparable, indeed jarringly monolithic, existing in the simultaneity of the moment and of the action. The *hamartia* or fatal flaw of a character often revolves around an attempt

---

34. Gilby, *Principality and Polity*, 24.

35. From Miguel de Unamuno's *Cómo se hace una novela* [*How a Novel Is Made*], in Wyers, *Miguel de Unamuno*, 58. For an excellent analysis of Unamuno's creation of the ultimate deconstructing self-reflective character, see Speck, "Making of a Novel in Unamuno," 52–63.

36. Cf. Bakhtin, "Dostoevsky's Polyphonic Novel," 5–46.

to smooth out, give temporal sequence, control the situation as if these realities can exist without utter entrenchment in the others.[37]

The way in which the novel is constructed further exposes the difficulty and the truth of the traditional *polis*. If we are to take the language of the relative-to-an-absolute seriously, it can only be grasped because the relative—for the time being, and it may be a long time— has taken the place of the absolute, as the effect takes the place of the cause.[38] Each particular thing, each act of existence, each exchange, glance, competing meaning, is on the *way of Being*, but like Dostoesvsky's polyphonic simultaneity, this *way* was never an easy ladder where each rung is an effect ideologically passed over as one ascends to the Absolute. Saint Thomas's rejection of God's self-evidence is done to magnify his inescapable non-mediated presence, too near to us to be self-evident.[39] Thus, this *way of Being* demands that each relative thing be exhausted, penetrated, overwhelmed—for the soul to know itself it must be, in a way, all things. This is why no prescriptive-based morality can constitute the soul, nor invoke the essence of conservational meaning.

What we see in *The Idiot*'s constantly intruding levels of narrative is the structural integrity of the Five Ways where meaning is not achieved by passing over Presence but as residing within. What takes us off course may keep us on it; the way up is the way down.[40]

> That the future is a faded song, a Royal Rose or a lavender spray
> Of wistful regret for those who are not yet here to regret,
> Pressed between yellow leaves of a book that has never been opened.
> And the way up is the way down, the way forward is the way back.
> You cannot face it steadily, but this thing is sure,
> That time is no healer: the patient is no longer here.[41]

---

37. Cf. *Problems of Dostoevsky's Poetics*, 28: "Dostoevsky attempted to perceive the very stages themselves in their *simultaneity*, to *juxtapose* and *counterpose* them dramatically, and not to stretch them out into an evolving sequence. For him, to get one's bearings on the world meant to conceive all its contents as simultaneous, and *to guess at their interrelationships in the cross-section of a single moment.*"

38. Cf. *ST* I, 2, ad. 2.

39. Cf. *Confessions* VII, 17, 23.

40. For a discussion of Heraclitus's oft quoted, highly suggestive fragment 60, see Kirk's commentary in Heraclitus, *Cosmic Fragments*, 105–12.

41. See Eliot's "Dry Salvages" in *Four Quartets*, 28.

It is in this sensation of Presence that *The Idiot*'s narrative is more truly reflective of existence, one where the eschatological precedes and informs knowledge rather than concepts mapping its course and placing fate and freedom erroneously at odds. When freedom and fate are opposed, the soul loses its bodily presence and its existential compact with the sharers of existence. Freedom becomes expansion of the ego, having no counterweight to return it to the communion of the common good. Fate in turn is seen only as a blind material force which must be suppressed by technology (abortion, genocide) in order to secure this ghost-in-a-machine freedom. But in this polyphonic narrative, we see the intermingling of freedom and fate which can strike at the truth of traditionalist locality, one that is deeply theological and personal, not because it is built from a naïve allegiance to a religious posture but because the soul-filled union with the particular and the relative inflames the common as uncommon good. This is a good where the joy and the guilt of the other is our own, where the common good of the *polis* mirrors the purgatorial power of the anteroom of heaven, where the dual intentionality of the human soul is fulfilled.[42]

Midway in the novel, we learn that Myshkin has been troubled by the paradox of "double thoughts"—how one can enact a choice with two contradictory intentions, one utterly noble and the other ignoble, and yet neither overwhelms the other.[43] This revelation is made known after an encounter with the boxer Keller, who is Myshkin's best man at his failed wedding to Nastassya; a request even more unbelievable considering the genesis of their relationship. Keller is a peripheral character, yet one who is always on the scene during decisive moments and one of several incongruous friendships Myshkin develops throughout the novel. Like many of the characters in Myshkin's orbit, his relation with the Prince reveals the latter's *deiformitas* not so much by the Prince's own actions but by Keller's spiritual evolution in relation to the Prince. At the outset of the novel, Keller is a more prominent member of Rogozhin's rowdy crew, leading the charge to crash Nastassya's birthday party, drunk and unruly.

42. Cf. Balthasar, *Christian State of Life*, 127: "But the hardest lesson to be learned there, the lesson that those who have been preoccupied with right and justice in this world will have to struggle to accept, is that there is no distinction of mine and thine even in matters of guilt, that they must see in every sin, by whomsoever it has been committed, an offense against the eternal love of God; that they must be disposed, therefore, to do penance, as long as may be deemed necessary by God, for every sin no matter who is its perpetrator."

43. Cf. Dostoyevsky, *Idiot*, 323–24.

This is the same party where our true *alter-Christus*, Nastassya, has assured certain characters of her long-awaited announcement of marriage; where she laughs in the face of the temptations and trappings of wealth offered to her by Totsky (who had made her his ward and then seduced her into becoming his mistress); where she humiliates her suitor Gavril Ivolgin, exposing his own mediocrity and financial ambition; where she briefly accepts Myshkin's proposal which is, at its root, an offer of salvation;[44] but runs off with Roghozin who is her fatality. Her refusal of Myshkin is a holy madness, she is too aware for her own good, and believes that her own death is preferable to imposing her presence on Myshkin and thus infirming and darkening the opacity of his soul. This preference Myshkin cannot understand. His likeness to Christ cannot go so far as to descend into hell, it has not yet united the cosmic Christ with the one on Holy Saturday.

> In the very face of this woman there was always something tormenting for him: the prince, as he talked to Rogozhin, had ascribed this sensation to one of infinite compassion, and this was the truth: even in the portrait, this face had called forth from his heart the whole suffering of pity; this impression of suffering, and even of suffering for this creature, never left his heart, did not leave him even now. Oh no, it was even stronger. But the Prince was dissatisfied with what he had told Rogozhin; and only now, in this moment of her sudden appearance, he realized, perhaps intuitively, what had been lacking in his words to Rogozhin. What had been lacking were the words that could have expressed horror—yes, horror! Now, at this moment, he sensed it fully; he was certain, was completely convinced, for particular reasons of his own, that this woman was insane.[45]

Her incongruity, her bodily soul, which refuses to abide by loss, would rather lose her life than live as a fraud or cause the fraudulence of another. Her madness is the most holy form of love, it is what caused

---

44. Nastassya Filippovna comes to discover Ganya's conflicting reasons for marrying her—his irrational passion for her as well as his desire to obtain her inheritance. His desire for Nastassya Filippovna perniciously unified with his destructive hatred for her, stemming from his rage over his own exalted self-image, his poor pecuniary circumstances and the resultant need to plot to marry someone with money whom he deems beneath his social standings. When he does pursue a marital engagement, Nastassya's repeated feigning and shirking his proposals only amplifies his conflicted desire and his hatred.

45. Dostoyevsky, *Idiot*, 407–8.

Christ to be put to death and it is what causes others to scorn, fear, lust after, and, very rarely, love her. For to love the Good one must not only know the Good but be wholly *of* it. With such love of Presence, Nastassya knew that freedom in this world lives within the fatal. She responded in kind, knowingly walking towards her death when she chose Rogozhin over Myshkin on the day of her wedding to the Prince. She alone understands the uncommon common Good, the play-of-Christ in both Rogozhin's descent and Myshkin's innocence. And while to all others, she is an intolerable ruin, a double nature, double personality, full of double promises and nonsensical contradictions, Nastassya is the only one who endures the stretching subordination of the soul. The wheel of fate turns, stretching us round and round by every act of our human freedom. Our freedom is also bondage: and only a God can save us.

Midway through the novel we are reintroduced to Keller, learning that he has been party to a plot to undermine and embarrass the Prince. With the help of Lebedev, they write a satirical article mocking Myshkin's idiocy, shared involvement with Nastassya, and stinginess with his ill-gotten inheritance. This is done on behalf of a simple and easily manipulated young man, Burdovsky, who fraudulently claims to be the son of Pavlishchev, the Prince's late benefactor. Keller concocts this scandal with visceral abrasiveness and, with Lebedev,[46] derives pleasure in seeing the plot unfold. His muscled physicality, extending to all facets of his personality, sharply contrasts the ethereal pacifism of the Prince. This attempt to extort money from the Prince failed and, for reasons inexplicable and yet cosmically natural, Keller becomes Myshkin's friend. At one point in the novel, Keller approaches Myshkin with a lengthy and impassioned apology, one which shows contrition and humility, and yet stops himself in the midst of his exhortation and confesses that he is also asking for money, and that his motives are twofold. The request for money wasn't the sole motivating factor for the apology. The apology, for Keller, stands independent of the pecuniary request and yet Keller admits that he realized midway through that the magnanimous nature of the apology can "naturally" be used for enticing Myshkin to give him money. Keller

---

46. Lebedev, claiming only to be the linguistic architect behind the slander pamphlet, is a character of double thoughts. He is introduced to us with Rogozhin on the train, becomes Myshkin's landlord for a time at the summer house in Pavlovsk, all the while acknowledging that it is Myshkin's genuine kindness which financially supports the widower's children.

claims the apology still comes from a region of genuine generosity while another and contrary motivation encroaches upon that generosity.

Keller:

> Listen, Prince, I've stayed on here since yesterday evening, first, out of special respect for the French Archbishop Bourdaloue (we were pulling corks at Lebedev's till three in the morning), but secondly and principally (I swear by all signs of the cross I'm telling the truth!) I stayed because I wanted to impart to you, so to speak, my full, heartfelt confession—and in this way to promote my own self-improvement. With that idea I fell asleep toward four o'clock, drenched in tears. Will you believe a man of noble nature? At the very moment I fell asleep, genuinely filled with inward and, so to speak, outward tears (because I finally was sobbing, I remember that!), a hellish thought occurred to me: 'And why not borrow some money from him after the confession, after all?' So I prepared my confession, you might say, like a piquant little dish flavored with tears, so as to pave the way with those tears and once you were softened up, have you hand over a hundred and fifty roubles. Don't you think that was dreadfully mean?

Prince Myshkin:

> Yes, except that certainly wasn't the way it was, it was simply a coincidence. Two thoughts occurred at once, it happens quite often. With me it happens incessantly. However, I don't think it's a good thing, and you know, Keller, I blame myself for that more than anything. You might have been talking about myself now . . . it is terribly hard to struggle against those *double* thoughts. I've tried. Heaven only knows how they come into being.
>
> The Prince looked at Keller with great interest. Apparently, the question of double thoughts had been on his mind for some time.[47]

We can see that these double thoughts have populated the entirety of the novel's polyphonic layers, so much so that characters possess double souls as well as souls completed only by others. Meaning is fragmented but not fragmentary, its unity is in the other and it is not easily won. The uncommon common good which we have sought all our lives will not unveil a straightened trail but demands everything be turned upside

---

47. Dostoyevsky, *Idiot*, 323–24.

down, just as the Prince ends where he begins, returning to the Swiss sanitorium lost of mind, utterly the same and entirely changed.

These double thoughts are there from the beginning and set the tone for the tension between fate and freedom which influences the entirety of the novel. Our Prince had arrived in St. Petersburg and both the passage there and his first port of call at the Yepanchins's secured his fate. The passengers he meets on the train, and those he encounters within hours of arriving in town, comprise the characters surrounding his gain and loss. On the train, he sits with Lebedev and Ragozhin, characters with double souls. The former sees each encounter as an opportunity to ingratiate himself with those of power or importance, receiving their favor. Ragozhin arouses Lebedev's interest as he is the heir of a wealthy merchant family and a stepping stone to others with greater influence. Upon hearing that the death of Rogozhin's father results in a tidy inheritance and has prompted Ragozhin's current return from exile, Lebedev fashions himself as indispensable to Ragozhin and his gang of rowdy followers. But when he learns of Myshkin's inheritance he becomes his right-hand man, and entreats him to rent his summer house. Myshkin is more pliable, more docile than Ragozhin, thus an easier mark and a more enjoyable companion. Lebedev is prone to lies, a drunkard, and a widowed father of a large family. Wholly aware of his weaknesses, he neither makes the effort to correct them nor to hide them. Yet our Myshkin finds something utterly redeemable about him and one cannot merely dismiss this assessment as the result of the Prince's naivete. Protective of his children, there is a sense that Lebedev's deceitful manner—which, again, he does not deny—is, for him, the way he puts his wits to use to secure a life above the poverty line. Curiously, he becomes friends with General Ivolgan who, having fallen from grace and perpetually off the wagon, is looked at with an equal mix of pity and snickering dismissal. The General *touches everything and caresses nothing*, and seeks, with desperation, to recover his own presence in the memory of others. For Dostoyevsky: "General Ivolgin, like all drunkards, was very emotional, and, like all drunkards who have sunk very low, he was much upset by memories of the happy past."[48] This friendship, which offers no social standing nor wins any favors for Lebedev, caresses his double soul. Their times together in drunken reverie ignited in each of them the holy form of recollection where sorrows needn't be forgotten but transform into a

48. Dostoyevsky, *Idiot*, 214.

glorious endurance transfiguring the past. The soul for once in its life triumphs in the reality that it is better "to be the poor servant of a poor master than to live and act as they do."[49] This is what they shared: to commune with saints and to taste the ocean on lips,[50] to be at every one of the far ends of meaning and find that they are held together by one body, and it is our own.

> But now I discovered the wonderful power of wine. I understood why men become drunkards. For the way it worked on me was not at all that it blotted out these sorrows, but that it made them seem glorious and noble, like sad music, and I somehow

49. *Resp.* 516d.

50. Cf. Neruda's "The Sea" in *On the Blue Shore*, 22:
I need the sea because it teaches me.
I don't know if I learn music or awareness,
if it's a single wave or its vast existence,
or only its harsh voice or its shining
suggestion of fishes and ships.
The fact is that until I fall asleep,
in some magnetic way I move in
the university of the waves.

It's not simply the shells crunched
as if some shivering planet
were giving signs of its gradual death;
no, I reconstruct the day out of a fragment,
the stalactite from the sliver of salt,
and the great god out of a spoonful.

What it taught me before, I keep. Its air,
ceaseless wind, water and sand.

It seems a small thing for a young man,
to have come here to live with his own fire;
nevertheless, the pulse that rose
and fell in its abyss,
the crackling of the blue cold,
the gradual wearing away of the star,
the soft unfolding of the wave
squandering snow with its foam,
the quiet power out there, sure
as a stone shrine in the depths,
replaced my world in which were growing
stubborn sorrow, gathering oblivion,
and my life changed suddenly:
as I became part of its pure movement.

great and revered for feeling them. I was a great, sad queen in a
song, I did not check the big tears that rose in my eyes. I enjoyed
them. To say all, I was drunk; I played the fool.[51]

This contact with Presence, this recollection of our originary
praxis is what Lebedev shared with the General, a transmission into the
incommunicable which is everything and yet missed by all. Lebedev's
friendship cannot be understood by others and that is a source of
frustration for him. Always after a night in this moving image of
eternity, he returns to the game of everyday affairs and thus returns
to the increasing oddity of his friendship that makes no worldly gain.
Lebedev, bonded to his trickery, cannot resist toying with the old man
when he discovers that his friend, during a drunken indiscretion, had
taken his money and secretly returned it only after Lebedev had realized
it had gone missing. When Lebedev deduces that it must have been the
General, he acts as if he is still searching for it. The General becomes
increasingly agitated, for the lack of the wallet's discovery increases his
shame. The General moves it again, now in plain sight, but Lebedev
continues the charade, acting as if he is unaware that the money is safely
found. Lebedev plays with the polity needed to keep the General's own
precious, though exaggerated, sense of dignity intact. The old man's
internalizing embarrassment leads to a disintegration of his health and
indirectly to his death. Lebedev recognizes his hand in the death of his
one true friend, knows it for its shame and knows of his own recoil. His
friend is now dead, his only confidant in the eternal who shared what
cannot be transmitted and whose death signifies the loss of Lebedev's
own temporary admission into the immediacy of Being. Yet he persists
as if this loss means nothing. Lebedev's double movements, half-fulfilled
actions present us with a strange truth. All things are directed towards an
end, but those beings who can reflect on the end, by their very reflection
scatter the end as an image is cast on broken glass. The good cannot be
coerced and its maintenance involves the most serious play. Lebedev and
the General only discovered this play when they, by inebriation, forgot
the world of social decorum and prescription and returned to the pre-
rational and the incarnational: sharers in the incommunicable:

> There is something at the bottom of every new human thought,
> every thought of genius, or even every earnest thought that
> springs up in any brain, which can never be communicated

51. Lewis, *Until We Have Faces*, 255.

> to others, even if one were to write volumes about it and were explaining one's idea for thirty-five years; there's something left which cannot be induced to emerge from your brain, and remains with you forever; and with it you will die, without communicating to anyone perhaps the most important of your ideas.[52]

But their play was built on weak and shifting sands and thus the balance between freedom and fate was uneven. Their double actions reveal the entanglement of a soul at war: one aspect desirous of the good in itself as entrenched *in* that very desire; the other a sobered and muted shell which only desired the good as an object to be achieved. The contradiction between the two brought out the lowest form of freedom-and-fate, one in which freedom and fate are wholly irreconcilable and at their root death is preferable to life, but death cannot be chosen for that would be too honest, too in contact with the *abyss*. Lebedev with all his schemes to achieve a social progress was perhaps looking for the social standing, opportune moment, position of prominence where he was free to exist without the lies or, perhaps less nobly, to be the architect of them. In either case, he sought liberation from a world which devoured and conquered and never gave anything to anyone meritorious.

On one occasion we actually see the double soul of Lebedev come bubbling to the surface; the soul inflamed by the moving image of eternity, the very one alluded to as the fruit of his comradery with the General but never witnessed. At one of Myshkin's impromptu summer terrace gatherings, Lebedev launches a linguistic gymnastic against the railroad's progress, dotting only to disfigure the agrarian landscape. But our mischief maker is reveling more in the delicious eloquence of his argument than in its meaning and consequence. He enjoys his voice, his stance, the way he pauses between critiques skirting scandal and passion. But as he is pressed to defend himself, as his argument advances, we see that he is forgetting the self as only constructed on social decorum and snobbish contrariety and, as if an octave of his voice automatically drops, he speaks the true and mournful loss of home and fidelity.

> The railroads alone will not pollute the 'water of life' but the whole thing is damned, sir, the whole trend of the past few centuries in its whole entirety, scientific and practical, may possibly really be damned . . . I challenge all of you, now, you

52. Dostoyevsky, *Idiot*, 413.

atheists: how are you going to save the world and where are you going to find a proper path for it? You men of science, of industry, cooperative associations, fair wages, and all of that? How are you going to do it? With credit? What is credit? Where will credit take you? . . . Without allowing any moral basis except the gratification of individual egoism and material necessity! Universal peace, universal happiness—out of necessity! . . . Not railway communication, my young impetuous lad, but the whole tendency of which the railroads may serve as, so to speak, the artistic representation. They speed around, clanking and rattling, all for happiness, they say, all for humanity! A certain thinker secluded from the world, complained, 'Mankind has grown too noisy and industrial, there is little spiritual peace.' And another thinker always on the go replied triumphantly to him, 'That may be, but the rumble of the railroad cars bringing bread to starving humanity is better, perhaps, than spiritual peace,' and walked proudly away from him. But I, the abominable Lebedev, do not believe in the cars that bring bread to humanity without a moral basis, for doing so may be coldly excluding a considerable part of humanity from the enjoyment of what is brought, as has happened already.[53]

In this double thought, we are confronted with the weakness of the human condition and the task of tradition. Progressivism is the perfect companion for a condition at odds with its nature. It is the promise of a teleological purposiveness, a rattling railroad bursting through the thicket, achieving its goal within the drive of ends justifying means. More so, it carries in itself its own justification by borrowing the same language of the moral template it actively seeks to annihilate. These double thoughts— the inclination of the soul to be awash in Goodness as opposed to dictating its own end as good—point us to the deeper double entelechy of the union of the will and intellect. The will's non-futural originary *praxis* is always in confrontation with the intellect's reflexive and anticipatory futurity. This confrontation, when in the midst of play, curves and shapes the soul in its *capax dei*, but when it loses its delicate balance, held by the presence of tradition in its immediacy, one aspect attempts to overwhelm the other. When this occurs, the double thoughts and double soul rise in conflict, and the common good becomes a non-sensible ideal or a solipsistic gratification, or both. The will achieves its futurity only in union with the intellect and the intellect achieves its placement or presence only

53. Dostoyevsky, *Idiot*, 392–93.

in union with the will. When either is stranded away from the other, then the futurity and the immediacy that their union unveils is detrimentally denigrated. In alienation from the pre-rational play of tradition, each becomes the trigger mechanism for the darkening of the soul and of a new form of collective good discoverable only in the image and likeness of that estrangement.

We find also the presence of a double soul in Rogozhin, who is often conceived as an anti-Christ figure but who has much of the makings of an *alter Christus*. This is the Rogozhin who competes with Myshkin for the love of Nastassya, but their loves are polar opposite and neither is fully Christ-like. Myshkin loves with a disembodied and ephemeral presence, one too fearful of touch to let the love be particularized into a passion. Myshkin is innocent but his suffering is a vicarious one, which he cannot process and which he refuses to place in the context of the cosmic Christ now flesh and blood. Our Prince's love has encircled the child at play, recited more than once the gaping terror of the guillotine, sought salvation for the consumptive Marie and for the mad and holy Nastassya, but these pieces of the *alter Christus* orbit him without connective substance, precisely because he refuses to act in a way that places him in-the-world.[54] He is not *of* the world: we are dealing with the presence of a holy innocent. But the task of that innocence is a difficult one: it is the question of retaining it when the in-the-world sweat and blood are not only acknowledged but enacted, where "human pride is exorcised and canonized."

> Habitual grace is a very different thing from a mere form of inertia; that it is not a sort of lightning conductor; that it is the most royally fruitful form of friendship, because it is the friendship of God; that it is the most magnificent nuptial garment because it is the seamless robe whitened by the blood of the Lamb—that it is, in a word, that fearful thing, the life of God in us: God Who thinks, God Who acts, God Who loves, through our minds, our wills, our hearts. It is the very goal and object of Christianity. It is the estuary in which all the sacraments, the seven streams of

54. Cf. Bakhtin, *Problems of Dostoevsky's Poetics*, 173: "In Myshkin this detachment from the ordinary relationships of life, the constant inappropriateness of his personality and his behavior impart to him a certain integrity, almost a naiveté; he is precisely an 'idiot'. The heroine of the novel, Nastassya Filippovna, also falls out of the ordinary logic and relationships of life. She, too, always and in everything acts in spite of her position in life. But characteristic for her is the violent emotional response. She is 'mad.'"

Paradise regained—meet and commingle. It is the culminating point of the ancient human pride exorcised and canonized: to becoming like gods—and of the eternal divine dream—to become man.[55]

To fulfill the reality that he is not *of* the world, he must be, like Christ, so heartbreakingly *in* the world that this potential *alter Christus* can actually live up to its origin. But this was Dostoyevsky's difficulty, as it is ours, and it invokes the genuine depth and difficulty of the uncommon common good. What Christ completes as fully *in* but not *of* the world can never be envisioned, let alone copied by us, and yet it is the very task of sanctification. This task needs a fertile ground, it needs tradition, not vacant progress. Tradition places the human person in the contact with Presence, by placing the will and intellect into their proper rhythm where futurity is discovered in saturated presence, and this presence stokes the life of transcendence. What must be conserved in tradition is the dynamism that we are wholly *in* and yet not *of* the world, and that neither can be retained without the other. Only then can true progress-as-transcendence be initiated, for meaning is not left behind but rediscovered in our participation within the moving image of eternity, in the historical and active encounter with tradition and the democracy of the dead, of those who have gone before.

Myshkin has the *in*-the-world innocence seen in his love of children, animals, and the little things that beg in corners. He also has the not-of-the-world oddness that acts not by prescription but by a connatural fidelity to something earthy and yet unworldly or uncommon. The *in*-but-not-*of* are discoverable only in the identification of the other. But when it comes to acting on that power, that uncommon good, Prince Myshkin stands as an inactive figure where the reactions of others in relation to him reveal his merely potential form of *alter Christus*. He is a cosmic Christ not yet ready to suffer unto death and descend into hell, though not unwilling. He is a Christ figure for a world already saved rather than one still fallen. He is no Christ overturning the temple tables or in the garden where everyone but himself falls asleep. Myshkin is nearing but has not yet approached the truth that the Our Savior turns the other cheek because he is too close to us, that every trespass is a bloodletting and a wounding. For someone like Nietzsche he is a Christ figure too

---

55. Debout, *My Sins of Omission*, 68–69.

weak to die, too weak to take in all of the world and be the other as other in order to be himself.

Rogozhin, on the other hand, is a figure ready to die, ready to become the other as other in order to be himself. He knows and incarnates the freedom and fatalism of Christ on the cross, carrying this truth within him but carrying it too savagely, refusing the grace that transforms suffering into a thing of love. His love is overly reified in contrast to Myshkin's fearful touch.

> On my bed, in the nights, I sought him whom my soul loveth: I sought him, but I found him not. I will rise now, and go about the city; In the streets and in the broadways will I seek him whom my soul loveth: I sought him, but I found him not. The watchmen that go about the city found me: Have ye seen him whom my soul loveth? Scarcely had I passed from them, when I found him whom my soul loveth: I held him, and would not let him go, until I had brought him into my mother's house, and into the chamber of her that conceived me.[56]

Both are driven to search for Nastassya by their needful loves, and each love is a hunt for the divine. Rogozhin seeks to complete (but knows not how) the soul as the other. Myshkin seeks to retain the other in its ownness, saving a life from any unity but its own. Rogozhin's deicidal love—a love closer to Good Friday—contrasts Myshkin's martylogical love which has not the substance for resurrection but languishes on in the *miseremini mei*.[57]

Together, these two souls constitute the most profound double thought, for each needs the other to complete itself and to be the uncommon common good of the *alter Christus*. Myshkin is grace without, or subconsciously withheld from, a substance to perfect; and Rogozhin is the cosmogonic in all its beauty and terror without the grace to become the Other. It is Rogozhin who has a filiation with the piteous Holbein Crucifixion and which causes him to pause in the oddity of that *in* but not-*of*-the-world figure; a figure so brutalized it must have at once seemed impossible for belief to exist, impossible for his disciples to believe this cadaver would resurrect in glory and be the Savior.[58] One evening in St.

56. Song 3:1–4.

57. Job 19:21.

58. For that intimate strangeness, see Sitwell's "Still Falls the Rain" in *Collected Poems*, 272:
Still falls the Rain

Petersburg, after their shared time in Moscow in their competitive pursuit of Nastassya—a time only referenced in the book but not experienced by the reader—Rogozhin and Myshkin have an exchange within the non-mediated. This encounter speaks to these two forms of *alter Christus*, as well as the double thoughts which disrupt their unity. At the end of the evening, after all the pleasantries have come and gone and Rogozhin is ready for Myshkin to leave his house, he delays the departure. Walking down the hallway towards the exit, a number of paintings hang on the wall, paintings his father picked up for a pittance at auctions, solely because he liked them. Only one painting had any value, the Holbein copy, and it is the one which causes Rogozhin to pause and lose his train of thought:

> Rogozhin suddenly stopped looking at the painting and walked ahead. No doubt his distraction and the strangely irritable mood that had come over him so suddenly might explain this abruptness; nevertheless the Prince found it odd that he would break off a conversation which he started and not even answer him. 'Tell me, Lev Nikolayevitch' said Rogozhin suddenly, having walked on a few steps. 'I've been meaning to ask you for a

---

Dark as the world of man, black as our loss
Blind as the nineteen hundred and forty nails
Upon the Cross.

Still falls the Rain
With a sound like the pulse of the heart that is changed to the hammer-beat
In the Potter's Field, and the sound of the impious feet

On the Tomb:
Still falls the Rain

In the Field of Blood where the small hopes breed and the human brain
Nurtures its greed, that worm with the brow of Cain.

Still falls the Rain
At the feet of the Starved Man hung upon the Cross.
Christ that each day, each night, nails there, have mercy on us
On Dives and on Lazarus:
Under the Rain the sore and the gold are as one.
. . .
Then sounds the voice of One who like the heart of man
Was once a child who among beasts has lain
'Still do I love, still shed my innocent light, my Blood, for thee.'"

long time, do you believe in God or not?' 'How strangely you ask
that and how strangely you look at me' observed the prince in-
voluntarily. 'I like looking at the painting,' Rogozhin murmured
after a short silence, as if he had forgotten his question again.[59]

Rogozhin shifts topics and does not wait for an answer from Myshkin. Instead, he opens the door to say goodbye to his companion. But
our Prince, not wanting to leave Rogozhin without an answer, tells of
four recent encounters. The first happened one evening walking with an
exceptionally learned man who treated him, Myshkin remarked, as if he
was his intellectual equal. This atheist was speaking as to why he doesn't
believe in God, but our Prince could not help but notice what he has
encountered before in similar conversations, that the disbeliever seems
to be conversing about something else; that his denial of God never hits
upon God but dances around it and rejects on the basis of a different
topic. This sensation is not elaborated but left as the fallow ground for
the next three stories. The second story causes Roghozin to roar with
laughter, perhaps at the *non-sequitur* intelligibility of the human soul—
namely that meaning doesn't always add up and actions, more than we
like to admit, betray our good sense. Two peasants and longtime friends,
neither drunk, are staying in the same room as they travel. For the past
few days one of the peasants, never a thief, well off by peasant standards,
and a Christian, begins to notice that the other has been wearing a curious silver watch on a fine beaded ribbon. This friendly and honest man,
so taken by the look of the watch and by a compulsion beyond himself,
no longer able to restrain himself, took a knife to his friend's back:

> took aim, raised his eyes to heaven, crossed himself, and bit-
> terly and silently prayed, 'Lord, forgive me for Christ's sake!' and
> cut his friend's throat with one stroke like a sheep, and took his
> watch.[60]

Rogozhin rocking back in forth in laughter responds:

> One fellow doesn't believe in God at all, while the other believes
> in Him so much he murders people with a prayer on his lips. No,
> my dear Prince, you could have never just invented that. Ha, ha,
> ha! No, that beats everything![61]

59. Dostoyevsky, *Idiot*, 228–29.
60. Dostoyevsky, *Idiot*, 230.
61. Dostoyevsky, *Idiot*, 230.

The third encounter involves how the Prince let himself knowingly be conned. A drunken soldier one night calls out to Myshkin to buy his cross, claiming it is silver and can be his for the reasonable sum of twenty kopecks. The cross, of old ornate Byzantine design with eight branches, dangled from a dirty blue ribbon and was made of tin and worth nil. But Myshkin agreed thinking it was not right to condemn "this peddler of Christ" for who knows what resides in his weak and drunken heart. The following morning, he comes across a young mother holding her six-week-old infant and crossing herself with ecstatic radiance. Myshkin turns to the peasant mother and asks why she made the sign of the cross, to which the young mother responds that the joy of a child's first smile overwhelms, as it does for God when a sinner turns to him and prays with his whole heart. In this last story, Myshkin illuminates the profundity of unreflective love. The wisdom of the mother permeates the double thoughts of the drunken soldier, of Lebedev, and the others who transmit, yet do not possess the good they transmit. This is what the atheist misses in his rejection of God as artificial template: Myshkin buys the cross because there is beauty in it exceeding and hidden in the fraudulence, just as there is sanctity for the peasant in prayer inside the ancient cathedral built by dominance and political supremacy. Travelers walk the hillside Tuscan towns unaware that such towers were built to defend and destroy, but still they dot the landscape in heartrending harmony, as if the fields, hills and valleys wave and bow at them. History and the historical movement of the heart are not always aligned, and there is a secret primal wisdom that defies reason and fact. When all else is lost (and all will be lost), this uncommon common Good, *Is*:

> Tell me honestly, I challenge you—answer me, imagine you are charged with building an edifice of human destiny, whose ultimate aim is to bring people happiness, to give them peace and contentment at last, but in order to achieve this it is essential and unavoidable to torture just one little speck or creation, the same little child beating his breasts with his little fists, and imagine this edifice to be erected on her unexpiated tears. Would you agree to be the architect under these conditions?[62]

62. Dostoyevsky, *Karamazov Brothers*, 308. For an article which sets out the shocking cruelties which render Ivan unable to accept the faith, to see it unworthy of belief: see Robert C. Wood, "Dostoevsky on Evil," in Barnhart, *Dostoevsky's Polyphonic Talent*, 1–24, esp. 6. "Ivan's phantasmagoria of human barbarity consists of actual scenes he has clipped from Russian newspapers. 1. Turkish soldiers cutting babies from their mothers' wombs and throwing them in the air to impale them on their bayonets. 2.

What the *alter Christus* possesses is not the answer but the *way*, the living intelligibility of the good when the good has simply vanished. This uncommon good cannot be managed or linearized, its eschatology is non-sequential and communicates only to one soul as heir to the world, and every soul may be the heir to the world, but the communication of this uncommon Good inflames the unity of the One. This contact and Presence of the divine so infused in us cannot be coerced out of existence even when all actions act to the contrary. Myshkin's peasant mother it was who imparted:

> the whole conception of God as our Father and of God's joy in man, like a Father in his own child—Christ's fundamental thought! A simple peasant woman! . . . Listen Parfyon, you asked me a question before, and here's my answer: the essence of religious feeling doesn't depend on reasoning, and it has nothing to do with wrongdoing or crime or with atheism. There is something else there and there always will be, and atheists will always pass over it and will never be talking about *that*.[63]

As Myshkin leaves the building, quite suddenly Rogozhin shouts from the top of entranceway asking if Myshkin still possessed that cross, to which our Prince replies that it is with him, around his neck. They exchange, spiritually and materially, that incommunicability which the atheist will always miss. Rogozhin nearly demands they exchange crosses and that by doing so they will be brothers. Myshkin, surprised, acquiesces and exchanges his tin one for Rogozhin's one in gold. This exchange will be brought up by Myshkin much later in the novel as they head to spend a final night as brothers in the room where Nastassya lay, dead by Rogozhin's hand, and after which Myshkin returns to deafness and silence, wearing that gold cross. Rogozhin's insistence, and the vulnerability of then inviting Myshkin back into his house for what will be a blessing by his mother, uncovers layers of divine surprises. We witness

---

Enlightened parents stuffing their five-year old daughter's mouth with excrement and locking her in a freezing privy all night for having wet the bed, while they themselves sleep soundly. 3. Genevan Christians teaching a naïve peasant to bless the good God as the poor dolt is beheaded for thefts and murders that his ostensibly Christian society caused him to commit. 4. A Russian general, offended at an eight-year old boy for accidentally hurting the paw of the officer's dog, inciting his wolfhounds to tear the child to pieces. 5. A lady and gentlemen flogging their eight-year old daughter with a birch rod until she collapses while crying for mercy, 'Papa, Papa, dear Papa.'" See also Wood, "Ivan Karamazov's Mistake."

63. Dostoyevsky, *Idiot*, 231.

that *non-sequitur* intelligibility, that craving for Presence so innermost in being that no generality, no ideal, no progressivism can acknowledge, let alone encounter.

> Finally, in silence, Rogozhin took the prince's hand and stood for some time, as though he could not make up his mind about something. At last he suddenly drew him after him and, in a barely audible voice, said, "come on." They crossed the first floor landing and rang at the door facing the one they had come . . . In the corner of the drawing room by the stove sat a little old woman in an armchair; she did not appear very old, in fact she had a rather healthy and pleasant round face, but her hair was completely white and, as could be told at first glance, she had entered her second infancy . . . Mother, said Roghzhin, kissing her hand, 'this is my great friend, Prince Lev Niko-layevitch Myshkin. We have exchanged Crosses. He was like a real brother to me in Moscow at one time, he did a lot for me. Bless him, Mother, as you would bless your own son. Wait, old lady, like this; let me fix your fingers right. But before Parfyon had time to do this, the old woman raised her right hand, with three fingers held up, and three times devotedly made the sign of the Cross over the Prince. Then, once again she nodded her head tenderly and affectionately to him. Well, let's be going Lev Nikolayevitch, said Parfyon. That's all I brought you here for.[64]

The *alter Christus* is the figure of the *un*common common good, one who appears as a weak sentimentalist or a soldier refusing to fall. He is every inconceivable unity, a pantheist's dream, overwhelmed in the visceral contact with the personal as faceless and the faceless appearing on our faces, recovering our presence in the divine. The *alter Christus* directs us to the true natural law as participation in the eternal, a participation which cannot hang on convictions, formulas or categories. It is the nature which exists against the grain, which takes the different path, not as reactionary but as natural to it. This Christ-likeness does not lead by the egoism of conviction, reaction, posture, or disposition which all reduce particular aims to a particular end, but elevates the particular into the uncommon as communion.

In question 90 of the *Prima Secunda* the objector argues that the essence of law, because chiefly concerned with *particular* human actions concerned with *particular* human matters, resolves itself with a *particular*

---

64. Dostoyevsky, *Idiot*, 232–33.

end. We can see in the Five Ways a companion critique, when the objector states the following:

> Further, it is superfluous to suppose that what can be accounted
> for by a few principles has been produced by many. But it seems
> that everything we see in the world can be accounted for by
> other principles, supposing God did not exist. For all natural
> things can be reduced to one principle which is nature; and all
> voluntary things can be reduced to one principle which is hu-
> man reason, or will. Therefore there is no need to suppose God's
> existence.[65]

The language of the common good can be misleading: is it "common"
as in "commonplace"? It must be present for all, but the all, as free, must
be prepared to enact and understand it as more than isolated prescriptions. In that sense, it is rare and far from commonplace. As communal,
it must unite with the universal, but its universality cannot be confused
with a mere generalization of meaning. The first objector attempts to
retain the locality inherent in human actions—that actions do not truly
resolve themselves in the general, and if they do, it is instead a confused
amalgamation of solipsistic desires manifested as an encompassing ideology. Such ideas cannot truly direct the human soul which, as unique and
incommunicable, is led *through* that uniqueness and incommunicability.
The companion objector in the Five Ways is also a timely one. When
God is seen as a nebulous overarching theme, the ordaining power of
the prescription, the particularity of human action is hard-tasked to find
any substantive connective meaning in relation to this emptied God. We
do not need to invoke God to explain the lifecycle of natural things nor
to explain our particular voluntary acts. If this were the case, the world
God created would align with a neurotic occasionalism, one ripe for the
post-Humean deconstruction of which we are still prisoners. Yet God
is innermost in all things and the truth of our particularity unifies in
Him who is Common to all. His uncommon Goodness is manifestly personal, intimate, individualizing each earthly other in the lover-beloved
relationship which creation endows upon each creaturely being. The *alter
Christus* reveals the common Good because, having stripped away the
double intentions which mask the relation between the particular and the
universal, he has unified them in his being; the universal is particularized
with his bodily soul and the particular takes on the endurance of the

65. *ST* I, 2, 2, arg. 2.

universal. He is thus a personal encounter with the common good rather than the common good being an amalgamation of individual convictions straining for some uneasy union, a lowest common denominator. That is why, for Saint Thomas, all particular matters are referable to a common good but *not* a common genus or species.

> Actions are indeed concerned with particular matters: but those particular matters are referable to the common good, not as to a common genus or species, but as to a common final cause, according as the common good is said to be the common end.[66]

Referable only to a common final cause, a divine finality innermost in us, the particularity of human actions is transfigured in our *capax dei*. The *alter Christus* leads because he does not lead and he reveals the universal not by plans, edicts, convictions[67] but by the very unmistakable particularity of his being.[68] This is cultivated by his pre-reflexive love of the Good which provides him with the endurance to transform the crucible of reflexive act into the wellspring of donative love—the true common good. This is why *The Idiot* unfolds in a polyphony of interactions and meanings so as to avoid an idea of the common good led by one's own limited rationality. It is both deconstructive and yet a recovery, as Rogozhin, Myshkin, and Nastassya act out the cycle of the *alter Christus*. They may not complete the revelation of the common good but instead each presents a failing *alter Christus*, and these *in-failings*, against all odds, point us to what does not fail: the Christ Person Who exists as the uncommon common Good.

---

66. *ST* I-II, 90, 2, ad.2.

67. As attributed to Saint Francis of Assisi: "Preach the Gospel at all times and if necessary use words." And when you do preach, it is because the words are not leading or designing or designating but in union with the sanctifying order of the pre-reflexive. From the words of Thomas of Celano who wrote the first biography of Saint Francis, three years after his death in Broocks, *Human Right*, 92: "[St. Francis] sometimes preached in up to five villages a day, often outdoors. In the country, Francis often spoke from a bale of straw or a granary doorway. In town, he would climb on a box or up steps in a public building. He preached to serfs and their families as well as to landholders, to merchants, women, clerks, and priests—any who gathered to hear the strange but fiery little preacher from Assisi . . . [so animated and full of zeal that] his feet moved as if he were dancing."

68. Benedict XVI, *Verbum Domini*, §93: "It is not a matter of preaching a word of consolation, but rather a word which disrupts, which calls to conversion and which opens the way to an encounter with the one through whom a new humanity flowers."

It is not enough to define morality as fidelity to one's own convictions. One must continually pose oneself the question: are my convictions true? Only one verification of them exists—Christ. For this is no longer philosophy, it is faith, and faith is a red color....I cannot recognize one who burnt heretics as a moral man, because I do not accept your thesis that morality is an agreement with internal convictions. That is merely *honesty* (the Russian language is rich), but not morality. I have a moral model and an ideal, Christ. I ask: would He have burned heretics?—no. That means the burning of heretics is an immoral act . . . Christ was mistaken—it's been proved! A scorching feeling tells me: better that I remain with a mistake, with Christ, than with you . . . Living life has fled you, only the formulas and categories remain, and that, it seems, makes you happy. You say there is more peace and quiet (laziness) that way . . . You say that to be moral one need only act according to conviction. But where do you get your convictions? I simply do not believe you and say that on the contrary it is immoral to act according to one's convictions. And you, of course, cannot find a way to prove me wrong.[69]

The *alter Christus—even and especially in-failing—*is a figure too good to be ordered to the world of reason. He is beauty in the dregs, one in being with Christ, the only Being who can save us from the relativizing, deadly power of our age. This uncommonly common good is unimaginable because it precedes noetic orientation, giving knowledge its image and direction. The common good involves arriving at a good once dispossessed. If this *communis* is a participation in the eternal law revealed to be the universal in the particular, the personal as communal, then what is possessed is the handing over of ourselves to the Other manifested in the local particularity of family and society. In our unreflexive love, we possess the Good *because* it exudes and infects others with joy; when we gain our reflexive ordination, the Good is present only by dispossession, for any reflection upon the uncommon common good, which refuses eidetic reduction, escapes our grasp. If we can endure and resist the temptation to reduce the Good to an egoical tautology of prescriptions and prohibitions, if we can guide ourselves towards the blindness of our originary love, then we may possess again the Good through the abandonment of our soul to the freedom of divine providence. This occurs when the joy and sadness of another is our own, when solidarity is

69. Bakhtin, *Problems of Dostoevsky's Poetics*, 97–98. Biography, letters, and notes from Dostoevsky's Notebook, St. Petersburg 1883.

not code for similar convictions, but the meaning of loving sharers in the universal incommunicability translated only by that which is innermost in all of us. Each of us is the heir to the world, but only when we are the other *as other*. For the good we seek is the good we can bring to God. What we gain is our participation in the eternal law, but our participation would add nothing to God if it did not dilate the heart and promote the growth of the soul:

> I have said that God is pleased with nothing but love; but before I explain this, it will be as well to set forth the grounds on which the assertion rests. All our works, and all our labours, how grand soever they may be, are nothing in the sight of God, for we can give Him nothing, neither can we by them fulfil His desire, which is the growth of our soul. As to Himself He desires nothing of this, for He has need of nothing, and so, if He is pleased with anything it is with the growth of the soul; and as there is no way in which the soul can grow but in becoming in a manner equal to Him, for this reason only is He pleased with our love. It is the property of love to place him who loves on an equality with the object of his love. Hence the soul, because of its perfect love, is called the bride of the Son of God, which signifies equality with Him. In this equality and friendship all things are common, as the Bridegroom Himself said to His disciples: I have called you friends, because all things, whatsoever I have heard of my Father, I have made known to you.[70]

The common good is not an object to be achieved or a secondary ethics of prescription, it is the intimate participation in the eternal law which inflames the property of love within the undivided soul. And because love is always relational then it is uncommonly common in the truest sense possible. It is this rare love of the common good which is at the heart of our subordinated ethics, subordinated because love is surrender to the other, and a chaste anarchism for it will only surrender to Love, having no master but Christ. The common good arrives at this truth not through the imposition of a religious template against meaning, for he is no idol. Neither is this common good, while compatible with the faith, arrived at by an adherence first to Revelation. This good, because entrenched in the moral life, is discoverable in the depths of the will and of the non-futural play of the will's originary *praxis*. In its secondary reflection, the moral good may encounter its naturally supernatural filiation

---

70. See John of the Cross, *Complete Works*, 150–51.

with the faith—because it springs from the same source—but it springs in a different way respective of its nature and order. That difference must be respected, because it is that difference which inculcates the creative endurance of the heart. Revelation is present and yet, stretched out by apocalyptic meaning, it carries the weight of the futural by anticipation and judgment. The common good of the genuine natural law is the trans-natural counterweight to that futurity. Unreflexively we are invested in the presence of Revelation, in the goodness of being divine playthings. The non-futurity of our moral ordination reveals revelation not to be a Hegelian stage of the Absolute, but that which is so near that it alone invokes transcendence. If morality loses the language of nearness, both the moral life as properly local/non-futural and the religious life so weighted in the futural, become what Nietzsche loathed—a careless passing over the beauty and terror of existence for an empty promise, empty because artificial, empty because it is nothing more than a manifestation of the ego hidden by language, conviction, discourse, aims and goals. This is the fate of all progressivisms and the temptation of any conservatism when it loses tradition as being-in-the-world, when it reacts against progressivism by acting like progressivism but only in reverse. It brings one to understand the great Wyndham Lewis when he remarked: "In a period of such obsessing political controversy as the present, I believe that I am that strange animal, the individual without any politics at all."[71]

> Mysticism keeps men sane. As long as you have mystery you have health; when you destroy mystery you create morbidity. The ordinary man has always been sane because the ordinary man has always been a mystic. He has permitted the twilight. He has always had one foot in earth and the other in fairyland. He has always left himself free to doubt his gods; but (unlike the agnostic of to-day) free also to believe in them. He has always cared more for truth than for consistency. If he saw two truths that seemed to contradict each other, he would take the two truths and contradiction along with them. His spiritual sight is stereoscopic, like his physical sight: he sees two different pictures at once and yet sees all the better for that. Thus, he has always believed that there was such a thing as fate, but such a thing as free will also. Thus, he believes that children were indeed the kingdom of heaven, but nevertheless ought to be obedient to the kingdom of earth. He admired youth because it was young and age because it was not. It is exactly this balance

71. See "Revolutionary Simpleton" in Lewis, *Enemy*, 183.

of apparent contradictions that has been the whole buoyancy
of the healthy man. The whole secret of mysticism is this: that
man can understand everything by the help of what he does
not understand. The morbid logician seeks to make everything
lucid, and succeeds in making everything mysterious. The
mystic allows one thing to be mysterious, and everything else
becomes lucid.[72]

Our reflections thus far have sought to spotlight the moral life in its
connatural mystique, one that does not entice the soul to rebel against
order—stymied by an imposed morality—but able to flourish outside the
law because the law is embodied in the person, as timely, personal, and
communal.[73] These reflections have utilized the natural theology setting
up the Thomistic Five Ways in order to help us identify the odd intelligibility of the moral life. What the will possesses is that pre-reflexive
self-evidence, that non-futurity of playful love, which gives meaning to
the futurity of the intellect only to receive its meaning as the intellect
protracts the will's desire and transforms the soul into the embodiment
of the uncommon good. In order to witness this uncommon common
good situated in the person, we turned to the polyphony of potential
Christ-like figures in *The Idiot*. Our task there was also to show how this
unveiling of the true common good shares the same well-spring as the
faith but arrives at the divine *via* a crucially different path, a difference
which must not be neglected. When it is obscured, the conservation of
the tradition falls prey to ignoring its ontological mysticism, its metaphysical personhood. It grounds its diminishing intelligibility in words,
sentiments, postures, empty commands which do not possess the faith's
revelatory power of the Word as different from all words. The conservative often imitates the faith in its ordination but fails to enact the faith's
lived-experience precisely because it is not born of revelation. Genuine
tradition is discoverable only in the orignary *praxis* which allows revelation to inhabit a fertile soul; it is compatible with revelatory meaning

72. Chesterton, *Collected Works*, 230–31.

73. Cf. Hartmann, "St. Thomas and Prudence," 65: "The good man our *spoudaios*
judges each thing correctly. Things appear to him as they truly are, for he possesses
true wisdom in the moral order. For him there is no opposition between appearance
and truth. 'Perhaps what chiefly distinguishes the good man is that he sees the truth in
each kind, being himself as it were the *standard and measure (kanon kai metron)* of the
noble and the pleasant' (NE, 1113a30). That which is the true and unqualified good is
the good that *he* desires and wishes for, for that is the good that appears to him. Thus
we see that the absolute good is that which *rules* his actions."

but it cannot act with its futurity. When it does, it becomes instead, like Gnosticism, a distorted image of the good, so close but so terribly far from the Real.

The time is at hand for conservatism to recover its originary *praxis*, to transcend the limits of its self-imposed and unclarified categories. As in concrete politics, so in thought itself there is a time, perhaps only a fleeting effulgence, in which the act can transform mere circumstance into new reality, thereby unveiling the existential efficacy of its nature as primal freedom. Now, whatever else may distinguish thought from action, clearly there is a radical likeness. This likeness is also discovered in the intellect's power to direct the will while leaving the will distinct from itself in the non-mediated presence of the Good. This unity transforms thought into action and action into a thought-filled directionality.

Whether it is conservatism's destiny or merely its good fortune the truth of the matter is that conservatism is faced with a historical opportunity and an intellectual obligation. Otherwise, like the liberalism it both supplants and competes with, it simply will not endure. Friedrich Hayek, in his justly famous essay "Why I Am Not a Conservative,"[74] complains that conservatives are men without principles. Not that they lack personal conviction and virtue but that they distrust, dismiss and then simply forget the necessary originary principles by which thought and action, each a transforming unity on the other, can be integrated into the world of ever changing realities. The soul as moving image of eternity is thus unable to inhabit a world as reflective of that moving image, creative and stable.

Ten Principles in Search of an Author: Tradition, Virtues, Limits

The conservative, the noble traditionalist, defends the necessity of *nomos* but not, or at least not adequately, its incarnating beauty as foundation.[75] Like dogma, prescriptions are the road signs, the cultural courtesies of immemorial usage and prudence, but they are not the destination of the

74. Hayek, "Why I Am Not a Conservative," 397–414. For conservatism to have found itself, however inchoately or uneasily, upon such a denial is egregious, contradictory and self-destructive. And it only confirms Hayek's complaint: for a principle founded upon such a denial can only be a pseudo-principle of thought.

75. Cf. Desmond, *Gift and the Passion of Beauty*.

human ethical life. They are the *rules* of the game but not the game itself. They do not impede the game, but again, they are *not* the game itself.

One is reminded of the odd paradox of Plato's *Protagoras*. For Protagoras, the great sophist and precursor of modern anti-nomian absolutism, there is no right or wrong, all is relative, and yet virtue *can* be "taught," as imposed; whereas for Socrates there clearly is right and wrong, but virtue *cannot* be taught.[76] To be in possession of oneself (*sophrosyne*) is less "self-control" or "temperance" or "prudence," than it is a knowing of oneself and, therefore, a way of being the form. But this cannot be "taught" (except by the progressive negative dialectic of *maieutic*), but must instead be re-collected. So virtue *is* knowledge but not teachable! In this, Kierkegaard is right: all truth is subjectivity and existential: to *have* the experience and *miss* the meaning, except after the fact, is the tragic essence of human action. The meaning can only be recollected, never taught. This recollection requires more than resolve, it requires faith.

When Russell Kirk set out his famous and admirable Ten Principles of Conservatism,[77] he understood them precisely *as principles*. It is not a question of disputing them within their order—for there is great efficacy and intelligibility to them—but of seeing them for what they are: not principles but conditional conclusions. These ten principles are the visible *effects* of a union with the world which prepares the soul for divine meaning. But to take these ten conclusions and place them in the lead as the foundational markers of tradition—effectively ridding them of their necessary subordination to the Good (which, in their own way, they claim to possess)—is to create a tradition in a vacuum. One must, with Péguy, always tell what one sees. Above all, which is more difficult, one must always see what one sees.[78] There is a world of difference between true principles and conditional conclusions: it is the difference between knowledge as *wisdom* and thinking as *ideological*. These ten principles are:

1. The conservative believes that there exists an enduring moral order.

2. The conservative adheres to custom, convention, and continuity.

---

76. Cf. Plato, *Prot.* 361a-b.

77. In *The Conservative Mind*, Kirk unveils six canons of conservative thought. Four decades later, he expanded those canons into "ten principles of conservatism," based on his later book, *The Politics of Prudence*.

78. Péguy, *Basic Verities*, 47.

3. Conservatives believe in what may be called the principle of prescription.

4. Conservatives are guided by the principle of prudence.

5. Conservatives pay attention to the principle of variety.

6. Conservatives are chastened by the principle of imperfectibility.

7. Conservatives are persuaded that freedom and property are closely linked.

8. Conservatives uphold voluntary community, quite as they oppose involuntary collectivism.

9. The conservative perceives the need for prudent restraints upon power and upon human passions.

10. The thinking conservative understands that permanence and change must be recognized and reconciled in a vigorous society.[79]

It is true that these ten principles are describing a set of circumstantial facts, namely that most conservatives do believe in this order. If one were to inhabit its social polity, observe and describe its members, this order would be the predominant classification. But this reaches only the level of a sociological awareness of the tradition. These are statements which are ontical at best, and, even if one relies on the other for its intelligibility—i.e., the continuity of the second principle requires the enduring moral order of the first; the fourth's principle of prudence requires an umbilical filiation with the sixth's awareness of our own imperfectibility—they do not reach beyond themselves to something other than themselves for a foundation. They reside within the conceptual appearance of these qualities as a disposition, attitude or approach. This is not to say that these qualities are not to be admired or that such a disposition does not aid the inculcation of the common good, but that they, by being described *as principles*, obscure our dwelling on the Good which first enables their descriptions. And because, "politics which sin against the laws of being, do so at their own peril,"[80] this pseudo-foundation is in danger of collapsing.

79. See Kirk, "Ten Conservative Principles," in *Politics of Prudence*.

80. Wilhelmsen, *Christianity and Political Philosophy*, 172: "They fall into either a tyrannical power which violates the body politic or into a chaos within whose vortex every faction within the community vies with all comers for the palm of power possessed by none." See also Spencer, *Social Statics*, 266–67: "Now the chief faculty of self-rule being the moral sense, the degree of freedom in their institutions which any given people can bear, will be proportionate to the diffusion of this moral sense amongst

What has *already* occurred is the loss of Being by the conflation of Being with idea, and this in turn amounts to the loss of the political mystique by the conflation of the *polis'* mystical locality with sentiment, attitude and disposition. Being is reducible to an imposed universal, and the always-preceding mystery which enables empirical, moral, and social clarity and certitude, is reducible to self-enclosed personal belief. Traditionalism, by attempting to undercut the deformations caused by a progressivist top-down approach often inflicts its own top-down vice-grip which cannot illuminate that the God we seek is a God of family and community, because he is not an ideational end-point but Trinitarian relation itself. True progress requires an outward transcending reach which is equally a deepening into the thicket of Presence, so that the very meaning of the Good we chase is invoked in the nearness of the family in the sheer relation with others. Bypassing Presence in favor of the promise of a futural presence never arrives at the "future" but tramples on a series of presences with diminishing returns until one reaches death. This twofold reduction seeks to combat the rapidly encroaching world of secularity, but can only offer flimsy universals rooted in private belief. And this is no weapon against the temptation to render fact equivalent with meaning.

I. The conservative believes that there exists an enduring moral order

This first principle is again not a principle, but a conditional conclusion. Linguistically, belief is the root, and thus reductively the originator of this enduring moral order. Because the moral order grounds itself on the conservative's own belief without pointing to *anything beyond itself,* then in this tautology of a cloaked idealism, the belief not only grounds the moral order but can as easily be its originator. If this principle is founded on belief, then this belief is girded by collective agreement and conviction. Put another way, upon what, other than agreement, is the conviction based? It cannot be based on the principle itself without begging the question. It is here indeed that a woeful conceptual confusion between principles, convictions, and true conclusions is most apparent and also most lethal. For we are immediately invited to consider the

---

them. And only when its influence greatly predominates can so large an installment of freedom as a democracy become possible. Lastly, the supremacy of this same faculty affords the only guarantee for the stability of a democracy. On the part of the people it gives rise wo what we call a jealousy of their liberties—a watchful determination like encroachment upon their rights: whilst it generates amongst those in power such a respect for these rights as checks any desire they may have to aggress."

divine providence and government a *theological postulate*: the very first principle of conservatism denies the possibility of rational penetration of the most fundamental tenet, not only of conservatism, but of human thought. Is this not to collaborate with modernity in reducing metaphysics and moral philosophy to non-binding religious conviction? More so, is it not a more reckless form of post-modernity's deconstructive ethics? If, for the post-modern, one can have the absolute, and develop a cohering system of rules by which this absolute meaning is engaged, it is done only within a linguistic enclosure. Within this enclosure the so-called game is afoot; the Christian can have God and follow his rules, but outside the enclosure one returns to the deconstructive relativism which refuses in advance any independent hierarchical intelligibility. There appears, as we indifferently scan the postmodern landscape, a penumbra of such enclosures—religious, sociological, and political—and if I choose to enter one of them, I may play by its game and invoke its respective universal, its eternally manifested meaning contained therein. However, by stepping out, I choose no longer to be constrained by that template, and return to myself without reference to anything independent and irreducible. In this first principle, we see a concession to the post-modern landscape, one which defends the absolute but does so only by constructing it within the same dramatic language game. This conservative principle is not only more reckless, but unknowingly more dishonest than its postmodern counterpart. Unable to recognize that conservatism has created its own artificial template and then enslaved itself by its own hand, the conservative signs his own death warrant. The existence of God here is not something recognized, it is something postulated, and neither Augustine nor Aquinas, nor even Plato nor Aristotle, would discern the influence of their thought here. Perhaps Henry of Ghent and the other fourteenth-century schoolmen, whose rise was coincident with the decomposition of the medieval synthesis, would, or a Pufendorf whose moral voluntarism identifies the natural law with religious disposition. In that first principle, we see Pufendorf's voluntaristic identification still intact, and the inclination towards the secondary ethics of prescription and prohibition as the essence of moral meaning. This is an ethics which tips its hat to God while vitiating his ontological givenness. True conservatism is more a political theology not because its basis is a template of religious experience, one against the natural *Scientia*, but because a genuine relationship with nature leads either by welcome (child's play) or exile (the cosmogonic) to the sacred. More and more, the locus of human goodness shifts from the following of command to interpreting it, and then to be the originator of it.

> ... a man would not even be sociable if he were not imbued with religion, and because reason alone in religion extends no further than to religion's capacity to promote the tranquility and sociality of this life; for so far as religion procures the saving of souls, it proceeds from a particular divine revelation. The duties of a man towards himself, however, emanate from religion and sociality together. For the reason why in some matters man cannot dispose himself at his own absolute discretion, is partly that he may be fit to worship the divinity, and partly that he may be an agreeable and useful member of human society.[81]

The language of the political mystique is more or less overlooked because the mystical is contrived as nebulous, flexible, a hold-all term used to encompass a multitude of dispositions. And yet it weaves itself back in, not by its own name but in its presence, when tradition is being defended. But any defense of tradition which relies on a defensive conservatism is doomed from the start. In such forms of defense, indignation and anger distract us from the silence and mystical incommunicability which prompts the tradition in the first place. We sense the silence in the fact that our answers are ill-prepared, that we are grasping for the light in the dark. We justify our tradition on the *belief* in an enduring moral orderer, but the basis for that belief is the conviction in that belief! We skirt atop the silence fearing it as weakness because we already forfeited its true defense when metaphysical meaning was suppressed. The silence is not weakness; it instead reveals the infirmity of such a conservatism.

II. The conservative adheres to custom, convention, and continuity

This is the principle of social continuity, by which is not primarily meant the delicate care for traditional social institutions as expressions of human nature's transcending activities in the world and called for by the very rational structure of his embodied presence to the world *via* those activities. This would require a connatural contact with divine agency which opens societies into their locality and concretizes the spiritual into every day act. No, what is meant here is that conservatives prefer the devil they know to the devil they don't. Fear guides this principle, perhaps an often enough reasonable fear of losing what has been so laboriously

81. Pufendorf, *On the Duty of Man*, 37–38.

created—but it is fear none the less. And what lurks beneath that fear is something of which *to be* fearful. If nature is our guiding principle, it is not only a prelapsarian one ordered by growth towards perfection, but also a fallen form of change ordered to death.[82] Because the first cause of the removal of God's grace is man,[83] this change-towards-death infiltrates, outwits, and transforms that originary change-towards-perfection. This nature cannot be managed and manicured for long. Nature satirizes man, as it is satirizing Hippolyte in his protracted dying. It gives him all the gifts endowed to beings with immortality, only to make him mortal— craving what is either the opposite of his nature or its lost truth, but in either case unachievable:

> Yes, nature is ironical! Why, he cried out suddenly, why does she create the very best human beings only to make fools of them later? She takes the only creature recognized on earth as perfect—she does this, and having shown him to mankind she has him say words that have caused so much blood to flow that had it been shed at one time mankind would have drowned in it! Oh, it's good I'm dying! I too might have uttered some dreadful lie, nature would have had it happen![84]

The postlapsarian is of a different nature, and no society can form a utopia on earth, either by reducing all to nature or creating an artificial template against nature. There must be a healthy fear of the cosmogonic: all nature carries without the inclination towards the good, but also the fallen temptation to recast the higher goods in the form of the lower. But because we must start from where we are and not from where we are not, no society in the image and likeness of a divine moral orderer can find either its image or likeness solely in fear. Fear is no principle. This is fear of the political mystique already suppressed by the conservative's woeful concession to convention. The fear is present because the *mythos* may be suppressed but it cannot be annihilated. The fear itself is a critical indicator of its sublated presence, having no other avenue but to align itself with the faith and attempt to take on the faith's non-demonstrability. But,

82. Cf. *ST* I, 109, 2.

83. ST II-II, 112, 3, ad. 2. The human person is the inventor of this disease, of this new form of nothing/nihil. Every shred of indirect causality or causal connection between man and God to implicate God as cause of evil is excluded. Good is diametrically opposed to evil: *"defectus gratiae prima causa est ex nobis."* The first cause of the absence of grace comes from man.

84. Dostoyevsky, *Idiot*, 309.

because conservatism is not faith, it may mimic the non-demonstrability of its principles but it cannot demonstrate, as faith does, the reasonableness of assent. Why? Because faith's reasonableness does not result from a non-sequitur revelatory ipsedixitism, but from the metaphysic of a connatural and transcendent engagement in the world, where man knows himself only in relation to others. When this engagement is suspended in favor of a prescriptive identity, fear—fear of the inability to defend its moral principles, fear of all change as suspect, fear of creativity—seeps in as a substitute for that mystique. Fear reduces morality to psychologism and establishes rather artificial dichotomies between belief *or* disorder, tradition *or* change.

This is the traditionalist dilemma most clearly seen in the Burkean struggle, which demands locality, where liberty cannot be settled upon abstract rule, but which fails to ground that liberty and natural right in anything which can emancipate itself from that abstraction.

> Government is not made in virtue of natural rights, which may and do exist in total independence of it,—and exist in much greater clearness, and in a much greater degree of abstract perfection: but their abstract perfection is their practical defect. By having a right to everything they want everything. Government is a contrivance of human wisdom to provide for human wants. Men have a right that these wants should be provided for by this wisdom. Among these wants is to be reckoned the want, out of civil society, of a sufficient restraint upon their passions. Society requires not only that the passions of individuals should be subjected, but that even in the mass and body, as well as in the individuals, the inclinations of men should frequently be thwarted, their will controlled, and their passions brought into subjection. This can only be done by a power out of themselves, and not, in the exercise of its function, subject to that will and to those passions which it is its office to bridle and subdue. In this sense the restraints on men, as well as their liberties, are to be reckoned among their rights. But as the liberties and the restrictions vary with times and circumstances, and admit of infinite modifications, they cannot be settled upon any abstract rule; and nothing is so foolish as to discuss them upon that principle.[85]

Conservatism is reducibly reactionary, and its prescriptive locality too weak to penetrate the incommunicability of the particular. Its reaction against a pandemic generality reacts, but offers no alternative but

---

85. Burke, *Reflections*, 60.

nostalgia or hostility. True conservatism, on the other hand, seeks the absolute and the universal, not as Icarus gazing at what will blind and destroy, not by constructing the absolute and then seeking it, but by connaturally inflaming the common good through the shared incommunicability of each person. Only an investment within the local and the personal can unveil the universal as it is, as utterly local and supremely personal. All metaphysics is local, as all politics is local: we can only start on the *way of Being* from where we are, and not from where we are not. This good is thus uncommon, not because it is an impossible idea, but because its wholly within-the-world presence is often overlooked in favor of an impossible idea, whether it be an ideal, value, universal, or goal. When favored as if it can achieve the unified movement of reality, as if its barren, Leviathan-like barrage of ideals can invoke the common good, then progressivism for the sake of movement itself takes over. Progressivism's so-called running towards futurity and progress is more anteriorly a running away from the lack of substance and reality in an ethics emptied of its cosmogonic and creative subordination.

Mysticism, for Eric Voegelin,[86] historically counters the forces of political ideology and its artificially imposed dogmatisms.[87] As such, a genuine mysticism would confront this principle of continuity precisely because custom and convention coinhere only with themselves *as custom*, with an oblique reference to a divine moral order as origin of the conviction of such belief as foundational. The conservative's outlet for a mysticism in convention and custom is a gnostic representation of it, and thus a suppression of mystical meaning as the only appropriate propaedeutic to a *polis* which keeps its originary subordinated ethics. In this reactive conservatism, custom and convention cannot be signifiers of an ethics subordinated only to human-in-divine courtship because, by being reducible to a theological postulate, they place that custom and convention as the prime identity of tradition, rather than its natural effects. Those who seek to inhabit the tradition in this reductive view become disposed to it, rather than encounter the mystique of a *polis* in its open locality. They do not come to it by witnessing it in the genuine sense of "witness"—as testifiers to its beauty and intelligibility by it being one with their bodily soul. Should they dismiss the tradition in favor of a progressive alternative, it is often argued by them that such customs

86. Voegelin, *Autobiographical Reflections*, 113.
87. Cf. Boczek, "Mysticism and Social Justice."

are merely rote ritual which have no meaning outside their own internal action. If conservativism places these conditional conclusions in the role of originary principles, these conclusions, now stripped of their proper entelechy, have no reference point but themselves. Ritual can only be understood as the recasting and recovery of the world as sacred because it constructs the sacral place where meaning can be revealed; where divine playthings reproduce divine work.[88] But if ritual is confined to a world already sequestered from the divine—by way of identifying ethical meaning with prescription, by reducing the moral order to a conviction—then ritual is no longer the earthly font, and has not the incarnational tools needed to create sacred space.

    III. Conservatives believe in what may be called the principle of prescription.

We have addressed this issue throughout as the prime misstep in ethical action. We will focus here on how the dominant language of prescription confuses the artificial state of the *polis* with the artificial and unnatural. These self-enclosed principles have set up a contradictory dichotomy. In one sense, the moral life is supposed to be the natural inclination of the human person. Yet, because this principle does not seek a foundation other than itself, we see how detrimental this prescriptive identification actually is. At first glance, we are presented with the naturalness of a divine moral orderer, but then the maintenance of this tradition requires something unnatural, counter-natural, restrictive and prohibitive. On the

---

88. Cf. Eliade, *Sacred and the Profane*, 29: "In reality the ritual by which he constructs a sacred space is efficacious in the measure in which it reproduces the work of the gods . . . for the religious man every world is a sacred world." There may be a sense in which knowledge is consensus/convention even within the Platonic noetic *polis*. There is no room for the isolated individual, i.e., outside the consensus in denial of the nomos. We not only "agree" on the meanings (*nomoi*)—more, we agree to abide by and conform to the *nomoi*. This may give the appearance of *doxa*, and in a high sense it is. That is, it is *doxa* not as "mere opinion" but *doxa* as reasonable consensus. This is different from "true belief" just as it differs from *noesis*. But it acts as a fundamental knowledge of the order of political things, which is to say of the human essence. The *physis* of *nomos* is the understanding that the nature of man is to create convention/consensus (meaning unlike Hobbes et al.'s state of nature philosophers, man is not reducible to convention/consensus). The philosopher sees this, but sees something more. It is that something more which renders him blind. He sees not too little but too much—and in the country of the blind the one-eyed man is king. Is this the tension between Socrates and Plato? And the tension between the King and the Philosopher? Is this the beginning of philosophical ethos/ethics?

one end, we have a community of souls, and then, on the other, an artificial convention becomes the homeless home for that community. There is nothing metaphysically unnatural about society, and it is not reducible to artificial convention, except insofar as convention is itself reducible to the natural creative expression of human nature. There is nothing more natural than tradition and social institutions. In their genuine instantiation as an intensive relationality, they are the illumination of human and divine meaning. They are neither something *made* on the analogy of transitive action, nor are they imposed as necessary consequences (i.e., social utilities) of a theological postulate. If man by nature really prefers the devil he knows to the one he doesn't, what can this mean but that man sees himself and the world as natural antagonists, even enemies to be separated by the artificial limitations and strictures of social rules and empty transcendent moral postulates. These lifeless prescriptive postulates pervert the relationship between the anticipatory futurity of the intellect and the non-futural immediacy of the will.

In point of fact, the Western tradition defines itself by holding that man and world are neither natural antagonists, nor in a deadly game of sublated authority. Indeed, there could have been no tradition otherwise. Man and world are made for each other; lose the one, destroy the other. We are by nature—not condition—rational animals, and reason as relational is communal and, as communal, is political. To call us rational makes little sense without it being understood within the body politic. And what does reason *reason* about? It reasons about its ordination, its human-and-divine entanglement rendering the true politic a mystical courtship. "The consciousness of being caused by the Divine ground and being in search of the Divine ground—that is reason."[89] Social and traditional institutions are not mere safeguards, devils we know; they are the outlets for, and expressions of, our transcendent presence in and to the world which is coextensive with our very nature. At tradition's heart is human freedom and liberty, not a priggish caution or niggling fear.

The principle of prescription defends immemorial usage, but from the basis of fear rather than wisdom. There do "exist rights of which the chief sanction is their antiquity."[90] The principle of immemorial usage is the great and characteristically Roman contribution to the concept of political authority, and marks Rome's only radical departure from

89. Sandoz, *Give Me Liberty*, 85.
90. Kirk, "Idea of Conservatism," in *Essential Russell Kirk*, 8.

Greek thought. It is a practical principle worthy of deep reflection. It is worthy also of genuine respect so long as we understand it in a non-modern sense—which is not possible if these conditional conclusions are being confused as foundational principles. This confusion renders immemorial usage inimical to philosophical reason, when it should be a reflection of the pre-reflexive mystical locality which prepares the soul for the ethical life. Forced into the position of a principle rather than an effect, immemorial usage functions in a defensive conservatism covertly to undermine, indeed deny, the distinction between speculative and practical reason. Immemorial usage is a fit *object* of knowledge in its speculative capacity, but it can hardly act as the principle by which it is itself, as a *praxis*, known and justified. To raise it to the *level of thought* is either to confuse or to ignore the distinction between the what-is-done-*as-done* and the what-is-done-as-*what*-is-done. When ethics moves from its primary political mystique to the secondary ethics of prescription, this is, to some degree, a natural shift—natural only if the secondary remains in filiation to that originary *praxis*:

> Since our natural world is also and necessarily connected in the closest way to the divine world . . . and since there is not and cannot be any impassible gulf between them, individual rays and glimmerings of the divine world must penetrate into our actual world, constituting all the ideal content, the beauty and truth, which we find in it. And man, who belongs to both worlds, can and must touch the divine world by an act of mental contemplation. And though living in the world of conflict and muffled disquiet, he enters into relations with the clear images from the kingdom of glory and eternal beauty.[91]

Morals are prescriptive, for otherwise they wouldn't be morals. Those who conceive morality as identical with morals—from the pragmatist to the positivist to the Protagorean relativist—would agree on the necessity of the prescription. The interesting and important thing to know is what it is about the prescriptive character of morals that makes them binding. And this cannot be immemorial usage, not because such use is invalid, but because its status as the object of rules, rules it out as a possible answer. To think otherwise is a simple category mistake. The enduring moral order constitutes continuity, and continuity evokes a moral order. Together, their constitution contains no reference beyond themselves. In a similar

91. Solovyov, *Divine Sophia*, 178.

manner, prescription is legitimized through immemorial usage, and immemorial usage justifies itself in the form of its own continuity. This continuity refers back to the enduring moral order which, as a principle based on *belief* and *conviction*, reduces prescription to a theological postulate originated by the ego. What *need* is there of that postulate if continuity and prescription are sufficient to restrain man and keep the devil at bay? Remember that the theological postulate is only justified in terms of need, not rational truth, and that once such a need is withdrawn it must collapse from the weight of its own non-necessity. This is the house made of straw, a house attempting to invite divine meaning within it after having exiled it from its foundations. Continuity and prescription justify each other. This going in circles is self-perpetuating, it seems, and thus constitutes whatever movement history and tradition may possess. And this tautologous self-perpetuation is, again, a mirror image of the current deconstructionism: within a linguistic enclosure meaning can abide by the absolute, but that absolute ceases to be once one tires of the language game. A conservatism of consequences masquerading as principles has trapped itself in such a game, unaware of its own trappings.

IV. Conservatives are guided by their principle of prudence.

The principle of prudence has little to do with the classic-medieval vir-tue of *prudentia* as the practical counterpart to the intellect's cognitive presence in the world. Rather is it a means of calculation, regulating and preserving the prior dual principle of prescriptive continuity as it devel-ops through history. Prudence here merely fine tunes the *nunc stans*, the *status quo* as a way of conserving the moral-political authority. Again, this is less a principle of/for thought than it is a warrant for inaction and a justification or not thinking. It enables us morally to prefer the devil we know to the devil we don't. It has perhaps a place within a conservative order to the extent that it is productive of social habits and dispositions, but it cannot be a part of that order *as a principle thereof.* Neither specu-lative nor properly practical but a sort of temperamental caution, this prudence permits, even encourages, us to yield to our yearning for safety. In this nature which guides and overthrows, which is inviting and exiling, prudence cannot merely be a safety net, for this is to render meaning static, and tradition the uncreative maintenance of the *status quo.* True prudence can at times be martyrological, imprudent, relentless, for it only subordinates itself to God, and God was, for a time, exiled from this world, dying, nailed to a tree:

> Everyone speaks to us of prudence, Lord, but of a prudence that is not yours, that we search for in vain in your Gospel. Jesus Christ, we give you thanks because You did not stay silent so as to avoid the cross, because You lashed out at the powerful, knowing that You were gambling with Your life . . . You do not want a prudence that leads to omission and that makes imprisonment impossible for us. The terrible prudence of stilling the shouts of the hungry and the oppressed . . . It is not prudent to 'sell all that you have and give it to the poor.' It is imprudent to give one's life for one's God and for one's brothers and sisters.[92]

Prudence is the very tremble of the soul as it balances its being within nature as purgative, perfective, and in its sheer cosmogonic indifference. It is a holy form of fear which motivates the inclination to recover our pre-reflexive union with the divine, to find it reflexively, not as an object to be achieved, reducible to consciousness, but to transform consciousness into the beautiful as Other.

> The mountains from their heights reveal to us two truths. They suddenly make us feel our insignificance, and at the same time they free the immortal Mind, and let it feel its greatness, and they release it from the earth.[93]

Prudence is that trembled presence in the world which knows when to hold and when to fold, when to act, and when to wait for the timeliness needed to act. It is this balance because it is so aware of the connatural divinity within the world, and denies neither the non-futural saturated presence of the will nor the anticipatory futurity of the intellect, knowing that the relationship between the two is the essence of each. When prudence is reduced to a temperamental caution grounded in the closed loop of consequences masquerading as principles, the fear which once stoked our *deiformitas* is muted and dulled. This is the false prudence of a moral orderer justified by continuity, and continuity cycled back as the evidence of the moral orderer. The maintenance of that continuity is then justified by prescription, and prescription is said to originate in the moral order again justified only by the presence of continuity. In this

92. Camps, *Oraciones a Quemarropa*, 17.

93. Belloc, *Path to Rome*, 230.

tautology, prudence is nothing more than hesitation. It is the golden mean of mediocrity.

V. Conservatives pay attention to the principle of variety.

From the prescriptive continuity sustained through prudence, this new principle of variety feels "affection for the proliferating intricacy of long established social institutions and modes of life,"[94] and holds that "there must exist orders and classes, differences in material conditions, and many sorts of inequality."[95] If we wonder why this is so, the answer should be clear to us by now: "if natural and institutional differences among people are destroyed, presently some tyrant or host of squalid oligarchs will create new forms of inequality."[96] We are back home again preferring the old devil we know.

The variety implicit in this inequality is nothing more than a necessary form of human finitude and imperfection. It neither encompasses nor expresses any fullness, let alone abundance, at the heart of the human creature. It is a strict function of an existential vacuity, and it issues in a moral hopelessness commensurate with social inequality. This variety, no longer a manifestation of finitude open to transcendence, but barred from it for fear of unbalancing the *status quo*, promotes a plurality of dullness. Having neither the concentrated vitality of true atheism nor the agonic defense of the divine, this variety is a spiritual malaise, an existential listlessness, which considers the activity of our finitude to be nothing other than the increasing fragmentation of meaning.[97]

The non-ideological conception of human finitude is something very different, resting on the essential and thus positive equality between

94. Kirk, "Idea of Conservatism," 8.

95. Kirk, "Idea of Conservatism," 8.

96. Kirk, "Idea of Conservatism," 9.

97. In an apt aside, Voegelin reflected on this variety of diminishing returns; see Voegelin, "Deformations of Faith." "It is a dullness which you frequently meet in our college environment. Anytime, you can find not only a student but also a faculty member who will simply tell you: 'I do not have any experiences of a divine reality, period.' And because he doesn't have them, or believes he doesn't have them, of course he has them, but in a different manner, but the assertion that he doesn't have them is to be considered an argument instead of assuming what it implies, that he is a somewhat dull, defective personality. And that is frequently in college environments. I'm speaking of course chiefly from a knowledge of social science departments; it may be different in theology or other departments, but it seems to be almost the majority of the faculty today."

man and himself, between man and man, between man and world. It issues in the social friendship coextensive with the nature of polity itself. Friendship and polity are impossible without equality; equality is the secret heart of friendship and thus polity. This primordial form of friendship explodes the rather miserly confines of an equality only before courts and after death. It is an equality not enforced by a prescriptive template, but the power of our shared incommunicability. We are each heir to the world because our being is in a non-mediated contact with the divine which distinguishes each of us, and which requires a reflection upon it which can never, of its own powers, catch up to that pre-reflexive contact. Our finitude is the recognition of the difference between our incommunicable immediacy and our reflexive difference. It is a finitude originating in immanence and understood only in transcendence. This finitude does not obscure mystical meaning but is its prerequisite. Thus, if a community requires equality, and if that equality is based on the meaning and nature of our finitude, then the *polis* can only be one which is mystical in ordination. Without it, it strains at an equality based either on a homogenizing socialism or which, with a reactionary conservatism, accepts inequality as variety, and finitude merely as limit, and not as gain.

The principle of a non-ideological conservatism is not a variety of unequals, i.e., class structure, but a diversity of equals. Human political society requires meaningful equality on this side as well as on the far side of eternity.

VI. Conservatives are chastened by their principle of imperfectibility.

The efficacy of these principles, estranged from any metaphysical givenness, find their plausibility and efficacy derived from a mixture of Scottish Calvinism and Stoic resignation. Human nature is always in the midst of its own imperfection—the whole of nature is ceaselessly groaning with the pangs of childbirth[98]—but is it actually characterized by imperfectibility? There is a dramatic chasm separating the painful awareness of our imperfection, and of a social order resolved to its irremediable imperfectibility. For the former, the sensation of our imperfection is intrinsically tied to our active *deiformitas*, as our potential for perfection. The latter instead remains static, seeing all yearning for perfection as not only inauthentic but as impossible and thus unworthy of effort. The sixth principle's linguistic confines betray an indebtedness to the modern view of

98. Rom 8:22.

man: Human nature suffers "irremediably from certain faults [and] man being imperfect, no perfect social order ever can be created."[99] In the most startling of ironies, this concessionary principle promotes a Hobbesian view of man in the name of combating the repercussions of that same leviathan state![100] This difference between imperfection understood only with real reference to perfection, and a concession to our imperfectibility divorced from any reference to perfection, has serious consequences.

In the Platonic language game,[101] our recognition of time requires that we are in contact with what rises above time, that our ability to encounter time as we move along its tide, means that, in a way, we are not swept along as other creatures are. The language of the temporal unveils our union with the eternal. In like manner, the recognition of our imperfection can only be grasped *because* we must already have some incomplete knowledge of perfection, but a knowledge nevertheless. How can we be aware of our imperfection if we had no metaphysical bearing within perfection? One only knows he is lost because the path he is on reveals that it is not the right way, and it does so because the soul in its nature is ordered to the Good. This concession to our imperfectibility is no peripheral concession, but one which strikes at the essence of human nature as understood within the divine mysticism of Being. This sixth principle destroys the load-bearing wall supporting the house. Having denied perfection in advance, what then is this imperfectibility? Without perfection both in the non-mediated contact with the will, and as a north star for the intellect, how can we define this imperfectibility? How can we say that the conservative's structure for managing this imperfectibility is more just or noble or intelligible than the radical liberal's? What has been surrendered in this concession is the degrees of being, without which meaning is utterly relativized. The intelligibility of Saint Thomas's *fourth way* has been wholly ignored.[102]

The difference between imperfections as degrees of perfection, and a thoughtless acceptance of imperfectibility, is that the former can still

99. Kirk, "Idea of Conservatism," 9.

100. Cf. de Jouvenel, *Power*, 55: "Hobbes seems to me to have given Leviathan only a shadowy existence, which was but the reflex of the only real life—that of the men composing him. What is certain, however, is that metaphor is always a dangerous servant; on its first appearance it aims but to give a modest illustration to an argument, but in the end it is the master and dominates it."

101. Cf. Peterson, "Language Game in Plato's *Parmenides*," 19-51.

102. Cf. ST I, 2, 3 *resp.*

be understood *as imperfections*. Within these degrees, we can recognize that no society on this side of eternity can be perfect, as no human happiness can truly fulfill our hunger for the divine.[103] In stark opposition, this conservative concession has lost its metaphysical basis on which to claim one finite and imperfect imitation of the good is more or less perfect than another. Its argument for accepting this imperfectibility, stripped of its filiation to the divine, is that believing in perfection issues pride in man, unleashes the ideological tyrants who usurp the distinction of perfection as their own. Moreover, it overlooks the reality that our inability to arrive at perfection in this world does not mean that we are not in a relationship with that perfection. Our willing union intelligibilizes our imperfection as a participant in the Good, thus rendering to imperfection not only a negative sense but also a positive one. The conservative carries only its negative view, and thus its basis for the upholding of tradition is circumscribed by an anti-rational fear. This is, again, the same concession to the postmodern linguistic enclosure where, within the game, I may have my absolute and play by its rules, but because this bubble survives only in reference to the conviction or belief in the absolute, once I step outside the game I return to the panoply of relative meanings with no reference to the divine.

> *VII. Conservatives are persuaded that freedom and property are closely linked.*

Kirk's principle is not wrong, but has it been given the foundational bearing needed to intelligibilize its meaning? When dealing with the question of finitude and equality, we must allow finitude's pre-conceptual reality to influence continually any conceptive understanding of it. Only then can such a finitude, naturally inclined to the mystical, reveal an equality not of generality and manufactured agreement. The conservative has found himself trapped in a vicious either/or: by rejecting socialism, he rejects the neutral and neutered form of imposed unity, but without the proper metaphysical underpinnings his alternative defense of variety becomes one of promoting inequality. It is thus either equality at the cost of the personal or inequality at the cost of the collective. But because the personal is understood only in the locus of the collective, when personhood is lost so is the genuine collective, and vice versa. In this principle, freedom to act out one's unique finitude requires the ability to possess

103. Cf. SCG III 26-41.

property, a space wherein the person is granted equal right to govern the locus of his endeavors, as well as to provide a *thisness* through which the dialogue of his own personhood unfolds. This principle is rightly attempting to address how equality as it pertains to human finitude is not one of a masked homogeneity, but one which corresponds to the unique intimacy of each person. Property is not ego-driven but is a mineness, a manifestation of the centrality of the soul to be the sole heir of the world "only because men are in it who are every one sole heirs as well as you."[104] Property cannot distinguish itself from a lifeless socialism by being an increasing manifestation of inequality. What it is in its primacy is the intimate accord of the soul in its locality. The soul made in the image and likeness of the divine is creative, and must make the world. This is not a world against nature or reducible to it as if man is merely a spectator, but of the creating of nature in its en-souled capacity. Property is utterly connected to freedom only insofar as property retains its mystico-metaphysical origin. It is the place of play in its profoundest sense; it is where the soul, in play, uncovers its own centrality. Each human person is not a cog in the wheel but the sole inheritor of the earth by being the other as other. Property in this respect reveals true equality, for in mineness I am the sole inheritor of the earth as the other is the sole inheritor. Since each of us is the other, we inherit ourselves only in the other. Property as the cosmogonic articulation of the ritual of sacred space.[105]

This places property deeper than possession, for property is the sacred space where actions and meanings begin in the numinous rather than strain to find the sacred in the relativity of the profane. Our courtship and communion with the other, with the sharers of the universe, begins not in the degrading slavery of homogeneity but in the uniqueness of a creational *locus*. For the conservative, the divine can exist in name only; its Presence was exiled the moment its evidence became consensus and conviction. Because of this, the defense of property is confined to protection of those convictions rather than the expression of the soul's own inheritance of the universe. The conservative rightly shuns any domineering form of profane secularity, but inappropriately uses

104. Traherne, *Centuries of Meditations*, 20.

105. Cf. Eliade, *Sacred and the Profane*, 22: "If the world is to be lived in, it must be *founded*—and no world can come to birth in the chaos of the homogeneity and relativity of profane space. The discovery or projection of a fixed point—the center—is equivalent to the creation of the world; and . . . will unmistakably show the cosmogonic value of the ritual orientation and construction of sacred space."

property as its defense to the exclusion of its deeper meaning within the mystical underpinnings of the *polis*. By identifying property solely as a bulwark against unwelcome intruders—for the conception of property is a reflection of the larger *polis*—traditionalist conservatism appears rigid and static, suspicious of change and unable to distinguish the advent of a progressivist ideology from the creative endurance which grows souls in communal meaning.

> To remedy these wrongs the socialists, working on the poor man's envy of the rich, are striving to do away with private property, and contend that individual possessions should become the common property of all, to be administered by the state or municipal bodies. They hold that by thus transferring from private individuals to the community, the present mischievous state of things will be set to rights, in as much as each citizen will then get his fair share of whatever there is to enjoy.[106]

VIII. Conservatives uphold voluntary community, quite as they oppose involuntary collectivism.

> A new shipment had arrived. I had been assigned to ramp duty, and it was my job to guard the luggage. The Jews had already been taken away. The ground in front of me was littered with junk, left-over belongings. Suddenly I heard a baby crying. The child was lying on the ramp, wrapped in rags. A mother had left it behind, perhaps because she knew that women with infants were sent to the gas chambers immediately. I saw another SS soldier grab the baby by the legs. The crying had bothered him. He smashed the baby's head against the iron side of a truck until it was silent.[107]

106. Leo XIII, *Rerum Novarum*, §4.

107. SS soldier Oskar Groning, in an interview with the German magazine *Der Spiegel*. Bazyler, *Holocaust*, 151. The descent into hell is both gradual and sudden. For a very long time it may be easier to take a life miles away with some form of technological apparatus—abortion—separating one from the act than to extinguish life with bare hands, to feel the other writhing for survival even to the last pallid spasmodic twitch of existence. How then does the soul get to such a point that a child can be bashed against a military truck until it is silent? Do such acts cause sleepless nights? Perhaps. Or perhaps we are underestimating the constant dance the soul must make in order to retain its filiation to the good. For Ivan Karamazov, they sleep all too soundly. For him it makes God unworthy of our belief. And that may be true.

A *polis* which incarnates a god unworthy of belief is itself unworthy of participation. The sacred spaces discoverable in locality, property and the *polis*, are drafted in the image and likeness of the divine. They set out the rules of engagement, how relationality must proceed to the betterment of the person and the collective. By doing so, their architectonics create an intensified hierarchy which hums and throbs with divine yearning. When democracies degenerate into abortion on demand, and genocide as the emerging *status quo*, we must examine carefully the blueprint of that *polis*. It is not simply a vicious dictator who destroys a democracy; something within that reality has instead festered for too long and is impatient in its corruptive force.[108] Progressivist liberalism is not the alternative to fascist socialism but its precursor.[109]

> In contemplation, the most important manifestation of the conflict between second and first reality is the construction of a system. Since reality has not the character of a system, a system is always false; and if it claims to portray reality, it can only be maintained with the trickery of an intellectual swindle. It is found wherever there is a system. Since this intellectual swindle is inherent in the conflict between second and first reality and in system construction, the will to swindle naturally originates here.[110]

The balance between an atavistic individualism and an overreaching central authority more isolating than the minotaur's labyrinth is never a splitting of the difference. In the fifth principle of variety, we saw how a problematic defense of inequality, employed to combat the dictatorship by collectivism, creates its own problems. If, as political actors, we are not participants in our metaphysical equality, as each sharer in a

---

108. Eliot, *Christianity and Culture*, 12: "By destroying traditional social habits of the people, by dissolving their natural collective consciousness into individual constituents, by licensing the opinions of the most foolish, by substituting instruction for education, by encouraging cleverness rather than wisdom, the upstart rather than the qualified, by fostering a notion of getting on to which the alternative is a hopeless apathy, Liberalism can prepare the way for that which is its own negative: the artificial, mechanized or brutalised control which is a desperate remedy for its chaos."

109. Less the norm than the exception, the modern secular state is no mere balancer of constituencies and interest blocks, the neutral umpire of competing interests. See Gottfried, *After Liberalism*, xi. "[Rather, the ideological direction of our time is] determined by the regime itself, both by its interests in destroying the remnants of an earlier civil society resistant to its power and by an evolving project of social reconstruction."

110. Voegelin, *Hitler and the Germans*, 108–9.

mystic incommunicability, then that inequality of classes, social and material conditions, is pressed into defending the personal against a bullish involuntary collectivism. But these differences in social class, material wealth, because based on an inequality and a systematization of personality, have not the unitive force to defend the personal. Instead, they antagonize—as socialism surely attests—much of the backbone of the social strata. The inequality which individualizes man, but does not give him personhood, is a poor defense against the tendency to a Marxist state. This inequality functions more on a solipsistic identification than on any form of relationality. If there is relationality, it is based on utility which only places the ego as driving force, and one ill-equipped even to desire or take-on the transforming union of becoming the other-as-other in knowledge. This eighth principle is a true statement of the conservative's preference, but it cannot defend this preference without discovering our true form of equality in the *mystical intensity of being-in-the-world*. Our true equality always eludes those who are confined to an artificial moral template, whether they be liberal socialist or reactionary conservative. The socialist reduces equality to utility just as the conservative does, but in different ways. The former demands a *carte blanche* homogeneity to overwhelm any social inequalities, only to produce the most horrendous form of inequality—a finitude fleeing transcendence. The latter's defense of property, tradition and locality as originating in inequality, serve as their protection against the progressivist uniformity. The conservative attempts to defend the social utilities which result in inequalities (i.e., social, moral, spiritual and financial) in order to secure its own boundaries, from the property lines to the city line. Neither is truly at odds with the other; lift the sheets and find the beast with two backs, each massaging the other into existence.

> Existence has been emptied of cognitive and communal con-
> tent, the most delicate areas of the personal and social life are
> given over to ideas, and exist only at the pleasure of the ascen-
> dant theory of human behavior. But these ideas, even the politi-
> cally conservative ones, assume the ideological style. No matter
> how contradictory they appear in the arena of public debate,
> they share the ideological pose, which is indeed an artifice.
> All perpetuate the rationalist impulse for the vain and rootless
> abstraction. The mind as the self-constituted Absolute forges a

path into the secret essence of its own manifestation, the world follows in tow as its creation.[111]

IX. The conservative perceives the need for prudent restraints upon power and upon human passions.

> What does "the fool" mean, you have to clarify. In Psalms 13, the 'nabal' (that is the word translated as 'fool') signifies the mass phenomenon of men who do evil rather than good because 'they do not seek after God and his justice, who eat my people as they eat bread' because they do not believe in divine sanction for acts of unrighteousness. The personal contempt for God will manifest itself in ruthless conduct toward the weaker man and create general disorder in society. That is the implications of the nabal.[112]

This principle and the final one are very much subsidiary to the prior principles. It is the language of checks and balances, and a reflection of the delicate dance the political soul must continually perform in the cultivation of the personal from the collective and the collective from the personal. But this reflection will only offer us a pale glimpse into that dance. Because this principle is yet another conditional conclusion, the foundation for the personal, the collective, the enduring moral order and its continuity hinge upon an ever-relativizing conviction which has already accepted that it is better to accept our mediocre imperfectibility than to recover how imperfection always points to perfection, even in its failing. In doing so, it promotes an ethics which is pressed into a leading position as if identical with wisdom, rather than being a true ethics in-failing—revealing the way of Being as the way of the Good, a way which transforms the soul. For the most part, the language of prudence is isolated along its negative axis as restraint, prohibition and stricture, rather than as a creative and loving activity which knows *when* and *how* to act. This focus on the prohibitive is a direct consequence of a *polis* built on an undiagnosed fear, surviving only because it maintains itself as an artificial template. The arguments between the libertarian and traditionalist conservative over the extent of reasonable checks and balances on individual action and government power is just such an example. They are not dealing with prudence in any creative or

111. F. Gilson and Simcox, "Whittaker Chambers Pro Mundum," 18.

112. See Voegelin's "Quod Deus Dicitur" in *Published Essays, 1966–1985*, 386; "Beginning and the Beyond," 173–232.

properly positive sense, but see it as an argument over which forms of restraint best curb deleterious acts and promote a more just society. In such thinking, the end is noble but the means are not fully conformed to that end, and thus could never lead the soul to it. If prudence is firstly restraint and prohibition it is an extrinsicized virtue and thus no virtue at all. If restraint is properly to arise from the soul and from the collective, it must arise innermost in their being as the natural response to a particular action. And while prudence, in a fallen world, cannot always inhabit a soul in its positive sense, when we limit its identification only to its nullity, we destroy its essential meaning in favor of one of its accidental conditions. Saint Thomas speaks of prudence both as a virtue belonging to the universal principles of reason and to the singulars who invoke those principles:

> As stated above (Article 1, Reply to Objection 3), to prudence belongs not only the consideration of the reason, but also the application to action, which is the end of the practical reason. But no man can conveniently apply one thing to another, unless he knows both the thing to be applied, and the thing to which it has to be applied. Now actions are in singular matters: and so it is necessary for the prudent man to know both the universal principles of reason, and the singulars about which actions are concerned.[113]

The dance of checks and balances is one where the universal is discoverable in the particular and the particular basks in the radiance of the universal. This is the creative understanding of prudence, and it requires a metaphysical foundation for its meaning. Stripped of its mystico-metaphysical union, we are left with only its vestigial meaning as restraint. This is the restraint which separates imperfection from perfection. This extrinsicized prudence does not combat hell on earth but, like the Maginot line, it is its comically tragic entry point.

X. *The thinking conservative understands that permanence and change must be recognized and reconciled in a vigorous society*

> Man has a body as well as a soul, and the whole of man, soul and body, is nourished sanely by a multiplicity of observed traditional things. Moreover, there is this great quality in the unchanging practice of Holy Seasons, that it makes explicable, tolerable, and

---

113. *ST* II-II, 47, 3, *resp.*

normal what is otherwise a shocking and intolerable and even in the fullest sense, abnormal thing. I mean, the mortality of immortal men. Not only death (which shakes and rends all that is human in us, creating a monstrous separation and threatening the soul with isolation which destroys), not only death, but that accompaniment of mortality which is a perpetual series of lesser deaths and is called change, are challenged, chained, and put in their place by unaltered and successive acts of seasonable regard for loss and dereliction and mutability. The threats of despair, remorse, necessary expiation, weariness almost beyond bearing, dull repetition of things apparently fruitless, unnecessary and without meaning, estrangement, the misunderstanding of mind by mind, forgetfulness which is a false alarm, grief, and repentance, which are true ones, but of a sad company, young men perished in battle before their parents had lost vigour in age, the perils of sickness in the body and even in the mind, anxiety, honour harassed, all the bitterness of living—become part of a large business which may lead to Beatitude. For they are all connected in the memory with holy day after holy day, year by year, binding the generations together; carrying on even in this world, as it were, the life of the dead and giving corporate substance, permanence and stability, without the symbol of which (at least) the vast increasing burden of life might at last conquer us and be no longer borne.[114]

We are now at our final principle, and it is an insight which craves an overthrow of the meanings of change and endurance. These terms, tossed around as givens, are of the ineluctable mystery of Being, so ingrained that even when forgotten their hold is still present in the language of conservation, temperance, and tradition, no matter how nebulous and ill-defined. "The conservative . . . favors reasoned and temperate progress; he is opposed to the cult of Progress, whose votaries believe that everything new necessarily is superior to everything old."[115] This is the bedrock conservative truism concealing the only unity in existence which does not fail, and it aches to be understood in its creative endurance,[116] in Gray's elegy,[117] in the messy business of life. We find it in our breath and,

114. Belloc, "Remaining Christmas," in *Conversation with an Angel*, 296.

115. Kirk, *Politics of Prudence*, 25.

116. Belloc, *Silence of the Sea*, 270–71.

117. Cf. Gray, "Epitaph," *Elegy*, 45:
Here rests his head upon the lap of Earth
A youth to Fortune and to Fame unknown.

when it is stilled, in sight obscured or recovered, it is the cyclical wearing down of the stone and yoke, day after day, under the name of "change," for polity's sake. Even if perfection comes of it, let us not forget, it is not manifestly a change towards perfection. Perfection may come and still all will be lost for us and must be preserved for the other. What is tradition? It is the cosmogonic march to death *moored* to the liturgical, to the holy day, to the ritual act of being, becoming somehow the merciful substance of beatitude. This is the mystical polis which the conservative blindly defends but rarely encounters. And this "mooring" is the true terminological essence hidden beneath the banal ipsedixitism, "temperate progress." This heartrending unity moves in and through us: it is among the crush of leaves underfoot, the bat squeak of sensuality and the whimper instead of the bang.[118] It is a nostalgia so pure, and yet it does not live or act by nostalgia, it is not a sequence of past events. What is being enshrined in tradition? It is the present in all its missed glory, while we seek a foothold in that moving image of eternity. Why this temperate progress,[119] this incarnational mooring? For we cannot live well without living *within* that moving image. In tradition, change moves towards death and beatitude, not as an either/or, but in a startling unity where fate and freedom create one flesh: our own, but only in the unity with the other.

> Mary stood outside at the sepulcher weeping, and as she wept she stooped down and looked into the sepulcher, and saw two

---

Fair Science frown'd not on his humble birth,
And Melancholy mark'd him for her own.

Large was his bounty, and his soul sincere,
Heav'n did a recompense as largely send:
He gave to Mis'ry all he had, a tear,
He gain'd from Heav'n (twas all he wish'd) a friend.

No farther seek his merits to disclose,
Or draw his frailties from their dread abode,
(There they alike in trembling hope repose)
The bosom of his Father and his God.

118. Cf. Eliot, "Hollow Men," 77–82.

119. Temperance may be a poor substitute, a rather lifeless translation for *sophrosyne*, which is more primordial in its ability as an ordering virtue. Peter Geach considered temperance as a "rather a humdrum common sense matter." What the Greeks express in *sophrosyne* is better captured as a "mooring." Cf. North, "Concept of *Sophrosyne*," 1–17. Also see van Tongeren, "Nietzsche's Revaluation of the Cardinal Virtues," 128–49.

angels in white, sitting one at the head and the other at the feet
where the body of Jesus had lain. And they said unto her, 'Woman, why weepest thou?' She said unto them, 'Because they have
taken away my Lord, and I know not where they have laid Him.'
And when she had thus said, she turned around and saw Jesus
standing, and knew not that it was Jesus. Jesus said unto her,
'Woman, why weepest thou? Whom seekest thou?' She, supposing Him to be the gardener, said unto Him, 'Sir, if thou have
borne Him hence, tell me where thou hast laid Him, and I will
take Him away.' Jesus said unto her, 'Mary!' She turned herself
and said unto Him, 'Rabboni!' (which is to say, 'Master'). Jesus
said unto her, Touch Me not, for I am not yet ascended to My
Father; but go to My brethren and say unto them, I ascend unto
My Father and your Father, and to My God and your God."[120]

A tradition is not great because it is traditional; it is traditional because it is great, and it is great because it is true: true to being, to man,
to itself, to God. It is time to stop whistling in the dark and survive the
maelstrom. Tradition is gone, authority is gone, order is gone. The past
is gone. This is not, as some would have it, abstract metaphysical theory:
it is ineluctable historical fact: it is where we start from. All gone are prescriptive objects of belief as transcendental safety pins holding our world
and our status together, safe, dry, and intact. There can be no restoration.
Life is lived in the other direction. We return to our tradition freely now,
not to learn *what* to think but *how* to think, for the proper utility of tradition is not prescriptive but educative. It is a recovery of the mystique in
our pre-reflexive play so that what is reflected upon is more than emptied
speculation.

One is reminded of Bergson's *Two Sources of Morality and Religion.*[121]
Bergson's closed and open moralities are distinct but not opposed. The
prescriptiveness of the closed has its source in the freedom of the open.
It is the distinction between, and relatedness of, the *condition* and the
nature. Nomos requires *arete* as aspiration to the Good. Even within the
nomoi, one must be able to see and to play the game of Being, for that is
true freedom in accordance with human nature in its relation to the divine principles of *nomos.* Prescriptions are not principles but rules which
require principles for their meaning. And thus the conservative "principles" are limited and insufficient in themselves, but not in conjunction

120. John 20:11–17.
121. Bergson, *Two Sources of Morality and Religion.*

with the true principles of human nature in which they attain the efficacy and beauty that Burke and Kirk seek. For condition presupposes nature as finitude presupposes the infinite, as the social signage of life presupposes the sacrament of the eternally present-in-passing moment.

The Sixth Principle Discursus: The Necessity to Place Imperfectibility within the Context of Transcendent Meaning

If we were to pose the question, where is suffering greater, purgatory or hell, any thoughtful answer would place us in the midst of paradoxical meaning. It would also place us at the heart of the difference between imperfection with reference to perfection, and imperfectibility resolved to remain within its own limitations. The conservative's refusal to make a foolish utopia on earth is at risk of creating hell on earth. Utopias and hell amount to the same thing: the belief that the will can rest independent of God. The liberal seeks to construct a progressivist ideality that satisfies all the will's cravings, and thus builds the Shangri-La where the will can rest in its own powers. The conservative responds by building, out of fear, a protective wall around tradition where everything ceases to advance. Under its nose and before its own eyes, conservatism is creating an edifice where it demands that the will rest, accepting its limits. It is not the true opponent of the liberal ideology but an alternative with the same reduction. This sixth principle acknowledges our finitude *as limit*, and abandons the meaning of limit precisely by forgetting that such limits are signposts guiding us in our open nature.

Is it unjust not to receive what one never wanted? Just as the body can go so far in self-neglect or abuse that it can no longer recover, why is it implausible that the soul can do the same? The body needs to want and do the right things. This we understand. But the soul? Why do we assume it need not? That it can survive its own neglect? We think this because we don't take the soul seriously while we take the body seriously. But it does not stand to reason. Does it really make no difference if the soul enters death with its self-inflicted disfigurements; or does it make every difference in the world? Can't the soul, like the body, go so far that it cannot return? We say of the addict or glutton that, sad as it may be, "he has brought this on himself" and it is "too late now for medicine or exercise or surgery—his condition is terminal." Is this less the case for the soul, or even more? If the medicine of confession and forgiveness is refused, isn't the condition of the soul terminal?

Hell is not "punishment" as such; it is self-inflicted separation, and in that sense perfectly just, even if heart breaking. At what point did Hitler or Mao or Stalin go too far? Is hell an "unjust punishment" or the inevitable consequence of their actions, just as cirrhosis might be the result for the alcoholic? Again—to think of hell as unjust punishment is to consider it unjust suffering. Is hell even truly living up to the level of suffering? Of course, the worst punishment of all would be separation from God when man wants God. Indeed, that would be unjust punishment.

Let's ask that strange question: where is suffering worse, hell or purgatory, and of course cases can be made for both. But suffering, what is it? Saint John Paul II remarks in his *Salvifici Doloris*:

> Man suffers on account of evil, which is a certain lack, limitation or distortion of good. We could say that man suffers because of a good in which he does not share, from which in a certain sense he is cut off, or of which he has deprived himself. He particularly suffers when he "ought"—in the normal order of things—to have a share in this good and does not have it.[122]

We suffer because we ought to share in a good from which we have been cut off, either by others or by our own undoing. But suffering here means the possibility of recovery. We suffer because we recognize we ought to be with the good of which we are deprived. That ought implies a want or desire to be reconciled with the good, to be liberated from the lack by and through which suffering comes into being. The issue is that in hell the person has freely decided he does not want God. Now the good of Man is to-be in God. But that good is won and re-discovered freely, as we are free beings. We are free to cover over the good of our nature so much so that it is terminal. If it can be terminal for the lesser, the body, wouldn't it therefore follow that what is contained in the lesser must necessarily be a reality for the soul as the greater and in a far more magnified and acute manner? Radical freedom means that I can freely undo that ought. The removal of grace is on our side, not God's: the first cause of the absence of grace comes from man and angels.[123] That removal of grace, continually perpetuated, can enter a terminal state! In essence, we can remove the

122. John Paul II, *Salvifici Doloris*, §71.

123. ST I-II, 112, 3, ad. 2.

"ought" that makes suffering truly suffering! Let's follow the logic and see how it terminates in a paradoxical reality:

a. If we understand we ought to be with God, this *ought* implies recognition of that lesser state. Ought is a recognition, a desire to be in the better state with God.

b. I am free to be unfree and choose not to desire God, not to want God in my actions. I am free to remove the "ought" which is the very trigger mechanism of suffering.

c. Human suffering functions in the recognition that I ought to be in a better state, God. But hell is the place for those who chose to make God the lesser state, to choose their sins over God. This would be the state of imperfectibility closed off from perfection rather than imperfection yearning for perfection.

d. If the persons in hell never wanted God, then how are they suffering in any way comparable to purgatory where the "ought" is most visceral and accentuated? In purgatory, man feels the sting of his imperfection, he desires God because he is not fully with him yet. The ought is clear: purgation unto reconciliation.

e. The worst and most unjust punishment of all would be separation from God when the person desires God, and God does not allow that reconciliation. This is not the case in hell. The separation is on man's side: he never wanted God. More precisely, he extinguished that desire in favor of imperfectibility devoid of its meaning because severed from its connection to perfection. Thus, how is hell truly punishment if he is getting exactly what he wanted: a place as far removed from God or without God. The punishment in hell is just. The symmetry of free will is intact.

f. Paradoxically, hell would be the worst of all situations, beyond imagining and beyond compare, and no greater punishment. But only the suffering in purgatory would truly vivify the principle of imperfectibility. Such souls would ardently crave contact with the best in their natures as unified in God. Only purgatory, as redemptive in its suffering, would therefore offer the greatest and truest experience of suffering, enabling human persons to be, as Kirk described it, chastened in their imperfectibility.

An imperfectibility forced to be satisfied with its own imperfection not only causes the tradition to suffer but sets up a structure where our suffering can no longer be intelligibilized by the hunger for perfection. It creates the gravest form of suffering, for it is the one which leads to hell rather than to heaven. And what is hell but an endless litany of persons and collectives throughout time attempting to create their own utopias? It is one thing to recognize honestly that no amount of earthly goods can fulfill us; it is quite another to refuse that desire as if it were detrimental. If we refuse properly to order and guide that desire *for perfection* here in the *polis*, how will we be prepared either to desire or to recognize perfection when it is ours to recover, for the first time? The soul will always be restless with ambition, and most of it is to be feared. But in spite of, or in some way *because* of it, we must let our hearts seek more than a mediocre goodness. We must strive for perfection with the ecstasy that it can be won, not as a dispossessed idea but as realm of fire, water, life and love to be lived in; imagining with Kazantzakis, the only ambition which is salvific, the abandonment of the self to divine providence; the total risk and solid ground of humility unto death, Francis at the foot of the Pope's throne, having asked for an imprimatur on his order, his life—his *voce mea ad Dominum*:[124]

> The pope riveted his eyes upon Francis. Francis of Assisi, he said slowly in a grave, exhortatory tone, Francis of Assisi, I discern flames around your face. Are they flames of the inferno or the flames of paradise? I have no confidence in visionaries who seek the impossible: perfect love, perfect chastity, perfect poverty. Why do you wish to surpass human bounds? How dare you presume to attain the heights reached only by Christ, the pinnacle where he now stands alone, unrivaled?[125]

Before further analyzing the intellectual uselessness of this principle, note that it is neither prescribed by nor evidenced within the continuity of the Western tradition from Plato to Aristotle to Augustine to Aquinas to Étienne Gilson, Jacques Maritain, Romano Guardini, Chesterton, Belloc, Balthasar, Dostoyevsky and Solzenitsyn, though it can perhaps be found in Marx.

In what sense can a nature, particularly a created nature, be imperfect? Let alone irremediably imperfect? Quite simply, in no sense

124. Ps 141:2 (Vulgate).
125. Kazantzakis, *God's Pauper*, 178.

whatsoever. God is done no service, as Étienne Gilson was so found of pointing out, when we attempt to glorify his transcendence by denigrating his creation. It is pathetically true that man makes mistakes, is ignorant, chooses evil, sins. But before we allow this real capacity for disorder to dictate our retreat into a social-moral-intellectual Fort Apache, three points are to be made.

If it is true that you can't tell a book by its cover, it is even truer that you can't tell a nature by its condition, even if that condition is, like the book cover, the first thing you see. Take any device, gadget, tool, creature, or even theory you like. Suppose you had never before encountered such a thing. You come across a device, something new to you. Depressing the keys, nothing happens. Of course, this really tells you nothing because you have no idea what *should* happen. Now, you can describe your discovery in the richest, even the most poetic detail. But you will *never know what it is* until and unless you know it in its perfection or essence. What would this broken device tell us? Nothing really. And what does the history of man tell the classifying sociologist? About as much. But *whatever* it tells us, *it cannot act as a principle* either of knowledge, interpretation, or action. The issue at hand is this: the human condition and the human nature are not the same. We cannot infer the latter from the former, but, as Aristotle would have it, we define the lower from and by the higher. There simply is no other way to understand things. Any analysis or description of the human condition is flawed and faulted unless it describes that condition in the light of its true nature, which is its perfection. Only in the modern condition has this capital distinction been lost, and with it philosophy itself. The result is always the same: moralism passing under the guise of wisdom, sequestering the mystique of the *polis* to irrational sentiment.

Secondly, although man often enough chooses evil, it is always and only on the condition that the object of his choice is presented to him, wrongly in fact, as good. Now this is not a moral but a metaphysical principle, and it is coeval with the primordial Western affirmation of the hegemony of Being that began even before Parmenides. Being and goodness are defined in terms of each other (how else could they be defined?) Just as the denial of Being is self-contradictory, so the choice of evil *as* evil is a nihilistic impossibility. Man, said Augustine, can only *approach* nothingness, he can never achieve it.[126] The essence of evil,

---

126. Cf. Augustine, *On Free Choice of the Will*, I.15.31.106–8. See also Maritain, *God and the Permission of Evil*.

said Hannah Arendt, is banality, impotence, emptiness.[127] Man always acts for a perceived good, even if he is wrong about the true nature of that perceived good. So that here, at the very heart of human wickedness, is a principle, not of human depravity or moral exhaustion, but of the goodness and perfection of human nature and of the efficacy of reason. Where is the root of this perfection? That which frightens so many traditionalists is the same which excited ages of classical and Christian philosophers. For the very possibility of human error is the necessary (therefore good!) consequence of the essential characteristic of human freedom. Interpreted by conservatism as anarchic and irrational impulse in need of chastening, it is seen by the Christian tradition as the specific consequence of human rationality, *as the very origin of order itself.* Only in the ideological age has freedom been opposed to reason, as in Gide and Sartre. But this cohabitation of freedom and rationality is perfectly natural. It is in fact that which Aquinas calls man's longer way through time and world distinguishing him both from beast and angel.

Because man can neither live in utopia nor be like an angel does not mean that he is imperfect. It means that his perfection does not reside in those ways of living and being. For the conservative "we are not made for perfect things."[128] Utopia, a perfect thing for man? Wouldn't a truer and deeper conservatism rather say that our perfection is not to be found in utopia, thus utopia would not even be a wistful idea for man. A galaxy of difference separates the two formulations. See again how this conservatism proves morally sterile in the face of socialist utopianism. It really says something like this to the socialist: "your ideal society is just too good for man; perhaps if men were angels they might be worthy of it. But alas man is not made for perfect things." To oppose socialism by such a means is perhaps the most revealing testimony to the total mental collapse of modern thought, a thought which opposes the real to the ideal, and the *mystique* to the *politique.*[129] But a genuine conservatism, tuned into the authentic tradition, does not see in socialism an unattainable ideal. It sees it as unfit, not good enough for the true perfection of man's created nature. Man is called, by his very nature, to something better than utopia. He is called to embody his ideals in the world itself and, finally, he is called to paradise. And heaven is no socialist republic; perhaps hell is.

127. Cf. Arendt, *Eichmann in Jerusalem.*
128. Kirk, "Idea of Conservatism," 9.
129. Cf. Péguy, *Temporal and Eternal.*

GOD SPEAKS: When you love someone, you love him as he is. I alone am perfect. It is probably for that reason that I know what perfection is and that I demand less perfection of those poor people. I know how difficult it is. And how often, when they are struggling in their trials, how often do I wish and am I tempted to put my hand under their stomachs in order to hold them up with my big hand just like a father teaching his son how to swim in the current of the river and who is divided between two ways of thinking. For on the one hand, if he holds him up all the time and if he holds him too much, the child will depend on this and will never learn how to swim. But if he doesn't hold him up just at the right moment that child is bound to swallow more water than is healthy for him . . . Such is the mystery of man's freedom, says God, and the mystery of my government towards him and towards his freedom. If I hold him up too much, he is no longer free and if I don't hold him up sufficiently, I am endangering his salvation. Two goods in a sense almost equally precious. For salvation is of infinite price . . . Because I myself am free, says God, and I have created man in my own image and likeness. Such is the mystery, such the secret, such the price of all freedom. That freedom of that creature is the most beautiful reflection in this world of the Creator's freedom. That is why we are so attached to it, and set a proper price on it.[130]

130. Péguy, "Freedom," in *God Speaks,* 28.

4

The Wear of Winning: God among the Miscellany: Saint Thomas's Five Ways

When suddenly at the midnight hour
an invisible troupe is heard passing
with exquisite music, with shouts—
do not mourn in vain your fortune failing you now,
your works that have failed, the plans of your life
that have all turned out to be illusions.
As if long prepared for this, as if courageous,
bid her farewell, the Alexandria that is leaving.
Above all do not be fooled, do not tell yourself
it was only a dream, that your ears deceived you;
do not stoop to such vain hopes.
As if long prepared for this, as if courageous,
as it becomes you who are worthy of such a city;
approach the window with firm step,
and listen with emotion, but not
with the entreaties and complaints of the coward,
as a last enjoyment listen to the sounds,
the exquisite instruments of the mystical troupe,
and bid her farewell, the Alexandria you are losing.[1]

1. Cavafy, "God Forsakes Antony," in *Complete Poems*, 30. See Kazantzakis's

T HE BOOK HAS BEEN an intended and sustained resistance to the press-
ured moral claims to unity as much as to the ethical deconstructionism
which denies in advance any unity beyond a manufactured one. The latter
has as many and more claims to a totalitarian mindsight than the former,
and its own atavistic relativism is but another form of manufactured unity.[2]
The intramural squabbles between a conservatism disconnected from its
roots and a progressivist liberalism fed by the perpetual consumption of
those roots has taught us just this: both demand a form of unity at all costs,
and while the nostalgic brand is far less offensive than the ideological one,
this *demand* itself cannot be overlooked. Demand—this "lust to rule"[3]—
invalidates in advance the movement of the unity of Being, and places
ethical action in a position diametrically opposed to true subordination,
and because of this it will demand subordination to the idols of its own
image.[4] The unity we seek speaks more to Christ tempted in the desert;
to Nastassya's refusal to accept the shady comforts of the lie only to be

---

memories of Cavafy and of this poem. Cf. Kazantzakis, *Journeying*, 74–79.

2. Cf. Nietzsche, *Will to Power*, §481: "In opposition to Positivism, which halts
at phenomena and says, 'These are only facts and nothing more,' I would say: No,
facts are precisely what is lacking, all that exists consists of interpretations. We cannot
establish any fact 'in itself': it may even be nonsense to desire to do such a thing. 'Everything is subjective,' ye say: but that in itself is interpretation. The subject is nothing
given, but something superimposed by fancy, something introduced behind.—Is it
necessary to set an interpreter behind the interpretation already to hand? Even that
would be fantasy, hypothesis. To the extent to which knowledge has any sense at all,
the world is knowable: but it may be interpreted differently, it has not one sense behind
it, but hundreds of senses.—'Perspectivity.' It is our needs that interpret the world; our
instincts and their impulses for and against. Every instinct is a sort of thirst for power;
each has its point of view, which it would fain impose upon all the other instincts as
their norm.; §635: We are in need of 'unities' in order to be able to reckon: but this is
no reason for supposing that 'unities' actually exist. We borrowed the concept "unity"
from our concept 'ego,'—our very oldest article of faith. If we did not believe ourselves
to be unities we should never have formed the concept 'thing.' Now—that is to say,
somewhat late in the day, we are overwhelmingly convinced that our conception of the
concept 'ego' is no security whatever for a real entity.

3. Nietzsche, *Will to Power*, §681.

4. Cf. See Saint Augustine on human responsibility, sermon 169, in *Augustine Day
by Day*, 253: "Your justification is from God but without your willingness to accept
it, that justification could not exist in you. Justice exists in the universe without you
willing it but it cannot be in you without you willing it. God made you to be a human being. If you were able on your own to make yourself just, you would have made
something better than that which God made. God made you without your consent but
he does not justify without your consent. He made you without your even knowing it;
he justifies you only with your willing consent."

defined by all as "mad"; to Camus's First Man[5]—"[who] goes right back to discover this secret: he is not the first. Every man is the first man and no one is. That is why he throws himself at his mother's feet."[6] There is something far too easily won in the unity achieved by the mind, and while this inclination may well be a natural one, unity itself is often quickened and obfuscated by desires unprepared for the task of unity, for egoisms which first manufacture and then manage it. Perhaps, instead, the task of true unity has been to endure the miscellany, and not only endure it but grow in its shadow and its warmth, always within the ways that truths have a *non sequitur* mystery to them. Each is its own *non sequitur*, eternally at play and utterly its own. Cannot the Five Ways find their meaning in *The Idiot* and through them a moral life which resides as much *contra mundum* as it is *pro mundum*? Why are we unable to endure the divine miscellany without reducing it to a penumbra of disintegrating absolutes? We are not searching for the Renaissance man but the *alter Christus*. We have instead created "men without chests,"[7] but perhaps this was the result of a unity itself forced upon the soul, demanding a conformity to a teleology, doing injustice to God, man and creation. There is a time which precedes the futural and must refuse its siren call, at least for the time being. Here creativity and play lay the sanctifying groundwork for the dark business of creative endurance and the life of beatitude won from suffering, but when reflection peers too dismissively at it, it is disregarded as mere miscellany, as extraneous and accidental in favor of an abstracted deterministic concept. But if God is eternal, would not a miscellaneous invocation of the good not only be as relevant but substantially more so than a teleological one, which finds its intelligibility in the mastery of a temporalizing order? The former is situated, yes, in time but appears almost indifferent to it as if it contains the secret of the heart so pure and true that it needn't anything else than the moment in which it resides. It bathes in the eternal, this aeviternal miscellany of play and *non-sequitur*. Even in the graveyard, it is the radical miscellany that evokes the prayer of the observer.

As we turn our attention to the demonstrations, we would be hard-tasked to deny any teleological meaning to them. Such an action would be yet another attempt to massage a unity against the real. By that same token, it would be too reductively easy to view them within a non-cre-ational teleology, given that the *exitus* and *reditus* structure is invested in

5. Camus, *First Man*.

6. Camus, *Notebooks*, 125.

7. Lewis, *Abolition of Man*, 25–26.

and patterned after an existential eschatology no longer as an end to be perceived but as a personal and incarnational realm to be lived in. The *eschaton* here invokes not only creational but un-created meaning. And because each of the Five Ways is arriving at that Being which must be innermost in all things, and not merely at an Aristotelian prime mover, then this non-derivative primacy, by which goods are utterly good in themselves, takes on a whole new meaning.[8]

Saint Thomas will arrive at unity, one which is not opposed to the existential miscellany but is instead its prime and living cause. Only a God most interior, existence itself, can endure and enjoy the otherness of creation. Each particular good carries with it the open nature of human-and-divine relation, a miscellaneous newness, wherein unity is enshrined and understood. The desire for unity is often urged on by fear, by a need to align with a certain and stable ground as if large parts of existence are dangerously flimsy and will break open at any moment. Existence is not flimsy but neither is it stable, and this moving image of eternity is understood not merely by a species or a genus but must be assimilated by each person—each as heir to the world having retained the child at play—tailored to the incommunicability of the individual soul. "*To Be* is the actuality of all actions, and for this reason it is the perfection of all perfections."[9] Thus, true unity never escapes this radical personalism, and if the demonstrations are to have any lasting merit they are directed towards the person arriving at a unity which is undeniable not because it is prescribed, demanded, managed, or manufactured, but because each diverse thing in existence, every numberless facet of difference, groans with the interiority of the divine Person.

> For blessed are those that never stopped
> standing calmly outside in the rain;
> to them will come all harvests,
> and their ripe fruit will be numerous.
> They will outlast any end

8. Cf. Renard, *Philosophy of God*, 35: "The first and second ways, for example, go far beyond mere Aristotelianism. Aristotle concludes to a first cause which moves only in so far as desired in the order of efficient causality. Indeed, it is not an easy matter to know just what Aristotle understands by efficient cause. Saint Thomas, on the contrary, posits the existence of a first unmoved mover *which by its action here and now* has an influx upon any actual motion."

9. Thomas, *De Pot.* VII, 2, ad. 9. Cf. Wippel, *Metaphysical Thought of Aquinas*, 174–76.

and any kingdom whose meaning is gone;
they will rise like rested hands
when the hands of all other classes
and nations are worn.[10]

The Five Ways begin with two prescient objectors, one capitalizing on the incongruity between an all-good God and an infective destructive evil, the other referencing the primacy of *natural* explanations for the natural order of things. Neither the problem of evil nor the scientific objection is to be overlooked or dismissed; with them Aquinas has offered us the indelible objections which remain within the hearts of the skeptic and the believer. If honest, we shall find that these objections unite the historical and the futural.

Darkness at Noon: The Objectors

> It seems that God does not exist; because if one of two contraries be infinite, the other would be altogether destroyed. But the word 'God' means that He is infinite goodness. If, therefore, God existed, there would be no evil discoverable; but there is evil in the world. Therefore, God does not exist.[11]

The first objector strikes at the devastating problem which Saint Thomas cannot yet fully address without the incorporation of the entirety of the Christian theo-drama. Having begun these demonstrations almost by virtue of a Pascalian wager, Saint Thomas is attempting to show all, but in particular those who do not believe but who accept the principles of the natural world, that through this natural world the evidence of God's existence is beyond any *reasonable* doubt and clearly therefore worth the risk of faith. The Five Ways are as much a sure-bet wager as a set of demonstrations, and while Saint Thomas never leaves God to one side in order to philosophize in isolation, he has undertaken a delicate dance to reveal that the truths of reason are indeed not only compatible with the truths of faith, but even *more* reasonable when leavened by the faith. Reason is compatible with faith because any true unity supports, not by sublation but by magnification, a spiritual assemblage of diverse and particular goods. The demonstrations unfold in such a way that should we peer into the structural experience of *any* particular and minute aspect

10. Rilke, "Poverty and Death," in *Book of Hours*, 199.

11. *ST* I, 2, 3, arg. 1.

of existence and see things as they are, we cannot miss the existence of the divine. The demonstrations are not about act-and-potency. They are *about* the pots and pans and pains and pleasures of the day, which are not to be either ignored or reduced to irrelevant or interchangeable examples of act-and-potency, but the very existentially essential realities to be understood.

There is a tension in this first objector that is only heightened by Saint Thomas's response:

> As Augustine says (Enchiridion xi): Since God is the highest good, He would not allow any evil to exist in His works, unless His omnipotence and goodness were such as to bring good even out of evil. This is part of the infinite goodness of God, that He should allow evil to exist, and out of it produce good.[12]

This response can in no way do justice to the problem of evil. Instead, Saint Thomas intentionally withholds any truly meaningful reflection, apart from opening a small window where there is a potential compatibility between the presence of evil and the infinite goodness of God. This may well be the seemingly weakest response not only in question 2 but in the whole of the *Summa*. But if we are to look at this response not only from the task at hand but also from the metaphysical *exitus* and *reditus* structure of the *Summa Theologica*, a different conclusion arises. As Saint Thomas addressed in the prior article, one can arrive at God by faith alone, by reason or by the confluence of reason and faith, and "there is nothing to prevent a man, who cannot grasp a proof, accepting, as a matter of faith, something which in itself is capable of being scientifically known and demonstrated."[13] These *ways* are a window into the soul of the world, and they are particularly important for those who haven't the faith but have the reasoning desire to know the world *as it is*. It is for the hearts and minds inflamed by the intelligibility of the natural world, for those who would voice independently the second objector's preference to remain with *natural* causes as sufficient explanations for the *natural* world, and are hesitant to dismiss the natural cause which is different for each diverse effect. Even though the truths of reason find their supreme compatibility with the truths of faith, this compatibility is most clearly seen in the process of a finding, a discovery, one that is natural and not compulsory. Why does Saint Thomas's response to such a pervasive difficulty as the problem of evil appear cursory at best? Because

12. *ST* I, 2, 3, ad. 1.
13. *ST* I, 2, 2, ad. 1.

it is the only authentic response he can give within the confines of natural reason not yet accepting the revelatory mystery of the God-Man. Christ alone was born to die, to suffer evil unto death, and to resurrect, making our death, when conjoined to his, one free of the degrading slavery of evil and, instead, the very path to our immortality. While Christ is the exceeding fulfillment of every speck of groaning nature, to see this fulfillment necessitates the graceful coming to terms with the reality that faith is beyond but not contrary to reason, and that the highest act of reason is to surrender to what is most reasonable, even if *not* demonstrable: to the faith. Only the faith can illuminate for reason the hidden agonies of death and suffering,[14] only faith can unravel the unfathomability that one body and one soul constitute one immortal person, yet the body dies and, yet still, our immortality cannot be a disembodied one; only faith can make a friend of death. Tolstoy again makes the point:

> I was stopped by a contradiction from which there were only two ways of escape: either what I called reasonable was not so reasonable as I thought it, or what I called unreasonable was not so unreasonable as I thought it . . . I also understood that, however unreasonable and monstrous the answers given by faith, they have the advantage of bringing into every question the relation of the finite to the infinite, without which there can be no answer . . . Faith is the force of life. If a man lives, he believes in something. If he did not believe that there was something to live for, he would not live. If he does not see and understand the unreality of the finite, he believes in the finite; if he sees that unreality, he must believe in the infinite. Without the faith it is impossible to live.[15]

14. Cf. Baring, "Dostoevsky," in *Poems, 1914–1919*, 38:
You healed the sore, you made the fearful brave,
They bless you for your lasting legacy;
The balm, the tears, the fragrant charity
You sought and treasured in your living grave.
The gifts you humbly took you greatly gave,
For solace of the soul in agony,
When through the bars the brutal passions pry,
And mock the bonds of the celestial slave.
You wandered in the uttermost abyss;
And there, amidst the ashes and the dust,
You spoke no word of anger or of pride;
You found the prints of steps divine to kiss;
You looked right upwards to the stars, you cried:
"Hosanna to the Lord, for He is just."

15. Tolstoy, *My Confession*, 42–45.

Saint Thomas has not sequestered faith from reason in the Five Ways but has instead entered without fear into the land of the blind, and in the country of the blind the one-eyed man is king, not the two-eyed man.[16] Saint Thomas closes one eye and plays the one-eyed man, leading reason by reason. Faith is never denied, it reinforces the desire to demonstrate God's existence in reason. Faith's own confidence in the truth of Being gives reason the horizon, the noetic distance to approach, in reason, what faith already possesses as the two-eyed man. Reason can then discover its pre-possessive reality in the divine and become transformed in order to approach what is beyond reason, no longer condemned to the unreasonable or irrational, but lovingly encountered as that which overwhelms the rational life because it is too good to be possessed but never too good to be true. The Five Ways are a wager and with all wagers they are a gamble and a risk. The gamble is not whether the demonstrations will have enough substance to merit affirmation beyond a reasonable doubt. Instead, by letting faith recede temporarily into the backdrop, by allowing reason to come to the truth by its own terms, Saint Thomas is trusting that this approach will place one into the hands of the faith in a connatural way, one reflective of our originary *praxis*, and not one of mere prescription and command.

This brief response to the dramatic incompatibility between evil and an all good, all creative God is telling. It is either the weakest answer of all or never intended to be an answer in the first place, as if the matter were settled and put aside. Evil is not a philosophical problem to be solved but a theological mystery to be endured. But to endure this mystery requires that reason reach a form of understanding arrived at only at the end of the demonstrations. Endurance requires grace and admission to the faith. This theological mystery is not without its own intelligibility and profound spiritual awakening but we would be amiss if we thought such a problem could be confined to the philosophical register, where only the *effects* of evil are seen and only the *effects* of God are understood, both in veiled ways. This problem requires that we understand those effects *as* effects, not only of particular causes but of entrenched underlying causes, to which we are intimately bonded. We must understand these prime causes as they interrogatively unveil our destiny and personhood. But this again requires, indeed demands, admission into the faith. Saint Thomas is preparing the *quinque viae* as such an admission, a journey

16. For a cogent utilization of H. G. Well's *Invisible Man*, see Flew, "Theology and Falsification," 48–49.

where reason concludes in each of the *ways* at the door to the divine. Should reason realize nothing other than that only this door can make sense of the natural world, then this "yes" is also a "yes" to the faith.

Thomas's response to the objector opens only the door to the compatibility between reason and faith, it does not presume to answer the prime situational difficulty encompassing the whole of the Christian theo-drama! The presence of evil, for Saint Thomas, does not logically invalidate by contradiction the supreme goodness of God. This, again, does not address the problem of evil *per se* but shows us that reason, in a world of competing goods and encroaching evils, *can still reason* to this all good God. Reasoning about a good God is not fundamentally contrary to a rational process which must take into account contradictions and irreconcilabilities. How has Saint Thomas advanced his argument? He has put Rational Man at ease: "have no fear, uncover what is there naturally, do not be afraid to encounter this Presence, this sensation of goodness, this spiritual miscellany that you have experienced before in the non-articulable wisdom of play. Let us hold off on the dark business of existence until you have more of the tools needed to endure it. For we must endure it and cannot stray from it, not even for a moment." He has also put Irrational Man at some dis-ease by acknowledging, without sugar-coating, the radical nothingness of evil. And for Irrational Man nothing is more real than nothing.[17]

Saint Thomas demonstrates God beyond a reasonable doubt because no natural cause is truly a first cause. This isn't to say we aren't the first cause of something else. In order to understand evil in its deadening devolution, we must understand how nothing which *is* receives its primal origination from us—we are never the true first cause. If, for Saint Thomas, man and angels are the first cause of evil[18] and the first cause of the absence of grace,[19] the adventurous lightness of the Five Ways have prepared us for the weight of this cross. What we have caused is the potential annihilation of everything that *is*, for the only thing we own is our own nothingness and the receding to nothingness is the only thing of

---

17. Cf. Beckett, *Malone Dies*, 16.

18. *ST* II-II, 112, 3, ad. 2.

19. Thomas, *In. Sent.* I, dist. 40, 4, 2: "It is . . . evident that the first cause of the absence of grace is purely and simply on the side of man to whom grace is lacking— because he had not been willing to receive it—on the side of God, there is no cause of the absence of grace, except once admitted that which is the cause on the side of man."

which we are first cause. We can reduce ourselves into preferring nothing over everything, death over life, non-being over Being.

Aquinas's response to the first objector is an invitation into the compatibility of the world in all its potencies as signatories of the divine. His response to the second objector places that natural world within its neediness for the supernatural.

The objector states:

> Further, it is superfluous to suppose that what can be accounted for by a few principles has been produced by many. But it seems that everything we see in the world can be accounted for by other principles, supposing God did not exist. For all natural things can be reduced to one principle which is nature; and all voluntary things can be reduced to one principle which is human reason, or will. Therefore, there is no need to suppose God's existence.[20]

Thomas's response:

> Since nature works for a determinate end under the direction of a higher agent, whatever is done by nature must needs be traced back to God, as to its first cause. So also whatever is done voluntarily must also be traced back to some higher cause other than human reason or will, since these can change or fail; for all things that are changeable and capable of defect must be traced back to an immovable and self-necessary first principle, as was shown in the body of the Article.[21]

The intelligibility of the natural world is as such an *invitation*, one that issues the need for natural principles to reveal their essential lineage from God as true first cause. This, again, is the magnificent existential dance which has developed and unified the entirety of question 2 as well as the whole of the *Summa*. His response to the first objector puts reason at ease to approach the natural world in all its givenness, withholding the reflexive testimony of the faith in favor of the non-reflexive courtship with the natural world. Now, as if making those preparatory steps into the faith, Thomas's response to the second objector unveils that all non-mediated courtship not only secures a more steadfast and connatural admission into the faith, but it must do so because it provides reason

20. *ST* I, 2, 3, arg. 2.
21. *ST* I, 2, 3, ad. 2.

with the basis for its reflexive activity, not its refusal. As reason *reflects* on various natural and voluntary actions, the power of the human soul is incarnated as the linchpin intelligibility which can alone comprehend the necessary and transcending relationship between changing things and an unchanging God.

The Supreme *Non-Sequitur*: The Unnameable

> The human spirit alone is able to comprehend something of the bond which exists between the instability of the world and the stability of God. By naming an object, as the poet does, man rescues it from the fate of dissolution.[22]

But the naming, requiring abstraction, endangers the unique particularity of the thing, left behind as "just" this or "merely" that. As we begin the Five Ways, we recognize that the odd knowledge of existence is in no way obtained in a concept but only in an existential judgment. This judgment is patterned into the structural unfolding of the Five Ways: each requires us to concede the existential judgment—God exists—at the end of the demonstration. These existential judgments announce themselves only after the futility of an infinite regress, and they invoke a pointing towards a necessity that cannot be enshrined in a conceptual identity, but must be present in order for such identities even to be possible.[23] What can to some extent reside within our conceptive viewing are those entities which carry potentiality, those finite things which possess life but only an aspect of it, which possess wisdom but only a degree of it, which possess existence but only a participation in it. What we are demonstrating could never fall under the spell of a non-creational teleological rendering precisely because we seek to demonstrate *To Be* itself, that very "thing" which refuses eidetic viewing and does so in order to make sight possible:

> Although existence is more perfect than life, and life than wisdom, if they are considered as distinguished in idea; nevertheless, a living thing is more perfect than what merely exists, because living things also exist and intelligent things both exist and live. Although therefore existence does not include life and wisdom, because that which participates in existence need not participate in every mode of existence; nevertheless God's

22. Fowlie, *Claudel*, 31.
23. Cf. Pegis, "Necessity and Liberty," 19–45.

existence includes in itself life and wisdom, because nothing of the perfection of being can be wanting to Him who is subsisting being itself.[24]

The structure of the Five Ways creates an intelligible movement where the futurity of the intellect and the saturated presence of the will both have an investment. This existentially grounded eschatology is not superficially limited to a conceptually managed teleology—as it would be for a metaphysics of non-creational essence and substance—but is one with the miscellaneous gratuity of existence. God's freedom is patterned into existence along with his directionality, thus each and every thing can get us to God; there is no need to pass over these effects, but rather to understand each thing in itself. Saint Thomas utilizes cause and effect to demonstrate God's existence beyond a reasonable doubt, but the effects which are traced are not passed over as indifferently ineffectual, but are each shown instead to reveal the presence of God as efficacious Other; each reveals its participation in God's *To Be*. Because Saint Thomas is demonstrating the only Being Who exists in his own right and thus must be existentially imprinted in all things, the structure of the Five Ways heralds an indebtedness both to our presence and to the nature of our souls to stretch beyond themselves in order to be themselves. These are *metaphysical* demonstrations in the most rigorous sense of the term. They arrive at that which stands beyond and beneath, the always preceding cause, thus aligning with our non-mediated intimacy. And this always-preceding cause is also the source to which all things are directed via their participation in *To Be*. This unstripped immediacy grasped primordially by the will is also the cause of the intellect's futural movement, and this movement does not spring from an extrinsicized template but from the utter depth of our unified nature. The *ways* were never a mere *teleology* but a viatoric reflection of our natures, and the ground both of the necessity and the possibility of a poetic of space and a poetic of temporality.

Each of the Five Ways abides by the following structural integrity:

1. *Each way starts from an in-the-world sensible experience, in sheer but not bare presence preceding conceptualization.*

Aquinas commences each way with an invocation of nature. Before he asks *what* we can understand of the sensible world, we are *in* the

---

24. *ST* I, 4, 2, ad 3.

givenness of sensory being. These demonstrations are not seeking to clarify *what* God Is in his essence, but *that* he is, and while this existential *thatness* is not delimited and finite, it is manifestly a with-*in*-ness. Thus, when Saint Thomas begins each demonstration with a bare laying out of the sensible world he does this to separate the demonstration from the temptation of the intellect to act as the guide rather than it being guided and subordinated to Being. The distinction between a demonstration conceptually overwrought with the question of God's *quiddity* and one which focuses on existence itself is reaffirmed by this first subtle step. The Angelic Doctor recognizes that God's *quiddity* is in no way inhibited by finite modes of existence; he is Existence itself. If his demonstrations were to commence with the question of *whatness*, in any respect, he would be dismissing God's existential primacy as well as undermining his effort to focus on a dramatically different order. Whereas relation for Aristotle is a question of an order of essences which do not fundamentally engage but only exist as eternal co-parts, Saint Thomas's demonstrations unveil an order of existence where relation requires engagement, union, desire, and the neediness of the Other for its fulfillment. For the Stagirite, the question of demonstrating the prime mover would always be one of *quiddity*,[25] for this is a non-creational enterprise, and one in which the language of *thatness* is never emancipated from quiddity.[26] For Saint Thomas, *before* he can ask into God's *whatness*, which is done in the question directly following the demonstrations,[27] he must show that this *whatness* can only be understood in an existential metaphysics capable of being compatible with the Christian God *as Uncreated*. This most minute act, commencing with a simple sense experience, supports a realist metaphysics as the natural fulfillment of empirical knowledge rather than its irreconcilable contrary. It places the human person *in* the *world* rather than in abstractions, showing that if we cannot get to God from where we are, we cannot get to God from anywhere. This in-the-world placement thus places the bodily soul (a union of the contributions of will and intellect) at the forefront of these ways. It makes the demonstrations an existential viatoric on the way to faith rather than a manufactured teleology.

25. Aristotle, *Phys.* VIII.

26. É. Gilson, *Spirit of Thomism*, 98–99.

27. Cf. *ST* I, 3 on God's simplicity. Here Saint Thomas asks the questions of quiddity: whether God has a body; is God composed of matter and form; composition or simple; perfect; composed of subject and accident and, in particular, demonstrates that God's essence and existence are identical.

As natural knowledge is always true, so is natural love well regulated; because natural love is nothing else than the inclination
implanted in nature by its Author. To say that a natural inclination is not well regulated, is to derogate from the Author of
nature. Yet the rectitude of natural love is different from the rectitude of charity and virtue: because the one rectitude perfects
the other; even so the truth of natural knowledge is of one kind,
and the truth of infused or acquired knowledge is of another.[28]

2. *Saint Thomas asks what we gather intellectually from sense experience*

After reconfirming our pre-reflexive contact with the bodily world, the
path of reflexive knowledge has its proper counter-balance. In this second
aspect of the argumentative flow of the Five Ways Saint Thomas commences reflection. Again, this is not reflection beginning in a Cartesian
mind or in an ideological materialist vacuity, but one which is earthy and
concretized by time, experience and change. This interrogative act places
the human person in its unique position on/as the horizon between time
and eternity. Each of the Five Ways considers a distinct though interrelated formality of limited reality: motion, change, and dependency; primacy in efficient causes; necessity; participation in relation to perfection;
an *arche* invoked in design and finality. Not only is God considered from
a different vantage in each of the *ways*—i.e., pure *Actus*, true first-cause,
necessary Being, absolute perfection, and the supreme end—so is the human person who is granted access to lift the veil of Being. While the Five
Ways transcend time as change, and time as the *hic et nunc*, they do not
avoid time as actual presence but rather see into the immediacy of time,
of the miscellany, its dependent relatedness to an independent fulcrum of
time, rendering the poetic of time possible.[29]

These demonstrations are all tributaries of the same Truth: the existence of God as the entrenched source of finite existence *because* he
is irreducible to it. The Five Ways are neither to be understood as temporal empirical demonstrations nor proofs which can stand alone. Each
demonstration refers to the other, not because each lacks a piece of the
puzzle but because in them Saint Thomas is revealing aspects about our
nature when confronted with the indivisible and inexhaustible reality of
the Godhead. These are genuinely metaphysical demonstrations which
reveal the empirical *to be* empirical only because the empirical certitudes

28. *ST* I, 60, 1, ad. 3.
29. Cf. Renard, *Philosophy of God*, 32–33.

are dependent upon a groundless foundation which refuses progression or regress. Thus, when this second step is encountered, what we are actually faced with is the uniqueness of our stance in existence. We are beings in flux reflecting on flux. This requires that the change we possess is not reducible to a temporal progression but instead reveals our spectatorship-participation in the moving image of eternity. The nature of these demonstrations transcends time, and thus in order to grasp this primal *thatness* requires we ourselves somehow, some way, transcend time. The time specific to our natures is distinct from all other creatures. These Five Ways are no mere teleological expression of the truth where at best a distant end is perceived, they are a viatoric courtship where our own aeviternal nature must be invoked and then utilized in order to concede to the dramatic existential conclusion of each of the Five Ways. In these first two steps, Saint Thomas has given our originary *praxis* its due and revealed the privileged access of the human soul. The union of the two prevents in advance a materialist conception of the world reducible to sensory experience or an abstractive rendering where the mind manages the teleological goals of existence. In this setup, God can be encountered naturally, not prescriptively or indeed forcibly. Each thing in the world is invested with divinity so that the human person can encounter the freedom to persist in the miscellany of any number of encounters with particular goods and still discover God and the hierarchical truth grafted innermost in each thing. Myshkin, the holy idiot, would understand. All creatures are immigrants in the land of Being: they never lose their native nothingness.

3. *The infinite regress*

God loves to multiply intermediaries.[30]

When we hear the term "infinite regress," not only is it generically understood, but the language of the "infinite" has been conflated with the "indefinite" as if interchangeable. In reality this regress, in divergent ways, carries with it both the manifestation of the indefinite and the intensity

---

30. Cf. Sertillanges, *Sources de la croyance de Dieu*, 65: "At the summit, the source, the activity; in the middle, the intermediaries, unique or multiple; and finally, the results which this activity produces. Multiply intermediary causes into infinity, and you complicate the instrument, but you do not fabricate a cause; you elongate the canal but do not make a source. To say that the intermediaries, if sufficiently multiplied, will serve as a cause, is like saying that a brush will paint by itself if the handle is long enough."

of the infinite. On the side of the natural, empirical object, any causally traced series of like specimens is not infinite but reducibly temporal and indefinite. None has the power to raise itself beyond or outside its own finite limitation. Each natural first cause, by potentiality, dependency, limit, materiality, reveals itself to be an intermediary cause. In essence, each natural cause is at its origination an "effect." And if the question is "did a natural cause, cause the world?" we realize that such a question is looking for a first in the order of causation, but how could a natural cause have caused the world if natural causes, bonded to potentiality, reveal themselves to be intermediaries? In a word, how could an effect cause the world? Is this not begging the question? But this series is an indefinite one precisely because the descriptive phenomena of these effects as material, changing, potential, and dependent render them within the temporal order and thus unable to rise to the level of the infinite.

> Again, whatever is caused as regards some particular nature cannot be the first cause of that nature, but only a second and instrumental cause; for example, since the human nature of Socrates has a cause, he cannot be the first cause of human nature; if so, since his human nature is caused by someone, it would follow that he was the cause of himself, since he is what he is by virtue of human nature. Thus, a univocal generator must have the status of an instrumental agent in respect to that which is the primary cause of the whole species. Accordingly, all lower efficient causes must be referred to higher ones, as instrumental to principal agents. The existence of every substance other than God is caused, as we proved above. No such substance, then, could possibly be the cause of existence otherwise than as instrumental and as acting by virtue of another agent. But it is only in order to cause something by way of motion that an instrument is ever employed; for to be a moved mover is the very essence of an instrument. We have already shown, however, that creation is not a motion. Hence, no substance besides God can create anything.[31]

On the other hand, the regress is one which indicates the infinite because the underlying unity of the ways reveals these demonstrations to transcend temporal succession and progression. The moment the regress is stopped, not by the things within the temporal and causal tracing, but by the demonstrator, then this indefinite regress is transformed into a

---

31. SCG, II, 21, 5.

re-collection of the infinite. What the human person recognizes in that invoked *ananke stenai* is the realization that this indefinite series of causes and effects, each reducible to a prior effect, is circling around and pointing towards an infinite which it cannot reach. There is an infinite distance between that indefinite regress and the source which alone has the power primordially to invoke its cessation as origin. But, at the same time, the demonstrator, the human person, who lifts this interrogative veil, realizes that any indefinite regress is stopped also by the power of our reflexive act to see things as they *are*. We are, in a way, freely seeing with the eyes of Being; seeing the unmistakable and undeniable presence of *To Be* itself. Our participation in the indefinite regress transforms it into a recollection of the infinite. This infinite cannot fully be recalled because its essence is unknown to us and exceeds our finite limitations. And yet our very recognition of this unknown infinite requires that we must be prepossessed in it. The moment we interrogatively enter the indefinite regress is the moment it is transformed from a natural ordering to a supernatural one, from an indefinite succession to a viatoric chasing of the infinite. Our pre-reflexive unity with the world prepares us to see that this unity has always been one in which we are wholly *in* because we are not wholly *of* the world. In our unreflexive love, we live out the indefinite regress in all its beauty and terror as we unknowingly prepare for the inevitable moment of reflection and transformation.

> I know as often as I measure my thoughts,
> how deep, how long, how wide:
> but you are is, and was, and will,
> and quiver within time.
>
> . . .
>
> I give you thanks, you mighty force,
> which ever gentler works on me
> in quiet and behind closed doors,
> so working days are pure again
> and contrast with my unclean hands
> like holy imagery.[32]

When we reflect on that process, when we noetically distance ourselves from our first connaturality, we transform, by that very act of reflection, the indefinite regress into an infinite one, with different meanings and dramatically different parameters. We have left the world of time (the indefinite) for the realm of the eternal (the infinite) only to know of that

---

32. Rilke, "Monkish Life," in *Book of Hours*, 87.

eternality because we remain in time. This the serious play of the indefinite and infinite regress. And God does so love to multiply intermediaries.

4. *The ananke stenai: the necessity to come to a stop*

> It wasn't the New World that mattered, which could have slipped into the sea. Columbus died having hardly seen it and scarcely knowing what he discovered. Life is what matters, life alone—the continuous, eternal process of discovering life—and not the discovery itself at all! . . . But I might add, however, that in every serious human thought born in anyone's brain there is always something left over which is impossible to communicate to others, even though one were to write whole volumes and explain the idea for thirty-five years; there will always be something left which cannot be coaxed out of your brain and which will remain with you forever; you will die with it, without ever communicating to anyone what is perhaps the essence of your thought.[33]

This *ananke stenai* is not a grasping of a different object or merely the mental recognition of a diverse order standing in total distinction from our own. What is arrived at in the Five Ways is not so much like a train journey which stops at a particular town or junction separate from our embarkation point. The stop of this *ananke stenai* is as much a *way*, because we are arriving not at an object *in* existence but existence itself. This is no substance-based existence where existence itself is reducible to a mode of essence and each eternal essence exists independently from the other, as if ships in the night persisting in their own eternality. Mentally admitting that a different order has never been the total integrity of the *ways*, it is the realization that we are, by our reflexive activities, stretched and protracted souls participating in that different order which is our *own difference*. The *ananke stenai* posits an order truly distinct from our own and yet paradoxically the difference is the identity, essence, and reality of our order. It reveals that God *is* and that we are *in* but not *of* the world. This *necessity* to a come to a stop in the order of existence reconciles the order of meaning to existence and permits meaning to be understood as *it is*.

> Whatever belongs to a being is either caused by the principles
> of that being's essence or comes to it from some extrinsic

33. Dostoyevsky, *Idiot*, 412–13. Hippolyte's last conviction for which he said he paid dearly.

principle . . . The 'to be' cannot be caused by the thing in itself considered formally or in its essence. Here I speak of cause in the sense of efficient cause, for in this case, the being would be its own cause; it would give its own 'to be,' a thing which is impossible. Hence, every being whose 'to be' is different from its essence, receives this 'to be'" from another.[34]

In chapter 1 of the *De Ente* Thomas attempts to outline no more than a map of the basic onto-metaphysical notions, being (*ens*) and essence (*essentia*). Three crucial points are to be made in this connection which must be kept clear and present to mind if we are at all to progress to an adequate understanding of the subsequent chapters:

- In the prologue Thomas states, as the fundamental noetic fact, the absolute intentional priority of being as the aboriginal ground, origin and terminus of thought, from which all our *thinking* arises and into which all our *knowledge* is resolved: "*ens autem et essentia sunt quae primo intellectu concipiuntur*."[35] *Ens* is the *primum apprehensum* in which man is totally immersed.

- But what does this participle *ens* signify? Is it the concrete being, the ontic essent, the existential individual, the subject of being? In a major sense Thomas indicates just that in paragraph 1, wherein he seems to take *ens* as the composite of which a constitutive element or principle is essence: "we ought to get our knowledge of simple things from composite things and arrive at what is prior by way of which is posterior . . . for this reason we must begin with the meaning of 'a being' (*ens*) and proceed to the meaning of an essence."[36] In other words, *ens* does not signify the *essence* of a thing; is therefore not identical with essence; is not essential in some sense; and is therefore in some sense accidental to the thing. Here *ens* seems to be act.

---

34. *De Ente* V.

35. *De Ente*, prooemium. See also DV, I,1; SCG II, 83, 31.

36. *De Ente*, prooemium. The particular procession from particular being to essence, underscores a dramatic difference in our understanding of essence. Essences are revealed as active, as unable to be separated from ontic ascent and thus must translated into our understanding of the demonstrations. We are not *beginning* with vacant essences but *arriving* with active essences which are none other than beings exercising natures.

- But on the other hand, Thomas goes on immediately to identify *ens* with the predicamental categories, as well as with the truth of propositions. As divided by the predicaments *ens* is in some way identified with essence because essence is derived from the predicamental character of being, because essence is such only as positive in reality, which, again, is to be predicamental. *Ens* and *essential* here are ontological notions taken *in abstracto* as the act of being: they are transcendental notions of affirmative being. And at no point is the proper notion of essence a logical notion. [/BL 1-3]

Thus essence may be called quiddity, form, nature for various and proper reasons but it is called essence because "through it, and in it, that which is has being": "*sed essential dicitur secundum quod per eam et in ea ens habet esse.*"[37]

Essence thus is the content of the definition signifying *ens* when that content is actual or actuated or positive (this is the real meaning of the discussion of negatives and privations: that although the being of truth has a greater extension than the being of the categories, nevertheless it is only as dependent upon the latter that the former can be conceived). Essence is a dual ordering to being: it is that *in* which a thing has being and is thus the subject of being. But it is also that *through* which *ens* has being, in which case *ens* is the subject of being and *essentia* a primary ontological constituent. In the first way, *ens* is categorically delineated in essential definition, while in the second sense Thomas is surely pointing to essence within the realm of formal causality. Only the *esse* of the *ens habet esse* can be seen, though darkly still, as the properly metaphysical notion pointing to an order of efficient causality.

Again: categorically and predicamentally *ens* is considered as if it were the same as *essential* which is equated with *ousia*. But it is the ontological composite (i.e., not in terms of matter and form, but in terms of *essentia* and *esse*) of which *essentia* is only, but crucially, a constituent.

If *ens* as participle is ambiguous (like *currens* as he who runs and the act of running) between the ontic subject of being and the very exercised act which *is* being, the two related participatorily through the very duality of Being itself in such a way that a) it is almost impossible to represent the one without the other, if indeed b) being is ever able to be represented at all for Aquinas—then *essentia* would seem to share a similar destiny. This reality must tie back to the program of the Five Ways.

37. *De Ente* I.

We can now intensify the meaning of *essentia* by considering it in relation to its uncovering in composite beings. Composite here of course means the union of form and matter, and not the union of *essentia* and *esse*.

The core of the problem as it stands at the commencement of chapter 2 is this: we have seen the ambiguity of both *ens and essentia* in such a way that no matter how *essence* is considered it is totally enwrapped in actuated being either explicitly in its connection with predicamental *ens* or as the ontological constituent which enables and delimits the self-reception of *esse* by *ens*, or implicitly as the dependency of beings upon actuated and essential beings makes clear.

But now, if we keep in mind that essence is an ontological principle of being, in fact fulfilling the function of the subject of being—then no longer can matter play that role as it did prior to Aquinas wherein matter would conjoin with form as the subject of form or being. But essence now is the formal principle: what possible role could matter perform? As a principle of ontological indeterminacy and noetic incapacity, matter cannot of itself be the essence. Essence is a) that by which a being is named a being and b) it is what is signified through definition. And as the definition of natural substance includes matter, therefore form alone cannot be the essence of a composite. Essence therefore embraces both matter and form, with form on a somewhat higher level.

"Form and matter are found in composite substances, as for example soul and body in man. But it cannot be said that either one of these alone is called the essence."[38] Essence here is not equated with form, or even nature, and certainly not concept. It designates the being of a thing in its total actuated condition, which in the case of man is to be an incarnate spirit. What is outside definition is outside the essence. If matter cannot be brought into the definition of man as properly reflecting the essence of man—then man of all material beings will be torn asunder. And if the notion of essence itself is cut off from its relation to actual being, then the irreducible reciprocity of *esse* and *essentia* in *ens*, which synthesizes both, is lost.

The problem again: if essence is indeed not matter and not form but both in the composite being, and if essence is signified by the definition which points to being in its reality (essence)—then how will the definition include matter? Matter individuates but the definition is universal.

38. *De Ente* I.

But then will the definition be applicable to a singular being? How can essence be kept from losing its moorings in actual being? These are the critical questions Thomas attempts to answer with his doctrine of designated matter and non-precisive abstraction.

If we are to think about Being, and thus to think truly, beautifully, and within the Good, it is a *necessity* to engage this stop which unveils this difference as such. This is why when we arrive at *To Be*, not as a facet of the truth but as the always preceding truth itself, our understanding of truth is transformed from an isolated external object or fact to the very habit of our acting being. The conformity of the thing to the intellect hinges not only upon the undividedness of the act of existence from that which is, but this undividedness or withinness is also a preceding truth, *a beyondness* and *priority* which forms the basis of all truths. When we possess truth through our conformity to it, we are possessed by that which is innermost and exceeding being:

> Consequently, truth or the true has been defined in three ways. First of all, it is defined according to that which precedes truth and is the basis of truth. This is why Augustine writes: 'The true is that which is;' and Avicenna: 'The truth of each thing is a property of the act of being which has been established for it.' Still others say: 'The true is the undividedness of the act of existence from that which is.' Truth is also defined in another way—according to that in which its intelligible determination is formally completed. Thus, Isaac writes: 'Truth is the conformity of thing and intellect;' and Anselm: 'Truth is a rectitude perceptible only by the mind.' This rectitude, of course, is said to be based on some conformity. The Philosopher says that in defining truth we say that truth is had when one affirms that to be which is, and that not to be which is not.[39]

The *ananke stenai* is our enactment of truth in this threefold manner. We are not solely admitting a mental difference but invoking our participation in that truth-filled transformation as our own. This stop or difference is not isolated from the world but is its foundational life. And yet, this difference cannot be arrived at through existence as if God is the highest rung on the ladder of beings. No matter how high we climb the ladder of finite, empirical, and material existents, the climb can and will proceed indefinitely. I may be circling around the divine but only *acknowledge* that I am in fact circling in the act of reflection. I admit the

39. DV I, 1 *reply*.

ananke stenai, this difference as such, which is also the very uniqueness of my own being which acts by a different time altogether. The journey, in a way, is directed always by its arrival or terminus or goal or end. It is because of this that the finite *actor*, either by weakness or by fear, prefers to see this goal through the path of least resistance, as a mentally admitted teleological end. Because Saint Thomas is arriving at the *existence* of God who alone can ground all existence itself, the *ananke stenai* cannot be the distant eternal, the end of an ideationally posited teleology. Only by reconciling the necessity to arrive at an end with the truth of Hippolyte's feverish claims that the end is not the discovery itself but the continuous, eternal process of discovering life, do we grasp the *in* but not *of* world reality of God. This *ananke stenai* speaks as much to our own nature which by its reflection on this difference is stretched beyond itself to be itself. This is the *homo viator* in its *deiformitas*.[40] This stop in the order of existence which transforms an indefinite regress to an infinite re-collection, has never been a generic universal understood through an artificially prescribed template. Because this stop is the always exceeding connaturalness uniting and distinguishing man and world, it is understood through that connaturalness, which is to say it is arrived at by way of the incommunicability of each human soul. The *ananke stenai* may be a universal truth but it is arrived at by what is innermost in us. It is the intimate contact of one soul affirming its own unique difference within the source of the difference as such.

1. *The pointing towards God: the strange certitude of a negative theology*

> Yet others arrived at a knowledge of God from the incomprehensibility of truth. All the truth which our intellect is able to grasp is finite, since according to Augustine, 'everything that is known is bounded by the comprehension of the one knowing;' and if it is bounded, it is determined and particularized. Therefore, the first and supreme Truth, which surpasses every intellect, must necessarily be incomprehensible and infinite; and this is God. Hence the Psalm (8:2) says, 'Your greatness is above the heavens,' i.e., above every created intellect, angelic and human.

40. Cf. See Saint Augustine on wayfarers, sermon 169, *Augustine Day by Day*, 17: "On earth, we are wayfarers, always on the go. This means that we have to keep on moving forward. Therefore be always unhappy about what you are if you want to reach what you are not. If you are pleased with what you are, you have stopped already. If you say; 'It is enough,' you are lost. Keep on walking, moving forward, trying for the goal. Don't try to stop on the way, or to go back, or to deviate from it."

> The Apostle says this in the words, 'He dwells in unapproach-
> able light' (1 Tim 6:16). This incomprehensibility of Truth is
> shown to us in the word 'lofty,' that is, above all the knowledge
> of the created intellect. John implies this incomprehensibility to
> us when he says below (1:18), 'No one has ever seen God.'[41]

Hippolyte is not wrong, there will always be something left unsaid which cannot be coaxed out of the soul and which will remain locked and within us forever. We will die, and even if volumes of thoughts have been written down, with each death a library burns and can never be rebuilt. All are equal in the graveyard: equally *unique*. The *ananke stenai* reveals the capacity of the soul to be transformed in its contact with the divine because this stop, pause, moratorium, stillness within the moving image of eternity, communicates itself to each of us, not in an extrin-sicized manner—which would not have the power to reach us—but to our own incommunicability. The beauty of the Five Ways is that Saint Thomas's certitude never discards the utter risk of a vigorous negative theology. In fact, what we point at beyond a reasonable doubt is the *Dio ignoto*, the cloud of unknowing, the mystery too near and too present to be understood in words. This is why God is the *un*moved mover, the *un*caused cause. In each of the Five Ways, we point at the utter openness of an "un": in the *fifth way* we arrive at a being which intelligibilizes and arranges the world but itself, as un-planned planner, needs no arrange-ment and is not reducible to any stream of intelligibility. Not only does this "un" dramatically distinguish itself from the ideological enclosure of a "self" in the modernist *self*-caused cause,[42] this source which does not need to justify itself places man within the certitude of the mystery of his own being. If the human soul is on the *confinium* of time and eternity, this is because we are in as much contact with the recognition of our own nothingness as with the profound reality that there is an infinite distance between ourselves and nothingness. *Abyssus abyssum invocat:*[43] we stand

41. Thomas Aquinas, *Comm. St. John*, prooemium, 6.

42. The Rig Veda beautifully speaks of that dramatic difference which sets the stage for language as parabolic. See its hymn "The All-Maker (Visvakarman)," in Koller and Koller, *Asian Philosophy*, 11: "You cannot find him who created these creatures; anoth-er has come between you. Those who recite the hymns are glutted with the pleasures of life; they wander about wrapped up in the mist and stammering nonsense."

43. Cf. Ps 42:1–3a, 7 (NIV): "As the deer pants for streams of water, so my soul pants for you, my God. My soul thirsts for God, for the living God. When can I go and meet with God? My tears have been my food day and night . . . Deep calls to deep in the roar of your waterfalls; all your waves and breakers have swept over me."

on the tightrope wire and all around us is either the abyss *as abyss* or the abyss as the unveiling certitude of God. In either case, it is each of us in confrontation with the total interiority of our personhood. Saint Thomas's demonstrations are not proofs which possess the object they prove, but are *ways* pointing towards an Otherness which, if possessed, is only possible because it pre-possesses us in the particularity of each soul.

> I'm still a novice concerning pain—
> that's how small I feel in this great dark;
> but if you are there, be heavy and break through;
> have your whole hand do its work on me
> and I, with my cries, on you.[44]

This pointing is directing us towards the door of the divine—because we do not know God's essence—and it is as much a recognition of the total Otherness of God as well as a metaphysical invitation to the faith. The world is too full of God, so much so that God's unique self-evidence is his unavoidable mystery.[45] No amount of tracing the natural causes can get us to God Who is the supreme *non-sequitur*, the surprise, the freedom in and of existence. His pattern is not in a straight line but in the loving miscellany of the lilies of the field and in the temple. It is directionality which ensures freedom and does not make closed natures. Teleology functions because natures are closed, because freedom must play second fiddle to the directionality completing a nature. This is perhaps why Sartre rejects God. We are looking for an *eschatology appropriate to open natures*. Not one which surrenders intelligibility for freedom but reveals utter freedom as the progenitor of our directionality. These natural causes get us to God only because they do *not* get us there. The distinction between their quiddity and their *to be* renders their movement one which ends where it began, a real stasis as much as a real movement, a desire for the futural but a remaining in the present:

> Whatever is not contained in the concept of essence or of quiddity comes to it from without and forms a composition with essence, because no essence can be understood without understanding its 'to be;' for I can know what a man or a 'phoenix' is and still remain in the dark as to whether such a being does exist in the world. Therefore, it is clear that the 'to be' is not the same

44. Rilke, "Poverty and Death," in *Book of Hours*, 165.

45. On the starting point of Saint Thomas's *prima via* see Owens, *St. Thomas Aquinas*, 169–91.

as essence or quiddity, unless perhaps there exist a being whose quiddity is its 'to be;' moreover such a being would have to be the One and the First . . . Consequently it follows in all other beings, that the 'to be' and the quiddity are distinct.[46]

The union of our will and intellect, the non-futural and the futural, we surrender to what these natural causes unknowingly encircle but never reach, that difference as such which enables, in the first place, this encircling or enshrining. This pointing is thus a surrender and a metaphysical invitation to the faith because we know beyond any reasonable doubt that God exists; that he exists not as distant eternal but so near that his self-evidence is his mystery, and that to fulfill our desire to know we cannot return to those natural causes which circle and speak but which do not reach him. The substance of faith incarnates this metaphysical surrender. It transforms this surrender, for it is the revelation of the faceless face, the one source which intelligibilizes our *in*-but-not-*of* the world yearning.

> When the mind's very being is gone,
> Sunk in a conscious sleep,
> In a rapture divine and deep,
> Itself in the Godhead lost:
> It is conquered, ravished, and won!
> Set in Eternity's sweep,
> Gazing back on the steep,
> Knowing not how it was crossed—
> To a new world now it is tossed,
> Drawn from its former state,
> To another, measureless, great—
> Where Love is drowned in the Sea.[47]

46. *De Ente* V.

47. Jacopone da Todi, "How the Soul by Holy Annihilation and Love Reaches a Condition that is Unknown and Unspeakable," in Underhill, *Jacopone da Todi*, 474–501, esp. 477.

The *Summa Theologica*:
Its Judicial Structure Revisited

That which rests in all creatures, and is distinct from all creatures, which all creatures know not, of which all creatures are
the body, which controls all creatures within, that is thy Self,
the immortal controller. So far, again, with regard to creatures.
Now with regard to the (individual) self. That which rests in
the breath, and is distinct from the breath, which the breath
knows not, of which the breath is the body, which controls the
breath within, that is thy Self, the immortal inner controller. The
Unseen Seer; the Unheard Hearer; the Unthought Thinker; the
Unknown Knower; there is no other Knower. This thy Self, the
immortal inner controller.[48]

The Five Ways are not only carried by a metaphysical architectonic
where that necessity to come to a stop in the order of reason prompts our
pointing to an origin in the order of beings, but they also have a judicial
structure. By opening each article with a set of objectors, Saint Thomas is
attempting to ensure that he demonstrates his argument without naively
dismissing or circumventing the contrary positions. If there is a truth to
be issued, it will not be prescriptively coerced, demanded by a skirting
of contrary positions—as if the objectors are merely straw men. Instead,
his response and reply to objections elicit from the objectors' missteps
their partial truths as the basis for the unveiling of the truth. These objections are the necessary confrontational movement by which meaning is
chastened and refined into wisdom—truth not reducible to fact but to
a unity of facticity always in view to the human and divine accord. The
sed contra is an act of presence. These demonstrations proceed through
reason but it is not a rational apparatus divorced from the tradition or
its lineage invested in all things. The Five Ways require man as an *open
nature* in order interrogatively to encounter the truths of these demonstrations. We may begin in the empirical but the empirical itself points
beyond its datum to the groundless ground. An open nature does not
mean an empty one, one which receives no meaning from without. It
receives its open accord because it understands that fidelity to the truth
is the opening of the soul. This is connaturalness transitioned into tradition, not substituted for it. In the *sed contra* all acts must find their genuine subordination, otherwise they will attach themselves to an artificial

48. Brhadaranyaka Upanisad, III, 7, in Koller and Koller, *Asian Philosophy*, 13.

pattern, a substitute and surrogate, a shadowy truth surfeited on a series of diminishing returns. In the *responsio* Saint Thomas, having referred to the tradition, now articulates it. The statement of the truth and the explanation of truth are not the same thing. This is the strange ecstasy and fright of our reflexive union with the Being-beyond-reflection. One can state the truth but may not know or even possess it, and in many occasions the statement is the nexus to the lie. The true statement, for instance that "God is Good," is both the fullest and most vacuous statement possible; its truth may be irreducible to us but the realization of its fullness or vacuity depends upon our participation in that incommunicability. This is the dramatic responsibility of our natures as moral actors. Transmitting the truth is not primarily a rational, intellectual invocation but an act; the intellect must be enacted by the activity of truth. The mystery of ourselves and God is incommunicable. This does not mean it cannot be transmitted to another but that this transmission does not proceed by the usual channels of empirical statement, where the soul making the judgment is a "neutral" part of the equation. Whether you are virtuous or not, the empirical fact that the "cat is on the mat" can be judged equally. It is a bare objectival statement and the transmission of its factical truth is transmitted via the statement and not so much by the courtship of the soul. When it comes to the truths of Being which more directly carry us up into our open nature, into our *deiformitas*, the statement of the truth—the *sed contra*—is a guide, but it necessitates that each person come to this truth by walking through its door, as if for the first time. This is why, as Saint Thomas sees it, God has set out more than one way to arrive at the truth: through reason, through faith, through faith and reason: because each of us, tailored to our personal incommunicability, must make the *way* or journey. Having begun with the objectors, not as straw men, but as ways to a discovery of the truth, Saint Thomas places himself in the position that the responsibility of demonstrating the truth cannot be cast off. If he is to argue that God is not self-evident but can be demonstrated, Saint Thomas accepts the responsibility that he must demonstrate those affirmations as truthful in a way conducive to truth. This judicial structure works hand-in-hand with our originary *praxis* as a rigorous and naturally supernatural unfolding of meaning precisely because the structure of the *Summa* situates us to experience truth in a manner free from prescriptive statement or reductive facticity. The *reply to objections* only augments the strength of this process. They complete the response, conforming to, while deepening, the *sed contra*, and return us to the beginning. The initial objectors are again not merely stepping stones to a truth more aptly described as an ego-driven stance, but to a truth which, as irreducible to all its expressions, is discoverable in any form of knowledge yearning for the truth. The replies to objections not only confront directly the objectors' positions but are also a sign of respect as well as a recognition of the dependency on the Other for our knowledge. This Otherness—because we are bodily souls—is not apprehended immediately but is manifested through the *longer way* of time, experience, and personal encounter. Just as God's effects take the place of his essence in the demonstrations, the objectors' positions take the place of the *Other* while we are fleshing out a closer approximation of the Truth. The objectors proffer reasonable doubt, utilizing the multiplication of intermediaries to argue an alternative view of the order of things, an alternative reading of the evidence. This reasonable doubt confronts knowledge and disrupts it, and this disruption allows truth to seep in. If genuine knowledge is only in the world and if it is through otherness that we understand ourselves, then this judicial structure is a safeguard ensuring that the process reveals truth in a truthful way. When truths are revealed in a way contrary to how truth is properly accessed in time, experience and the relation with the other, we fail to be participants in truth. Access to it requires that *longer way*. In this judicial process, Saint Thomas reveals that we don't grasp truth through *methodic* doubt but by *reasonable* doubt. The former attempts to keep otherness at bay at the cost of reducing Being to an Idea, whereas the latter recognizes that the highest knowledge of truth requires that the recipient be engaged in the enactment of that truth. This is possible only if truth is always dialogic, always a discovery of the other *as other*. The objectors, having taken the place of the Other, enable the abstractive argumentation of the *summa* to have substance, weight, and bearing outside the mind and in the world. This judicial structure is not only the scaffolding for the demonstrations and for the whole of the *Summa*, it is itself an exercise in meaning. There are layers of wisdom being incarnated in this structure and, for the Five Ways in particular, it is an essential supporting structure for the internal design of the demonstrations. The intelligibility of beginning with sense experience leads to the infinite regress and then to the necessity to come to a stop at a divine origin. This internal structure is supported by that overall judicial intelligibility emblematic of the *Summa Theologica*. That overall structure creates the essential checks and balances to the logic of the demonstrations and shows us a moral and intellectual structure which is not artificial and extrinsicized, achieving what such a prescriptive structure desires: glorious truth freed from distraction, illusion, and untruth.

The First Way: All Is Becoming

The first and more manifest way is the argument from motion. It is certain, and evident to our senses, that in the world some things are in motion. Now whatever is in motion is put in motion by another, for nothing can be in motion except it is in potentiality to that towards which it is in motion; whereas a thing moves inasmuch as it is in act. For motion is nothing else than the reduction of something from potentiality to actuality. But nothing can be reduced from potentiality to actuality, except by something in a state of actuality. Thus, that which is actually hot, as fire, makes wood, which is potentially hot, to be actually hot, and thereby moves and changes it. Now it is not possible that the same thing should be at once in actuality and potentiality in the same respect, but only in different respects. For what is actually hot cannot simultaneously be potentially hot; but it is simultaneously potentially cold. It is therefore impossible that in the same respect and in the same way a thing should be both mover and moved, i.e. that it should move itself. Therefore, whatever is in motion must be put in motion by another. If that by which it is put in motion be itself put in motion, then this also must needs be put in motion by another, and that by another again. But this cannot go on to infinity, because then there would be no first mover, and, consequently, no other mover; seeing that subsequent movers move only inasmuch as they are put in motion by the first mover; as the staff moves only because it is put in motion by the hand. Therefore, it is necessary to arrive at a first mover, put in motion by no other; and this everyone understands to be God.[49]

The demonstration from motion involves not only change but all becoming, corporeal and even spiritual.[50] Movement here means the process of becoming actual. From our bare, first sensory experience we see that some things are in motion and some are not. The swingset moves and then ceases to move, the flag in the wind, the pendulum, the acorn changes to become the oak, and so much more. Movement is not

49. *ST* I, 2, 3 *resp.*
50. See Saint Thomas on obediential potency, DV, XXIX, 3, ad. 3.

something confined to a materiality permanently severed from the spiritual. If the soul is the form of the body, then change and becoming are how that form is encountered:

> At the very beginning of my life in the village, when I would sometimes meet—especially at midday—the noisy crowd of children running home from school with their satchels and slates, with their cries and laughter and their games; then my soul suddenly went out to them. I don't know just how it was, but I began to have a kind of intense feeling of happiness every time I met them, I would stop and laugh from sheer happiness, seeing their little legs flashing in perpetual movement, the little boys and girls running together, their laughter and their tears (for many of them managed to fight, cry, make up, and start playing again, all on the way home from school), and I forgot all about my sadness.[51]

This dramatic universe of motion is not the tail-end of experience but its core memorial meaning. If it can be demonstrated that God's very existence is the *élan vital* of that movement, then all spiritual and material meaning discovers its perfection in him. We are entrenched in a world of change and our perception of this change is also in change. All is in a state of flux. Even in the stillness of the quiet darkness of evening, the motion never ceases: the stillness is never divorced from the flux; indeed it may render it visible for the first time. Our intellect begins reflexively to engage this change. We understand that whatever is in motion is brought into movement from something else. We are participants as well as spectators in this moving image. We participate in it by our knowledge of the movements exterior to us, by the movements we engage, and through the process of our own becoming, material and immaterial, which affect our participation in this moving image. All is this process of becoming, and yet while we are subsumed in this change we are not submerged by it, we are recognizing this change as it is a moving image of eternity. As participants who can recognize this moving image always in movement, we realize that all change is the reduction or transition from "potentiality" to "actuality," from acorn to oak, child to man, student to graduate. This change is the closing of the gap from potentiality to actuality so that all actual states arrived at through this process never extricate themselves from becoming. Every enactment of their actuality is also a filiation with their potentiality. Anything moved from potentiality to actuality is done

51. Dostoyevsky, *Idiot*, 76–77.

so by what is already in a state of actuality. What makes one domino move is another actually moving domino. What makes the wood not just the potential for heat but actually hot is actual fire. All is actually existing but existing in a miscellany of trading and transitory states. The actually hot wood has the potential to be cooled not by its own powers but by external things which are actually cool and can reduce that wood's potential to hot actuality, thus bringing it to its same or similar temperature. We begin to enter the *indefinite* regress: no existent can be both potential and actual at the same time and in the same respect. It is either one or the other, not both—it is either hot or cold, fire or not fire, moving or not moving. The domino can't be potentially moving and actually moving at the same time in the same respect; the fire can't be potentially hot and actually hot at the same time. The rain must actually fall and, when it does, only then does it have the potential not to rain. Here we begin to see the shift from an indefinite regress to a re-collection of the infinite. All natural existents appear as moved-movers. But if moving/changing things aren't both potentially moving and actually moving at the same time in the same respect this means that the object does not and cannot bring itself from a state of potentiality to actuality. Again, it requires something else already actually moving to put it into motion. With Aristotle:

> If, then, God is always in that good state in which we some-times are, this compels our wonder; and if in a better state this compels it yet more. And God is in a better state. And life also belongs to God; for the actuality of thought is life, and God is that actuality; and God's self-dependent actuality is life most good and eternal. We say therefore that God is a living being, eternal, most good, so that life and duration continuous and eternal belong to God; for this is God.[52]

Aristotle's prime mover and Saint Thomas's *un*moved mover share the language of the indefinite regress as pointing towards the perfection of the divine. But there are differences between these two original movers which cannot be overlooked. Only Saint Thomas's can truly be reconciled with freedom, providence, and creation. While Aristotle concludes to a first cause whose movement is confined to the order of efficient causal-ity, Saint Thomas is far beyond an essentialist understanding of the first mover. He posits the existence of a first unmoved mover whose action is eternally present and is innermost in any actual motion. Thomas, unlike

---

52. *Metaphysics*, 1027b–73a.

much of Thomism, also recognizes the position of the interrogative soul whose participation unveils the mystery of that infinite *To Be* beneath and immanent in all things because wholly transcendent.[53] Together the Five Ways reveal an intelligibility to the universe that is unlike any non-creational teleology. Aristotle's prime mover is the highest identification of the Good but not a personal one or one which can make our reflexive acts rise beyond themselves *to be themselves*. Creational meaning fulfills the good which Aristotle sensed as encompassing but which he could not place. The prime mover is the distant eternal, somehow originating an efficient causality which in a non-creational world has no origin. In the Aristotelian apparatus, there would be no real sense of relation between God and man even if man possessed the good which alone God possesses most fully.[54] Saint Thomas, on the other hand, is seeking in this *first way* that transition from an indefinite regress where God is but the highest conglomeration of all exemplars, neither personal nor relational, to a re-collection of the infinite which, as the ground of existence, makes possible the personal and relational.

53. Cf. Hart, *Hidden and the Manifest*, 175: "It is one thing for a theologian simply to assert that God's 'mode of causality' is utterly different from that of the creature, and that therefore God may act within the act of the creature without despoiling the latter of his liberty, but such an assertion is meaningful only if all conclusions that follow from it genuinely obey the logic of transcendence. As primary cause of all things, after all, God is first and foremost their ontological cause. He imparts being to what, in itself, is nothing at all; out of the infinite plenitude of his actuality he gives being to both potency and act; and yet what he creates, as the effect of a truly transcendent causality possesses its own being, and truly exists as other than God (though God not some 'other thing' set alongside it). This donation of being is so utterly beyond any species of causality we can conceive that the very word 'cause' has only the most remote analogous value in regard to it. And, whatever warrant Thomists might find in Thomas for speaking of God as the first efficient cause of creation (which I believe to be in principle wrong), such language is misleading unless the analogical scope of the concept of efficiency has been extended almost to the point of apophasis."

54. Fascinatingly, we can see this struggle between the identification of the highest principle as Prime Mover versus a preliminary form of Unmoved mover as far back as the Rig Veda, Koller and Koller, *Asian Philosophy*, 7–13:

"Whence this creation has arisen—perhaps it formed itself, or perhaps it did not—the one who looks down on it, in the highest heaven, only he knows—or perhaps he does not know."

"The All-Maker is vast in mind and vast in strength. He is the one who forms, who sets in order, and who is the highest image."

"Our father, who created and set in order and knows all forms, all worlds, who all alone gave names to the gods, he is the one to whom all other creatures come to ask questions."

We cannot proceed to infinity or, more precisely, arrive at the infinite by tracing an indefinite series of moved movers, each arriving at the same neediness of the other for its reduction from potentiality to actuality. When tracing the indefinite litany of effect to cause, we realize that what is moving is brought about only by something actually moving, and that this cause was also once potentially moving and was also brought into movement by a preceding cause. Every preceding cause was once a potentiality requiring something actual to make it actually move. Every actual thing participates in potentiality, the potentiality to be in a differing actual state brought about only by another. We realize that by tracing things which always participate in becoming would amount to an endless tracing. If everything was once in a state of potentiality, then nothing would have begun. But things did begin as evidenced by the empirical reality that things are in a state of potentiality and actuality. This is not a tautology but the return to the undeniability of a world always reconstituting itself, always actual because always becoming something other at the hands of the other.

If every natural actuality arrives at its actuality at the hands of another, which itself arrives at its actuality at the hands of another, we ask the question "what could be the origin of becoming, how can anything which participates in potentiality have initiated this movement when such states need something other for their reduction to actuality?" Only God's existence as pure actuality, infinite actual existence, as the first mover Who puts things into motion, Who first brought all things from potentiality to actuality is this totalizing Other. God is an *un*moved mover and not a moved mover. The actual things of the natural world are moved movers: they are in a state of actuality which always carries the potentiality for another state. Both their potentiality and their present actual states are moved into actuality by another already in that actual state. Moved movers: the fire *moves* the wood to be hot but it itself is *moved* to be fire by the lighter. Natural things in actuality are not pure *Actus*, they are not *un*moved movers. No movement in nature can be the primal movement of things. Since every actual movement in nature began in a state of potentiality (and has the potentiality to return to potentiality) none of them can be the true "first" that put them into motion. And we cannot, as the objector would have us believe, account for one thing which cannot account for itself by another which cannot account for itself *ad infinitum*, for thus the whole cannot be accounted for: *reductio ad absurdum*. If we begin in sheer potentiality nothing would have begun. Yet a world of things, which always partake in potentiality, does exist! The origination of its movement, beyond any reasonable doubt, cannot be derived from any aspect of the natural world which before all else signifies its *need* to be moved so that it can be a moved mover.

> Others came to a knowledge of God from his eternity. They saw that whatever was in things was changeable, and that the more noble something is in the grades of being, so much the less it has of mutability. For example, the lower bodies are mutable both as to their substance and to place, while the heavenly bodies, which are more noble, are immutable in substance and change only with respect to place. We can clearly conclude from this that the first principle of all things, which is supreme and more noble, is changeless and eternal. The prophet suggests this eternity of the Word when he says, seated, i.e., presiding without any change and eternally. 'Your throne, O God, is forever and ever' (Ps 44:7); 'Jesus Christ is the same yesterday, today, and forever' (Heb 13:8). John points to this eternity when he says below (1:1), 'In the beginning was the Word.'[55]

We have arrived at the *ananke stenai*, that necessity to come to a stop in the order of reason which unveils a stop or origin in the order of being. God's existence is pure actuality, always actually existing and thus not dependent on anything else for his actuality. He is the *un*-moved mover, the infinitely actual mover, who instantiates the process of becoming because he is irreducible to it. Movement requires, as its first mover, the existence of something that "was" never in a state of potentiality, something always actual, an un-moved mover. From our connatural experience of the world, the world itself in its intelligibility discovered in its neediness for the other reveals, beyond a reasonable doubt, the existence of an *un*moved mover. Why is it God? Because all of the natural world are moved movers and no moved mover is a "first" order of movement but an intermediary one. How could an intermediary order of movement initiate, let alone sustain, becoming? But there is a world of becoming, thus it is necessary something has initiated it and sustained itself. Since it cannot be a moved mover, it must be a mover not in need of any reduction from potentiality to actuality for its movement, and this unmoved mover we call God. What exactly this God is in essence is a mystery beyond the reach of reason but reason, beyond any reasonable doubt, points to the certitude of this mystery.

55. Thomas Aquinas, *Comm. St. John*, prooemium, 4.

The Rosary of Tears: *Sed Contra* Courtesy

One moment—be quiet—don't say anything—stand still, I want
to look into your eyes. Yes, stand like that; let me look. Let me
bid farewell to a human being. He stood still, very pale, his hair
wet with perspiration, clutching rather oddly at the prince with
his hand, as though afraid to let go of him. Hippolyte, Hippolyte,
what's the matter? cried the Prince. One moment—enough—
I'm going to lie down. I'll just have one sip to the health of the
sun.[56]

This First Way may invoke a temporal succession to articulate its
logic but it is not reducible to that succession, and in its essence it resides on a metaphysical plane irreducible to change. But so little is this a
denigration of change in the Greco-Roman-Stoic style that it has, on the
contrary, elevated change—the miscellany of actual existence, this rosary
of tears we call life—to the vehicle of privileged access to the divine! For
if we cannot get to God by means of the miscellaneous minutiae of the
world, then we cannot get to God. But we *can*, and so we *must*. If, when
we speak of act-and-potency as conceptual abstractions divorced from
actual things, the danger is to empty the world *as world* of foundational
meaning. If we keep tracing the causes in nature we would go on indefinitely, each thing requiring something else to bring it into actuality. In
order to avoid this *reductio ad absurdum*, we realize that this process of
change in nature would never have begun "in the first place" without a
Being who, as *un*moved, is not in becoming, not in time and its succession. The demonstration begins in sense experience and thus midway,
in an infinite thicket of intermediaries. When it points to its origin, it
points to a mystery beyond the empirical realm which grants the empirical realm its full intelligibility and certitude. We may proceed from effect
to cause but, for the lesser to direct us to the greater, we must somehow be
in possession of the greater. The empirical and scientific world of change
only makes sense because of the metaphysical, *not as its antithesis but as
its foundation*, just as the moved movers cannot help but circle around
and point us to that difference as such, to that beyond time-and-becom-
ing *un*moved mover, God, Who loves to multiply intermediaries as the
privileged access to his love.

56. Dostoyevsky, *Idiot*, 402.

The eternal order did not need to be forced and ratified by a template of ideality over and against the natural world. The demonstrations are a lesson in the co-naturalness of the natural law and moral order. The moral order in the image and likeness of God is unique and distinct from all else, but it is not the antithesis of natural meaning as if it survives only by a protective sequestering. If the bodily soul is given a chance to encounter the good of the world as it manifests non-reflexively, then when does it reflect of the Good? The divine, understood as the only fulfillment of natural yearning, as the *un*moved mover, is seen as the necessary source and fulfillment of becoming. Now note the judicial structure of the argument as previously discussed. Can the world as effect be accounted for only by the evidence of the natural order? Alternatively, does the evidence of change point to a culprit-qua-cause of change? God is in the dock. Is he responsible (guilty) as culprit/cause or is there some reasonable doubt, a natural explanation that will acquit him of responsibility independent of his *sed contra* courteous confession of responsibility? Saint Thomas plays prosecutor: God is responsible for becoming-qua-world as its necessary cause as unmoved mover. The evidence can be explained in no other way. Guilty as charged . . . Next case.

The Second Way:
Efficient Causes and the Recovery of Freedom

The second way is from the nature of the efficient cause. In the world of sense, we find there is an order of efficient causes. There is no case known (neither is it, indeed, possible) in which a thing is found to be the efficient cause of itself; for so it would be prior to itself, which is impossible. Now in efficient causes it is not possible to go on to infinity, because in all efficient causes following in order, the first is the cause of the intermediate cause, and the intermediate is the cause of the ultimate cause, whether the intermediate cause be several, or only one. Now to take away the cause is to take away the effect. Therefore, if there be no first cause among efficient causes, there will be no ultimate, nor any intermediate cause. But if in efficient causes it is possible to go on to infinity, there will be no first efficient cause, neither will there be an ultimate effect, nor any intermediate efficient causes;

all of which is plainly false. Therefore, it is necessary to admit a first efficient cause, to which everyone gives the name of God.[57]

The *second way* appears as the flipside of the first demonstration and, in many respects, it is the same demonstration but from a different vantage. Yet, this difference is essential. What is learned is neither repetitive nor unnecessary; it is received again for the first time and this time with a view to defending a radical freedom as existing only within an eschatology. The first demonstration reveals its intelligibility through the neediness and passivity of the world—that each natural thing in its state of becoming always requires something other than itself to convert its potentiality to actuality. Instead of focusing on the neediness of the world, this essential repetition dramatizes the intelligibility and activity of the world as capable of enacting meaning, event, decision, choice, and all forms of actions. While the first demonstration depicts a world in need aligned with holy infliction, the second way reveals the world in the hidden meaning of potency as active power. This is a natural world too full of life, so that if the garden is ignored, it grows wild and lifts even the concrete stepping stones and finds room to expand within crevices. This unrelenting expansion can be seen in the spiritual and the corporeal, the immaterial and the material. It is the source of pain which prompts Hippolyte to seek suicide as his only refuge. Seeing so much raw power pass over his infirm body, deemed unfit to take on its life, is a merciless taunt. And it is the same cosmogony which causes him to hesitate, to stretch his body, to protract over time and space, aligned with his soul and to live a little more. It is also the source of Sartre's nausea at the recognition of the *de trop* excess of existence.

> We degrade providence too much by attributing our ideas to it out of annoyance at being unable to understand it. But again, if it is impossible to understand it, then, I repeat, it is hard to answer for what it is not given to man to understand. And if that is so, how am I to be put on trial for not having been able to understand the true will and the laws of Providence? No, we'd better leave religion alone. Besides, I've said enough. When I read these lines the sun, I'm sure, will have risen and resounded in the sky, and its immense incalculable power will pour forth upon the world. So be it! I shall die gazing straight at the source of power and life, and I shall not want this life![58]

57. *ST* I, 2, 3, *resp.*
58. Dostoyevsky, *Idiot*, 387–88.

From our first sensible experiences of the world we see life brimming with power and activity, each facet of existence buzzing in an unrelenting divine indifference which makes us more certain that the sun will rise and fall each day than of the fulfillment of our own intentions. Rather than viewing the world from the naked passivity of potentiality-to-actuality, we are beginning from actuality, from all the efficient, making, producing, active ordering and initiating causes which populate and dominate the world we inhabit. This may be the inverse of the first demonstration and may end with a companion conclusion, but the *way* is telling. This world of vibrancy and power cannot be passed over, not only because it is where we *are* but because its power itself constitutes our own. Each action has the power to spur on another. The essential business in St. Petersburg prompts Myshkin to leave the safety of Switzerland and to find his only relatives. Making introductions at the Yepanchin house was the seat of that efficient or making cause whereby he casts his eye on Nastassya's haunting photograph, and that glance was enough to be the making cause of his love and his pity. Heavy clouds are the active cause of rain, the rain is the active cause of vegetation and the vegetation is the efficient cause of the animal's nourishment, and that nourishment is the efficient cause of the animal's procreation. The idea for a house is the active cause of the blueprints, the blueprints are the active cause for the foundation, the foundation is the active cause for the house structure, a structure which is the efficient cause for the walls, and the walls become the making cause for the decoration and paint. We cannot end this ceaseless ordered cycle of power and activity that affects the body and the soul, the widely understood and the mysterious, the nebulous and overlooked reaches of consciousness and being. There is order throughout the chaos. This reflects more the intelligibility of the moral miscellany as respective of free natures with directional movement, than a non-creational teleology at odds with freedom. In the human realm, the so-called free choice sets in motion an order of consequences from first to last. And yet of course, to give the hard determinist his due, that free choice is itself determined by efficient causes themselves stretching back indefinitely. And one must be careful here not to infiltrate Saint Thomas's open and free nature with a determinist prescriptivism under the guise of a teleology more appropriate to a closed rather than to an open nature.

Our reflexive action intellectually gathers a structure to these making causes. We understand that they exist within a cycle of priority, an intelligibility as to how the order unfolds. The news of pressing business "must" precede the autumn's train ride where Myshkin meets Ragozhin and embarks on their shared fate in a way similar to how clouds precede the rain, and the rain precedes, so as to make possible, the vegetation. This priority is signified in a twofold manner: a temporal and an intelligible priority. Lastrites may occur prior to the moment of death, but this temporal priority does not extend into the realm of Being and causality. The rites do not cause the death, as the rooster's crow does not cause the sun to rise. But in the order of priority, the order of temporality is unmasked to be a necessary one. Not only does the pressing business come temporally prior to embarking the train, it is the intelligible priority which must occur so as to issue in the motivation to take the journey.

In this chain of making causes each is dependent on the other. As in the *first way*, something already in actuality is required in order to transform another from potentiality to actuality. This interdependency reveals that no efficient cause can emancipate itself from that cycle of dependency; if one cause is removed the other causes cease to exist. Every efficient cause is a made-maker as much as it is a moved-mover. This dependency means that each making cause is ultimately dependent on a prior efficient cause which is itself revealed to be the effect of a prior cause. We cannot proceed in an indefinite regress where each natural cause circles but cannot reach the source, the difference as such, required for its existence. The *second way* shows not that the divine is far beneath and at an inaccessible depth, *but at the very surface of things*,[59] that mystery confronts us in all things as primordially "given" in all existential acts, not excluding but radically including the ethical/moral act as subordinate and-as-free. Causality is not the opponent of freedom but is its accompanying precondition, rendering determinism both naïve and irrelevant, indeed as quaint as its putative opposite, indeterminism. Saint Thomas does not need to leap over the Chinese wall erected by Kant and positivism, or blow it

---

59. The incarnate oddness where certainty reveals mystery and is never truly opposed to it, places us within the power of Christianity. See C. Gilson, *Political Dialogue*, 197–98: "To be possessed and dispossessed, at once, of the fullness of Christ protects man and allows him to survive the death he already is. The intensity of the mystery constantly overthrows man, outwitting the non-freeing powers of nature. The mystery is experienced therefore as a "super-affirming negation." See Pseudo-Dionysius, *Divine Names*, in *Complete Works*, IV, 6. The heart of the church is also a *hyper-icon* surrounded by the iconic which, as reflection, points towards the entrance way but cannot direct man inside its imageless face. This agitated possession/dispossession, as certainty no longer diametrically opposed to uncertainty, is how the church as body of Christ provides for the reality that man is *in* but not *of* the world. The world constantly overturned by Christ is no longer *of* itself, and is itself *in* but not *of* the world.

up like Nietzsche or live *as if* it weren't there. Thomas can quite calmly walk through it because it is a mirage, an illusion of vanity that comes from living in the desert of mere thought too long. Both rationalism and romanticism are united in sentimentality.

> Man is master of his acts and of his willing or not willing, because of his deliberate reason, which can be bent to one side or another. And although he is master of his deliberating or not deliberating, yet this can only be by a previous deliberation; and since it cannot go on to infinity, we must come at length to this, that man's free-will is moved by an extrinsic principle, which is above the human mind, to wit by God, as the Philosopher proves in the chapter 'On Good Fortune' (Ethic. Eudem. vii). Hence the mind of man still unweakened is not so much master of its act that it does not need to be moved by God; and much more the free-will of man weakened by sin, whereby it is hindered from good by the corruption of the nature.[60]

Each natural efficient cause is the master of its effect as each human being is the master of his deliberate actions. The universe hums with power and activity, but all this activity depends upon an immediacy with a causal origin of true priority. Whereas each natural efficient cause has *relative* priority, it is never absolutely prior and instead always reveals its own status as an effect, as an inherent neediness. But if there is a world of efficient causes which are only relatively prior, how can this freedom-to-cause be existent in the first place without a cause which in its efficiency is absolutely prior? The question is: can a natural cause be the first efficient cause? The answer is no, beyond any reasonable doubt, precisely because every natural efficient cause reveals, through its union of act and potency, its unabashed intermediary status. The reality of its intermediary status renders it unable to be a first. And if there is no first there are no intermediaries, but there are intermediaries, therefore there must be a first-as-difference-as-such: a first which is necessary, commanding the fates as the source of the fates, and the difference-as-such, which enables the freedom of the intermediaries to act as efficient causes.

> All things in the world are moved to act by something else except the First Agent, Who acts in such a manner that He is in no way moved to act by another; and in Whom nature and will are the same. So there is nothing unfitting in an angel being moved to act in so far as such natural inclination is implanted in him

---

60. *ST* I-II, 109, 2, ad.1

by the Author of his nature. Yet he is not so moved to act that he does not act himself, because he has free-will.[61]

God is the first efficient cause, the *un*made maker, Whose very efficient causality reveals the marriage of the fated and free. Who in essence this Being *is*, we cannot wrap our minds or hands around. The "un" in unmoved mover is our affirming of the certitude *as* mystery. But we know beyond a reasonable doubt that the entanglement of responsibility and providence, freedom, and the cosmogonic, align in him.

While the first demonstration depicts a world so consumed with neediness that it is inflicted and groaning for the other, the *second way* reveals the same world expanded in its vibrancy and power. And if the human person is the horizon between time and eternity, then our souls are also that borderline between utter neediness and cosmogonic power, and there is no way to extricate ourselves from one in favor of the other. It is precisely the belief that such extrication is possible which constitutes the gravest sins in the name of either the protection of an artificial freedom or an equally artificial concession to fate.[62] It is the unity of the two that cuts away and shapes the soul in its character, and the impossible balance between the two reveals the *alter Christus*. The soul is in utter need and yet possessed of a power unlike any other creature on earth. This neediness is not the opposite of freedom, and that power is not the assurance of its existence. It is the strange and often unforgiving union of the two which constitutes human freedom, a radical freedom possessive of a divine directionality, a freedom understood only as it situates itself inside the fatal. There is no overriding theme sitting atop existence, no point A getting us to point B without the unsought particulars of time and chance. And yet, the presence of path is there, not dictating the intermediate actions but found within them, enjoined in all the myriad choices that are disconnected.

> God moves man's will, as the Universal Mover, to the universal object of the will, which is good. And without this universal motion, man cannot will anything. But man determines himself by his reason to will this or that, which is true or apparent good. Nevertheless, sometimes God moves some specially to the

---

61. *ST* I 60, 1, ad.2.

62. One need look no further than the Charlie Gard case. See Camosy, "Learning from Charlie Gard." See also the appendix, "Case in Point," "The Grandest of All Refusals: Abortion's Pogrom against Contingency," 295.

willing of something determinate, which is good; as in the case
of those whom He moves by grace.[63]

All of Myshkin's actions unfold in a polyphonic miscellany. There is
no naive teleological theme grafted into the narrative. And yet there is,
again, a pattern in the disconnections, not overriding them, but living in
the freedom and responsibility of our personal choices. Because the utter
neediness of the world is our own neediness, and its total power courses
also through us, freedom and fate dance as one. Everything has inevitability and direction, and every end and every beginning is nevertheless surprising and haunting. The knife rests on the table at Rogozhin's;
Nastassya at one time lets it graze her own hands; it is the knife held in
Rogozhin's hands, stalking the hotel corridor preparing to bludgeon the
Prince. Myshkin's epileptic fit saved him from fate only to be reaffirmed
through the death of Nastassya and his return to deafness. The knife that
kills Nastassya remains within lineage of the guillotine and of the man
who slits his friend's throat on impulse but begs for forgiveness before-
hand. Nastassya's death was fated from the beginning and it haunted every turn of the novel and yet it posed no imposition on freedom. Because
of this, fate stings with the recognized reality that another end, another
way was once possible. This is the creative endurance of souls living on
the horizon between time and eternity, fate and free will, the non-futural
and the futural:

> "Did you intend to kill her before my wedding, just before the
> ceremony, at the door of the church, with the knife? Did you or
> not?"
> "I don't know if I did or not," Rogozhin replied dryly, as if
> he was rather surprised at the question and did not answer it.
> "Did you ever bring the knife with you to Pavlovsk?"
> "No, never," he said, then after a silence added, "All I can tell
> you about the knife is this, Lev Nikolayevitch: I took it out of a
> locked drawer this morning, because it all happened this morn-
> ing sometime before four o'clock. It was always here between the
> pages of a book. And—and there was something else that was
> strange: the knife seemed to go in three or four inches, just un-
> der the left breast, and no more than half a tablespoon of blood
> came out of her chemise, no more than that . . . That's when the
> stab goes straight into the heart."[64]

63. *ST* I-II, 9, 6, ad. 3.
64. Dostoyevsky, *Idiot*, 637.

There is a very real sense wherein that eschatological and absolute end must be the *limiting* factor essential to moral actions while at the same time be the *un*-limiting sphere that accommodates human freedom as being in the image and likeness of God. The end must be both the source of moral limit and the freeing source of our anthropological or metaphysical transformation. Is this a contradiction in terms, as Sartre would see it, or is this at the very heart of the power of the Christian God as our end? The problem becomes how to articulate an eschatology indebted to Aristotle while going clearly beyond him. This is precisely what the Five Ways achieve. Is there metaphysical freedom in the metaphysics of Aristotle? Can a strict Aristotelian teleology set out for a prime mover accommodate the implications of a creator God? Additionally, if we articulate the creator God to be within the template of an Aristotelian teleology, originally set out for a prime over, without a deepening of that teleology into eschatology (i.e., the free act of entering into image and likeness) are we not in fact promoting a serious loss of freedom? The teleology of the prime mover is one of limit and never envisioned for that metaphysical freedom cultivated in creational causality and in its corresponding image and likeness. It is only incorporated within the language of the Thomistic *un*moved mover as first efficient cause through a total transformation. Aristotle's metaphysical finality ultimately overwhelms the freedom that the *Nichomachean Ethics* sought to defend. Aristotle could envision intermediary acts of freedom but in an effort to make sense of the intelligibility of the universe, the finality must override the potency of that freedom, rendering it null and void. In a sense, Arisotle is caught in a catch-twenty-two: finality is necessary to intelligibilize freedom within the context of a world and a situation, but if it is present *as finality* it overwhelms and destroys freedom. This is the unavoidable predicament of a non-creational order in which existence has no real role to play except as a mode of essence. Saint Thomas's finality, while needing to invoke the intelligibility of the universe, cannot undermine the freedom which makes that universe meaningful. Because the universe is a personal ordination the stakes are immeasurably higher.

Without an "end" you might have environment but you could not have a *situation* which all moral quandaries are: *what* shall I do and *why* shall I do it, *here & now*? It is true that all ethical acts and decisions are, so to speak, situational, but this is so precisely because and insofar as they involve a relation to an end, for it is exactly this that defines a situation as what it is: a particular complex or matrix of actuality and possibilities the order and meaning of which can only be determined (i.e., in decision) in relation to the end willed or recognized. By its very nature, a situation refers beyond itself to a *possible* end: in other words, there is no such thing as an absolute situation (*except* in relation to an absolute end): the "human condition" taken as a universal situation would be such an absolute situation. Also, the very idea of an absolute or supreme or final or perfect or complete end already involves the notion of situation in order that it may be realized or approximated or actualized in ethical action. Thus, there are no absolute rules (as there are in speculative knowledge) that can be invoked to determine *a priori* the relation of a situation to its end; this role is performed by *prudence*.

Lebedev, for example, participates in the attempted extortion of the Prince's inheritance money, when in fact he knows that Burdovsky is not Pavlishchev's heir. This is by definition an ethical act of moral decision, that is, it is an act or decision specifically human in that it employs or puts to use human freedom: *it directs action*: but in order to direct action, there must be, also by definition, something in accordance with which action is directed, and this is the end or good. Now, parenthetically, it is clear that in such an instance, that is, in such a concrete and particular situation in which possibilities and ends are pondered, no absolute or *a priori* rules can be invoked in order to determine the activity, except in the most general or universal way: i.e., "one must always seek the good" holds here; but *what* the good of the situation is in no way is predetermined: if it were, then the moral act or ethical decision could not be a moral act or ethical decision, and man would not be man. Instead, I decide in terms of a particular instance/situation and thus in regard to a particular/specific end/good (e.g., money needed, personal dislike, jealousy). Still this particular situation and this particular end are only actualized—because man is a temporal/durational/historical being—in the light of a totalizing unity or perfection, which is a final end (whether or not this dependency is consciously recognized or not). So that the order of specific ends and particular situations hangs from a prior ethical decision in relation to the final end: e.g., "what kind of person is it that I want to be?" or "what kind of man should I be in order to be happy with myself in myself?" Now, again, this does not deny what we have already affirmed, namely that there are no *a priori* rules; rather does it confirm it. For this totalizing end, again, says nothing in *concreto* about the means of its actualization in a given situation, although it gives the situation its meaning and its direction precisely *as* a situation.

Sartre's concept of *project*[65] which totalizes and unifies all ethical activity is appropriate in this regard, and it is not so very different, *formally* considered, from Aristotle and Aquinas. One could object that we are being hyper-rational to suppose that each little gesture has reference to some ultimate whole or that many/most decisions are made in terms of such an end. In other words, it may well be that the vast preponderance of all decisions are made on whim/feeling/compulsion and the like. But this will not do as an objection. It fails on two counts:

1. Such a conception is un-reflective and thus un-philosophical. In other words, even if it were true, all it says is that most men live unexamined lives, which, we know from Socrates, is not worth the living, whereas we are examining the true essence of human activity; what it means, in other words, for man *to be* man.

2. More importantly for our purposes, however, is that such a conception of the alleged thoughtlessness of ethical activity (i.e., its meaninglessness) is itself already, as Sartre has shown, a moral choice in relation to a totalizing end which bestows meaning and direction on particular situational acts. If one sees one's personal decisions in no other terms than those, for example, of the immediate pleasure of the moment, or as indifferent because in essence unfree—well then there is in this *already* a moral decision, is there not, a conception of man in his finality, albeit one that denies both the essence of moral decision, human finality, and thus even of situation (for immediacy is not duration, nor is it temporality, nor is it history). There is no way out of the ethical circle, any more than there is any way out of the ontological, metaphysical, or hermeneutical circle: to step out of the circle is to deny action just as it is to deny being: and neither can be denied without contradiction. And more: to deny action is to deny what we began by accepting, namely the situation: in seeking to explain human activity, we have explained it away. This is the contradiction. "The end (*finis*) has the same role in relation to the practical order as the self-evident principle has in speculative matters."[66]

What has been set out so far in the first two demonstrations of the Five Ways is a structure that moves us beyond an Aristotelian teleology

---

65. Cf. Sartre, "Pursuit of Being," 3–32.
66. *ST* I, 82, 1, *resp.*

and can effectively respond to the Sartrean critique. The relationship between the neediness of the first demonstration and the power and activity of the second place, freedom in situations where limit is not the rejection of freedom but where it is sharpened and refined.

Whenever the prime mover is explained, it is difficult not to see everything else being "caused" by the prime mover. If the prime mover is the eternal and foundational origin of reality and if the rest of nature follows a sort of teleological end, then is there any space for freedom? The prime mover works as the source of being and reality. Such a source seems to be far off, non-relational, and unchanging, aside from causing the "primary motion."[67] The first mover, for Aristotle, "must be essentially immovable."[68] When this kind of being is the source of reality, one must question whether reality could have attributes opposed to this source, particularly will and desire. And while it is easier to see that man could possess attributes of will and desire opposed to the prime mover since the prime mover does not create man—it is much more difficult to envision how the human person could have genuine attributes opposed to God in a creational metaphysics. The prime mover is a being that is perfectly still and does not need anything. Would not man be of the same kind of nature? And even if the human person is no longer in Aristotle's universe, if like-unto-like is a primal truth of a creational metaphysics and if that relationship of human likeness to divine likeness is set within or added to a metaphysically unaltered Aristotelian teleology, have we, contra-intuitively, the makings for the loss of genuine creational freedom? If we place that Christian sense of like-unto-like within the unaltered Aristotelian teleology, have we not set out persons to act in the image and likeness of the divine end which will quite possibly limit them and remove their freedom because that divine end is, teleologically speaking, by its very nature a limit, stop, and cessation? It is not, as in the Five Ways, a door to the divine which, when opened, reveals our freedom. In Saint Thomas's existential metaphysics, our natures are open natures *because* we are existentially dependent on the one being Whose essence is identical with his existence. We are not substances limited within by the impregnable boundaries of our substance but a nature requiring the existential otherness of the divine for its perfection, an otherness which is personal and relational.

67. Cf. Aristotle, *Met.* 1079.
68. Aristotle, *Met.* 1079.

The Cause Celebre

The issue of causation is at hand: the prime mover does not cause like the creator God causes, and thus: does the fact that the creator God causes out of nothing liberate us from the problem of freedom, or does it make it all the more difficult? Does the Aristotelian teleological structure, which in some respects ensures *moral* freedom and therefore the moral ethical act, have a serious shortcoming vis-à-vis *metaphysical* freedom?[69] Metaphysical freedom is the free non-mediated *pre-disposition* of man-in-the-world that allows moral freedom to be a reflection of his more primal freedom—that, being on the horizon between time and eternity, the human person, is *unlike* any other natural creature:

> A bird was singing in the tree above him and [Myshkin] began looking for it among the leaves; suddenly the bird took wing and flew away, and at the same moment he, for some reason re-called the 'gnat' in 'the hot sunshine,' about which Hippolyte has

69. For Pope Emeritus Benedict XVI, there is a twofold sense to conscience and the collapse of these two can cause a reduced understanding of our moral comportment. In the late Medieval and Modern eras, the more epistemological notion of conscience as decision-maker/choice obfuscates the more primal/original notion of conscience as ontological/pre-cognitive foundation (recollection, habitus, inherent good). This ontological or pre-cognitive foundation is what we are striving for when articulating the metaphysical freedom that allows man truly to be free, to lose or gain his essence, or happiness or end. This is freedom as pre-condition for moral freedom. See Ratzinger, *On Conscience*, 40: "There is an ontological inner tendency within man, who is created in the likeness of God, towards the divine. From its origin, man's being resonates with some things and clashes with others. This anamnesis of the origin, which results from the god-like constitution of our Being, is not a conceptually articulated knowing, a store of retrievable contents. It is, so to speak, an inner sense, a capacity to recall, so that the one whom it addresses, if he is not turned in on himself, hears its echo from within. He sees: That's It! This is what my nature points to and seeks. The possibility for and right to mission rest on this anamnesis of the Creator, which is identical to the ground of our existence . . . nothing belongs less to me than I myself. My own 'I' is the site of the profoundest surpassing of self and contact with Him from whom I came and toward whom I am going . . . It is the longing for a truth that does not just make demands of us but also transforms us through expiation and pardon. Through these, as Aeschylus puts it, 'guilt is washed away,' and our own being is transformed from within, beyond our capability. This is the real innovation of Christianity: The Logos, the truth in person, is also the atonement, the transforming forgiveness that is above and beyond our capability and incapability. Therein lies the real novelty on which larger Christian memory is founded, and which indeed, at the same time, constitutes the deeper answer to what the anamnesis of the Creator expects of us."

written that 'it knew its place and took in the general chorus,' but he alone was 'an outcast.'[70]

Man is not a being with a *ready-made essence* that defines his end. If this were the case, his moral actions would be futile reflections of freedom subsumed by the *determined* teleological end prescribed by his essence, just as a brute animal has a determined nature to a determinedly natural end prescribed by his essence. On the other end, we cannot deny essences in order to defend freedom because all we would be defending would be a freedom unworthy of defense: a deontological will-based desire with no direction, no transcendence. But rejecting Sartre and turning to Aristotle does not offer a valid option for the Christian if there is moral choice, but all these choices and their particularities cannot compete with the necessity of the teleological end. In Aristotle's metaphysics, the freedom of moral choice is subsumed by the over-riding primal end necessarily and teleologically prescribed and completed in each being's essence. If this is true, how are we free if the end of our nature is already prescribed and thus unfree? And yet, on the other hand, there must be an intelligible pattern to existence. The teleology cannot be thrown away but must be deepened so as to accommodate the nature of man to be in the *image* and likeness of the creator God. That image and likeness entails a profound metaphysical freedom to strive to live up to an image that has no end, that pulls up our essences and protracts our souls in yearning because we don't exist in our own right.

This is the central wisdom of the Five Ways. Saint Thomas is not demonstrating a prime mover, nor is his argument for efficient causation one which is merely the first in a temporal series. The inclusion of existence is the dramatic difference which enables teleology to be deepened into an eschatological relation. No longer are enclosed essences directed towards an end which cannot truly affect them but which only confers finality and overrides the freedom of their intermediate choices. This new directionality transforms the soul through freedom because the completion, the arrival of the end, is the reception of our being in its own incommunicable and distinct fullness.

Let us not forget that Saint Thomas begins his demonstrations in concrete sensible lived experience. All abstraction, no matter how spiritual, how complex, is only possible because it turns upon the particularity of the little thing. The metaphysically abstract language of the Prime

---

70. Dostoyevsky, *Idiot*, 406.

Mover conceptually conveys an un-relational distant eternal which itself does not need or possess freedom and thus, whether rightly or wrongly, one must question whether the natures of every being moving towards this end could possess a real or intrinsic sense of freedom, if by "freedom" one means the sense of the agony and ecstasy within the hunt for our image and likeness set out in Christianity. The *alter Christus* in all of us is asked to be in the inexhaustible image and likeness of that Person Who as Being has no end. This kind of free will is what is found within the life of love which is transcendent, personal, and transformational. As Augustine says of God's love in the *Confessions*, "you are good and all-powerful, caring for each one of us as though the only one in your care,"[71] so that freedom means fulfilling our Form by breaking, paradoxically, the confines of that formal or essentialist end. In the first two demonstrations, the relations between passivity and activity, neediness and power, unveil the tension between freedom and finality within a teleology. When Saint Thomas dramatically alters the Aristotelian worldview so that his *un*moved mover is existence itself, he has transformed the teleology into a living *eschaton*. Fate, here, is no longer the enemy of freedom but can be its perfection, and if the finality we freely choose is the true finality, neither illusion nor lie, we possess a radical freedom Sartre could only have suspected but could not grasp, let alone acknowledge.[72]

The Third Way: The Gratuity of Existence

The third way is taken from possibility and necessity, and runs thus. We find in nature things that are possible to be and not to be, since they are found to be generated, and to corrupt, and consequently, they are possible to be and not to be. But it is impossible for these always to exist, for that which is possible not to be at some time is not. Therefore, if everything is possible not to be, then at one time there could have been nothing in existence. Now if this were true, even now there would be nothing in existence, because that which does not exist only begins to exist by something already existing. Therefore, if at one time nothing was in existence, it would have been impossible for anything to have begun to exist; and thus even now nothing

71. *Confessions* III, 11, 19.

72. See Sartre on counter-finality in his two volumes of the *Critique of Dialectical Reason*.

would be in existence—which is absurd. Therefore, not all beings are merely possible, but there must exist something the existence of which is necessary. But every necessary thing either has its necessity caused by another, or not. Now it is impossible to go on to infinity in necessary things which have their necessity caused by another, as has been already proved in regard to efficient causes. Therefore, we cannot but postulate the existence of some being having of itself its own necessity, and not receiving it from another, but rather causing in others their necessity. This all men speak of as God.[73]

A cosmological demonstration begins in non-mediated sensible experience and attempts to show, from effect to cause, the necessity for a first cause that is purely actual, needing nothing other than itself for its existence, and thus alone able to be the existential foundation for all finite existence. Saint Thomas's Five Ways are all cosmological demonstrations, but this third demonstration on the relation between possibility and necessity is considered the prime cosmological argument.[74] In this demonstration, passivity and intermediary causation are discovered to be attributes of finite existence as a total gift.

> There was neither non-existence nor existence then, there was neither the realm of space nor the sky which is beyond. What stirred? Where? In whose protection? Was there water bottomlessly deep?[75]

Before we embark on this *third way*, we should briefly distinguish the first demonstration's use of potentiality and actuality from the third demonstration's application of possibility and necessity. In commonplace parlance, the language of potentiality and possibility appear interchangeable, and while they are related terms, their meanings express a shift in argumentation from an empirical emphasis to a metaphysical one. In the *first way*, the question of existence resides unspoken, but in the *third way*, existence itself is the fundamental question at hand. This is the linchpin of all five demonstrations, the estuary from which the surrounding demonstrations flow, receiving support and nuance in their meanings. In demonstration one, Saint Thomas is looking at the world of becoming. Potentiality is a question of empirical state and not whether

73. *ST* I, 2 *resp.*
74. Cf. Feser, "Thomistic Proof," 117–46.
75. Rig Veda, in Koller and Koller, *Asian Philosophy*, 6.

something exists or not, or exists necessarily or contingently. Whether or not Myshkin is actually in an epileptic fit does not directly refer to the Prince's existence, only to his present state. Whether or not the water is potentially hot or actually hot is not a question of its existence except indirectly through the longer way of dependency which always circles around the mystery of existence. Aquinas in the first and second ways has taken that longer way, he has pointed to the truth of the world in all its neediness and in all its powerful activity as an indefinite series of intermediaries groaning for their shared origin. In the *third way*, he is now ready to approach directly that "*un*" in *un*caused cause, that faceless mystery which faces us, too near to be seen.

Possible or contingent things are nothing other than existence in its gratuity; these things do not contain the necessary warrant for their existence. The Swiss sanitorium where Myshkin begins and ends is not necessary for his or its own existence. It may have a "borrowed necessity" but not absolute necessity. Myshkin requires this place in order to convalesce, as air is a borrowed necessity for the continuance of life. Neither the sanatorium nor the air we breathe truly raise themselves to the level of necessity.[76] It is not necessary for possible things to exist; they would not and could not exist unless they are made or caused or created by something else—their existence must be brought into being by something else and is thus open to generation and decay. What the *longior via* of the first and second demonstrations has clearly revealed is a world made entirely of possible beings. The indefinite cycle of dependency, whether masked in power and activity or seen for what

---

76. Air may be far more in the image and likeness of true necessity than the sanatorium, but once the specific human dimension is added to existence, does not the language of necessity change, or at least the language of borrowed necessity? For Aristotle, leisure is the union of pleasure and happiness which allows us to live blessedly (*NE* 1338a1). It is the end for the sake of itself, the only end which truly distinguishes us from brute animals. Thus, if this distinction constitutes us as humans, in a way strange and profound, leisure's borrowed necessity carries the same importance, and more, than the very air we breathe which does not distinguish us as humans. Cf. *NE* 1177b6-18: "The activity of the practical virtues is exhibited in politics and in affairs of war, and actions concerning these seem to be un-leisurely. Actions in war are completely so, for no one chooses to fight a war for the sake of fighting a war . . . But political action is also un-leisurely, and beyond taking part in political activity itself, this type of action seeks to gain power and honors, or at least, happiness for the politician himself and for his fellow citizens, and is different from political science [theory], which is clearly sought as being different. So among virtuous actions, political actions and actions in war are superior in nobility and greatness, but they are un-leisurely, aim at some end, and are not choiceworthy for their own sake."

it is, unveils the endless penultimate nature of all finite existents. And since no intermediate cause can come into being without a first cause, if all the natural world is comprised of nothing but intermediate causes, then nothing would be. But there is a world, a world full of causes that did not have to be, that were not necessary, that are possible and thus gratuitous and in that sense "absurd." The metaphysical reality of the gift of existence places us pre-thematically within the intensity of the Creator God. The gratuity which faith can unveil is here pressed up against us in a non-mediated union. Our existence is not necessary. What then does this mean? We are at the door of the divine when we uncover the unmistakable gratuity of existence. This gratuity begins to reveal itself in the Greek understanding of unity:

> First, if in a number of things we find something that is common to all, we must conclude that this something was the effect of some one cause: for it is not possible that to each one by reason of itself this common something belongs, since each one by itself is different from the others: and diversity of causes produces a diversity of effects. Seeing then that being is found to be common to all things, which are by themselves distinct from one another, it follows of necessity that they must come into being not by themselves, but by the action of some cause. Seemingly this is Plato's argument, since he required every multitude to be preceded by unity not only as regards number but also in reality.[77]

Determining whether or not that gratuity is a gift or an absurd *de trop* curse, as freedom is such an either/or, is discoverable only in the language of the faith. But this faith has its metaphysical preamble in these Five Ways and most particularly in the third demonstration. Can existence be lived without acknowledging its gratuity, if not its absurdity? And if we accept this radical contingency, what then do we do? For Lebedev's apocalypse, the damned sought the gifts of God as if a right, an obligation on God's part. The recipient is no longer receiving a gift but an entitlement. The third horse of the apocalypse comes because the gratuity of the world has been battered into non-existence by supply and demand:

> I'm rather good at the interpretation of the Apocalypse, and I have been interpreting it for the last fifteen years. [Nastassya] agreed with me that we've arrived at the time of the third horse, the black one, and of the rider who has a pair of balances in

---

77. Thomas Aquinas, *De Pot.* III, 5, *resp.*

his hand, for everything in our present age is weighed in the scales and everything is settled by agreement, and all people are merely seeing their rights: 'A measure of wheat for a penny, and three measures of barley for a penny.' And, on top of it, they still want to preserve a free spirit and a pure heart and a sound body and all the gifts of the Lord. But they won't preserve them by seeking their rights alone, and there will therefore follow the pale horse and he whose name was Death, and after whom Hell followed.[78]

We never leave the sanctifying particularity of lived experience. If we do, we will never get to God because we have separated ourselves from contact with both metaphysical and spiritual gratuity. If we are going to get to God, we are going to find him where we are, and not where we are not. From our un-reflexive contact with the world we encounter nature full of presences, some intruding and some receding, many in cycles, others lasting for lengthy periods of time while still others only for days, and some only moments—some remarked upon, many more left unremarked. We gather intellectually that this world of changing presences is a world resplendently full of possible things, each facet of existence under the dominion of generation and decay, birth and death, the springtime of our years recalled more vigorously in the autumn leaves. Is it not a stunning sensation to come to the realization that everything around and within us points to God primarily through its gratuity? [79] Even, indeed especially, existentialist absurdity is but another name for gratuity, as perhaps Camus came to see.[80]

78. Dostoyevsky, *Idiot*, 192–93.

79. One could object that matter itself does not corrupt but, after each corruption of the substantial form, it continues to exist united with another form just reduced from its potency. But if this be the case, then matter must have some necessity not of itself. And that is precisely our argument. An eternal world of corruptible beings is not intelligible without a being that has some necessity either from another or from itself. A corruptible being that is actually existing, must at some point cease to exist. If it never ceases to exists, never corrupts, that can only be because it has the power not to corrupt. But such a being is by that reality incorruptible. Cf. Renard, *Philosophy of God*, 40. See Saint Thomas's refutation of Corruptible Ungenerated and Incorruptible Generated, in Thomas Aquinas, *Comm. De Caelo*, 1, lect. 29.

80. Camus, *First Man*, 288: "When I was young I asked more of people than they could give: everlasting friendship, endless feeling. Now I know to ask less of them than they can give: a straightforward companionship. And their feelings, their friendship, their generous actions seem in my eyes to be wholly miraculous: a consequence of grace alone."

Each thing need not be and exists only through the borrowed necessity or the desire of something else which itself requires *another other*. The beauty of the *third way* is that gratuity places us within the realm of the eternal and then hints that this eternal must be of a personal order. In terms of the temporal: if everything in nature *need not be* then at one time nothing would have been in existence. I can forget or delay this dramatic truth by remaining within the temporal succession, the indefinite regress, but in doing so I am not living according to my nature on that horizon *between* time and eternity. If everything in the world is a possible being nothing could have been in existence in the "first place" because nothing would have been necessary to have caused all these possible things. We know there was a time when nothing was, as much as we know that nothing cannot cause anything whatsoever. Even if the world were "eternal"—it would for Saint Thomas still require an eternal dependence upon a being with no beginning in Being. Again, even if the world had no *beginning in time*, it would still be forever dependent for its existence on a necessary being. And yet the existence of the world is the beginning-of/as-time (at least as change in its relentless tick-tock passage). Therefore, not all beings are merely possible. Non-existence cannot be thought nor can it be engaged without the inclusion of existence as a preface: the *Is* in *Is*-not contrasting what we cannot conceive. This is a place unlike any other, it is not bound by limit, time, pause, duration, succession. This is the eternal prepossessed in us in order that we can know time, change, succession, duration, and limit. Not only is existence a gratuity, the fact that we are prepossessed in the eternal invokes a higher ordered gratuity, for while the former skirts around the language of gift, the latter begins to strike at the divine nature needed to bestow a gift. A gift requires a giver and the giver must be a person, not an impersonal prime mover. The metaphysics of the Five Ways places us in Being not merely as prime mover but in the most powerful of mysteries. Being is this *un*caused cause, this different source that is not merely the highest in the order of beings but that *difference as such*. We grasp it only in the "un," in the certitude of the mystery. At the very same time, this *un*caused cause, while faceless to us, is not without a face—it never retreats into the abstract Aristotelian orderer. The inclusion of the question of existence is not an inessential addition but instead turns the tables upside down. Our existence is not necessary and our knowledge of this contingency requires our prepossession in that Necessary Being. This prepossession cannot be achieved by our own powers. It is the non-necessary deliberate gift of Being as God. The *un*caused cause, from the side of natural reason, may be faceless but it subtly outlines the reality that there *Is* a face, that this *Is* a personal encounter, and that these *ways* are placing us at the door of the divine which is the door to the revelatory gifts of the faith. God is not something far off, but inhabits the reality of every possible thing and everything in the natural world is a possible thing. If everything in the world can *not*-be, then nothing would be, but, again, there *is* a world. This world full of beings that can *not*-be, reveals its gratuity, and only from there do we understand what necessity truly is. I can either proceed along the indefinite regress of beings that can *not*-be—where each reveals its gratuity only to be ignored—or I can recognize that gratuity, thus transforming that indefinite regress into a re-collection of the infinite. This re-collection is a rediscovery of my non-mediated prepossession in the divine, a prepossession gifted to me, allowing me to encounter the eternal in the temporal and to uncover the universal in the particular. Most intimately I learn that all my acts of knowledge begin in the personal, not only my own personhood but from within the Person Who makes the act of knowledge-in-Being possible in the first place. God is the only necessary Being and thus the only Being that is truly needed in its own right.

> The *Existent* was here in the beginning, my son, alone and without a second. On this there are some who say, the *Nonexistent* was here in the beginning, alone and without a second. From that Nonexistent sprang the Existent. But how could it really be so, my son? he said. How could what exists spring from what does not exist? On the contrary, my son, the *Existent* was here in the beginning, alone and without a second.[81]

The Fourth Way: A Connaturally Illuminated Moral Order

> The fourth way is taken from the gradation to be found in things. Among beings there are some more and some less good, true, noble and the like. But 'more' and 'less' are predicated of different things, according as they resemble in their different ways something which is the maximum, as a thing is said to be hotter according as it more nearly resembles that which is hottest; so that there is something which is truest, something

81. *Chandogya Upaniṣad*, XI, in Koller and Koller, *Asian Philosophy*, 25.

best, something noblest and, consequently, something which is uttermost being; for those things that are greatest in truth are greatest in being, as it is written in Metaph. ii. Now the maximum in any genus is the cause of all in that genus; as fire, which is the maximum of heat, is the cause of all hot things. Therefore there must also be something which is to all beings the cause of their being, goodness, and every other perfection; and this we call God.[82]

From the gratuity of existence, we proceed to the shared principles of exemplarity and complementarity. This world of active neediness does not exist in its own right. Each natural being is a participated being. And because this participation is grounded upon the gift of existence, it reveals a startling relationship between immanence and transcendence, and of the mystery of beings made in the image and likeness of God.

Still others came to a knowledge of God from the dignity of God; and these were the Platonists. They noted that everything which is something by participation is reduced to what is the same thing by essence, as to the first and highest. Thus, all things which are fiery by participation are reduced to fire, which is such by its essence. And so since all things which exist participate in existence (esse) and are beings by participation, there must necessarily be at the summit of all things something which is existence (esse) by its essence, i.e., whose essence is its existence. And this is God, who is the most sufficient, the most eminent, and the most perfect cause of the whole of existence, from whom all things that are participate existence (esse). This dignity is shown in the words, on a high throne, which, according to Denis, refer to the divine nature. 'The Lord is high above all nations' (Ps 112:4). John shows us this dignity when he says

---

82. *ST* I, 2, 3, *resp.* Cf. *De Potentia*, III, 5, *resp*: "The second argument is that whenever something is found to be in several things by participation in various degrees, it must be derived by those in which it exists imperfectly from that one in which it exists most perfectly: because where there are positive degrees of a thing so that we ascribe it to this one more and to that one less, this is in reference to one thing to which they approach, one nearer than another: for if each one were of itself competent to have it, there would be no reason why one should have it more than another. Thus fire, which is the extreme of heat, is the cause of heat in all things hot. Now there is one being most perfect and most true: which follows from the fact that there is a mover altogether immovable and absolutely perfect, as philosophers have proved. Consequently, all other less perfect beings must needs derive being therefrom. This is the argument of the Philosopher (*Metaph.*ii, I)."

> below (1:1), 'the Word was God, with 'Word' as subject and 'God' as the predicate.[83]

Our sense experience is forever in contact with a world of gradation. Nature is no mere external attribute but the realm of being, and its material flux is a companion to our own in its perfection and disorder. If when man fell creation fell, this presupposes that nature is an extension of our being as we are an extension of it, as necessary as our heartbeat and our breath. It is no wonder that when the most important expressions must be laid bare, they never retreat into abstract terms but attempt to breathe life into these numinous obscurities of the heart with the pulse of the world, its waves, vistas, clay, and mud—this is Péguy's carnal creature, "a body kneaded from the clay of the earth, the carnal earth."[84] To say we are *in* but not *of* the world is misunderstood if the world is viewed merely as a gateway to something other. It is precisely because we are not *of* the world that we experience its immanence in ways which chasten the soul and permit the recovery of its own truth and participation in the mystery of Being. Nature may be the backdrop of Being but so is Beauty[85] and without it the soul could not learn its own yearning:

> The prince left and walked on mechanically wherever his steps hastened to lead him. In early summer in Petersburg there are sometimes lovely days—clear, hot, and still. As if on purpose,

83. Thomas Aquinas, *Comm. St. John*, prooemium, 5.

84. Péguy, *Portal of the Mystery of Hope*, 45. See also Rilke, *Sonnets to Orpheus*, §29:
Silent friend of many distances, feel
how your breath is enlarging space.
Among the rafters of dark belfries
let yourself ring. What preys on you will

strengthen from such nourishment.
Come and go with metamorphosis.
What's your most painful experience?
If what you drink's bitter, turn to wine.

In this huge night, become
the magic at the crossways of your senses.
Be what their strange encounter means.

And if the earthly forgets you,
say to the quiet earth: I flow.
Speak to the rushing water—say: I am.

85. DN IV, 5. See also Schindler, "Love and Beauty."

this was one of those rare days. For some time, the prince wandered aimlessly. He did not know the city well. Sometimes he
would stop and pause on street corners before certain houses,
in squares, on bridges; once he entered a pastry shop to rest.
Sometimes he would watch the passer-by with great interest, but
most of the time he noticed neither the people nor where he was
going. He was in a state of painful anxiety and his nerves were
on edge and at the same time he felt an extraordinary craving
for solitude. He wanted to be alone and give himself completely
passively to this agonizing tension, without seeking to escape
it.[86]

Confronted by and imbedded in this world of gradation, we gather the efficacious presence of the moral life. The intellect realizes that such degrees
of *more and less* are assigned insofar as they resemble or are compared
to other things. And these resemblances are looking for their respective
maxims because without that exemplar they could not exist; of necessity
they refer to their absolute source. And this source is no mere stopping
point; it carries itself in all resemblances. It is the Good that turns all
other virtues upside down in yearning for its source: "beauty like that is
strength. One could turn the world upside down with beauty like that."[87]

Where do these resemblances or comparisons originate? In a
standard in which all resemblances and comparisons must originate;
a standard in which the maxim and perfection of all these qualities is
contained. Such a standard is an endlessly open nature, and because it
carries all the perfections housed within participated beings, it is more apt
to call it a groundless ground. If the moral order works by degrees, and if
the source of these degrees carries the perfections of all its participations,
then moral order is not primarily imposed by an extrinsicized
prescription but instead invoked by our originary *praxis*. The former
loses the source of genuine subordination and thus subordinates itself
only to the tautology of the ego. The latter, embedded in the non-futural
here-and-now saturated presence of the Good, subordinates to nothing
but this source innermost in all things. Such a morality is more a listening
and a touching[88] than a sight, for the sight of the moral order comes *after*
contact with it, not *before*:

86. Dostoyevsky, *Idiot*, 243.

87. Dostoyevsky, *Idiot*, 101.

88. DA 423b26–4a9 Cf. C. Gilson, *Metaphysical Presuppositions*, 57: "Aristotle uses
'touch' as an analogy for the soul as an exteriorized nature, as that which is potentially

> The human good is that which possesses an aspect of fittingness for the being of man. The goodness appeals to us, it beckons and invites us to act for it. The reason does not create the good, rather the reason discovers it. The presence of the good is the primary requirement for the proper activity of our practical reason. Thus Thomas teaches that man is bound to the good not by means of a law which imposes it from without upon us, but through the discovery of the reason and the perfective qualities of the good. In being the creatures that we are, we are *already* related to, 'bound to,' God. It is, for Thomas, the task of human reason to discover and acknowledge this 'obligation' or intentional bond in an explicit manner.[89]

While there are many natural standards, each is bonded to potentiality, intermediacy, and thus each is non-necessary. The natural order is always an indefinite regress as well as an indefinite progression. We can always discover something *more* beautiful, *more* good, *more* perfect. The natural world is always on the hunt for its exemplar and every natural standard, through its participation and neediness, reveals itself to be along the *longer way*. Natural standards are thus *constructed* standards, put together, transformed and taken apart by their needful participation in otherness for their existence.[90]

These resemblances take us to the very heart of the question of moral foundation. When, for example, moral categories are rooted in

---

all things because it is the meaning or the combining/unifying principle of its sensible constituents. Unlike the other senses, touch does not have a medium between the sensible and the sense organ and therefore the world is immediately apprehended."

89. Hartmann, "St. Thomas and Prudence," 70. One of the most original, because deeply true, accountings of Saint Thomas on prudence. The existential efficacy is never overlooked. Dr. Hartmann diagnoses such a misstep as a downgrading of natural law to a set of rules independent of Being rather than far closer to an ancillary of natural love. It is the task of reason to *discover* the good and true and then to promulgate them as laws. While most Thomists would agree on this directionality, when they overlook how being existentially manifests itself in the good, in the realm of providence, they collapse that distinction in favor of the promulgation. In doing so, the command has no grounding intelligibility outside itself.

90. Cf. *De Pot.* III, 5, *resp*: "The third argument is based on the principle that whatsoever is through another is to be reduced to that which is of itself. Wherefore if there were a *per se* heat, it would be the cause of all hot things that have heat by way of participation. Now there is a being that is its own being: and this follows from the fact that there must needs be a being that is pure act and wherein there is no composition. Hence from that one being all other beings that are not their own being, but have being by participation, must needs proceed. This is the argument of Avicenna (in Metaph. viii, 6; ix, 8). Thus, reason proves and faith holds that all things are created by God."

feelings, those categories appear to have no continuity: one man's sin is another man's virtue.[91] The Good is confined to relativity but is never truly confined, for what is *relative* can only be so because it is *related* to something other than itself. We must have an idea of perfection in order to understand imperfection as a degree of perfection. Without a standard that contains all these perfections, and indeed causes these gradations of goodness, truth and beauty, we couldn't say anything is *more or less* good, true or beautiful in the first place because there would be no purely actual Good, True, or Beautiful to which to refer. And without that purely actual Good, there would be no participated goodness, no relative goodness where one man's virtue is another man's sin. In other words, we stop and realize that we cannot go on indefinitely in more and less, because at the root of more and less, of resemblances, is its dependency on a source. But this source is not placed atop existence, it is a good capable of universality *only* because it speaks to the intimacy of each person as the sole heir of the universe:

> There is still an awful lot of centripetal force on our planet, Alyosha. I want to live, and I do live, even if it be against logic. Though I do not believe in the order of things, still the sticky little leaves that come out in the spring are dear to me, the blue sky is dear to me, some people are dear to me, whom one loves sometimes, would you believe it, without even knowing why; some human deeds are dear to me, which one has perhaps long ceased believing in, but still honors with one's heart, out of old habit.[92]

All natural standards are participated resemblances, more or less rooted in a unique standard that contains all perfections. And if it contains all perfections, if all resemblances refer to this standard, then our knowledge of this good is not discovered primarily by accepting a template of order but by an in-dwelling within our own connatural participation in this groundless ground, this *un*measured measurer. If all natural standards and every natural identification of the beautiful is a measured-measurer, man can be called the measure of all things only because he is able to reflect on his own status as a measured-measurer. This reflection will return us to the movement of the Five Ways, where our neediness

91. Cf. Russell, "Science and Ethics," 223–43.

92. Dostoyevsky, *Brothers Karamazov*, 230.

and our activity reveal our penultimate nature.[93] Even Protagoras had a point. To satisfy that penultimacy we must see it for what it is as a unique intermediary. By our ability to reflect on that intermediary nature we not only have the *ability* to go beyond that status, we are *already* beyond it. Morality is not something "put on"; it is the naturally supernatural disposition of our beings as reflexively penultimate. In order to be ourselves we must go beyond our nature,[94] recovering our prepossession in the only true finality which confers our participation in it. The only *way* to recover this prepossession is to become united in being to its exemplar. It is not enough to *know* the good, one must *be* the good in order to *have* the good which all by *nature* seek in order *to be* happy.[95] The enactment of the moral life is irreducibly the enactment of a human life, as a human-and-divine courtship.

> It must be said that every being in any way existing is from God. For whatever is found in anything by participation, must be caused in it by that to which it belongs essentially, as iron becomes ignited by fire. Now it has been shown above (I:3:4) when treating of the divine simplicity that God is the essentially self-subsisting Being; and also it was shown (I:11:4) that subsisting being must be one; as, if whiteness were self-subsisting, it would be one, since whiteness is multiplied by its recipients. Therefore, all beings apart from God are not their own being, but are beings by participation. Therefore, it must be that all things which are diversified by the diverse participation of being, so as to be

93. On our penultimate nature, see C. Gilson, "Groundwork for the Christian *Polis: Noli Me Tangere*," 241–70.

94. Cf. Maritain, *Approaches to God*, 26: "So man awakened to the sense of Being does not only know that God exists and is self-subsisting Existence, he also knows that because of the very fact God is absolute ontological generosity and self-subsisting love; and that such transcendent love causes, permeates, and activates every creature. Though human reason is helped in fact by revelation to know more perfectly these natural truths, reason is enough, the natural forces of the human mind are enough, for man to know that God is self-subsisting Love, as He is self-subsisting Intellection and self-subsisting Existence. And we should also know, through the Gospel revelation, through faith, as the creature is concerned, God should not only be loved by that He loves, I mean with the distinctive madness of love, and that there can be relations of friendship, mutual self-giving, community of love, and the sharing of common bliss between God and His intelligent creatures: a fact which implies the supernatural order of grace and charity."

95. This is the difference between the philosopher, lover of wisdom, and the *philodoxa*, lover of opinion, in the *Republic*, 480a.

more or less perfect, are caused by one First Being, Who possesses being most perfectly.[96]

God's existence is no mere highest in the order of eternal essences. As the only Being Who exists in his own right, all things originate and refer to him. He is the *arche* and the *telos*, the beginning and the end. This necessary Being is *necessary* not because it is the first cause that set things into motion and lets them spiral disconnectedly, or connectedly only by a mirror image of diminishing reflections. It is such a reductive view of God which, unable to realize our connaturalness in the Good, that constructs an ethics of demand and prohibition and political correctness.

This *fourth way* reaches the same conclusion as the Anselmian argument of "that than which nothing greater can be conceived." But whereas Anselm, arguably, started in concept[97]—nevertheless situated in the world and in the revelatory imprimatur of the faith—Saint Thomas took the *longior via* through existence and experience and showed how *more and less* require a source that contains all those perfections. God is no univocal standard. As *un*measured measurer nothing can yearn for perfection without referring to God. More still, nothing can exist without referring to God. What Anselm and Aquinas recognized is that Being is never merely an entity but the *Way.* If there were no way for things to be, there would be things. But there are things; therefore there is a way for things to be. In every culture and time there are a plurality of traditions, social mores, customs which are considered more or less fitting, given a particular situation. The etiquette of the funeral, wake, and wedding are as such constructed standards, *ways* to be, which in varying degrees of perfection, resemble and refer to the super-natural *Act* of the Good. Historical or traditional standards are themselves swept up into the tide of "more and less," they are resemblances of the highest standard, and as resemblances they require a standard which, again, contains all the perfections. Moral objectivity is rooted in a super-natural source, otherwise there would be no right or wrong, good and beautiful, and there would be no legitimate constructed standards, because there would be no perfect Good to which those resemblances refer. There would be no tradition.

The denial of final causality in favor of situational efficacy can neither be accepted nor naively dismissed. If the natural law loses its contact

96. *ST* I, 44, *resp.*
97. Cf. C. Gilson, "Search for a Method," 51–128.

as primarily a natural love,[98] ethics tends to overlook the situational necessity of developed standards in favor of an absolute standard. But by overlooking the situation such an ethics, often in the name of God, creates the grandest constructed standard imposed upon the world as it obscures our connatural access to God. The situation cannot be a situation without reference to the Absolute; relativities cannot proceed indefinitely without surrendering to the Absolute which makes those finite relations possible. Neither can the situation be ignored, for it is the place in which we begin and through which we realize that there is a *way* for things to be. All metaphysics is local as all morality is local, as is all politics. And this participation is again a personal one. If this *un*measured measurer contains all perfections in which we participate, we participate only because we are gifted with this participation. We are radically contingent beings and our relationship with the only necessary Being reveals that God's decision to allow us to participate in his perfection is not one conceived by a distant impersonal eternal but one which makes each of us heir to the world.[99] As Existence, God is the prime heir, having created in freedom and perfection the world for himself: *les jeux sont fait . . .*

> The active intellect, of which the Philosopher speaks, is something in the soul. In order to make this evident, we must observe that above the intellectual soul of man we must needs suppose a superior intellect, from which the soul acquires the power of understanding. For what is such by participation, and what is mobile, and what is imperfect always requires the pre-existence of something essentially such, immovable and perfect. Now the human soul is called intellectual by reason of a participation in intellectual power; a sign of which is

98. Cf. Torrell, "Collationes in Decem Preceptis," 235: "The law of divine love is the standard for all human actions."

99. The maxim of perfection cannot be an indifferent and impersonal orderer. If so, it would elicit the interior difficulties and determinisms of a prime mover. How can the source of perfection not include, so as to ground and fulfill, the trajectory of the finite personhoods which seek out those very perfections? To deny this would be equivalent to Schopenhauer's dismissive derision of those relativistic positivists who envision that those things which lack intelligence gain their intelligence by their own powers which by virtue of lacking intelligence do not possess said powers! This tautology is wholly confounding. The fourth demonstration therefore evokes dramatic implications. The unmeasured measurer is the perfect Being because perfection requires the *dramatis persona* of a supreme personhood enabling all other persons participatory access into his open nature as lodestar making possible those finite personhoods as living and realized.

that it is not wholly intellectual but only in part. Moreover, it reaches to the understanding of truth by arguing, with a certain amount of reasoning and movement. Again, it has an imperfect understanding; both because it does not understand everything, and because, in those things which it does understand, it passes from potentiality to act. Therefore, there must needs be some higher intellect, by which the soul is helped to understand.[100]

The Fifth Way: Authority as Authorship

The fifth way is taken from the governance of the world. We see that things which lack intelligence, such as natural bodies, act for an end, and this is evident from their acting always, or nearly always, in the same way, so as to obtain the best result. Hence it is plain that not fortuitously, but designedly, do they achieve their end. Now whatever lacks intelligence cannot move towards an end, unless it be directed by some being endowed with knowledge and intelligence; as the arrow is shot to its mark by the archer. Therefore, some intelligent being exists by whom all natural things are directed to their end; and this being we call God.[101]

Saint Thomas begins each of the *ways* within the particularity of sense experience, and in the final demonstration he reaffirms sensible experience as not primarily a means to conceptual or abstract knowledge but as an attribute of the grandeur of the living world.[102] Our arrival at immateriality is not a divesting of the material in a quest for true knowledge, but

100. *ST* I, 79, 4 *resp.*

101. *ST* I, 2, 3 *resp.*

102. Cf. É. Gilson, *Terrors of the Year Two Thousand*, 16. "There was in the thirteenth century a philosopher to whom the sight of the world did not give nausea, but a joy ever new, because he saw in it only order and beauty. Man did not seem to him a Sisyphus hopelessly condemned to the liberty of the absurd, for he read in his own heart the clear law of practical reason. On all sides, within as well as without, a single and self-same light enlightens the understanding and regulates things, for the spirit which is found in them reconstructs them in the mind according to the order of the same creative intelligibility. This harmony of thought and reality which in our time Einstein describes as the most incomprehensible of mysteries, does not astonish our philosopher, for he knows its source—that same God Whose pure existence is at the origin of all reality as well as of all knowledge. And what is liberty for created man, unless it be to accept himself lovingly, even as his Creator wants and loves him? What is it to act as a free man unless it be to regulate the will according to reason, and reason itself according to the divine law?"

a prime contact with uncreated *To Be* as what is innermost in creation. This immateriality is not an avenue to leave the world but to return to it with a truer anatomy of sensation. The *ways* are a recovery of our bodily soul, they unveil the personal immateriality at the heart of every miscellaneous and unremarkable passage of time, event, and encounter. What is immateriality for the human person but materiality bonded to the sacred, for we get to God from where we are and not from where we are not? Our bodily souls need a world in which to enact the universe. This reminder of the centrality of the world is crucial to this demonstration, to the demonstrations as a whole and to the entirety of the Summa's *exitus and reditus* structure. The *fifth way* is called teleological because it seeks to demonstrate that God exists through the manifold order of nature, and that God *is* designer. But, again, the non-creational language of a teleology cannot encompass what these Five Ways have achieved.[103] The inclusion of existence means that if God is shown to be the designer, it is *because* he is the personal interiority intelligibilizing the natural world and not a mere end to be perceived, existentially disconnected from the world. The meaning of God as *authority* is metaphysically grounded in this *fifth way* as *authorship*. We are made to be active participants in his image and likeness and through that participation we find ourselves, like God, wholly *in* and yet not *of* the world. God's full immanence and transcendence reveal that this authority is not extrinsically invoked but one of connatural existential imprimatur. His freedom to create a world of non-necessary beings means that his authority *is* most originally his authorship. This authorship is the very *way* in which beings are in that divine loving freedom so often revealed in the non-reflexive immediacy of play, the gift of existence.[104]

> Some attained to a knowledge of God through his authority, and this is the most efficacious way. For we see the things in nature acting for an end, and attaining to ends which are both useful

103. Cf. *ST* I, 8, 4, *resp.*: "For whatever number of places be supposed, even if an infinite number be supposed besides what already exist, it would be necessary that God should be in all of them; for nothing can exist except by Him. Therefore to be everywhere primarily and absolutely belongs to God and is proper to Him: because whatever number of places be supposed to exist, God must be in all of them, not as to a part of Him, but as to His very self." The shifting from a non-creational understanding of existence to a creational one, with an uncreated source, dramatically alters the human composition and our readings of the Five Ways.

104. Cf. O'Rourke, "Creative Diffusion in Aquinas," in *Pseudo-Dionysius and Aquinas*, 225–74.

and certain. And since they lack intelligence, they are unable to direct themselves, but must be directed and moved by one directing them, and who possesses an intellect. Thus, it is that the movement of the things of nature toward a certain end indicates the existence of something higher by which the things of nature are directed to an end and governed. And so, since the whole course of nature advances to an end in an orderly way and is directed, we have to posit something higher which directs and governs them as Lord; and this is God. This authority in governing is shown to be in the Word of God when he says, Lord. Thus the Psalm (88:10) says: 'You rule the power of the sea, and you still the swelling of its waves,' as though saying: You are the Lord and govern all things. John shows that he knows this about the Word when he says below (1:11), 'He came unto his own,' i.e., to the world, since the whole universe is his own.[105]

From our first experiences, we see a world full of design, brimming with relentless pattern and order, from the cycle of the seasons, the manner in which a body heals, the movement of the stars, the physical laws, the gravitational pull not only of the body but of the soul. When Myshkin reflects on Hippolyte's manifesto, he thinks of the gnat which knows its place in the bright sun and within the chorus of existence. These things, all in harmony, serve to remind him of his place as an outcast and calls to mind Switzerland in the first year of his cure, still unable to speak properly, still deaf to the world. The final *way* returns to the world because it is no mere material set of data, objectively distinct and spiritually inert. It is the *way* to God because it is God, both in his presence and his absence, the certitude and the confounding mystery of his existence. The world is invitation and exile and it alone can dispossess us of all things so that we may arrive at the door of the divine, too full of God ever to be opened on its own.

> One bright, sunny day he went for a walk in the mountains and walked for a long time, tormented by a thought that, try as he might, seemed to be eluding him. Before him was the brilliant sky, below—the lake, and around, the bright horizon, stretching away into infinity. He looked a long time in agony. He remembered now how he had stretched out his arms towards that bright and limitless expanse of blue and wept. What tormented him was that he was a complete stranger to all this. What banquet was it, what grand everlasting festival, to which he had

105. Thomas Aquinas, *Comm. St. John*, prooemium, 3.

long felt drawn, always—ever since he was a child, and which he could never join? every morning the same bright sun rises; every morning there is a rainbow on a waterfall; every evening the highest snowcapped mountain, far, far away, on the very edge of the sky, shows with a purple flame.[106]

As outcasts on that horizon between time and eternity we can see the world for what it *is* as much as miss it altogether. This step *back*, because of our fallenness, is always dangerously close to a step *out* of existence. We must remain within its presence as we are protracted by it, stretched in yearning for the Other. In this state, we gather intellectually that this sensible world which inhabits our soul acts in patterns and predictable designs in order to obtain the best result. Again and again, the world acts for an end, every miscellaneous aspect of existence acts for its own *non-sequitur* finality. Flowers move towards the sun, the cactus conserves water, the life cycles march on relentlessly indifferent to our own end. The end for us does not devour freedom but is the way in which freedom acts, but figuring out how this is true takes a lifetime, it is the essence of the *longior via*. All things act for an end, this is the way of Being, and so Nastassya accepts her fate as Myshkin returns to silence. We are burdened with the gift of intelligence which obscures our acting towards an end, but we cannot ignore the truth that things which lack intelligence *always* act intelligently. The flower which lacks intelligence moves intelligently, vacant planetary matter travels "designedly," orbiting through space following an invisible trajectory. All the things of Spring, the grass, the buds of the trees, the bee's pollination—none of them recalls its own march as it acts towards its respective finality.

We act for an end but our knowledge of this end reveals our finality to be both certain and yet a mystery. All of creation marches towards an order as we march towards the abyss, because the end is withheld from us and the order which was once present, at a distance, recedes when we act upon it. We are asked to be as *To Be* is—the order and the end. We do not follow the order like the rest of creation. Our moment of reflection separates us from the march. Our original and non-mediated intimacy with Being had always and unknowingly prepared us in its play to become identical with our finality, so wholly unified in love, that we can live outside its direction and beyond its march. One is here reminded of that other tale of holy fools in *Brothers Karamazov*. At Zosima's funeral we

---

106. Dostoyevsky, *Idiot*, 406.

find Alyosha transfigured by an encounter, a mystical caressing of the visible and invisible world. Overwhelmed, he becomes like his dead master and falls in surrender to the Other:

> Filled with rapture, his soul yearned for freedom, space, vastness. Over him the heavenly dome, full of quiet, shining stars, hung boundlessly. From the zenith to the horizon the still-dim Milky Way stretched its double strand. Night, fresh and quiet, almost unstirring, enveloped the earth. The white towers and golden domes of the church gleamed in the sapphire sky. The luxuriant autumn flowers in the flowerbeds near the house had fallen asleep until morning. The silence of the earth seemed to merge with the silence of the heavens, the mystery of the earth to be touched by the mystery of the stars . . . Alyosha stood gazing and suddenly, as if he had been cut down, he threw himself to the earth . . . It was as if threads from all those innumerable worlds of God all came together in his soul, and it was trembling all over, 'touching other worlds.' He wanted to forgive everyone for everything, and to ask forgiveness, oh, not for himself! but for all and for everything, 'as others are asking for me,' rang again in his soul.[107]

When the saintly Zosima died, his rotting corpse causes much commotion and scandal. How could this saintly man die and not be immune to the ravages of decay? His sainthood must be crowned in incorruptibility, with the scents of water and pine and roses. But Zosima taught more to the earth, to the dust and to the essential failings of the soul in love; that the soul must always be in-failing as it groans for God. The musk of death became a stench revealing what he taught all along: he is no otherworldly figure, he is a bodily soul made of earth and clay and mud, one in the body of Christ. This *alter Christus* is of the world and will not lose that *way* when he acts towards an end.[108]

107. Dostoyevsky, *Brothers Karamazov*, 262.

108. Any serious examination of this demonstration cannot ignore the chastening anarchism at root within existence. Within us and all of existence, there is a double existence: growth, change, generation toward perfection and growth, change, generation toward death. The former, try as it might, can never—contra Pelagius—outwit the latter. Only in the merciful grace and sublime audacity of the incarnation does death become the handmaiden for our change toward perfection. Without a serious recognition of the cosmogonic indifference permeating all things and placing us within the beauty and the terror of existence, we play into the hands of those who dismiss such demonstrations as mere naïve whistling by the graveyard. See Dawkins, "God's Utility Function," 85: "The total amount of suffering per year in the natural world is beyond

In this world, we have things which lack intelligence acting in an intelligent manner, not acting fortuitously but designedly reflecting a designer, an authorship. And we have those beings that can act intelligently towards an end because they possess the knowledge of that end. But that knowledge is not possessed as an empirical fact, but prepossessed in us and known reflexively only by dispossession. The end is a Being Who is personal, and yet nothing encloses this Person, no separation is in place which limits him from ourselves so that through that limit we can see him. We are blind as we act towards this end which by reflection appears futural and distinct from us, but by action is a non-futural hiddenness wherein to know the True and Good we must *be* the Beautiful. There are two orders of beings: 1) beings which never fail to act intelligently but do not possess intelligence and 2) beings which act intelligently and can fail to act intelligently because they do possess intelligence but possess it by dispossession and thus by gift. In either case, the prime source of that intelligence is not situated within the beings by their own right. The reality of our neediness, intermediary status and non-necessity reveal that intelligence, beyond a reasonable doubt, to originate in a Being other than ourselves.

> You darkening ground, with patience you bear the walls.
> And perhaps you grant for an hour the cities to last,
> and grant yet two hours the monasteries and churches,
> and give yet five hours of misery to the redeemed,
> and look upon the farmer's work for seven hours yet—
> Before you become again forest and water and wilderness
> Growth
> in the hour of incomprehensible terror and death,
> where you demand from it all

---

all decent contemplation. During the minute that it takes me to compose this sentence, thousands of animals are being eaten alive, many others are running for their lives, whimpering with fear, others are slowly being devoured from within by rasping parasites, thousands of all kinds are dying of starvation, thirst, and disease. It must be so. If there ever is a time of plenty, this very fact will automatically lead to an increase in the population until the natural state of starvation and misery is restored. In a universe of electrons and selfish genes, blind physical forces and genetic replication, some people are going to get hurt, other people are going to get lucky, and you won't find any rhyme or reason in it, nor any justice. The universe that we observe has precisely the properties we should expect if there is, at bottom, no design, no purpose, no evil, no good, nothing but pitiless indifference."

your incomplete image back.
Just give me time and I'll love the things as no one
ever did
until they all have become wide and worthy of you.[109]

We cannot proceed indefinitely, explaining nature by natural things that cannot account for themselves: the root cannot account for its blossom; the blossom cannot account for its movement towards the sun, as we cannot account for our existence by displacing it on another existent which itself cannot account for its existence. All things act as if intelligently. Either they do not themselves possess that intelligence or they possess it only by supreme gratuity. Thus, the origin of this intelligence cannot be in intermediary and possible beings, because if there was no first in the order of intelligence and design there would be no intermediaries. But there are these intermediaries—God loves to multiply intermediaries—thus, beyond a reasonable doubt, I must conclude to an intelligent designer as the free root and origin of intelligence; the *arche* and *telos*, the end to which all things act, in order to obtain the best result. This *un*caused authorship is the necessary being, pure *Actus*, for it alone would be able to endow beings with order and purpose.

These natural things without intelligence are endowed with intelligent actions and thus point beyond themselves. Our bodily souls endowed with intelligence turn, looking for a source, for we know that its authorship always exceeds the bounds of our beings. This excelling is what constitutes our human nature as only resting when its rests in God. The *fifth way* may be coined as intelligent design, but this designer is no demiurge forming substances from pre-existing matter. This is a designer who handed over his own existence to be the ground of the design, the maintenance of the design, and the fulfillment of the design. This authority has given his life twice for this entrenched authorship, once in creation and once on the cross. He gives his life for the first time every day when he communicates to each person that he or she is the sole heir of the universe. This *un*designed designer, this *un*caused authorship frees each of us to be the sole heir, for when we act intelligently, when we act the way of our being which is on the borderline between time and eternity, the path has never been trod before. As he is the *Way* we are the way in and to him.

---

109. See "Monkish Life" in Rilke, *Book of Hours*, 85.

What will you do, God, when I'm dead?
I am your pot (when I crash into potsherds?)
I am your drink (when I go bad?)
I am your cloak and your career;
without me you end up losing making sense.

. . .

I fret about you, God.[110]

---

110. Rilke, "Monkish Life," in *Book of Hours*, 47. Cf. Martin, *Balthasar and Russian Religious Thought*, 202: "It is not insignificant that the first two books of Rilke's *The Book of Hours: Prayers to a Lovely God*, 'The Book of Monkish Life' and 'The Book of Pilgrimage,' are marked by a distinctly Russian mode of mystic spirituality, the imprint of his two journeys to Russia in 1899 and 1900. In these poems Rilke adopts the persona of a Russian artist-monk who enjoins a prayerful dialogue with God."

Postscript:
Laughter and the Love of Friends

In Defense of Miscellaneous Goods

A ND SO OUR SEEMINGLY random miscellany of readings centering on Dostoyevsky's *The Idiot* and Saint Thomas's Five Ways, the questions of play and originary praxis, condition and nature, *nomos* and *arete*, signage and sacrament—all these categories possess perhaps the unity in our being-in-the-world open natures.

The miscellany of this book is not about forcing an order but recognizing that existence does abide by a profoundly lingering openness to God and to ourselves united as open natures. The presence of this miscellaneous collection is an effort to resist the temptation to unify before existence has taken hold, before we have subordinated our wills to its interiority which throws ourselves so far beyond ourselves in order to be ourselves. We unify out of fear of the abyss, fear that the order will not appear, and a deeper fear that the perfection of the order is in fact that it does not appear, that it never reduces itself to an eidetic vision. The order, the patterns of the good we see from afar, disappear the moment we act upon them. We let ourselves believe that the good is as such a futural object enclosed apart from the randomness of existence. We then cease to act from where we are and instead proceed from where we are not. In doing so we lose the encompassing reality that if there are things there is a *way* for things to be. When we act, the way becomes hidden and in its place is a world pulsing in the divine miscellany. Unable to see that this miscellany is the manifestation of the way appropriate to free beings on the borderline between time and eternity, we refuse our divine subordination and attempt to extract that way from the meandering vicissitudes of existence. If there are things, there is a way for things to be. We lost trust in the way which is a reflection of our radical freedom. By trying to resurrect that vision of the good by our own powers, the more it disappears the more we confuse its hiddenness with an emptied anticipation of something more to come. We prepare a world to be passed over in Nietzsche's sense. Only when the world is too full can anticipation be driven by the Good to the Good. The futural and the non-futural must always be in play.

We are not trying to extract from the miscellany an overarching theme but to show that if unity is present it is always what is innermost, contingent, unique, incommunicable, where each is the sole heir to the universe. This is a recovery of ethics as non-futural, of that playful originary *praxis* which provides reflection with a living and not an artificial basis. The miscellany is a bulwark against the temptation for an untimely unity. Only a unity which is timely, which understands that if there are beings there is a *way* for beings to be, can unify the heart in the Truth. If Thomists or conservatives or liberals begin in the futural they begin in an artificial basis which can never arrive at the natural law as love. This is the necessary preparation to intellectual and moral and political reflection. The existential miscellany of the world in which each soul is its sole heir, is itself a preamble to unity as the demonstrations are a preamble to the faith. If all of existence is in groaning, then knowledge on this side of eternity is entirely perambulatory. When we force unity before letting existence existentialize our particularities, we act as if we can walk without a *way*. All metaphysics is local not only because it is enacted in a local sphere but because it originates in the *hereness*, the locus of our incommunicable endeavors.

This book has been an exercise in withholding from the temptation to elicit meaning too soon. In our fallen condition, everything is an endless process to elicit meaning. Perhaps only the poets bathe in the truth which prepossesses and without which we could not be dispossessed and in search of its meaning. But this withholding is not abstraction, it is not an aptitude only for the intellectual, it is the true font of unity open to all. It is an *anamnesis* so sweet and pure that in it we crave the lost wisdom of childhood. In fallenness, we retain always a filiation with our original nature and it is essential we keep it near. What the child at play has is what we have lost: we became thinkers only after we had ruined ourselves as knowers.[1] This rootless eliciting of meaning, unity, order, should remind us, indeed chasten us, in the reality that we have ruined ourselves as knowers.

Perhaps by condition there can be claims to need an overwrought moral order. But when condition is divorced from nature it is no longer condition at all. Condition is always a condition *of*. And without nature there is nothing which condition conditionalizes. To create an ethics based on a human condition divorced from nature is to envision an ethics for an aspect of existence which simply does not exist. More still, these prescriptive moral orders, these so-called necessary evils, attempt to extract a pattern of unity but are instead a wayless forgetting. The *non sequiturs* which populate our lives are the intelligibility of the ethical life and through them alone do we recover the unity not extrinsicizied but connatural to our status as divine playthings.

Is it not strange that the most peripheral of characters, Yevgeny Pavlovitch Radomsky, would be the kind benefactor, the friend who visits Myshkin regularly upon his return to the sanitorium. Pavlovitch, a retired soldier, wealthy and formerly Agalya's suitor, was scarcely remarked upon throughout the novel, and yet he was different from all the other people Myshkin had come to know of late.[2] His warm intentions and intercessions helped the Prince return to Switzerland and to the place where the Prince had once before found his voice and his heart. Describing himself as a "completely superfluous person in Russia,"[3] Pavlovitch is this extraneous, unremarked passerby. He finds his way not only to visit his sick friend at least once every few months, but to have understood the hidden transfiguration which occurs when nothing else but the love of the Good populates the bodily soul.[4] This is a friendship born of passing half-conversations, brief interludes of kindnesses which often preceded those tawdry and cruel distractions. Pavlovitch, escaping all our attentions, themes, and designs, had been present all along; the peripheral

1. Cf. Pegis, *Introduction to St. Thomas*, xxiv.

2. Dostoyevsky, *Idiot*, 640.

3. Dostoyevsky, *Idiot*, 640.

4. Cf. Schürmann, "Theo-logically/Eschatologically Oriented Values," 33: "Love is the soul of all theo-logically/eschato-logically oriented exhortation and imperatives, a love that responds both vertically and horizontally to the experience of God's eschatological love, or rather, that structures everything in an 'incarnational' manner, seeing God in one's neighbor and one's neighbor in God."

witness who alone could recognize the good stranger on the outside looking in, casting his eye to another on the outside looking in.

> Schneider frowns and shakes his head more and more each time;
> he hints at a complete breakdown of the intellect; he does not yet
> say positively that the illness is incurable, but he allows himself
> the most melancholy intimation of that possibility. Yevgeny Pav-
> lovitch takes this very much to heart, and he does have a heart.[5]

---

5. Dostoyevsky, *Idiot*, 640.

Appendix

Case in Point

A society without God—a society that does not know Him and treats Him as non-existent—is a society that loses its measure. In our day, the catchphrase of God's death was coined. When God does die in a society, it becomes free, we were assured. In reality, the death of God in a society also means the end of freedom, because what dies is the purpose that provides orientation. And because the compass disappears that points us in the right direction by teaching us to distinguish good from evil. Western society is a society in which God is absent in the public sphere and has nothing left to offer it. And that is why it is a society in which the measure of humanity is increasingly lost.[1]

The Grandest of All Refusals: Abortion's Pogrom against Contingency and the Historical Defection within the Language Game of Choice[2]

There is no worse philosophy than a philosophy which despises nature. A knowledge that despises what is, is itself nothing; a cherry between the teeth holds more mystery than the whole of idealistic metaphysics.[3]

---

1. Benedict XVI, "Church and the Scandal of Sexual Abuse."

2. Earlier selections of this appendix were published; see C. Gilson, "Grand Refusal."

3. Maritain, *Degrees of Knowledge*, 335; Maritain, *Peasant of the Garonne*, 45.

A N ETHICS IN-FAILING IS one which, because it does not lead but adheres to the trans-noetic intelligibility of existence, can experience—as connaturally bonded to the good—the infectious disharmony of moral evil. It experiences those machinations as prime defections from the Good, not needing to place or proffer its position as the "better" or the "truer" perspective. Rather, the subordinated ethics encounters the truth not from an isolated stance or position, but from the ground where *all* so-called stances or positions are forms of defections even, and if they are noble ones. It is this ground which particularizes the universal into something incommunicable and thus truly capable of communion. In this living region of Being, ethical enactment is seamlessly united to the metaphysical and mystical as one incarnate body *politique*. The ethicist *is* mystic, and because the ground of truth refuses to be bifurcated, this authentic metaphysician participates in the revelation of the Good and Beautiful against the backdrop of stances *as* defections. This is the truer historical cartography which Étienne Gilson considered the mark of the genuine philosopher.[4]

Let us then take that most deceitful of moral defections, abortion, and attempt to experience its desertion, not by proffering an alternative perspective or stance which, albeit noble, is unable to communicate the truth, having already distanced itself from the effulgence of true-Being. Let us not so much speak of natural law but allow it to reveal its own irreducible ground against the falsehoods which depend upon its intelligibility for their defections. Trust that all freedoms, true and false, are wedded to fate: this is the interior essence of the subordinated ethic which will not surrender to anything, precisely because it is unified to the numinous ground of the beautiful from which it is gracefully inseparable. This is not historicism but genuine historical exegesis, an awareness that Presence permeates all time and, because it refuses to be reduced and thus raised to the level of eidetic consciousness, it is often recognized in those historical actions which erroneously seek to raise it into the eidetic, making it a haphazard gnostic reflection of the ego. We shall look at abortion in a twofold manner, divided into two main sections:

4. See É. Gilson, "Forgotten Transcendental: Pulchrum," 6: "The whole of Dante's work suggests that Beatrice remained the liberating force of his lyrical powers, because she had formerly presented to his gaze that excruciating beauty possessed by some bodies which promise more than a body can hold and something other than a body can give."

1. *The Grandest of all Refusals: the Historical Defection*: here we will encounter abortion's defection from mystery as it cascades along the historical tides which seek to manage Being into an insubordinate ethic.

2. *Advocatus Diaboli: The Language Game of Choice*: once we have caught sight of its fully self-enclosed apparatus drifting against Being-as-such, abortion leaves itself open to being exposed as a cowardly linguistic defection. The project of abortion historically dismembered from Being has made itself a full-blown perspective insubordinate to reality itself. As such, unlike Being which refuses eidetic dissection, the great "gift" of any lie, so historically rampant, is that it exists only in a realm where there is no life but at best only copy theory of life. The abortion position may be dictatorially encompassing by sheer brutish will, but as a meaning connected to and in the service of the incommunicable, it is dramatically vacant, laughably vacant where it not so terrifyingly ugly. And because pro-abortion advocacy is not entrenched in, and intelligibilized by, reality but instead lays about as a brazen bubble populated with pure solipsistic ideational meanings, it can only be extorted into "reality" by fearmongering, intimidation, and that deceitful form of emotional pandering that is itself a form of fearmongering and intimidation. Abortion cannot help but show itself not to be knowledge at all but the ignorance that depends on truth by way of defection. While the pro-life position has sometimes made the misstep of making itself a mere stance and defending itself on the ground of its own self-perception, whether that be solely a religious or affective argument, it can reconnect to the incommunicable communion of Being. Abortionism, on the other hand, can only persist by making itself antagonistically weaker to the point of implosion. Abortion is thus the grandest of all refusals, not only a pogrom against contingency but a litany of unearthly defections.

The Grandest of all Refusals: the Historical Defection

In his 1929 work *Three Reformers*, French Catholic philosopher Jacques Maritain referred to modern Western society as a "homicidal civilization." When he died in 1973, *Roe v. Wade* had only just been handed down in the United States. Almost fifty years later, this ruling is the capstone (indeed the gravestone) and inevitable result of our "homicidal civilization" and it can be cartographically traced to the rampant rationalism that left no room for the irreducibility of the human soul. As we have seen throughout, it is the other *as* other that constitutes both knowledge and love among the miscellany of Being. The very incarnation of otherness is the unborn child. The denial of that otherness is also, and therefore, the denial of ourselves at its deepest root. It is not only sin, which it is; it is the suicide of the soul.

The historical deconstruction of the soul is, in some form or another, the loss of the philosophical principle of intentionality, which is man's foundational relationship with, and dependency on the world for his knowledge and activity. It is this loss which is at root in the prolonged collapse of the soul, and the protracted suicide of Western man. The loss of this foundational relationship is ultimately the denial of key fundamental presuppositions, those non-demonstrable irreducible facts of existence, by and through which I begin my discourse and journey as a being in the world. These are not stances or positions, but the ineluctable ground that anchors all fidelity and defection. The three key presuppositions are as follows:

- I am in the world; I do not need to prove it and I cannot deny it; the world in all its fullness and miscellany is the *irreducible* ground of the possibility of my knowledge and action.

- I know myself only in the face of otherness; I do not need to prove the self or otherness and I cannot deny them; self and otherness are the *irreducible* constituents of being human.

- I am free; I do not need to prove free will and I cannot deny it. Free will is found in the *irreducible* newness of each person's free rational activity of the will. It is not absolute, nor need it be, and the precondition of its choosing is intelligence and self-mastery, requiring time and, especially, societal and familial assistance. It is not absolute and it can be poisoned at the well of childhood by the ugliness of the broken home and a demonic culture of death.

One may call these presuppositions hopelessly naive preconceptions, but they are the *irreducible* and unbroken ground of the possibility of knowledge and action. If we do not accept these presuppositions, we expose ourselves to a deeper naivete—the view of the world as, at best, a reductionist construct out of sense data and power-driven social conflict.

The loss of these presuppositions has allowed the emergence of determinism, behaviorism, positivism, and all the other forms of postmodernist secular nihilism. If the world, self, otherness, and free will are not irreducible facts by which I begin my activity as a knower, then we leave ourselves open to reducing the world, the self, otherness, and free will to these empty secular myths.

Man's unseemly fascination with the reductionist pseudo-certitudes and arrogant pretensions of natural science and psychologism have dictated and dominated much of human action, and is at the heart of the malignant neglect of these intentional presuppositions. Such neglectfulness contributed to the deterministic worldview of the human person as a mere microorganism within that cell of determinism. The world of connatural meaning was thus "bracketed" and then discarded; any remains became a reconstituted world: a series of relativist subjectivisms overflowing into an endless series of hidden determinisms that eviscerate and emasculate all responsibility and which lurk in the deceptive language of tolerance, equality, and rights. In all these terms an abundant nihilism reigns, removing the absolute sense of Good and Evil in human action as well as the accountability that naturally aligns itself to a natural law ethics of ends, limits, and natural objective goods.

Without these pre-eidetic presuppositions we are unable to know ourselves. We are unable to perceive or engage or confront the genuine irreducibility of each person. We are left to an extorted examination of the reductive residuum: behavior, genetics, environment, and political obsession. Is this not the essence of ideology and its bloodless abstractions which are blind to the primal beauty and terror of existence and which subvert the civilizational shapes of historical finitude and friendship? It is marked by a hubris in the former and an irreverence in the latter, both bordering on the diabolical.

After the loss of a genuine intentionality, the soul straddled a state of existential listlessness, neither residing fully within the body nor in the world nor in Being. The soul, unable to be accounted for either by the prevailing behaviorisms or the radical ideologies became, strangely enough, the unnecessary appendage, a cumbersome, meddlesome Medieval hangover restricting man from the new, unlimited, and will-based meaning of the world. What is lost is the fundamental truth that the soul is neither reducible to matter, nor yet is it self-enclosed, both of which erroneous preconceptions can be employed to justify the unjustifiable and deny the undeniable, namely the irreducible otherness of the unborn child.

In this simplistic intellectual Pelagianism, the soul was no longer the "noble carrion" of Gerard Manley Hopkins that finds itself more alive as it "lay wrestling with my God."[5] Instead the carrion carcass of this empty spirit lay in wait and in the service of those lifeless abstractions that seek only to annihilate. As it was severed from or reduced to the body, the soul was picked over for its leftover meanings, meanings that could be deformed and pressed into the service of the prevailing right wing, but especially left wing ideologies. What connects them as positions outside and hostile to the faith is that each dispenses with the route, what we have insistently called with Aquinas is the *longior via*, the longer way. The rightist refuses to traverse it, while the leftist annihilates it; the leftist dilutes the mystery of existence, while the rightist reifies it. The soul thus became nothing more than a gossamer slip of a "word" to hide the modern tyrant: the ideologue with all his atheistic secularisms and vulgar political attitudes.

The soul, no longer the form of the body, was further bracketed as either a strictly religious category or reduced and resituated into that absolute vacuity known as "world spirit" or the so-called tide of history. Each a stance with allegiance only to its own insubordinate ethic. The soul became an alien category outside the world of natural meaning with nowhere left to turn except as the reward of resentment in the many romantic pessimisms unleashed in response to the Enlightenment. The soul became "personality". Yet such pessimisms, more often than not, drowned out and dried up in a penumbra of materialisms as deep and as dark as Marxism and Fascism.

The last counterfeit substitute for the principle of intentionality, and with it the relevance of the human soul and its originary affectivity, dried up in the deflation of European idealism and rationalism in the aftermath of the First World War. In its ruins a profound homelessness befell both theological and philosophical truths, so much so that they became transient perspectives wasting away in the many half-way houses that had all collapsed in the gutters of World War I and the postmodernist crisis that followed and lingers still. One might recall Schopenhauer's sad dilemma: if there is no God to be comprehended, then the world is barren and meaningless because man has no pattern by and through which

---

5. See "Carrion Comfort" in Hopkins, *Gospel in Gerard Manley Hopkins*, 216.

to accomplish God-likeness. But poor Schopenhauer's only consolation, the denial of the will-to-live through his noble escape hatch of forgetting the will in an endless aesthetic, was only to be terribly mismanaged by Feuerbach's fervent and materialistic God usurpation. But this was also overthrown, further crystallized in the usurpation of the personal in favor of the collective where all are equally soulless products of a constructed social contract.

In this thicket of non-being the last meaning of the soul was to be emptied. Its deconstruction began by removing the soul's intentional relationship to the world, and to God, but it required more: namely, a newfangled version of the "soul" *as* individual but with no other responsibility than to the continued and relentless affirmation of the *aisthesis* self. Paradoxically, the loss of the personal in favor of the social collective did not obliterate the individual but rather reaffirmed it in a radically new light! The great levelers, secularism and materialism, hand in hand would unleash the totalitarian reign of the individual built on an atomistic solipsism and pure perspectivism wherein power determines the context and content of the constructed individual, granting absolute right to gender or race or class or the so-called ideals of civilization. With the mask of objectivity removed, one is left with the struggle for power. And in this struggle *solidarity trumps objectivity*. Solidarity in guilt drowns even the objectivity of the evil act.

If we are to accept the parameters of God usurpation, then we must accept the following:

- there is nothing, no soul residing within man, he is what he makes of himself in the immanent or rather transient, and

- if there is no "soul," neither is there any rootedness directing knowledge and action. The human person has no other, knowledge has no object other than the self, and the self has no object other than itself! The human subject is its own subjective content.

Among the most pernicious repercussions of the reordering of man's noetic primacy are the dramatic alterations done to free will. Historically, freedom allowed itself to be reduced when we conceived it as a kind of perspectival grasping of some distant "universal" superimposed over and against the world. Once the inauthentic sense of freedom was linked to Christianity, as for instance in Kant, and subsequently condemned, so too of course was any genuine sense of a natural light (*lumen naturale*) given by God. When solidarity trumped objectivity, free will fell to the *reduction to choice* so esteemed by the liberal tradition. Choosing among a plurality of indifferent alternatives constituted freedom, and indifferentism reigned because man decided to be *beyond* good and evil. The only meaning left was the meaning construct known as the "absolute right" of the individual to secure his own content. It is no surprise that the genocide of abortion continues unabated, thriving under the deformed meaning of women's "rights"!

The soul and its existential privilege vanished into a self-induced coma, a hall of mirrors of pure perspectives where the human person can no longer call out from the abyss of the soul to the abyss of Being: *abyssus abyssusm invocat*. We begin and end without otherness, having no beginning or end but the totality of the I which is itself a mere construct. Insofar as "knowledge" has any meaning, the world is "knowable" but only as a plurality of fantastical and shifting constructs. This "knowledge," so divorced from the incommunicable ground which enables communion and irreducibility, can only thrive and perpetuate itself—like abortion itself—in the annihilatory, against existence, by the insubordinate refusal to dialogue within the game of Being-as-such. It *has no meaning behind it*, thus losing its character as sign, but countless constructed meanings or "perspectives." God is an empty fiction. Nietzsche proclaimed the death of God, and his postmodernist offspring proclaim the death of the soul, and this proclamation is far more powerful because it does not even need to be spoken. Now there is no faith but the faith in the relativity of all opinions and there is no absolutism but absolute relativism. Only our own needs interpret the world: our drives and their for-and-against, every drive as a kind of *lust to rule*, each with its perspective which it *compels* all other drives to accept as norm. When one drive becomes so powerful that it forgets or rejects or denies or covers up the fact that it is itself just a relative interpretation, then hierarchies, power structures, "ideals" are built up—and these must be deconstructed and brought back to the only fact of the doctrine of post-modernism: that there are no facts; there is no universal rational ground for interpretation—there is only a multitude, a pluralism of perspectives. And this passes for freedom. What child stands a chance against it? Children are doomed—if not already in the womb—to shoot their way out of immanence, as at Columbine and Parkland.

But this is a deadly moral Ponzi scheme run by more-than-Dickensian knaves and imposters, wolves, thieves and mercenaries, a Potemkin village masking the emptiness of the lie: deducing the non-existence of truth from the arbitrary refusal to seek the truth. This is an ideology wherein only the possibility of truth is too impossible to entertain. This is the soul-less soul and goal-less goal of the protracted suicide of the West described by James Burnham a half century ago.[6] The Western intellectual is, oddly enough, strung out on the very contagions that anesthetize the mind, curdle the heart and debase the will, rendering arid and impotent the natural inclinations to truth, action, and love—making even basic endurance or survival *problematic*. Man falls, as Maritain noted, all the while thinking he is rising, mistaking this betrayal for freedom.

In sum, the loss of the soul requires a series of related *denials* fully accomplished in the modern/postmodern world. The human person first denied any *center of unity* in the so called object of cognition. To do so, he went far *beyond* the Kantian critique of *imposing subjective limits on knowledge* by denying any radical metaphysical otherness on the part of the so called object at all. This denial is far-reaching, because it dismantles any foundation rooted in self-presence or the perception of Being which acts as the independent arbiter and criterion of truth, whether this foundation be God, Nature, or Reason. Even subjectivity in the Cartesian sense is a mere construct, a *fiction* along with God, Being, and Truth.

Thus, after denying:

- any center of unity,

- any notion of foundation or reference point or bottom line, postmodernism is also

- the denial of *meaning*.

The postmodern loss of the soul thus goes farther than any modern existentialism, which looked for meaning in a transcendently meaningless world. Not only is there no transcendent meaning, but the very *idea* of

---

6. Cf. Burnham, *Suicide of the West*. See also Eliot, *Thoughts After Lambeth*, 32: "The world is trying the experiment of attempting to form a civilized but non-Christian mentality. The experiment will fail; but we must be very patient in awaiting its collapse; meanwhile redeeming the time: so that the Faith may be preserved alive through the dark ages before us; to renew and rebuild civilization, and save the World from suicide." Cf. Leslie, *End of a Chapter*, iii: "It was while invalided in hospital during the Great War that I began to record notes and souvenirs of the times and institutions under which I had lived, realizing that I had witnessed the suicide of the civilization called Christian and the travail of a new era to which no gods have been as yet rash enough to give their name, and remembering that, with my friends and contemporaries, I shared the fortunes and misfortunes of being born at the end of a chapter in history."

meaning is *repressive*. No longer connaturally tethered to fate, freedom must have no direction, no *ananke*, no ever-deepening eschatology which illuminates the intelligibilizing miscellany of human into divine creative action. Freedom held at odds from fate becomes an (im)pure directionless will-based lust as purely free and yet entirely fatal. Having no direction, it has one overarching direction, becoming more and more identical with material death so as to outwit Being and resurrect its own disconnected image severed from reality. The soul thus perished in a fundamental self-referential *solipsistic relativism*.

Where do we go from here? How do we re-introduce the world, a reintroduction that goes beyond the limited scientific or sentimental re-introductions that fell short of bringing back the soul? Unfortunately, in this present, empty, and homicidal state, the re-affirmation, re-articulation, and re-grounding of the soul often appears as a kind of aesthetic speculation, a mere vague expression of a counterfeit transcendence in a world that appears fundamentally un-transcendent. We are circling here the basic distinction we discussed earlier between classical-medieval and modern thought. Modern thought is ideological *because* it does not allow the possibility of knowing the world but only of knowing *ideas* about the world. Thus it builds upon an *idea* of man, an *idea* of history, an *idea* of culture and tradition, an *idea* of politics, all of which emerge concretely as *ideals* of man, history, culture, tradition, and politics. All stances and perspectives unable to recover the ground of their betrayal. But what are ideals to the modern mind? They are *values*: subjective, personal, idiosyncratic, non-binding, and cognitively empty values. Does it make one whit of conceptual, philosophical difference which values are "embraced" or "cherished" when the very understanding of values as ideals, and ideals as ideas, and ideas as beliefs is the common and determining factor in our conception of man? Can even a conservative social order endure with such a contradiction lodged in its heart?

If this is what makes modern thought ideological, what makes it modern is this. All its claims can be traced, even in their merely apparent mutual exclusivity, to the guiding movements of modern philosophy, primary among which are the following: the attempt to divide the world into a radical incompatibility between ideas (luminosity) and things (opacity), as in Descartes;[7] the move to reduce the world to an aggressive

---

7. See Amo, *De Humanae Mentis Apatheia* [*On the Impassivity of the Human Mind*]. A selection of Amo's dissertation is translated by Lewis: see Amo, "Anton Wilhelm Amo: Introduction."

APPENDIX   283

partisanship of willfulness versus unintelligibility, as in Kant; the trans-figuration of the world into Pure Idea, as in Hegel; the degeneration of the world into Pure Action, as in Marx; the overcoming of the world through Pure Power, as in Nietzsche. Truth comes to be ideas as functions of the Pure Self: whether these ideas are abstract or concrete, metaphysical or historical, pragmatic, empiricist, positivist, or idealist is not the impor-tant point. What is important is that the world becomes either a radical beyondness or a sheer immanence equivalent to selfhood. Does it matter which head of the Gorgon we prefer to gaze at? In either instance, the world becomes an idea-logos, an *artificial construct.*

But where then is this transcendent meaning? How can we rise above and outside the greatest evil, i.e., the all-too-present denial of evil? It seems that we are so far down the path of annihilation that the region of transcendence which affirms the irreducibility of the soul is practi-cally inaccessible to postmodern man. All human actions call forth their own unrepeatability. What actualizes our relation in the world is that our actions cannot be retrieved; they are fundamentally final because finite. This irretrievability that forms the tapestry of finite actions is the appearance of history, thus rendering this history as well as all its forma-tions unrepeatable. This finality in every action means that the human person can actively close himself off from, and thus forget, the activity of transcendence. As Saint Anselm knew, all we own is our own nothing-ness—but so too can we approach to a kind of nothingness, said Saint Augustine, by allowing an empty and dangerous nihilism to prefigure, situate, and resolve our actions.

Modernity is the age of the monster, the dynasty of terror. The un-fathomable penetration of nihilism has broken open and has perhaps per-manently severed man from tradition. Yeat's slouching rough beast *has been born.* We have replaced tradition with a new anti-tradition, one that de-ritualizes, de-sacramentalizes, and thus de-traditionalizes existence. This new "tradition" denies death through death and kills as it denies it is killing. Thus the "weasel word" abortionist language of "termination."[8]

In this most severe crisis, can man go home again? What does this mean? Can we look to the traditional vision of transcendence, of man

8. Note the systematic corruption of language: from pro-life which represents a fundamental responsiveness to existence, young and old, to "anti-abortion advocates" now to "abortion foes." If language is the house of Being, then the corruption of lan-guage *is* the corruption of the soul. For the utilization of such obscurant terminology see for example Hellmann, "Abortion Foes."

rising up to the universal good? Has the tradition of transcendence been so historically annihilated that, by invoking it, man is invoking only an alien empty category—yet another stance as defection—that can only distract from the problems of modernity?

If the absolute is discoverable only in the particular and the particular is characterized by man's *towardness* to a world of creativeness, adventure, and non-sequitur, the *longer way* of Aquinas, then abortion's *pogrom against contingency* has in praxis destroyed man's access to the divine and thus to himself. This massive interdict on intentionality, transcendence, and freedom has restructured and deformed our historical givenness and reduced it to a series of empty finite moments anchored to the self-enclosed realm of necessity at best, and whim at worst. Because the participants in existence have knowingly or, even more perniciously, thoughtlessly embraced the present de-ontological system, rejections of the Christian vision, anticipated by Maritain, are materializing as the major obstacle to the relevance of the faith.

Is there hope? The foundation, the *arche*, like the soul, cannot help but manifest itself even if only in-authentically. We see these inauthentic forms in the rabid consumerism and pornographic obsessions that feed the vapid individualism and how, most particularly, political liberals give greater gravitas and an almost idealistic fanaticism to other moral, environmental, and political issues while rendering abortion a solely emotional issue. What does this mean? The absolute may always be *there*, but if it is not in a form that befits human nature it is *as if* it does not exist. We live in the forgetfulness of Being, in the endless foundering in the nothing, the no-where of truthlessness. It is time to recollect Being as God. And, as Étienne Gilson noted in his little-known but prophetic 1948 talk *The Terrors of the Year Two Thousand*: "Not a sin, not a moral fault is there which is not first of all an error made to the detriment of intelligible light, in violation of the laws of the supreme reason."[9]

If we are to come home again, if we are to reaffirm the irreducibility and primacy of the soul and of the meaning of human life, it is not enough to invoke the pieties of transcendent meaning. In this world, calling forth transcendence in order to save the soul has more often than not subsumed the particular and all the activities of our everyday active life under the systematic umbrella of a static lifeless set of "universal goods," "eternal verities" and human rights. In this crisis of modernity, even the basic

---

9. É. Gilson, *Terrors*, 17.

acceptance of modernistic renderings of "transcendent" universal goods has actually aided the continued thoughtlessness that unleashed the terror of modernity and the tyranny of abortion in the first place. Why? Because the meaning of "transcendence" in this world-homelessness is nothing more than an escape hatch, a hidden concession that blindly accepts that the soul, its irreducible foundation and its transcendence, are strictly outside-the-world religious categories. As a fundamentally alien category, the soul is unable to contribute to meaning, because now there is no inherent or natural meaning left to discover or augment! In the depth of this crisis, any breakthrough would be quickly relativized by the prevailing perspectivisms that have conquered every arena of thought, particularly the academic, and among the academic even those pockets of professional Thomists who see "objectivity" as an emergency exit from the trials of historical temporality.

Christianity, sorting through the intellectual and spiritual carnage, is presented with two competing unacceptable alternatives: the soul reduced to a material principle, or an irreducible principle of merely religious sentiment. Of course, Christianity chose the latter stance, the lesser of two evils. But this modern religious choice was fraught with a minefield of defections, desertions, and denials, because both alternatives carry the same fatal flaw: the blind allegiance to a reductive rendering of the natural world. This promotes an ethics inflicted by the same deontological impasse as the abortionist ethic: severed from its life-giving subordination to and originary affective union with Being which alone illuminates the natural law not as prescriptive but as dynamic, inviting, and incarnational. The former seeks to defend what the latter refuses but has not the tools to illuminate what *Is*! This flaw not only creates the unnecessary opposition between the body and the soul but issues in the exact same conclusion for both alternatives: when the soul is relegated to a strictly religious category it terminates in separating God from Being. The soul is left to remain outside the region of the current confines of meaning, far flung into the homelessness of nonbeing, again contributing nothing but hollow religious sentiment and "values" and appeals to a tradition already emptied of its intelligibility and transcendence.

Before man proclaimed God's death, he had already buried natural meaning, and to accomplish that last rite, he had already killed off the soul. Underneath all of this persisted the anesthetized extraction of Being from the world and this extraction happened at night and behind our backs. Being is not in the soul, nor in the world, and, now, nor in

God. Being is nowhere to be found. Without incarnational Being there is no meaningful direction to human knowledge and activity, nor a consubstantial intellectual exegesis of the world, nor a tran-substantial sense of man in God. All of these unities are now but phantom apparitions of a stale and primitive religion.

Before the moral collapse came the metaphysical collapse, and before the metaphysical collapse was the epistemological collapse. All these implosions cannot help but point towards the remnants of soul which mirror the contemporary, humanistic and effete figure of Christ: a half-dead corpse dragged through the centuries[10] pardoning while condoning all sins until there is no such thing as sin because it has lost all of its meaning.

While it was once possible to be, like Maritain, without contradiction, politically liberal and theologically faithful, since Roe vs. Wade this is now an impossibility. In many respects, man cannot go home again; we are strangers in a strange land; as *homo viator*, we are without a way home. We live in the annihilation of the given, and abortion is unfortunately debated within this context-without-content. The classic moral vision is suppressed in all its real forms, the ground of its activity is uprooted; at most it is a shadow-land of frail bloodlines of recollection, remembrance, regret, and forgiveness. These frail bloodlines convey the evils of abortion, but haven't the metaphysical strength to articulate the reasons why abortion is the profoundest existential defection, desertion, and betrayal. In a moral vision constrained by the loss of Being, Christianity is limited to waging a defense of life through emotional affectivity and a proclamation of traditional values that more often than not fall on deaf ears. The human person and world are no longer in a relationship of mutual obligation and implication. Absolute right knows no obligation. It is sheer insatiable demand, demand even and especially for the blood of the innocent.

Catholicism and its intellectual tradition by no means equated the soul to the Kantian consciousness or the Hegelian spirit. For our tradition, the paradoxical mathematics of the human person is that *one* soul united to *one* body equals *one* human person. The logic of perfection is that the soul is the principle of life, and that it is inseparably and existentially discoverable only within the world. The soul's situatedness within the human person, connaturally understood within the world, grounds

---

10. Nietzsche, *Antichrist*, §31.

religious insight. Thus, unlike the consciousness emptied of everything but itself, the Catholic soul was never a merely religious or solipsistic phantasy. We cannot defend human life by positing the soul as a merely subjective religious category!

To confront the homicidal culture of death we must reject its empty and reckless moral platitudes and return to the origins of ethics. Again, the moral collapse began in the metaphysical collapse, which is itself founded on an epistemological collapse. Thus, if we can delineate the metaphysical evil of abortion through reflective meditations on the meaning of temporality, contingency, intentionality, freedom, and history, then, and only then, can we secure the possibility of a more powerful ethics to defend life, and this is what we have attempted in our meditations thus far. Powerful, because it refuses to lead, to raise, and thus reduce truth to a collection of facts disassociated from living communion.[11] We can re-affirm what it means to be man as rational animal (which is an unfortunate term to begin with), but we must uncover it as it is re-awakened in Gabriel Marcel's *homo viator* (man as wayfarer), in G. K. Chesterton's everlasting man, in Kierkegaard's stages on life's way, in Pascal's wager. The loss of the soul is the loss of the principle of intentionality and what is this loss but the continued neglect of our relatedness in and to the world? The loss of the soul is reflected in the prolonged historical mismanagement of "rational animal" and its terrible disservice to reason! Reason, as the distinction between man and animal has been overused and precariously applied, resulting in a latent and widespread neglectfulness of the senses, passions, and the genuine meaning of Saint Thomas's *longior via*. The disposition of this "rational animal," with its litany of dead "concepts," "ideas," "abstractions," "substantial forms," and "acts and potencies," has more often than not obliterated the genuine insight of metaphysics:

---

11. This is an ethics as jarring as the figure of Christ which no sociological interdict can reduce to a religious figure in general. Christ is utterly universal in his particularity and communal through his incommunicability. When speaking of a natural law ethics we see it as wholly unified to the body *politique* not in general, not as vacant *ideal* but as wedded to the somatic unity of the figure of Christ as inescapable in its transcending particularity. This is an ethics which *is* truth itself necessarily preceding reflection, diagnosis, debate, and discussion so as to *enable* reflection, diagnosis, debate, and discussion. Identical with Being-as-such it takes on the invocation of law because it is as things *are*. Christ is not a figure *in* time, but the figure *of* time. The natural law ethics is not a prescriptive stance *in* or *beyond* time, but the living ledger *of* time which intelligibilizes freedom and fate through their always-unified dance.

Being outstrips all of our thoughts, ideas, and meanings and it must do so in order for man to have genuine thought and action in the first place!

The moment reason was pressed into the service of laying conceptual concrete over what it considered an "unwieldy" existence, the minute it made a direct highway of "clear and distinct ideas" to answer or frame such problems as immortality or, especially, the existence God, it lost everything. It might not be so much of a stretch to say that in the endgame of a degenerate and decadent metaphysics lies scientism/behaviorism/determinism because that decadent metaphysics pays only lip service to Being and God as parts of an elaborate word game.

It is the soul to which the body is united and for which it exists, the two coming together in what the theologian Romano Guardini called a "holy association" as the unity of man, requiring time and the world for its journey[12]—it is this soul which possesses a logic of its own. The French writer Georges Bernanos, who knew the vast cemeteries under the moonlight to be the graveyard of modern man, also knew "that everything beautiful in the history of the world has originated without anyone's knowledge, from the mysterious accord which exists between the humble and burning patience of man and the gentle mercy of God."[13] The communion of man in political association is the least of exceptions. The isolating speculations of political and philosophical angelisms and materialisms are deformities that make up ideologies but unmake societies. But it is by the soul's self-understanding, through its presence in and to the world that make it habitable; the transcendental disposition of man binds him to creation. This is the longer way, but the surer way, and it is incompatible with any ideology.

A cherry between the teeth holds more mystery than the whole of idealistic metaphysics and ideological politics, and thus more reality than the entirety of their subsequent materialisms with their overflowing secular banalities. A child in the womb is the holy and full incarnate mystery of a cherry between trembling teeth; it is the savor, the meaning inherent in and spanning from the birth of the little sparrow to the sacrament of last rites.

---

12. Guardini, *Prayers from Theology*, 28.
13. Bernanos, *Les grands cimetières sous la lune*, 51.

Advocatus Diaboli: The Language Game of Choice

Now is the time to show that the cherry between trembling teeth carries more meaning than the whole of abortion ideology. We have experienced the moralistic charade of abortion which persists only within its own alter reality and we have witnessed the hidden Presence of Being within the historical missteps which allow abortion to persist. Let us play—quite literally—devil's advocate and take hold of the constructed reductive reality which lives by defection and persists via annihilation. Our aim is to look at some of the crucial arguments in favor of abortion and see what response, what apologetic, can be employed effectively to counteract those claims. In doing so, we are not seeking an alternate position or stance, for that would be to concede to a relativism, a plurality of non-hierarchical perspectives. Instead, we seek the interior truth of the fourth demonstration: what is relative persists only in relationality, and relation, logically and metaphysically, is necessarily understood within the context of a *primum efficiens*, an absolute perfection. If we deem the relative as the manifestation of freedom and the absolute as the prime manifestation of fate, the former is free only because the latter lies above the cycle of limited freedom and its directional binding. If there were no absolute, there would be no relations to an absolute and more still, there would be no limited freedom by and through which one acts either via defection, as in the case of abortion, or in harmony with freedom, for there would be no order appointed from eternity, transcending all causes in order to invest them with freedom. All is relative by way of being related to an absolute. We seek the rediscovery of the ground where freedom and fate coexist and are not bifurcated by the ego insubordinated by its own false wisdom. The pro-lifer is thus wayfarer ever mindful of home. What truths, if any, are present and what are missed in the pro-abortion position, and what arguments might we be we missing when we defend life? If all freedoms are indelibly a form of fate, let us see what unfolds when following the abortionist "logic." The world is naturally supernatural and is entreating us to enter into the harmony of our originary subordination and incarnational penultimacy. It reveals that if there is a resolution it cannot be worked out on the *natural* plane or, more precisely, the world is, again, naturally supernatural and to sequester it to some artificial conception of the "natural" world is to do a disservice to that natural world! Thus, we will utilize arguments from absurdity to show something fundamental is missing in the pro-abortion argumentation so that we become more cautious that we do not make similar ontological missteps in the exegesis of what it means to be for life.

Here are the thirteen interrelated arguments we are to confront:

1. "Life" may begin at conception, but *human* life does not: how is a single cell a person? It is not; it is a collection of cells no more advanced than a fleck of skin.

Scientists determine life as something that has the capacity to grow, metabolize, respond to stimuli, adapt, and reproduce of its own accord. So do philosophers. The metaphysician, physicist, and physician, if honest, should find a natural preliminary agreement regarding life. And for this living *action* to occur, what precedes potentiality is actuality.[14] From zygote to blastocyst to embryo there is not one point in which the unborn is inanimate; there is actual *being* from the moment of conception, with heartbeats at day twenty-four and brain waves at day forty-three, both of which are well before the end of the first trimester. It is alive and it is human. Therefore, it is a *human life* that is being taken. And it is not only innocent human life but proto-innocent. The willful taking of innocent human life is called murder.

Emily Letts, a twenty-five-year-old woman who filmed her own abortion, pronounced, "Yes, I do realize it was a potential life. I have a special relationship with my ultrasound."[15] The problem is that potentiality

14. Cf. Clarke, "World of Change," 109–22. See our discussion of Saint Thomas's First Way in the book.

15. Letts, "Emily's Abortion." For an even more horrendous accounting see Amelia Bonow (activist for #Shoutyourabortion, author of a book of the same name as well as an upcoming children's book defending abortion) sit down with children, on a children's YouTube channel, "Hilo Kids," and explain how abortion is part of God's plan, that it is "pro-life" and just like going to the dentist. For transcript sections and intelligible commentary see Desanctis, "Leave the Children Out of It," paras. 5–10: "Innocent young children, perhaps heretofore unwilling to go along with this bizarre construct, are the latest target in the quest to normalize the killing of the unborn, and Bonow's video is a prime example. 'They just suck the pregnancy out,' she tells the children of her own abortion procedure. 'It was like a crappy dentist appointment or something. Do we want people to just have all those babies?' she later asks one of the kids. When he shakes his head no, evidently being led in this direction by her questioning, Bonow asks, 'So what do we do with them?' The child, now clearly baffled, offers tentatively: 'Put them up for adoption?' Bonow is not pleased. 'I feel like if I am forced to create life, I have lost the right to my own life,' she replies. 'I should be the one to decide if my body creates a life.' She also insists that the phrase pro-life is propaganda, and that she is actually pro-life, while those who oppose abortion are not. Later, a child asks what God thinks of abortion. 'I think it's all part of God's plan,'

cannot exist without actuality. Her "potential" relationship with her child is *only* recognized because she is *actually* relating to her child, which is in actual existence. The child is only a "potential" child before the moment of conception. Remember: potentiality cannot exist without actuality. I have all the potential to respond to a student's question, but that potential can only be realized, addressed, and actualized because I am an actual human being with the potential to respond! Emily Letts misunderstands the *grammar of existence*. The unborn child is conceived, it is an actual living being, an actual human child who has *potential* options such as growing more, being born, going to school, preferring soccer over football. Emily Letts could only speak about a potential or possible child if there were nothing actual to look at or nothing actual to abort! The very sonogram which she holds would have to depict an empty womb to depict a potential child in its *logical* truth. The fetus is alive; it is *human*: it is a *human* life.

The language of abortion is thus intentionally misleading. And we should be bothered by misleading language.[16] Such language is not a

_____

Bonow explains." When Plato in the Republic speaks of the four forms of declining government (timocracy, oligarchy, democracy, tyranny), with each more rotten than the next, what differentiates the slow and often decadent rot of democracy from tyranny is that the former still hides its sins, still attempts to cover them over through the use of sophistry and deceptive language games. The latter heralds its sins *as* virtues. Is this not our present culture, where a vicious form of eugenics is touted on a children's show as not only normal but praiseworthy? More still, for Plato, the soul of a society is first written large in the hearts of its citizens. See *Resp.* 435e: "Must we not agree that in each of us there are the same forms [*eidos*] and habits [*ethe*] as in the Polis? And from nowhere else do they pass there." The organization of the society is therefore *not* a set of standards prescriptively outside man, society must be formed by the soul's turning around (*periagoge*) from the day that is really night to the night that is truly day (*epanados*) That is why it is almost impossible for those with an inclination towards goodness and justice to survive a tyrannical society. *How* and *where* are they to ratify that inclination in such a corruptive culture, and in what relation will they find the Other who nurtures their souls? Plato acknowledges a political and civilizational intentionality, where we know ourselves in the face of otherness. In a society where abortions are not only performed with normalizing frequency, but children are being indoctrinated en masse, what is lost almost in its entirety is any sense of an *epanados*: the ascent of the soul from the day that is night (*nykterine*) to the night that is truly (*alethine*) day. See also 2 Cor 2:15–16 (NASB): "For we are a fragrance of Christ to God among those who are being saved and among those who are perishing; to the one an aroma from death to death, to the other an aroma from life to life."

16. Wittgenstein, *Philosophical Grammar*, §46: "One is inclined to make a distinction between rules of grammar that set up 'a connection between language and reality' and those that do not. A rule of the first kind is 'this colour is called "red,"'—a rule of

game, not *mythos* or parable, but its deadly opposite. We should seek out the truth that is veiled—veiled so as to prepare us—for the Beautiful and Good which we must become like in order to recognize and appreciate.[17] "For the gods may be said to love the cryptic and dislike the obvious."[18] Instead the abortion jargon hides the truth in language which refuses to be parabolic precisely because it cannot be! If its language were grounded on the incommunicable communion of beings in Being, it could not speak its platform which must exist only as a series of non-sequitur defections having no reference other than to its own solipsistic ideology. Abortion speaks about whether or not one should *have* a child, and as such is reversing the logical meaning of "have" in terms of potentiality and actuality. All choices by their nature reflect necessity, and the true efficacy of freedom is unified to fate, not idolatrously opposed to it.[19] When I make a choice, I am down one path and not another. The "choice" to have the child ended at the moment of conception. In this sense, the pro-life position is truly the pro-choice position because it reflects that choices have limits. The child in the womb is present, that isn't in dispute. Otherwise the question of abortion would be a non-question! When abortionists speak of *having* the child, more appropriately it should be termed as destroying, terminating, ending that child's existence. And while abortion advocacy does circle around that language by calling the abortion a "termination," it unites that termination with "having" (as birth) the child, which is an inappropriate logical correlation, and more so a dangerous moral and spiritual one. Many are misled into thinking the termination amounts to not having the child when in fact, the child is *already* present, the child is "had" and the abortion is instead the killing of that life. You cannot terminate and choose to have or not have a child at the same time. You terminate because you *already* have a child. Otherwise, if you do not *have* a child why do you need to terminate it? I choose to have a child because there is no child. I terminate or abort or end life because there *is* life, there *is* a child already "had". Again, we should be wary when language misleads us. We should ask *why* it is misleading us.

the second kind is '~~p=p'. With regard to this distinction there is a common error; language is not something that is first given a structure and then fitted on to reality." See Harris, *Language, Saussure and Wittgenstein*.

17. Cf. Plato, *Symp.* 212a.

18. *Brhadaranyaka Upanishad*, IV, 2, in Koller and Koller, *Asian Philosophy*, 15.

19. Cf. See the Myth of Er, Plato, *Resp.* X. See also Voegelin's discussion of the Pamphylian myth in Voegelin, "Republic," 3:46–134; also Voegelin's relating of the Myth to the Gospels in Voegelin, "Gospel and Culture," 59–101.

2. Is a fetus *really* a person? Let us look at the *person* argument from another angle, four to be precise:

   a. *When a fetus gets to a certain size, it is then and only "then" a person.*

Since when does size determine value? Is a toddler worth less than a teenager because the toddler is smaller? What size determines our personhood, and who determines that? And yet, isn't it telling that in a perverse manner the abortionist is invoking the logic of the fourth demonstration? By demarcating a particular size or place as the point in which life is "finally" a person, has it not invoked a hierarchical order where all other lives are lesser and relative to that apex point of absolute acceptability? And in doing so, yet again, has it not logically misread the relationship between potentiality and actuality? It has thus demanded the completion or fulfillment of the hierarchical in those things that are subordinate, secondary, and penultimate within the order of causation. Abortion language has demanded that the very order which cannot lead, but must follow upon true priority, and must impossibly replace that essential priority which it needs to exist! How laughably absurd if it were not so ugly. This is no mere denial of the divine, or an emancipation from its shackles, this is no intellectual atheism, but a wholly dependent divine reimagining in a way Hegel had already advanced almost 200 years prior![20]

   b. *We can abort a fetus before he or she feels pain.*

We agree that fetuses are less developed than we are. But may we kill them because they are so? People in their sleep, on anesthesia, or with certain health conditions do not feel pain. Can we kill them? Why does level of development or susceptibility to pain determine value? This is again a dim and juvenile, yet scandalous, reimagining of the fourth demonstration. How important it is for us to see that the abortionist's illogic is not only so much contrary to the truth but an uncreative and wholly dependent re-configuring of the truth. The fact that we can recognize its reconfigured reductionism nevertheless provides us passage back to the

---

20. Hegel, *Logic of Hegel*, §237. See Shestov's analysis of Hegel, *Kierkegaard and the Existential Philosophy*, 5–6: Shestov rejects that rampant Hegelian revolutionary rationalism which "accepts from the Bible only what can be 'justified' before rational consciousness [for] it never for a moment entered into Hegel's mind that in this lies the terrible, fatal Fall, that 'knowledge' does not make a man equal to God, but tears him away from God, putting him in the clutches of a dead and deadening 'truth.'"

ground which is not a stance or a position but the truth of things as they *are*.

c. When the baby is born, he or she is "now" a person.

Since when does location determine value? Am I worth more inside a house than I am outside on the lawn? There are many pro-abortion advocates who believe we should value the baby in the womb—but only at a certain stage of development. So which is it? Inside or outside of the womb? Why does environment determine value? Did the astronauts, once beyond *terra firma*, simply evacuate their human value? And abortion is permitted in many states up to nine months, and even post birth "termination" or afterbirth abortion has been proposed,[21] preferring such a term over infanticide on the idea that the infant outside the womb is not yet a person. We are to remain mindful that a hierarchy of improper values is continuously imposed in order to promote abortion. The abortionist's penumbra of "absolute" benchmarks are fallacious and cannot help but be so. The litany of standards claiming to amount to a human person, e.g., in the womb at seven or eight or nine months, outside the womb, outside the womb but alive for nine months, are all secondary causations. As secondary, each enters absurdity not only attempting to justify the unjustifiable but attempting to lead when it cannot. In the second demonstration, the Angelic Doctor shows us that all natural "first" causes are not true first causes, each reveals its temporal priority but never an ultimate ontological priority housed *within* itself. As such, all natural standards are signposts pointing towards their dependency on a standard that is unmade so it can truly make those natural "first" causes. And now of course with the rush to "legalize" postpartum "termination," the "logic" must again change.

---

21. "Afterbirth abortion" is yet another example of the deceptiveness of language which is the natural bedfellow of the abortionist ideology. This is by definition infanticide, but cloaked in clinical and so-called palatable language. See Giubilini and Minerva, "After-Birth Abortion," 261–63: "When circumstances occur *after birth* such that they would have justified abortion, what we call *after-birth abortion* should be permissible . . . We propose to call this practice 'after-birth abortion', rather than 'infanticide', to emphasize that the moral status of the individual killed is comparable with that of a fetus . . . rather than to that of a child. Therefore, we claim that killing a newborn could be ethically permissible in all the circumstances where abortion would be. Such circumstances include cases where the newborn has the potential to have an (at least) acceptable life, but the well-being of the family is at risk."

d. Before a baby reaches viability, it can be aborted.

Does degree of dependency determine value? Infants are completely dependent on others for sustenance. Can we kill them because they are dependent on us? Why does viability outside the womb determine value? Has there ever been one person utterly self-sufficient? If we claim to be so, does not our very causation among other things betray us repeatedly throughout our lives? Whenever total independence and self-sufficiency have been politically touted as "virtues," "ideals," or essential attributes of a *human* society, they are soon accompanied by a civilizational decline and fall, one that is barbaric and unnatural. More on this point momentarily.

3. Does a fetus really have a soul? Babies born with severe health issues; is it not better to abort? The embryo in the womb is smaller than a grape seed; how is this wrong?

Religion here is the great defense against abortion but it also is utilized by pro-abortion activists to lessen the pro-life stance with such claims that this is "just a religious idea," "this idea of the soul is something only believed in by religious fanatics but not *really* real."[22] Believers have to be made aware that their faith is grounded in reason and our arguments for the soul precede religious identifications. Plato demonstrated the existence of the soul as the principle of *living* things beyond a reasonable

---

22. It is certainly lamentable that the once-precise language of the separation of church and state has become so flexible, vague, and nebulous as to permit all sin by denying sinfulness, at least within the realm of the state. This division has become an escape hatch from the natural law which is *natural* because it is not merely a command or prescription but the prime invocation of Being upon which all beings, indubitably secondary, depend. The demonstrations for the existence of God repeatedly reveal a world which is naturally supernatural. Church and state derive their meanings in differing degrees, from the same source, nature, which conveys to both their ineluctable secondary statuses. Thus, both cannot help but encounter the supernaturalness upon which all things find communion. To argue that a religious rejection of abortion should be disregarded as having no value to matters of the state, functions because it has gnostically misread that difficult and elusive distinction. Neither church nor state is emancipated from its secondary, subordinated, or penultimate status. Both are responsive to Being for their actions and the companion enactment of their laws. A law of the state which permits abortion by citing, as defense, its distinction from religious ideas, creates an in-subordinated tautology which can exist only by defection, where law is nothing more than a circular reflection of wills, wants, and whims irreverent to Being, acting as an ordering principle when they could never be such orderers except by imitation.

doubt in the *Phaedo*[23] as did Aristotle in the *De Anima*.[24] Saint Thomas, for example, appropriates those great themes as do modern-day scientists when they speak of life as the capability for growth, change, response to stimuli, reproduction, and so forth. This is not some so-called patriarchal Western idea but a recognition of primacy and true actuality within living things which spans all cultures:

> This Self is simply described as 'Not, not.' It is ungraspable, for it is not grasped; it is indestructible for it is not destroyed. It has not attachment and is unfastened; it is not attached and (yet) is not unsteady.[25]

The great atheist Sartre knew that his atheism could only be effective if he avoided scientific categories, because such categories affirm the philosophical principle of the soul and by extension, God.[26] The soul is not some esoteric term but the foundation of classic and indeed modern science with its divisions of species, genus, and so forth. The soul is understood as the animating principle of the body. If things were purely passive, purely material, purely potential, no life could happen. The argument that the baby in the womb is no bigger than a grape seed works against the abortionist who then claims there is no soul. For how can this purely material, passive "grape seed" grow and change without the potential to grow and change? And remember: there can be no such thing as pure potentiality! We can only speak of potentiality because there is something actually present. One cannot go from less to more without, in actuality, that maxim, without actuality as always present enabling the transition from potentiality to actuality. The child in the womb, yet without heartbeat or legs, could not gain heartbeat or legs if only in a state of potentiality—if it were purely material—which by the fact of its existence is absurd. By existing, it is not only in a state of mere potentiality. That which has the potential for heartbeat and legs gains those things because it already possesses a principle of actuality which allows that growth. The paper in my hands has all the potential to drop to the ground but as something as close as possible to pure potentiality and pure materiality,

23. Plato, *Phaed.* 70c–84b, 102b–107c; *Resp.* 608e–12b; *Phaedr.* 245c–24ca; *Symp.* 201a–12c; *Min.* 81a–b. See also Apolloni, "Plato's Immortality of the Soul," 5–32. Ficino, *Platonic Theology.*

24. DA 405; Met. 71b–76a; Phys. 194b29–30; DC 279a17–30; See also Adamson, "Aristotelianism and the Soul," 211–32.

25. *Brhadaranyaka Upanisad,* IV, 4, in Koller and Koller, *Asian Philosophy,* 22.

26. Sartre, "Being-for-Itself," 119–300.

it cannot do so without the aid of my hands. If the child in the womb is mere matter, it could do nothing, it would be like that paper destroyed by time rather than raising itself to its dignity. The potential for that child to read, learn, skateboard, laugh, cry is *because* it is *already a human soul.* That zygote in the womb is not a plant, for a plant, whether it be tiny or massive—mustard seed or oak—does not have the potential to laugh, learn, inquire, graduate, nor will it, because that is not its *actual* nature. "He is a man who is to be a man; the fruit is always present in the seed."[27] Actuality must precede potentiality and, more than that, informs the being of what potentialities are *intrinsic* to its nature.[28] That zygote, blastocyst, and embryo are actual human souls with the potential to do *human* things. Therefore, it is *already* a human life.

4. Here is a two-part question: This whole talk of the soul seems to reveal a difference in dependency as key to the abortion argument. My soul and body no longer are dependent on my mother, but the unborn fetus is wholly dependent on the mother for nine months.

27. Tertullian, "Apology," in Coxe et al., *Ante-Nicene Fathers*, 3:17–60, esp. §9: "For us murder is once for all forbidden; so even the child in the womb, while yet the mother's blood is still being drawn on to form the human being, it is not lawful for us to destroy. To forbid birth is only quicker murder. It makes no difference whether one take away the life once born or destroy it as it comes to birth. He is a man who is to be a man; the fruit is always present in the seed." See also "Apocalypse of Saint Peter," 146, esp. §25: "And near that place I saw another strait place into which the gore and the filth of those who were being punished ran down and became there as it were a lake: and there sat women having the gore up to their necks, and over against them sat many children who were born to them out of due time, crying; and there came forth from them sparks of fire and smote the women in the eyes: and these were the accursed who conceived and caused abortion."

28. This pandemic confusion over the relationship between potentiality and actuality is used to perpetuate a myriad of moral corruptions such as abortion, infanticide and the viewing of animal consciousness as more worthy of protecting than a human life. See Singer, "All Animals Are Equal," in Regan and Singer, *Animal Rights and Human Obligations*, 215–26, esp. 156: "Would the abolitionist be prepared to let thousands die if they could be saved by experimenting on a single animal? The way to reply to this purely hypothetical question is to pose another: Would the experimenter be prepared to perform his experiment on an orphaned human infant, if that were the only way to save many lives? (I say "orphan" to avoid the complication of parental feelings, although in doing so I am being overfair to the experimenter, since the non-human subjects of experiments are not orphans.) If the experimenter is not prepared to use an orphaned human infant, then his readiness to use nonhumans is simple discrimination, since adult apes, cats, mice, and other mammals are more aware of what is happening to them, more self-directing and, so far as we can tell, at least as sensitive to pain, as any human infant. There seems to be no relevant characteristic that human infants possess that adult mammals do not have to the same or a higher degree."

Isn't that dependency a criterion which shows why abortion is a rational and reasonable choice? Secondly, how is that dependency fair on the mother? The unborn do not have the right to use the woman's body for nine months. The feminist mantra: It is my body, my choice. Keep your laws out of my uterus!

For one, we must ask, is the baby inside the mother's womb really the mother's body? Genetically, that unborn baby does not have the same genetic markers as every other part of the mother's body. Your leg is genetically yours, your arms, your womb, your ears, but not that zygote. It is indubitably genetically *other*.

Let's proceed with an absurd example revolving around the seemingly sensible lines: "It's my body, it's my choice." If I put an explosive in my body and let it detonate in a public area with a potential for casualties, is that my so-called right? Most would argue against such a right but then uphold abortion as a right, on grounds that it, unlike the bomb scenario, does not hurt anyone else; that it is a private affair of one's own determination over one's own body. But is that entirely true or true at all?

The unborn life in the womb is, again, *not* the woman's life, neither genetically nor anthropologically.[29] Not only philosophy but science has confirmed that the unborn baby is not the mother's body; it is something undoubtedly *other*. So if detonating the bomb inside of my body is prohibited on the basis of killing others—let alone the serious injunction against killing oneself—am I not killing another human life when I abort the child? How is abortion any different than the detonation of the bomb? In both cases, through my body I destroy person or persons other than my own body, and in both cases do damage to myself, physically, spiritually and morally. Whether indeed that damage is *felt or reflected upon or acknowledged* is a different question. But the damage *is* present, for abortion is demonstrably a violation of what *is*, in favor of a series of defections which must function by inverting the order of potentiality and actuality and then violating the secondary status of natural standards.

So that we can proceed, let us clarify the requirements of free will or free choice. *Because* I am *able* to make a choice, I am *therefore* responsible for that choice, and thus responsible for the necessity into which I

29. The late great atheist Christopher Hitchens was honest enough to recognize this point; see *God Is Not Great*, 220: "[An] unborn child seems to me to be a real concept. It's not a growth or an appendix. You can't say the rights question doesn't come up. I don't think a woman should be forced to choose, or even can be . . . as a materialist, I think it has been demonstrated that an embryo is a separate body and entity."

place myself. Free will is not divorced from responsibility but umbilically linked to responsibility. The responsibility of a doctor is to treat patients, and not to uphold that duty means that the doctor is held responsible for his or her actions. This is the *necessity* imposed upon him by the consequences of his free choice to be a doctor.

The unique essence of womanhood is that we carry life; this is a primal, foundational responsibility on which the history of existence itself rests. Is it easy? No. But when has easiness been the arbiter of goodness and reward? Is it fair? What does that even mean? Freedom is often misinterpreted as being free *from* responsibility, but this is clearly not the case. If we are free from responsibility, then we are not free. To be free from responsibility would be equivalent to an unthinking object which cannot choose, as the inanimate stone is wholly free from responsibility and not culpable should it fall or be thrown. Our actions have consequences, this is a sign of our freedom and of our responsibility, and thus of an intrinsic fairness. Womanhood means that women are unique, the bearers of existence; the bearing of life is intrinsically bound up in our essence and in the historical form of existence. We are free to *abstain* from motherhood, like the nun, but once pregnant we *are* mothers, and mothers don't kill children and are responsible, indeed guilty, if they do. Again, a woman is only *potentially* a mother and a man is only *potentially* a father when the sonogram shows an empty womb.

It is often claimed that the baby in the womb is wholly dependent on the mother whereas those adversely affected by the bomb in the park are independent beings obviously capable of life outside the womb. This distinction between dependency and independency becomes the criterion which renders the abortion morally acceptable and the bombing morally unacceptable. But is that true, is the logic of this argument tenable? Is it even a viable criterion?[30]

Does the unborn baby not have the "right" to use a woman's body for nine months? If we go down this path of argumentation we end up revealing a cycle of dependency where none would have a right to live! How do nine months in the womb reflect a deeper dependency than eighteen years of total dependency on the public school system, or five years on welfare, or three years in rehab after a car crash, or depending on the optometrist to make glasses for sight, or depending on the farmers for your food, or your grandparents in a nursing home for the final decade,

30. It is, of course, yet another secondary and relative standard attempting to invoke a *primum efficiens* status which it cannot achieve.

which may become your parents, and then your husband, and then you and then your child when he or she is grown old and infirm? Are any of us utterly and totally self-sufficient human beings? If that be true, we'd be gods or, even more so, God himself. The blatant fact of our birth, growth, decline, and death are undeniable testaments to our dependency on others. This is an inescapable fact of existence, that to exist requires dependency upon otherness from which none is exempt. This primal truth of existence is violated by the logic, or lack thereof, of abortion. By indicating that dependency is one of the prime motivations for abortion, the abortionist implies there is a state which exists in life free of dependency, and more absurdly, that this is the so-called *natural* or normal state. Tell me where that state exists?[31] Can you envision this state anywhere? And historically, when such a state is conceived, these so-called utopias are but the ideas of molochs, a reflection of that Biblical Canaanite god who demanded child sacrifice. Utopias are never planned without gas chambers, death camps, and the wicked ideologies with which the twentieth century has scarred our historical landscape. It is why Pope Francis spoke of abortion as Nazi eugenics with white gloves,[32] as hiring a hitman. This is not hyperbole, but the unmasking of a lie built by misleading language and matured in cruelty masquerading as mercy. If we go down the cycle of dependency argument whereby dependency is the criterion for abortion and independency is not, then, let's at least be honest, none would have the right to live!

Let us look at this common claim of the pro-abortion movement, "my body, my right," from a different angle. Historically it has extended as a sociopolitical injunction against the government, banning it from meddling where it has no right to meddle. The government should not tell women what to do with their bodies. In 1999, Hillary Clinton said:

> Being pro-choice is trusting the individual to make the right decision for herself and her family, and not entrusting the decision to anyone wearing the authority of government in any regard.[33]

31. Cf. Arendt, *Origins of Totalitarianism*, 475–77.

32. Pope Francis, "Incontro del Santo Padre Francesco": "Lo dico con dolore. Nel secolo scorso tutto il mondo era scandalizzato per quello che facevano i nazisti per curare la purezza della razza. Oggi facciamo lo stesso, ma con guanti bianchi. [I say this with pain. In the last century the whole world was scandalized by what the Nazis did to create the pure race. Today we do the same, but with white gloves.]"

33. Clinton, Remarks at National Abortion Rights Action League Anniversary Luncheon in Washington, DC, in 1999. See in Kengor, *God and Hillary Clinton*, 191.

This more than implies that morality cannot be legislated. Is that appropriate or fair even? Are we not entering a problematic quandary if we say that some moral choices can be legislated but others are inexplicably free from such burden? If choices are free from responsibility then they are not *free* choices.

Look again at the following statement: "It is my body, it is my choice." Let us rephrase that. It is the rapist's body, it is the rapist's choice to rape with his body. What's the problem with such argumentation? Well, you may say that in the case of the rape it is another person being violated which renders the rape reprehensible and capable of being legislated on moral grounds. But haven't we already clarified that it *is* another person being violated with abortion? It clearly is, that cannot be denied scientifically, genetically, or philosophically. And it is innocent human life, indeed proto-innocent human life. The second line of defense is to argue that the unborn child wholly depends upon the mother and cannot live outside the womb. But, again, how is this a permissible argument in favor of the abortion? Have we not already revealed a world utterly entrenched in dependency, in which none self-emancipate from such need? Let's press the absurdity to its limits: a social worker is caring for someone who is severely brain damaged. Without the social worker's care, monitoring of life support, the patient could not live. If we can abort the unborn child on the basis of the child's dependency on the mother, then the social worker has the *obiter dicta* right to violate and murder his patient on a similar totalizing dependency.[34] We would certainly call the latter not only absurd but unjust, immoral, and cruel. If we are speaking fairly and honestly, how can we not call the former, the abortion, unjust, immoral, and cruel? One of the cornerstones of law and relation is fairness. If one person is held accountable for a crime, but another who commits the same crime in similar circumstances is released scot free, we would see this as a lapse not only in the law but in the expression of free will as universally applicable. If we cannot see the permission of abortion as a glaring transgression of human rights, i.e., the rights of the unborn, how can we prosecute the father who beats the three-day-old infant to death, or the care-worker who steals from and abuses the Down syndrome patient? The unborn may be wholly dependent on the mother

---

34. We have obscured the reality of our universally shared dependency as the natural expression of our dependency on the divine. This dependency is no mere ontological fact; it is the basis of any meaningful sense of gift.

for existence, but how long is a three-day-old baby going to survive if left to its own devices, or the patient with advanced dementia?[35]

Let us return to the Hillary Clinton remark: "Being pro-choice is trusting the individual to make the right decision for herself and her family, and not entrusting the decision to anyone wearing the authority of government in any regard." It sounds generous, but isn't something amiss here? Trust is something earned, not in-born. We are free beings with the tools for goodness, but our freedom accords us with the responsibility to enact that goodness, to participate in its courtship. We have to earn trust and work hard at it. Laws are present to encourage trustful behavior precisely because we do miss the mark, we do fall short, we do lie, steal, cheat, and murder. The primary function of the law, for Saint Thomas, is to make persons good, *simply*. The secondary function of the law is to curb the behavior of those willfully opposed to the good. It is problematic when the latter function of the law overshadows its primary duty, which often occurs because the law is drafted with an eye to the good not in itself—*simpliciter*—but according to some ideal or perspective—*secundum quid*—only fleetingly participating in the Good *as such*. This distinction between the *simpliciter* and *secundum quid* is a primal expression of an ethics with proper subordination versus one untethered from its connatural subordination in Being.

> For if the intention of the lawgiver is fixed on true good, which is the common good regulated according to Divine justice, it follows that the effect of the law is to make men good simply. If, however, the intention of the lawgiver is fixed on that which is not simply good, but useful or pleasurable to himself, or in opposition to Divine justice; then the law does not make men good simply, but in respect to that particular government. In this way good is found even in things that are bad of themselves: thus a man is called a good robber, because he works in a way that is adapted to his end.[36]

35. This returns us to the fallacy of self-sufficiency. No unborn child, infant, toddler, teenager, young adult, adult, or elderly person is without dependencies on persons and things other than themselves for their existence. This includes the network of dependencies indelibly actualized by existing and the ones which are in degrees of potentiality precisely because existence abides by contingency. If the argument of totalizing self-sufficiency is to work, then there would simply be no existents in the first place . . . except perhaps God. How strange to be denying God by such an erroneous logic and yet by that logic constructing an idol.

36. *ST* I-II, 92, 1.

What is even more problematic is an understanding that law can be suspended in certain matters because its sometime participants possess an absolute right—but only in certain situations—rendering them the arbiter of the Good. This is yet another example of attempting to make a measured measurer, i.e., a woman's participation in goodness and justice, identical with the unmeasured measurer, i.e., the originary basis for such participation. How dangerously absurd and untenable such a position is, when its very implementation demonstrates that a woman's judgement is *not* the primary adjudicator. The very fact that this judgement is an inviolable right but only in the specific instance of abortion is a contradiction in terms. If the absolute is affected by potentiality, contingency, and happenstance it is clearly not the absolute and not therefore an absolute right! For all the abortionist's claims to respect freedom, it has trampled on the very interlocutors of freedom. The fact that such a view of women's rights has been discovered, drafted, and concluded to historically, demonstrates that this perspective is not the unmeasured measurer but very much measured and in need of measure, mean, and legislation. How is it that there is a pandemic acceptance to trust that *all* women will know what to do with the unborn child in their wombs. How will *all* women miraculously know the truest thing to do during this most overwhelming and life-changing circumstance, when we do not, nor should we, always and *naively* trust *all* women to pay their bills, or trust *all* women never to commit felonies, or trust *all* women never to commit arson or murder? How is it that women are suddenly paragons of virtue *only* when it comes to abortion rights? This is more than a bit disingenuous. It is a dangerous precedent.

Finally still, is the feminist mantra *actually* pro-woman? Does not abortion downgrade what it is to be man and woman by diminishing the man's responsibility for the child, and then mishandling that responsibility by handing it over to the woman? The woman, through the totalizing decision to terminate, must act both as if she is wholly responsible for the pregnancy while, oddly enough and at the same time, ridding herself of all responsibility because it is her absolute right to terminate. Do not forget: responsibility and absolute right are diametrically opposed terms. Responsibility requires contingency, dependency, a relation participating in the absolute whereas absolute right leapfrogs over the messy business of the vicissitudes of existence. The father, now off the hook, is divested of his responsibility as duty of care, which is then placed on the woman, only to be transformed into a right that completely strips her of that very responsibility. If she decides to keep the child, then the child is her responsibility and can be extended to the father, sometimes by legal force. If at any time within that pregnancy she changes her mind, then the responsibility for the child somehow erodes into a universal right, where not only is the parental responsibility for the unborn child a non-question, so too is the father's responsibility denied by the artificial terminology of a woman's right. When has a genuine right ever eroded human responsibility as relationality in and towards others? The fact that this so-called universal right to abortion cannot co-exist with any form of human responsibility unmasks this "right" as both empty and destructive. The child in the midst of this battlefield between absolute right and responsibility is equivalent to Shroedinger's cat! The woman is wholly responsible for the decision to terminate, and thus wholly outside the jurisdiction of responsibility and responsible action, for responsibility implies a duty of care to something other than herself, which has been barred from the abortionist illogic: it is her body and her right, *ens totum*. The absolute right of abortion is thus like the absolute right of my lungs to function in relation to my body. It is not the chosen responsibility of my lungs to provide a duty of care to my heart and extremities but the absolute function of my body in a seamless somatic unity. By making abortion an absolute right, the abortionist destroys the very freedom it sought to give the woman in the first place, for it has displaced responsibility from its participants—mother and father—and denied what makes responsibility meaningful: otherness, contingency, degrees of right and wrong, and freedom. If abortion is done in the "name" of free will and if to do so divorces such freedom from responsibility, then such a fallacious argument impales and dismembers the very free will it seeks to enhance.

5. In life, many potential opportunities change. How can we say that depriving someone of a future is unfair if choice by its nature claims one possibility while leaving other future possibilities unclaimed? If abortion invokes limits how is it bad? Every choice by its nature limits you from other alternative potential choices. If free will invokes parameters, what is wrong with limiting the number of children I have by way of abortion?

The language of planning by its nature means something *has not* yet happened and you are planning for it. I have not been accepted into medical school but making plans for it, once I am accepted into medical school, that part of the plan has finished or completed itself. I can no longer "plan" to get into medical school as I already am accepted into medical school. All choices are finite, and that plan has reached its conclusion. I can plan for other things but no longer that prior plan. Choices, again, by their nature invoke finitude or limit. This is the language of potentiality, and in terms of the unborn child, the planning for that child ended the moment the child is actually in existence, irrelevant of dependency or whether it is wanted or not. One can no longer plan to limit the number of children once the child exists. Strip the language to its truth, for language can and does gravely mislead and we must be suspicious: we may be led to the slaughter by all-too-corrupted convenient language. When that zygote or blastocyst or embryo or unborn child is present, one can plan to remove its own distinct life or not. It is dishonest language to speak of *planning* to *have* the child when the child is already present and the plan, whether planned or not, has already reached its finitude and been realized. Dante, in the *Inferno*, placed fraud below certain murders such as a crime of passion.[37] Why? Because one animal may snap the neck of another in the heat of the moment but the way in which human beings can fraudulently deceive others in language and action, is unique and terrifying. We must be on guard, we must be vigilant.

6. Abortion is already legal; if it is legal it is good. Why try to change it? Why argue what is considered legally sound?

A weak argumentation which, by nature, shouldn't need clarification but, by condition, often does. Slavery was legal! Does that make it good? Of course not. Such logic implies that laws are truer, more foundational and more valuable than human conscience. It implies further that human conscience and our participation in existence is utterly dependent on legal rules for its complexion and cultivation, which may be partially true but not primally true. In fact, it is the other way around. Human conscience and our participation in *natural* existence is what cultivates human laws, for *we* draft human laws. If we indicate that laws *ipso facto* decide human conscience then the human law becomes a leviathan, a monster in control of us, rather than the shepherd guiding us and reminding us of what is good and true or failing to remind us of what is good and true. Furthermore, if our conscience is utterly dependent on legal rules for its complexion, then this would be yet another example of

37. Alighieri, "Inferno," *Divine Comedy*, cantos xviii–xxx, pp. 143–250; Alighieri, *La Vita Nuova*, canto 34.

an in-subordinated ethics, where secondary *aisthesis* perspectives claim a primacy they do not possess. More still, such laws would place freedom in opposition to fate, for the law would be good only if we follow it, closing our natures by copying its rule. The truer expression of the law is good because our likeness to it and the law itself are both participations of Being *as such* which frees us through conformity. When we conform to Being, that source which is groundless, which is the *un*caused cause, the *un*measured measurer, the first which has no beginning and end, we conform to an open nature, where fate is the estuary of freedom.

7. The child is not "wanted." How is it "fair" to let it live?[38]

There are so many hidden dangers utilizing the language of "wanted" and "unwanted." Desires by their nature change all the time. How many times can you honestly say that you wanted something, believed it was essential for your happiness, and it turned out either partially true, not true at all, or one of your biggest regrets? One of the reasons we have to earn trust is that we are free beings who have to grow into our natures. The tree is treelike, it is a fixed nature we can all grasp. But to say the man is manlike doesn't quite cut it.[39] Our natures are measured not by growth and decay, not by materiality like the tree, but by knowledge and, therefore, by wisdom which takes time, patience, understanding to cultivate. The drug addict desires peace, and peace is a good desire, but *how* that desire is manifested in the quick fix is not good at all. Desire and *how* desires are manifested are often not aligned. In order for judgment to be sound it must rest on that which is intrinsic and bedrock. If judgment rests only on desires and whims which change all the time, we would have chaos, anarchy itself and, more than that, deep unhappiness.

More still, when we begin to value human beings by their worth, by their attributes, by qualities which are more desirable than others, have

38. See John Rogers's (Democratic representative of Alabama) ruthless ipsedixitism: "Some kids are unwanted . . . So you kill them now or you kill them later. You bring them into the world unwanted, unloved, then send them to the electric chair. So you kill them now or kill them later." See sage commentary by Desanctis, "Democratic State Rep. Makes Horrifying Pro-Abortion Comment."

39. Cf. Maritain, *Approaches to God*; Pascal, *Pensees*, §72: "For after all what is man in nature? A nothing in relation to infinity, all in relation to nothing, a central point between nothing and all and infinitely far from understanding either. The ends of things and their beginnings are impregnably concealed from him in an impenetrable secret. He is equally incapable of seeing the nothingness out of which he was drawn and the infinite in which he is engulfed."

we not set out a dangerous precedent? Nazi Germany has the same ideology of the abortion clinic because both invoke the language of "wanted" and "unwanted" as prime motivation for their actions which in both cases is death for a massive population. The originary founder of Planned Parenthood is Margaret Sanger, who was a known eugenicist. Eugenics, as she argued, required the segregation and compulsory sterilization of undesirables, from Down syndrome, welfare minorities, homosexuals, those with diminished IQs. One may claim that I am invoking a "guilt by association" fallacy, that just because the founder of Planned Parenthood supported eugenics does not mean the abortion industry is enveloped by that same ideology. But in both eugenics and in abortion the prime motivating factor for the majority of abortions is that the child is "unwanted." A population is decimated in the name of a "greater good." There are 3,000 abortions on average in the United States per day, 321,384 abortions were performed by Planned Parenthood alone in 2016[40] and 56 million on average occur per year worldwide.[41]

The language of the "unwanted" child has all sorts of dangers and, while some draw real sympathy, the hierarchical order of goods must be clarified.

a. I cannot "afford" a child:

This is a serious concern and what a situation to be in, to be poor, struggling, and without support. But the abortion only plays into the eugenic ideology. Prolife advocates should be prolifers, meaning they work to support the good of the whole person each step of the way throughout life. Being poor is a serious concern, but in the order of things being poor is a state of existence which as existence itself is always better than non-existence. There are ways to improve quality of life, there are no ways to bring someone back from death, from the dismemberment of an abortion. The "I cannot afford a child" argument only truly works *before* conception; otherwise the problematic ideology of eugenics stemming from dependency and "unwanted" attributes is supported. More absurdly but more to the point: if the mother also has a toddler, why not kill the toddler rather than the unborn child? If the argument for the abortion

40. Planned Parenthood, "2016–2017 Annual Report." According to a January 2017 Guttmacher Institute report, 926,200 abortions were committed in 2014. See Jones and Jerman, "Abortion Incidence," 17–27.

41. Singh et al., "Abortion Worldwide 2017."

is on whether or not the child can be afforded—and is thus unwanted because unable to be afforded—then the toddler in need of glasses, child-care, more substantial food and clothing is much more expensive than the baby. The mother may save more money killing the toddler than the unborn child. The response may be that the mother has bonded with the toddler and, again, "wants" the toddler. But we have returned both to the ideology of preference argument and secondly demonstrated the fact that desire cannot nor should not be the foundation for judgment. How can the mother know she will not love or want the unborn child, how can she make a judgment about life on something as mercurial and changing as desire? How is that fair to herself and to the separate life inside her?

b. The child has Down syndrome, it's better to abort.[42]

In England, there have been such screenings and subsequent abor-tions on demand for children with Down syndrome that this population is in real decline. This is not a cure for Down syndrome; this is a message to that community that their lives are not worthwhile. There is a slippery slope to the "unwanted" child argument and we must recognize that none of us is the ideal human being, whatever that may mean. Whether it is ad-diction, dyslexia, Down syndrome, overweight, underweight, too short, and on and on. The moment we hinge abortion on the language of "un-wanted" characteristics none of us is emancipated from its cruel fate. We must also ask ourselves: when was intelligence the fundamental identity of the human person? The scientists who created the camps were genius-level IQ's, as were the creators of the atom bomb or the massive freeway systems meant to separate race into wealthier and poorer parts of town. But, of course, intelligence is a prime indicator of the human person, and the child with Down syndrome is at a disadvantage. But intelligence is

42. For a detailed argument on this position, see Singer, *Practical Ethics*, 182: "In Chapter 4 we saw that the fact that a being is a human being, in the sense of a member of the species Homo sapiens, is not relevant to the wrongness of killing it; it is, rather, characteristics like rationality, autonomy, and self-consciousness that make a differ-ence. Infants lack these characteristics. Killing them, therefore, cannot be equated with killing normal human beings, or any other self-conscious beings. This conclusion is not limited to infants who, because of irreversible intellectual disabilities, will never be rational, self-conscious beings. We saw in our discussion of abortion that the potential of a fetus to become a rational, self-conscious being cannot count against killing it at a stage when it lacks these characteristics—not, that is, unless we are also prepared to count the value of rational self-conscious life as a reason against contraception and celibacy. No infant—disabled or not—has as strong a claim to life as beings capable of seeing themselves as distinct entities, existing over time."

not genuinely intelligent if it is merely the ability to process a preponderance of data in a moral vacuum. Intelligence is in the *service* of the truth, which is good and beautiful. "Rational animal" reflects wisdom, not mere intelligence. Intelligence, unlike wisdom, is often at the service of death and disease rather than life. It is called "progress" but is instead barreling toward a dead end. Animals have intelligence, plants act intelligently, but wisdom is cultivated when we reflect on our surroundings and uncover what brings about life, and not death. To utilize our intelligence thus requires reflecting on the otherness of existence, on our relations with others. Thus, if our nature as rational animal is understood only in the context of the unpacking of wisdom within our relationality with others, then the child with Down syndrome has just as much a capacity for wisdom, to reflect on life, and to be a source of our own reflection of life and wisdom. When we destroy others, destroy the environment, propagate lies, build cities and institutions that are ugly and geared towards death, we obscure and even lose our own access into what it means to be human, to be open natures. Here is the most serious of questions: how then is the killing of a Down syndrome baby the way to understand our human nature if we understand ourselves *only* in our *living* context with others? Killing the marginalized is tyrannical by nature and self-destructive of the killer's humanity.

There are more arguments for infanticide, for the practices of euthanizing those who are a burden on society. Did these arguments populate the culture out of nowhere or are they the product of an abortion-mindset? And while we understand triage care, where care should be devoted to those in most need and then work down from there, that is very different from refusing care on the basis that the value of a life depends primarily upon external attributes, such as whether they are wanted or not, whether they contribute to society or not. The culture of abortion is beyond a specific self-enclosed abortion, it is influencing our conscience quietly and behind our backs. It is surprisingly easy to forget the good and find oneself a participant in death. Has not history repeatedly taught us this lesson? If we accept the logic of abortion, we accept a culture where life is valuable only because of what that life can "produce," what so-called "progress" can be made by that intellect. If the language of "wanted" and "unwanted" is permissible in abortion, and which cuts across all genders, all sexual orientations, all races, then how is it not a perfect, scarily perfect propaedeutic to refusing care to the elderly, to supporting the infanticide of the toddler who has Down syndrome and is just a bit too much to handle, to the murder of a child just not living up to his or her potential? There are many pro-abortion scholars who advocate infanticide[43] and for what is termed a merciful or dignified euthanasia for those unable to be contributive members of society. Richard Dawkins and Peter Singer, both pro-abortion and pro-infanticide,

43. Peter Singer, Michael Tooley, Francesca Minerva, Richard Dawkins, and Stephen Kershnar, to name a few. For a defense, albeit brief, of infanticide, see Dawkins and Singer, "Richard Dawkins Interviews Peter Singer." Dawkins considers killing those with Down syndrome as a form of alleviation of suffering. In a sense he is invoking that strange line from the Gospels that it is better they are not born. But is he? Let us think about Christ's remarks regarding those who betray the Son of Man: "The Son of man indeed goeth, as it is written of him: but woe to that man by whom the Son of man shall be betrayed: it were better for him, if that man had not been born" (Matt 26:24, DRA). The phrase is not "better off dead," but rather "better not to have been born"; they do not mean the same thing. As Augustine notes in "Free Choice of the Will": better to be alive and sin than not sin because you are not able to sin. Thus, Christ is not stating that Judas' existence is not worth his life and thus it is better we end his life and be dead, because the fact of existence is always greater than non-existence, and the reality of freedom is always more perfect than un-freedom. It is better Judas exist than be dead. But if he is to exist and sin the way he did, it would have been better never to have been born. But Judas *was* born and that cannot nor should not be undone, undoing his existence by stating "better off dead" is a denial of the good of the gift of existence, whereas if it is stated "better never to have been conceived or to exist" it is a just statement. Thus, once born, existence is far greater than non-existence and in all his sinfulness, once he exists, his sinfulness (his betrayal of the good) is still better than him choosing death or sinning against the gift of life. Again, Judas *was* born, and once born, this existence is always better than non-existence whereas never to have existence in the first place is a perfectly just or good statement. But Judas did have existence—thus death is not an option towards the Good, it isn't going to get Judas to the good of Christ's statement "better not to have been born." Judas's sin against life is not merely to crave death but to go against life so fully as never to have had life. Thus, Christ's statement (better not to have been born) in all its magnitude is just and merciful as a reflection on the gravity of Judas's sin. Because the sin against life is so deep into the meaning of fraudulence, it isn't merely the degree of fraud that skews the order of reality, it's not even wanting death which is a part of life, but denies reality or life in the first place! And thus, is it cruel to deny man what he did not want in the first place? If man didn't want life, to say "better not to have been born" is a merciful and just statement. But only Our Lord knows whether the interiority of the soul is completely akin to the sin against life; that is another aspect of God's mercy and justice: that his knowledge/omniscience is without limits as the source of Freedom and thus knows our sin not merely in its utter limitations (as sin is nothing but limitation) but knows it in the lost or violated freedom or Goodness needed to turn away and prefer that limit and sin. Thus, God sees into the very caverns of ours soul knowing ourselves better than we do, and thus knows the full truth in our turn away from God. The urgency expressed in the line "better not to have borne" clearly shows us the essential need for Christ and the utter and total lostness we are to ourselves when we deny him.

rightly recognize the failed logic of abortion. If the abortion is defended on grounds of location—i.e., inside the womb, this cannot hold up as an appropriate criterion! The child outside the womb, unwanted and helpless, is effectively the same as the one still inside the birth canal. What is permissible today will become mandatory tomorrow.

Let us not forget that the question of life is bound up in the question of death. Since when are death and dying not a contributive part of society? We learn in the natural process of life and the natural process of death. In abortion we hide both life and death; we prevent both from the unfolding of their experience and meaning.

8. Some will argue that being pro-choice is more inclusive of homosexual, transgender, non-binary people. The argument proceeds as follows: abortions reflect a more inclusive approach for those who do not identify themselves in traditional family roles. Because abortions reshape the way we understand family as well as the meaning of sexuality as divorced from procreation, it therefore plays the architectural role in helping along the inclusivity of such minorities.[44]

Hillary Clinton once asked Mother Teresa why there hadn't been a woman President, to which Mother Teresa responded: probably because she had been aborted.[45] With forty to fifty million unborn aborted each year, and the majority coming from minority populations who struggle with

---

44. See this most interesting upcoming article on the recovery of gender as the recovery of human responsibility: Oncale and Delaney, "Maternal Femininity and Paternal Masculinity," 44–55.

45. See Fitzpatrick, "Marching for Life, Mother Teresa, and Mrs. Clinton." See also Teresa of Calcutta, "Whatever You Did unto One of the Least, You Did unto Me": "The greatest destroyer of peace today is abortion, because it is a war against the child, a direct killing of the innocent child, murder by the mother herself. And if we accept that a mother can kill even her own child, how can we tell other people not to kill one another? How do we persuade a woman not to have an abortion? As always, we must persuade her with love and we remind ourselves that love means to be willing to give until it hurts. Jesus gave even his life to love us. So, the mother who is thinking of abortion, should be helped to love, that is, to give until it hurts her plans, or her free time, to respect the life of her child. The father of that child, whoever he is, must also give until it hurts. By abortion, the mother does not learn to love, but kills even her own child to solve her problems. And, by abortion, that father is told that he does not have to take any responsibility at all for the child he has brought into the world. The father is likely to put other women into the same trouble. So abortion just leads to more abortion. Any country that accepts abortion is not teaching its people to love, but to use any violence to get what they want. This is why the greatest destroyer of love and peace is abortion."

finance, with making ends meet, we can see how true Mother Teresa's response is. Heterosexual, homosexual, African, Caucasian, Indian, interracial gone, decimated. Eighty percent of abortion clinics are disproportionately in minority neighborhoods. *If that is not a whiff of eugenics, what is?* A whole generation which could dialogue about these issues, decimated. How does an approach which destroys life in all its different facets cultivate inclusion? That's not only a minor oxymoron but a glaring contradiction! Isn't society about defending minorities, those that are defenseless. Aren't the unborn, especially the unborn of so many minorities and groups on the fringe, the most defenseless?

9. What about rape and incest?

It is telling that this argument is championed numerous times, when most abortions are not because of these two crimes. In 2004, 1.5 percent of abortions were performed because of rape and/or incest.[46] Without minimizing the seriousness and heartbreak of such situation, we must *still* ask ourselves: because we have been victimized do we really have the right to victimize others? Because, again, the child is someone other, genetically and anthropologically. We do not combat crime with crime. It is not fair to be a victim, but it is far worse to become the victimizer. If it is permissible for the victim to become the victimizer, then the world could have no legal system, no moral code but destruction.

10. What about the life or health of the mother?

Like rape and incest, this is the camel's nose under the tent. It is an argument from the extreme rather than the mean, which is suspect not only in law but in daily life. The preponderance of abortions are derived from the arguments from *preference* and *want*. Apart from that, while the life of the mother is a serious question and requires love, support, and patience, we must ask ourselves, again out of fairness, is it justifiable that one should die without his or her consent for the life of another? Furthermore, do we arrest a person on the *potential* that he or she may commit a crime? Do we execute someone on the *possibility* that he or she may commit a murder? No. Then why do we permit and indeed *demand* the death of the child on the *possibility* that its life may adversely affect the mother's? The "health of the mother" argument has also been utilized in a vague way extending, more often than not, to cover the psychological

46. Finer et al., "Reasons US Women have Abortions," 110–11. See Also Lewin, "Rape and Incest: Just 1% of All Abortions."

health of the mother, i.e., the fact that she does not "want" the baby. And thus we return to *that* dangerous ideology.

11. If there are spontaneous abortions, why not artificial abortions?

There are spontaneous and accidental deaths, such as an undiagnosed heart defect causing the young athlete at the prime of his life to be found dead. If we follow the logic of arguing for planned abortions because there are spontaneous abortions, then I can justifiably affirm an absurd but relevant example. If there are spontaneous deaths, why not artificial deaths such as murder, death from torture, death from abuse, death from systematic starvation, death from death camps, death from child neglect, death from euthanasia, death from abortion?

12. Abortion is merciful population control to alleviate environmental and social stresses.

Not only a disingenuous argument but contradictory to its core. The claim that abortion is a "green" solution lowering carbon emissions because it is an effective form of population control is an infirmed argument from the start. How is it at all possible that life could be protected by its own destruction and by the annihilation of the most innocent of lives? Such faulty reasoning is on par with the deadly illogic of Nazi Germany. The idea of an ideal community opposed to any horrific agenda is in and of itself an intelligible goal. But when we see the ratification of such a plan in the barbarism of cruel mass extermination, it is abundantly clear that such a programmatic evil, as *causal* impetus, could never *effect* an ideal community as solution. Abortion, the annihilation of life, has no causal capacity to issue the effect of life in any respect. This is quite simply a contradiction in terms, a non-starter that has attempted to start for far too long. Thus, the desire for, and effective implementation of, a greener planet as echoed in Pope Francis's *Laudato si'*, is connaturally tied to a living respect for *all* life and a recognition of the interior family unit which first and continually evokes civilizational meaning.[47]

47. Francis, *Laudato si'*, §155: "Human ecology also implies another profound reality: the relationship between human life and the moral law, which is inscribed in our nature and is necessary for the creation of a more dignified environment. Pope Benedict XVI spoke of an 'ecology of man,' based on the fact that 'man too has a nature that he must respect and that he cannot manipulate at will.' It is enough to recognize that our body itself establishes us in a direct relationship with the environment and with other living beings. The acceptance of our bodies as God's gift is vital for welcoming and accepting the entire world as a gift from the Father and our common home,

Perpetuating the myth that a large population is wholly at odds with economic development and the primary cause of famines, conflicts, and poor environmental situations neglects the reality that human life itself—indeed the life of the proto-innocent—does not cause environmental degradation. Instead, the tools implemented as handmaidens of our deceptions are the culprits. The absurdist correlation between environmental friendliness and abortions-for-population-control, function within the same missteps as the current gun control arguments. No amount of gun control law will prevent such catastrophes such as Parkland. For all the progressivist mocking of our bourgeois mid-twentieth-century culture[48] there quite simply was not a gun problem or a drug problem or a sexual violence problem within schools. A constant tinkering with laws shows a corruption within the soul of the society;[49] that laws are merely prescriptive, reflective of our defecting conditions and not an instrument revealing the good of our natures. The culture itself has produced such violence because the very mindset which believes it is not only permissible but laudable to kill unborn children has become the very soul of the community. Evils are never self-contained, ideas have consequences, and the civilization of death which begins at the womb permeates whatever life remains.[50] Columbine and Parkland are the heartrending examples of the abortive culture. A culture that kills the unborn promotes the protracted

whereas thinking that we enjoy absolute power over our own bodies turns, often subtly, into thinking that we enjoy absolute power over creation. Learning to accept our body, to care for it and to respect its fullest meaning, is an essential element of any genuine human ecology. Also, valuing one's own body in its femininity or masculinity is necessary if I am going to be able to recognize myself in an encounter with someone who is different. In this way, we can joyfully accept the specific gifts of another man or woman, the work of God the Creator, and find mutual enrichment. It is not a healthy attitude which would seek 'to cancel out sexual difference because it no longer knows how to confront it.'" The *Republic's* often misunderstood notion of *koinoneo*, of a communizing, or an enriching of the family bonds to extend beyond bloodlines, as a blueprint for the *polis* seeks to evoke that umbilical connection that a noble civilization finds its entelechy within the familial structure. See *Republic* 464a–b.

48. For a defense of bourgeois values see Wax and Alexander, "Paying the Price." This article, only controversial to ideologues, and genuinely color-blind, was met with progressivist vitriol. Rather than examine its issues and talking points seriously, the hurling of fashionable victimization terms, from "a white male dominated patriarchy" to "cultural appropriation," was in full gear.

49. Plato, *Resp.* 338a–39a.

50. The abortive culture is most certainly reflected in the gun, drug, and pornographic sexual exploitative problems that have marred the youth of our generation. Each of these problems is causally linked to death, both bodily and spiritually.

death and/or suicide of those fortunate enough to survive. Such a pernicious mindset also ignores the reality that the tools and artifices we make can also be used for good. What is the point of a greener environment if we are destroying the very generations that should enjoy the rewards of a more pristine earth? Demanding such a vicious solution amounts to Kierkegaard's untruth cloaked in velvet—"velvet-clad mercenary souls."[51] Are we really to believe, after centuries of innovation and creative *techne*, that the problems of famine and pollution require mass extermination?

> The world's food problem does not arise from any physical limitation on potential output or any danger of unduly stressing the environment. The limitations on abundance are to be found in the social and political structures of nations. The unexploited global food resource is there, between Cancer and Capricorn. The successful husbandry of that resource depends upon the will and actions of men.[52]

A growth in population is precisely what the culture and the environment need in order to encourage a better quality of life in all registers from physical, sociological, societal to moral and spiritual. A much-needed growth in population does not inevitably lead to unmanageable stress on vital resources, but can instead encourage more people to develop new and innovative solutions to the problems confronting humanity.[53] Population growth thus ultimately encourages the creation, replenishment, and recycling of more resources. The more life, family, and community buzzing and brimming within a society, the more that society has to adapt creatively and innovate, thereby elevating its living standards and find solutions to resource scarcity.

> We, too, are at a moment when the world is creating new resources and cleaning up the environment at an ever-increasing rate. Our capacity to provide the good things of life for an ever-larger population is increasing as never before. Yet the conventional outlook perhaps because of a similar lack of imagination—points in exactly the opposite direction. When the doomsayers hear that oil can be obtained from various kinds of crops, they say: Yes, but it costs much more than fossil fuels. They do not imagine the cost reductions from increased

51. Kierkegaard, *Moment*, 44.

52. Hopper, "Development of Agriculture," 202. See also Kasum, *War against Population*; Mosher, "Too Many People?," 1–17.

53. Cf. Simon, "Population Growth's Effect," 311–512.

efficiency that will inevitably take place in the future, and they do not foresee that the total cost of energy, already a very small part of our economy, will become even smaller in the future. And when they hear that the rich countries are becoming cleaner and less polluted with each decade, the doomsayers say: But what about the poor countries? They do not imagine that the poor countries, when they become richer, will also eventually turn to becoming cleaner rather than dirtier, as the now-rich countries have done. Again and again they do not imagine the adjustments that individuals and communities make that create more resources, invent better technologies, and overcome environmental problems.[54]

If China is to be the litmus test in population control, one should take heed of its evil towards unborn children, an evil more visible than our own culture of abortion, but no different, for both are homicidal in act and red in tooth and claw.

> The parents were hunted down and the mother injected with poison to induce an abortion. The report said after 'the baby was pulled out inhumanly like a piece of meat,' it was still alive and began to cry before doctors slung the defenseless child into a bucket [of water to drown] and left it to die.[55]

Are we not reminded of Kermit Gosnell and the shocking cowardice of the media? Any other story of a mass murderer and the media coverage would be wall-to-wall and yet there was little to none as evidenced by the empty seats reserved for the media at the trial.[56]

> But Gosnell changed things for [filmmaker Ann] McElhinney. 'I got an education on abortion because of researching and investigating this story,' she tells me. In the case of Gosnell, she has focused not only on the unborn who died and the infants born

54. Simon, *Ultimate Resource 2*, 16.

55. Nikolas, "Outrage over Picture of Chinese Forced Abortion at Nine Months."

56. How strange that Brett Kavanagh is accused of a sexual offense more than thirty years ago and with little to no evidence. This accusation must be investigated. Not only was it investigated, it was given a Senate hearing and nonstop media coverage. Kermit Gosnell's crime far exceed the unsupported allegations against Justice Kavanagh. Why wasn't the media covering this story? Why were the media seats empty at that trial? Again, we are faced with that untruth cloaked in velvet. Both Kavanagh and Gosnell are about abortion, the former commits its act mercilessly and the media turns a blind eye, the latter may have the opportunity to impose abortion restrictions, and with that the media was all eyes.

alive and then killed, but also on 'two vulnerable women' who died there, one a young African American and one a refugee, she points out, adding: 'Hundreds of African-American babies were born alive and then murdered. Where is the outrage for those black lives that matter? Progressive Pennsylvania with all of its government agencies couldn't have cared less. Where's the outrage for that?' Gosnell's clinic was the epitome of what Pope Francis refers to as a 'throwaway society'.[57]

If this is population control at all, it is a form of eugenics, destroying the lives of those who would have come from ethnic minorities and underprivileged families, the very children whom generations before defined America as the place where, with hard work, dreams can materialize. Perhaps after all, it is population we need, we were not born to be alone and the cultures which advocate for contraceptives, not the opposite of, but the precursor to, abortion, find their population rates decreasing as happiness decreases.[58] Surely this is not a coincidence. The fallacy of the slippery slope may be a logical fallacy but it is not a moral or existential one. The assertion that with contraceptives, abortion rates would all but perish may make some form of superficial logical sense, but the existential reality is that not only do abortion rates rise, so too do the incidence of STDs.[59] In such a slippery slope, the deeper logic is entirely

57. Lopez, "Gosnell, Game Changer."

58. West, "What Mary Eberstadt Told Notre Dame about 'Humanae Vitae'": "Contraception promotes abortion-on-demand because it encourages career plans that depend on delaying children until later in life. If an unexpected pregnancy interrupts such plans, she said, abortion is more likely to be considered. Eberstadt also argued that the legalization of contraception and abortion are tied to another. She said movements towards the legalization of abortion always begin as birth control devices become more popular and available. 'Legal reasoning justifying freedom to contracept has been used to justify freedom to abort. You can't have one without the other.' Eberstadt mentioned that support for contraception is not universal. She said many African nations have 'resisted the attempts of reformers to bring them into line with the secular Western sexual program.' She quoted an open letter written by Nigerian-born author Obainuju Ekaocha in response to a contraceptive initiative by billionaire Melinda Gates: 'I see this $4.6 billion buying us misery. I see it buying us unfaithful husbands. I see it buying us streets devoid of innocent chatter of children . . . I see it buying us a retirement without the tender loving care of our children.' In contrast to Africa's resistance to contraception, Eberstadt noted the demographic decline of Japan, where, she said, loneliness is pervasive, especially among the elderly, who often die alone."

59. See Centers for Disease Control and Prevention, "Use of Contraception." Also see United States Conference of Catholic Bishops, "Greater Access to Contraception." For the clear link between STDs, abortion, and contraceptive usage, see Klick and

missed. Contraception's totalizing culturally disseminated disregard for the sanctity of life, which divorces the sexual act from its purpose as *pro-creative*, is not going to issue a sudden regard for the very same sanctity of life it banished! When the unwanted pregnancy arises, the contraceptive mentality *becomes* the abortive. The contraceptive culture *is* the abortive culture of death, and a culture that destroys its own members from within, is no culture at all. The slippery slope is how the camel's nose slips under the tent and with it, sins beget all more vicious ones.

13. *Arguments that claim abortion tinkers with the natural order just do not work.* We have adopted medicine and technology that "tinkers with the natural order"—antibiotics, vaccines, and anesthesia, for example—to which we do not give a second thought. We prolong life beyond what the "natural order" would permit and allow it to happen where it otherwise would not (in vitro fertilization, for example). Abortion might be bad, but arguing that it changes the natural order as evidence of its evil is an insufficient argument.

We speak of technology, of scientific advancement, of technological determinism, and without much thought see the following terms as synonymous: "progress," "advancement," and "goodness." Every advance is considered good in and of itself, as if, against the order of existence, the good of technology is good regardless of consequences. There is also the theory of historicism, a bedfellow of relativism, which claims that all human beings are bound by their own time and place, and that when we imagine in our arts and culture and history books another time period it is a *reimagining* in which we indoctrinate the past with our cultural sensitivities and peculiarities. Time is passing and, as such, we cannot lay hold of the past but only reimagine it in the fleeting present. As such we are products of our time and place. To condemn or praise our time and place as worse or better than another historical period is a fruitless exercise, for we haven't the power to emancipate ourselves from our limited cultural and temporal restrictions to gain true sight of another cultural epoch. This would be true except for the fact that we *do* recognize other times and places and these other times and places communicate to us, which would be prohibited if no time or place could exceed its own time and place but was locked from within. Yet the idea that we do reimagine and

Stratmann, "Effect of Abortion Legalization," 407–33.

indoctrinate the past and future with our perspectives and agendas, well, when you read Hegel, you'll understand how real that is.

The question of technology[60] is very much the question of the natural order, and together reveal the human participation in the natural order which is the specific *historical* order. Human beings who have the capacity to think and to know are *alone* historical beings. There are animals and plants throughout history, but only humans who reflect on the order of time and the moral exigencies of existence are *historical* beings.

Let us ask a laughable but serious question, one that brings us back to the ire of the gods angered at Prometheus for bringing man fire, and through fire, technology, and with technology the leisure to reflect on the natural order becoming thereby *historical* beings bound up in human and divine moral meaning.

If electricity was a necessity for the creating of the gas chambers in which eight million died, was it worth it? If electricity was a necessity for the abortion industry which kills over fifty million per year, is this advancement worth it? We can cite all the good of electricity of course, and the creation of most things is first good and then perverted for evil. But let us be aware that advancement is a risky business. What advances also advances us into separation and to loss. We are to some real extent products of our time and place, and we are products of a world populated by electricity, by internet and paved roads, and lights which light stores open at all hours, and hospitals with life-giving machines all in need of power. We cannot imagine a world without the technology which shapes us, for it is so unified with our historical form, so unified that it may be vampiric at our own hands. What technology does is throw us forward into situations undreamt, and when we act on desire, then we must be aware that the technology may not be reined in, and "causes" great evil. The desire for advancement which is a natural desire can only be fulfilled as natural *through* truth. When Hitler's final solution switched from trucks barreling through the streets shooting off guns, to gas chambers, that was an "advancement" in killing effectively. But such a technological progress was not good, it was instead a deadly advancement disengaged from the conserving stance of the good, freed to wind up in one of the many dead ends of existence.

So, how can we employ the argument that abortion tinkers with nature and is thus a defection, an evil, when historical existence, indeed

---

60. Cf. Heidegger, *Question Concerning Technology*; McLuhan and Powers, *Global Village*.

human existence itself has always been a tinkering with nature? The manifestation of specifically *human* existence was, for the Greeks, the manifestation of *techne*, the root word of technology. *Techne* means "making" and reflects our freedom, that unlike the animals we can reflect and construct and imitate our unique natures through technology. The manifestations of technology from fire, to the wheel, to bridges, to the construction of towns and communities and cities, appear more befitting of our free nature than the isolation of the wild, because as companions to free will, they invoke responsibility and consequences. As the bee buzzes and the spider spins its web in accordance with their natures, that *tinkering* is not itself contrary to our natures but how our free nature freely act out our natures. But in order to freely act out their natures it must be done in a way that respects nature rather than violates it, as abortion clearly does. When forty to fifty million are killed each year, that is forty to fifty million persons unable to place their unique imprint or tinkering or enacting of their natures on existence. We speak of goodness in two ways: goodness that is called *simpliciter*, and goodness that is called *secundum quid*. The first means simply good in itself, and the latter means good but only according to something. The infamous cat burglar who can get into Fort Knox is a "good" burglar but that is goodness *secundum quid*—according to effective breaking and entering—not goodness *simpliciter*, for it is not good to steal. So many advancements are good, but only good *secundum quid*, as the construction of the hydrogen bomb was certain good—*secundum quid*—according to the efficiency of bomb-making. But goods only according to *secundum quid* are akin to the snake eating its own tail; they serve only themselves and in doing so destroy others. The argument that defends abortion because medicines also tinker with nature, thus both are good, commits a logical fallacy, collapsing the distinction between *secundum quid* and *simpliciter*. These are the logical lacunae at the heart of Bentham's utilitarian recipe for evil: the greatest good for the greatest number, and aside from a massive begging of the question, both Stalin and Hitler invoked it in their genocidal quest for the "greatest good." As do the abortion architects of evil. It is the greatest evil for the greatest number. In truth, the end does not justify the means, it specifies the means. And a good end requires good means.

Our discussion about electricity and technology hit at something deeper and truer. What humans create, and tinker with, are not inessential attributes but the defining characteristics of human nature. Thus, when we reflect on advancements and progress we must ask ourselves:

are these advancements and progress according to the good itself or only good according to some view, some ideology, some desire or some whim which will not, because it cannot, better us, but only destroy us before we have the eyes to see what is lost.[61]

> Remember, O most gracious Virgin Mary, that never was it known that anyone who fled to thy protection, implored thy help, or sought thy intercession was left unaided by thee. Inspired with this confidence, I fly to thee, Mary, Virgin of virgins, Mother of Jesus Christ; to thee do I come; before thee I stand, sinful, sorrowful and trembling. O Mistress of the World and Mother of the Word Incarnate, despise not my petitions, but in thy mercy hear and answer wretched me crying to thee in this vale of tears. Be near me, I beseech thee, in all my necessities, now and always, and especially at the hour of my death. O clement, o loving, o sweet Virgin Mary. Amen.[62]

61. Objection: Don't like abortion, don't have one. Don't like a T-shirt, don't buy one. Don't like Cornell University, don't go to Cornell. This is a catchy motto but fails the logical test wholeheartedly. It assumes that abortion involves only your body, which we have already undermined. Secondly, do we say, don't like being raped, then don't get raped. Abortion is a *having*, something occurring both within the body of the mother and the child. The unborn child, who does fight and squirm against the abortion in the second and third trimesters, has no say in what is happening to his or her body, which science has affirmed is a separate genetic person.

62. Attributed to Saint Bernard of Clairvaux, "Memorare," in *Coeleste Palmetum*, 734.

Bibliography

Adamson, Peter. "Aristotelianism and the Soul in the Arabic Plotinus." *Journal of the History of Ideas* 62 (2001) 211–32.

Aertsen, Jan A. "Method and Metaphysics: The *via Resolutionis* in Thomas Aquinas." *New Scholasticism* 63 (1989) 405–18.

Aeschylus. *Oresteia*. Translated by Christopher Collard. Oxford: Oxford University Press, 2002.

———. *Tragedies and Fragments of Aeschylus*. Translated by Edward Hayes Plumptre. 2 vols. Boston: Heath, 1909.

Alighieri, Dante. *The Divine Comedy (The Inferno, The Purgatorio, The Paradiso)*. Translated by John Ciardi. New York: NAL Trade, 2003.

———. "The Inferno." In *The Divine Comedy (The Inferno, The Purgatorio, The Paradiso)*, translated by John Ciardi, 16–270. New York: NAL Trade, 2003.

———. *La Vita Nuova*. Translated by David Slavitt. Cambridge: Harvard University Press, 2010.

Amo, Anton Wilhelm. "Anton Wilhelm Amo: Introduction & English Translation." Translated by Dwight K. Lewis. https://www.academia.edu/32648027/Anton_Wilhelm_Amo_Introduction_and_English_Translation.

Anselm, Saint. *The Devotions of St. Anselm*. Edited by C. C. J. Webb. London: Methuen, 1903.

———. *Proslogium, Monologium, Cur Deus Homo, Guanilo's In Behalf of the Fool*. Translated by Sidney Norton Deane. Lasalle, IL: Open Court, 1962.

"The Apocalypse of Saint Peter." In *Ante-Nicene Fathers, Vol. 9: The Gospel of Peter, Apocalypses and Romances, Commentaries of Origen (1896)*, edited by A. Menzies, translated by A. Rutherfurd, 141–48. Buffalo: Christian Literature, 1896.

Apolloni, David. "Plato's Affinity Argument for the Immortality of the Soul." *Journal of the History of Philosophy* 34.1 (1996) 5–32.

Ardley, Gavin. "The Role of Play in the Philosophy of Plato." *Philosophy* 42.161 (1967) 226–44.

Arendt, Hannah. *Eichmann in Jerusalem: A Report on the Banality of Evil*. New York: Penguin, 1994.

———. *The Human Condition*. Garden City: Doubleday, 1959.

———. "Martin Heidegger at Eighty." *The New York Review of Books* 17.6 (1971) 41–55.

———. *The Origins of Totalitarianism*. New York: Harcourt, 1973.

Aristotle. *The Basic Works of Aristotle*. Edited by R. McKeon. New York: Random House, 1941.

Augustine, Saint. *Against the Academicians and The Teacher*. Translated by Peter King. Indianapolis: Hackett, 1994.

———. *Augustine Day by Day*. Edited by John Rotelle. Totowa, NJ: Catholic Book Publishing, 1986.

———. *Augustine: On the Free Choice of the Will, On Grace and Free Choice, and Other Writings*. Edited by Peter King. Cambridge Texts in the History of Philosophy. Cambridge: Cambridge University Press, 2010.

———. *City of God*. Edited by Vernon Bourke. New York: Image, 1958.

———. *Confessions*. Translated by Henry Chadwick. New York: Oxford University Press, 1998.

———. *Day by Day with Saint Augustine*. Edited by Donald X. Burt. Collegeville: Liturgical, 2006.

———. *Nicene and Post-Nicene Fathers: First Series*. Vol. 3, *St. Augustine: On the Holy Trinity, Doctrinal Treatises, Moral Treatises*. Edited by Philip Schaff. New York: Cosimo Classics, 2007.

———. *On Free Choice of the Will*. Translated by Thomas Williams. Indianapolis: Hackett, 1993.

Bachelard, Gaston. *Intuition of the Instant*. Translated by Eileen Rizo-Patron. Evanston: Northwestern University Press, 2013.

Baker, Kenneth. *Fundamentals of Catholicism*. Vol. 2, *God, Trinity, Creation, Christ, Mary*. San Francisco: Ignatius, 1983.

Bakhtin, Mikhail. "Dostoevsky's Polyphonic Novel and Its Treatment in Critical Literature." In *Problems of Dostoevsky's Poetics*, translated by Caryl Emerson, 5–46. Theory of History and Literature 8. Minneapolis: University of Minnesota Press, 1984.

———. *Problems of Dostoevsky's Poetics*. Translated by Caryl Emerson. Theory of History and Literature 8. Minneapolis: University of Minnesota Press, 1984.

Balthasar, Hans Urs von. *The Christian and Anxiety*. San Francisco: Ignatius, 2000.

———. *The Christian State of Life*. San Francisco: Ignatius, 2002.

———. *Church and World*. Translated by A. V. Littledale. Montreal: Palm, 1967.

———. *A First Glance at Adrienne Von Speyr*. San Francisco: Ignatius, 1981.

———. *The Glory of the Lord: A Theological Aesthetics*. Vol. 4, *The Realm of Metaphysics in Antiquity*. San Francisco: Ignatius, 1989.

———. *The Glory of the Lord: A Theological Aesthetics*. Vol. 5, *The Realm of Metaphysics in the Modern Age*. San Francisco: Ignatius, 1991.

———. *The Moment of Christian Witness*. Translated by Richard Beckley. San Francisco: Ignatius, 1994.

———. *Our Task: A Report and a Plan*. San Francisco: Ignatius, 1994.

———. *A Theology of History*. San Francisco: Ignatius, 1994.

———. *Who Is a Christian?* Translated by Frank Davidson. San Francisco: Ignatius, 1993.

Baring, Maurice. *Poems, 1914–1919*. London: Secker, 1920.

Barnhart, Joe E., ed. *Dostoevsky's Polyphonic Talent*. Lanham: University Press of America, 2005.

Barrett, William, and Henry D. Aiken, eds. *Philosophy in the Twentieth Century*. New York: Random House, 1962.

Bazyler, Michael. *Holocaust, Genocide, and the Law: A Quest for Justice in a Post-Holocaust World*. Oxford: Oxford University Press, 2016.

Beckett, Samuel. *Malone Dies*. New York: Grove, 1956.

———. *Oh les beaux jours*. Paris: Minuit, 1963.

———. *Samuel Beckett's "Waiting for Godot."* Edited by Harold Bloom. New ed. New York: Bloom's Literary Criticism, 2008.

Belloc, Hilaire. *A Conversation with an Angel: And Other Essays*. New York: Harper, 1929.

———. *The Path to Rome*. London: Allen & Unwin, 1916.

———. *The Silence of the Sea*. London: Cassell, 1941.

———. *Verses*. London: Duckworth, 1910.

Benedict XVI, Pope. "The Church and the Scandal of Sexual Abuse." *Catholic News Agency* (2019). https://www.catholicnewsagency.com/news/full-text-of-benedict-xvi-the-church-and-the-scandal-of-sexual-abuse-59639.

———. "Meeting with Artists." Vatican City: Libreria Editrice Vaticana, 2009.

———. *Verbum Domini*. Vatican City: Libreria Editrice Vaticana, 2009.

Benson, Stella. "The Secret Day." In *Twenty*, 3–5. New York: Macmillan, 1918.

Bergson, Henri. *Matter and Memory*. Translated by Nancy M. Paul and W. Scott Palmer. London: Allen & Unwin, 1970.

———. *The Two Sources of Morality and Religion*. Translated by R. Ashley Audra and Cloudsley Brereton. Notre Dame: University of Notre Dame Press, 1991.

Bernanos, Georges. *Les grands cimetières sous la lune*. Paris: Plon, 1938.

Bernard of Clairvaux, Saint. "Memorare." In *Coeleste Palmetum*, edited by Wilhelmi Nakateni, 256–57. Paris: Dessain, 1879.

———. *On Grace and Free Choice*. Translated by Daniel O'Donovan. Kalamazoo, MI: Cistercian, 1988.

———. "On the Love of God." In *Late Medieval Mysticism*, edited by Ray C. Petry, 54–65. London: SCM, 1957.

———. *Some Letters of Saint Bernard*. Translated by Samuel J. Eales. London: Ballantyne, 1904.

Berry, John Anthony. "Tested in Fire: Hans Urs von Balthasar on the Moment of Christian Witness." *Melita Theologica* 62 (2012) 145–70.

Boczek, Macon. "Mysticism and Social Justice." Paper given at the 29th Annual International Meeting of the Eric Voegelin Society (September 2013). https://sites01.lsu.edu/faculty/voegelin/wp-content/uploads/sites/80/2015/09/Macon-Boczek.pdf.

Borges, Jose Luis. *Labyrinths: Selected Stories and Other Writings*. Edited by James E. Irby. New York: New Directions, 2007.

Breton, Stanislas. *The Word and the Cross*. Translated by Jacquelyn Porter. New York: Fordham University Press, 2002.

Broocks, Rice. *The Human Right: To Know Jesus Christ and to Make Him Known*. Nashville: Nelson, 2018.

Burke, Edmund. *Reflections on the Revolution in France*. Oxford: Oxford University Press, 2009.

Burnham, James. *The Suicide of the West: An Essay on the Meaning and Destiny of Liberalism*. Chicago: Regnery, 1985.

Burrell, David B. *Knowing the Unknowable God: Ibn Sina, Maimonides, Aquinas*. Notre Dame: University of Notre Dame Press, 1992.

Cafavy, C. P. *The Complete Poems of Cavafy*. Translated by Rae Dalven. New York: Harcourt, 1976.

Camosy, Charles C. "Learning from Charlie Gard." *First Things*, August 2017. https://www.firstthings.com/web-exclusives/2017/08/learning-from-charlie-gard.

Camps, Luis Espinal. *Oraciones a Quemarropa [Point-Blank Prayers]*. La Paz: Jesuitas, 2015.

Camus, Albert. *The First Man*. Translated by David Hapgood. New York: Vintage, 1996.

———. *The Myth of Sisyphus and Other Essays*. New York: Vintage, 1991.

———. *Notebooks: 1951–1959*. Translated by Ryan Bloom. Chicago: Dee, 2008.

Caputo, John D. *Heidegger and Aquinas: An Essay on Overcoming Metaphysics*. Bronx: Fordham University Press, 1982.

———. *The Mystical Element in Heidegger's Thought*. New York: Fordham University Press, 1986.

Carnap, Rudolf. "The Elimination of Metaphysics through Logical Analysis of Language." In *Logical Positivism*, edited by Alfred Jules Ayer, 60–81. Westport, CT: Greenwood, 1978.

Catholic Church. *Catechism of the Catholic Church*. Vatican City: Libreria Editrice Vaticana, 2000.

———. *The Office for the Dead: According to the Roman Breviary, Missal and Ritual*. Toronto: Gale, 2010.

Centers for Disease Control and Prevention. "Use of Contraception and Use of Family Planning Services in the United States: 1982–2002." December 2004. https://www.cdc.gov/nchs/data/ad/ad350factsheet.pdf.

Chenu, Marie-Dominique. *Introduction a L'Etude de S. Thomas d' Aquinas*. Paris: Vrin, 1993.

———. "Le Plan de la Somme Theologique de S. Thomas." *Revue Thomiste* 45 (1939) 93–107.

Chesterton, Gilbert Keith. *The Catholic Church and Conversion*. San Francisco: Ignatius, 2006.

———. *The Collected Works of G. K. Chesterton*. Vol. 1, *Heretics; Orthodoxy; The Blatchford Controversies*. San Francisco: Ignatius, 1986.

———. *The Everlasting Man*. San Francisco: Ignatius, 1993.

———. "Jesus or Christ." *The Hibbert Journal* (1909) 746–58.

———. *Saint Francis of Assisi*. New York: Doubleday, 2001.

———. *St. Thomas Aquinas: The Dumb Ox*. New York: Doubleday, 1956.

———. *William Blake*. Cornwall: House of Stratus, 2000.

Clarke, William Norris. *Explorations in Metaphysics: Being, God, Person*. Notre Dame: University of Notre Dame Press, 1995.

———. "The Limitation of Act by Potency: Aristotelianism or Neoplatonism." *The New Scholasticism* 26 (1952) 167–94.

———. *The One and the Many: A Contemporary Thomistic Metaphysics*. Notre Dame: University of Notre Dame Press, 2001.

———. "The World of Change: Act and Potency." In *The One and the Many: A Contemporary Thomistic Metaphysics*, 109–22. Notre Dame: University of Notre Dame Press, 2001.

Clavell, Luis, and Alfonso Perez de Laborda. *Metafisica*. Rome: Armando, 2006.

Clemo, Jack. "On the Death of Karl Barth." In *The New Oxford Book of Christian Verse*, edited by Donald Davie, 291. Oxford: Oxford University Press, 1981.

———. *Selected Poems*. Newcastle: Bloodaxe, 1998.

Chrysostom, Saint. *Nicene and Post-Nicene Fathers of the Christian Church*. Vol. 10, *Saint Chrysostom's Homilies on the Gospel of Saint Matthew*. Edited by Philip Schaff. Whitefish: Kessinger, 2010.

Copleston, Frederick, and Bertrand Russell. "The Existence of God: A Debate." In *A Modern Introduction to Philosophy*, edited by Paul Edwards and Arthur Pap, 473–90. New York: Free Press, 1965.

Cornford, Frances Darwin. *Poems*. Hampstead: Priory, 1910.

Cornford, Francis Macdonald, trans. *Plato and Parmenides: Parmenides' Way of Truth and Plato's Parmenides*. London: Routledge & Kegan Paul, 1939.

Coxe, A. Cleveland, and Allan Menzies, eds. *Ante-Nicene Fathers*. Vol. 9, *The Gospel of Peter, Apocalypses and Romances, Commentaries of Origen (1896)*. Buffalo: Christian Literature, 1896.

Crane, Hart. *Complete Poems of Hart Crane and Selected Letters*. Edited by Langdon Hammer. New York: Library of America, 2006.

Crespi, Franco. "Absence of Foundation and Social Project." In *Weak Thought*, edited by Gianni Vattimo and Pier Aldo Rovatti, translated by Peter Carravetta, 253–67. Albany: State University of New York Press, 2012.

Curd, Patricia, ed. *A Presocratics Reader: Selected Fragments and Testimonia*. Translated by Richard D. McKirahan. Indianapolis: Hackett, 2011.

Davie, Donald, ed. *The New Oxford Book of Christian Verse*. Oxford: Oxford University Press, 1981.

Dawkins, Richard. "God's Utility Function." *Scientific American* 273.5 (1995) 80–85.

Dawkins, Richard, and Peter Singer. "Richard Dawkins Interviews Peter Singer." *The Genius of Charles Darwin*, June 15, 2008. https://www.richarddawkins. net/2009/06/peter-singer-the-genius-of-darwin-the-uncut-interviews-richard-dawkins-2/.

Debout, Jacques. *My Sins of Omission*. Translated by J. F. Scanlan. London: Sands, 1930.

Desanctis, Alexandra. "Democratic State Rep. Makes Horrifying Pro-Abortion Comment." *National Review,* May 2, 2019. https://www.nationalreview.com/corner/democratic-state-rep-makes-horrifying-pro-abortion-comment/.

———. "Leave the Children Out of It." *National Review*, January 9, 2019. https://www.nationalreview.com/2019/01/shout-your-abortion-activist-group-video-children/.

Descartes, René. *The Philosophical Works of Descartes*. Translated by Elizabeth S. Haldan and G. R. T. Ross. New York: Cambridge University Press, 1955.

Desmond, William. *Ethics and the Between*. Albany: State University of New York Press, 2001.

———. *The Gift and the Passion of Beauty: On the Threshold between the Aesthetic and the Religious*. Eugene: Wipf & Stock, 2018.

———. *Hegel's God: A Counterfeit Double?* Aldershot: Ashgate, 2003.

———. *The Intimate Strangeness of Being: Metaphysics After Dialectic*. Washington, DC: Catholic University of America Press, 2012.

Doctorow, E. L. *Reporting the Universe*. Cambridge: Harvard University Press, 2004.

Donoso Cortés, Juan. *Essay on Catholicism, Liberalism, and Socialism: Considered in Their Fundamental Principles*. Translated by Madeleine Vincent Goddard. Reprint, Boonville, NY: Preserving Christian Publications, 1991.

Dostoyevsky, Fyodor. *The Brothers Karamazov*. Translated by Constance Garnett. New York: Macmillan, 1922.

————. *The Brothers Karamazov*. Translated by Richard Pevear and Larissa Volokhonsky. New York: Farrar, Straus & Giroux, 1990.

————. *The Demons: A Novel in Three Parts*. Translated by Richard Pevear and Larissa Volokhonsky. New York: Vintage, 1995.

————. *The Karamazov Brothers*. Translated by Ignat Avsey. Oxford World's Classics. Oxford: Oxford University Press, 1994.

————. *The Idiot*. Translated by David Magarshack. London: Penguin, 1955.

————. *The Idiot*. Translated by Frederick Whishaw. London: Vizetelly, 1887.

————. *The Idiot*. Translated by Henry Carlisle and Olga Carlisle. New York: Signet, 2010.

————. *The Idiot*. Translated by Richard Pevear and Larissa Volokhonsky. New York: Vintage, 2003.

————. *Polnoe Sobranie Sochinenii*. Leningrad: Nauka, 1985.

The Douay-Rheims New Testament of Our Lord and Savior Jesus Christ. Compiled by Rev. George Leo Haydock. Monrovia: Catholic Treasures, 1991.

The Douay-Rheims Old Testament of the Holy Catholic Bible. Compiled by Rev. George Leo Haydock. Monrovia: Catholic Treasures, 1992.

Du Bos, Charles. *What is Literature?* London: Sheed & Ward, 1940.

Duffy, Francis P. "President Eliot Among the Prophets." *Catholic World* 89 (1909) 721–32.

Eckhart, Meister. *Breakthrough: Meister Eckhart's Creation Spirituality in New Translation*. Translated by Matthew Fox. Garden City, NY: Image, 1980.

Eliade, Mircea. *The Myth of the Eternal Return: Cosmos and History*. Princeton: Princeton University Press, 2005.

————. *The Sacred and the Profane: The Nature of Religion*. Translated by Willard R. Trask. New York: Harcourt, 1959.

Eliot, T. S. *Christianity and Culture*. London: Harvest, 1967.

————. *Four Quartets*. New York: Mariner, 1968.

————. "Hollow Men." In *T. S. Eliot: Collected Poems, 1909–1962*, 77–82. New York: Harcourt, 1968.

————. *Thoughts After Lambeth*. London: Faber & Faber, 1931.

————. *T. S. Eliot: Collected Poems, 1909–1962*. New York: Harcourt, 1968.

Fabro, Cornelio. *God in Exile*. Translated by Arthur Gibson. New York: Newman, 1964.

————. *Participation et Causalité selon Saint Thomas d' Aquin*. Belgium: Publications universitaires de Louvain, 1961.

Fackenheim, Emil. *Metaphysics and Historicity*. Milwaukee: Marquette University Press, 1961.

Feinberg, Joel, ed. *Reason and Responsibility: Readings in Some Basic Problems of Philosophy*. Belmont, CA: Dickenson, 1968.

Feser, Edward. *Five Proofs for the Existence of God*. San Francisco: Ignatius, 2017.

————. "The Thomistic Proof." In *Five Proofs for the Existence of God*, 117–46. San Francisco: Ignatius, 2017.

Ficino, Marsilio. *Platonic Theology*. Vol. 1, *Books I–IV*. Translated by Michael J. B. Allen and John Warden. Cambridge: Harvard University Press, 2001.

Finer, Lawrence B., et al. "Reasons US Women Have Abortions." *Perspectives on Sexual and Reproductive Health* 37.3 (2013) 110–18.

Fitzpatrick, Sean. "Marching for Life, Mother Teresa, and Mrs. Clinton." *Crisis Magazine*, January 2016. https://www.crisismagazine.com/2016/marching-for-life-mother-teresa-and-mrs-clinton.

Flew, Antony. "Theology and Falsification." In *Reason and Responsibility: Readings in Some Basic Problems of Philosophy*, edited by Joel Feinberg, 48–49. Belmont, CA: Dickenson, 1968.

Fowlie, Wallace. *Claudel*. New York: Hillary, 1957.

Francis, Pope. *Gaudete et exsultate*. Vatican City: Libreria Editrice Vaticana, 2018.

———. "Incontro del Santo Padre Francesco con la Delegazione del Forum delle Associazioni Familiari." Vatican City: Libreria Editrice Vaticana, 2018.

———. *Laudato si'*. Vatican City: Libreria Editrice Vaticana, 2015.

Frank, Joseph. *Dostoevsky: The Years of Ordeal, 1850–1859*. Princeton: Princeton University Press, 1990.

Gadamer, Hans-Georg. *The Beginning of Philosophy*. New York: Continuum, 1998.

———. "Plato's Parmenides and Its Influence." *Dionysius* 7 (1983) 3–16.

———. *Truth and Method*. Translated by William Glen-Doepel. 2nd ed. London: Sheed & Ward, 1979.

Geach, Peter Thomas. "The Third Man Again." *Philosophical Review* 55 (1956) 72–82.

George, Robert P., ed. *Natural Law Theory: Contemporary Essays*. Oxford: Oxford University Press, 1992.

Gilby, Thomas. *Principality and Polity: Aquinas and the Rise of State Theory in the West*. London: Longmans, 1958

Gill, Mary Louise. "Aristotle's Metaphysics Reconsidered." *Journal of the History of Philosophy* 43 (2005) 223–41.

Gilson, Caitlin Smith. "Efficacious Prayer, Suffering, and Self-Presence." In *Immediacy and Meaning: J. K. Huysmans and the Immemorial Origin of Metaphysics*, 153–264. New York: Bloomsbury, 2018.

———. "The Groundwork for the Christian *Polis: Noli Me Tangere*." In *The Political Dialogue of Nature and Grace: Toward a Phenomenology of Chaste Anarchism*, 241–70. New York: Bloomsbury, 2015.

———. "The Grand Refusal: Abortion's Pogrom against Contingency." *Human Life Review* 34.3 (2013) 48–58.

———. *Immediacy and Meaning: J. K. Huysmans and the Immemorial Origin of Metaphysics*. New York: Bloomsbury, 2018.

———. *The Metaphysical Presuppositions of Being-in-the-World: A Confrontation between St. Thomas Aquinas and Martin Heidegger*. New York: Continuum, 2010.

———. *The Philosophical Question of Christ*. New York: Bloomsbury, 2014.

———. *The Political Dialogue of Nature and Grace: Toward a Phenomenology of Chaste Anarchism*. New York: Bloomsbury, 2015.

———. "Rebellion of the Gladiators." In *The Political Dialogue of Nature and Grace: Toward a Phenomenology of Chaste Anarchism*, 13–65. New York: Bloomsbury, 2015.

———. "The Search for a Method." In *Philosophical Question of Christ*, 51–128. New York: Bloomsbury, 2014.

———. "St. Thomas and the Paradox of Mediation and Intentionality." In *Immediacy and Meaning: J. K. Huysmans and the Immemorial Origin of Metaphysics*, 17–94. New York: Bloomsbury, 2018.

Gilson, Étienne. *The Art of Misunderstanding Thomism*. West Hartford, CT: St. Joseph's College, 1966.

———. "Autour de Pompanazzi." *Archives d'Histoire Doctrinale et Litteraire du Moyen Age* 28 (1961) 163–278.

———. *Being and Some Philosophers*. Toronto: Pontifical Institute of Mediaeval Studies, 1952.

———. *The Christian Philosophy of St. Thomas*. New York: Random House, 1956.

———. *The Elements of Christian Philosophy*. New York: Mentor Omega, 1963.

———. "The Forgotten Transcendental: Pulchrum." In *Elements of Christian Philosophy*, 159–63. New York: Mentor Omega, 1963.

———. *God and Philosophy*. New Haven: Yale University Press, 1941.

———. *History of Christian Philosophy in the Middle Ages*. London: Sheed & Ward, 1965.

———. *Intelligence in the Service of Christ the King*. New York: Scepter, 1978.

———. *Jean Duns Scot: Introduction à ses positions fondamentales*. Paris: Vrin, 1952.

———. "Les Terreurs de l'an Deux Mille." *Revue de l'Universite d'Ottawa* 19 (1949) 67–81.

———. *Linguistics and Philosophy*. Notre Dame: University of Notre Dame Press, 1988.

———. *Methodical Realism*. Translated by Philip Trower. Front Royal, VA: Christendom University Press, 1990.

———. *The Philosopher and Theology*. Translated by Cecile Gilson. New York: Random House, 1962.

———. *Reason and Revelation in the Middle Ages*. New York: Scribner's, 1966.

———. "Regio dissimilitudinis de Plato a Saint Bernard de Clairvaux." *Mediaeval Studies* 9 (1947) 108–30.

———. *The Spirit of Mediaeval Philosophy*. Translated by A. H. C. Downes. New York: Scribner, 1940.

———. *The Spirit of Thomism*. New York: Harper, 1964.

———. *The Terrors of the Year Two Thousand*. Toronto: St. Michael's College, 1984.

———. *The Unity of Philosophical Experience*. San Francisco: Ignatius, 1999.

Gilson, Frederick. "And Dwelt Among Us." Unpublished, 1994.

Gilson, Frederick, and Thomas Simcox. "Whittaker Chambers Pro Mundum." *Hillsdale Review* 4.3 (1982) 18–31.

Giubilini, Alberto, and Francesco Minerva. "After-Birth Abortion: Why Should the Baby Live?" *Journal of Medical Ethics* 39 (2013) 261–63.

Gonzales, Philip. *Reimagining the Analogia Entis: The Future of Erich Przywara's Christian Vision*. Grand Rapids: Eerdmans, 2019.

Gonzalez-Reimann, Luis A. *The Mahabharata and the Yugas: India's Great Epic Poem and the Hindu System of World Age*. New York: Lang, 2002.

Gottfried, Paul Edward. *After Liberalism: Mass Democracy in the Liberal State*. Princeton: Princeton University Press, 2001.

Goyette, John. "On the Transcendence of the Political Common Good: Aquinas versus the New Natural Law Theory." *The National Catholics Bioethics Quarterly* 13.1 (2013) 133–55.

Gray, Thomas. *Elegy Written in a Country Churchyard*. New York: Limited Editions Club, 1938.

Grene, David, and Richmond Lattimore, eds. *Greek Tragedies*. Vol. 2, *Sophocles*. 2nd ed. Chicago: University of Chicago Press, 1992.

Groeschel, Benedict. *The Journey toward God: In the Footsteps of the Great Spiritual Writers—Catholic, Protestant, and Orthodox*. Ann Arbor: Servant, 2000.

Guardini, Romano. *Meditations Before Mass*. Translated by Elinor Castendyk Briefs. Bedford, NH: Sophia Institute Press, 2013.

———. *Pascal for Our Time*. Translated by Brian Thompson. New York: Herder, 1966.

———. *Prayers from Theology*. Translated by R. Newnham. New York: Herder, 1959.

———. *Sacred Signs*. Translated by Grace Branham. Wilmington: Michael Glazier, 1979.

Hackett, W. Chris. "The Soul and 'All Things': Contribution to a Postmodern Account of the Soul." In *The Resounding Soul: Reflections on the Metaphysics and Vivacity of the Human Person*, edited by Eric Austin Lee and Samuel Kimbriel, 307–29. Eugene, OR: Cascade, 2015.

Halliwell, Stephen. *Aristotle's Poetics*. Chicago: University of Chicago Press, 1998.

Hanfling, Oswald, ed. *Life and Meaning: A Philosophical Reader*. Oxford: Blackwell, 1987.

Harris, Roy. *Language, Saussure and Wittgenstein: How to Play Games with Words*. New York: Routledge, 1990.

Hart, David Bentley. *The Beauty of the Infinite: The Aesthetics of Christian Truth*. Grand Rapids: Eerdmans, 2003.

———. *The Hidden and the Manifest: Essays in Theology and Metaphysics*. Grand Rapids: Eerdmans, 2017.

Hartmann, Herbert. "St. Thomas and Prudence." PhD diss., University of Toronto, 1979.

Hartshorne, Charles. *Anselm's Discovery: A Re-examination of the Ontological Proof of God's Existence*. LaSalle, IL: Open Court, 1991.

Hayek, F. A. *The Constitution of Liberty*. Chicago: University of Chicago Press, 1978.

———. *The Road to Serfdom: Text and Documents*. Edited by Bruce Caldwell. Chicago: University of Chicago Press, 2007.

"Why I Am Not a Conservative." In *The Constitution of Liberty*, 397–414. Chicago: University of Chicago Press, 1978.

Hegel, Georg Wilhelm Friedrich. *Faith and Knowledge*. Translated by Walter Cerf and H. S. Harris. Albany: State University of New York Press, 1988.

———. *The Logic of Hegel*. Translated by William Wallace. Oxford: Oxford University Press, 1904.

———. *The Natural Law*. Translated by T. M. Knox. Pennsylvania: University of Pennsylvania Press, 1975.

———. *Phenomenology of Spirit*. Translated by A. V. Miller. Oxford: Oxford University Press, 1977.

Heide, Gale. *Timeless Truth in the Hands of History*. Cambridge: Clarke, 2012.

Heidegger, Martin. "Art and Space." Translated by Charles H. Seibert. *Man and World* 6 (1973) 3–8.

———. *Basic Problems of Phenomenology*. Translated by Albert Hofstadter. Bloomington: Indiana University Press, 1982.

———. *Basic Writings*. Edited by David Farrell Krell. Rev. and exp. ed. San Francisco: HarperSanFrancisco, 1993.

———. *Being and Time*. Translated by John Macquarrie and Edward Robinson. New York: Harper & Row, 1962.

———. *Discourse on Thinking*. Translated by J. M. Anderson and E. H. Freund. New York: Harper & Row, 1966.

———. *Early Greek Thinking.* Translated by David Farrell. Krell and Frank A. Capuzzi. New York: Harper & Row, 1975.

———. *The End of Philosophy.* Translated by Joan Stambaugh. New York: Harper & Row, 1973.

———. *The Essence of Reasons.* Translated by Terrence Malick. Evanston: Northwestern University Press, 1969.

———. *The Essence of Truth.* Translated by Ted Sadler. New York: Continuum, 2002.

———. "The Existential Structure of the Authentic Potentiality-for-Being which is Attested in the Conscience." In *Being and Time,* translated by John Macquarrie and Edward Robinson, §295–301. New York: Harper & Row, 1962.

———. *Hegel's Concept of Experience.* Translated by J. Glenn Gray and Fred D. Wieck. New York: Harper & Row, 1970.

———. *Hegel's Phenomenology of Spirit.* Translated by Parvis Emad and Kenneth Maly. Bloomington: Indiana University Press, 1988.

———. *History of the Concept of Time: Prolegomena.* Translated by Theodore Kisiel. Bloomington: Indiana University Press, 1985.

———. *Identity and Difference.* Translated by Joan Stambaugh. New York: Harper & Row, 1969.

———. *An Introduction to Metaphysics.* Translated by Ralph Manheim. New York: Doubleday, 1961.

———. *Kant and the Problem of Metaphysics.* Translated by James S. Churchill. Bloomington: Indiana University Press, 1963.

———. *The Metaphysical Foundations of Logic.* Translated by Michael R. Heim. Bloomington: Indiana University Press, 1984.

———. *Nietzsche.* Translated by Joan Stambaugh et al. San Francisco: Harper & Row, 1991.

———. *On the Way to Language.* Translated by Peter Donald Hertz and Joan Stambaugh. New York: Harper & Row, 1971

———. *On Time and Being.* Translated by Joan Stambaugh. New York: Harper & Row, 1972.

———. "'Only a God Can Save Us Now': An Interview with Martin Heidegger." Translated by David Schlender. *Graduate Faculty Philosophy Journal* 6 (1977) 5–27.

———. *Parmenides.* Translated by Andre Schuwer and Richard Rojcewicz. Bloomington: Indiana University Press, 1992.

———. *Phenomenological Interpretations of Aristotle.* Translated by Richard Rojcewicz. Bloomington: Indiana University Press, 2001.

———. *The Phenomenology of Religious Life.* Translated by Matthias Fritsch and Jennifer Anna Gosetti-Ferenci. Bloomington: Indiana University Press, 2010.

———. *The Piety of Thinking.* Translated by J. G. Hart and J. C. Maraldo. Bloomington: Indiana University Press, 1976.

———. *Plato's Doctrine of Truth in Philosophy in the Twentieth Century.* Edited by Henry D. Aiken and William Barrett. New York: Random House, 1962.

———. *Plato's Sophist.* Translated by Andre Schuwer and Richard Rojcewicz. Bloomington: Indiana University Press, 1997.

———. *Poetry, Language, Thought.* Translated by Albert Hofstadter. New York: Harper & Row, 1971.

————. *Ponderings II–VI: The Black Notebooks, 1931–1938*. Translated by Richard Rojcewicz. Bloomington: Indiana University Press, 2016.

————. *The Principle of Reason*. Translated by Reginald Lilly. Bloomington: Indiana University Press, 1991.

————. *The Question Concerning Technology and Other Essays*. Translated by William Lovitt. New York: Harper & Row, 1977.

————. *The Question of Being*. Translated by William Kluback and Jean. T. Wilde. New Haven: Yale University Press, 1958.

————. *Schelling's Treatise on the Essence of Human Reason*. Translated by Joan Stambaugh. Athens: Ohio University Press, 1985.

————. *What Is a Thing?* Translated by W. B. Barton Jr. and Vera Deutsch. Chicago: Regnery, 1967.

————. *What Is Called Thinking?* Translated by J. Glenn Gray and Fred D. Wieck. New York: Harper & Row, 1968.

————. *What Is Philosophy?* Translated by William Kluback and Jean. T. Wilde. New Haven: Yale University Press, 1958.

Heidegger, Martin, and Eugen Fink. *Heraclitus Seminar, 1966–67*. Translated by Charles H. Seibert. Tuscaloosa: University of Alabama Press, 1979.

Hellmann, Jessie. "Abortion Foes March into Divided Washington." *The Hill*, January 18, 2019. https://thehill.com/policy/healthcare/425941-abortion-foes-march-into-divided-washington.

Heraclitus. *Heraclitus: The Cosmic Fragments*. Translated by G. S. Kirk. Cambridge: Cambridge University Press, 1954.

Herbermann, Charles G., ed. *The Catholic Encyclopedia*. Vol. 9, *Laprade-Mass Liturgy*. New York: Robert Appleton, 1910.

Hesse, Hermann. "Thoughts on Dostoevsky's *The Idiot*." Translated by Stephen Hudson. *The Dial* 73.2 (1922) 199–204.

Hildebrand, Dietrich von. *Man, Woman and the Meaning of Love: God's Plan for Love, Marriage, Intimacy, and the Family*. Bedford, NH: Sophia Institute Press, 2002.

Hitchens, Christopher. *God Is Not Great: How Religion Poisons Everything*. New York: Hachette, 2007.

Hopkins, Gerard Manley. *The Gospel in Gerard Manley Hopkins: Selections from His Letters, Poems, Journals, and Spiritual Writings*. Edited by Margaret R. Ellsberg. Farmington, PA: Plough, 2017.

Hopper, W. David. "The Development of Agriculture in Developing Countries." *Scientific American* 235.3 (1976) 200–17.

Huizinga, Johan. *The Waning of the Middle Ages*. Mineola, NY: Dover, 2013.

Hulme, Thomas Ernest. *Speculations: Essays on Humanism and the Philosophy of Art*. Edited by Herbert Read. London: Routledge & Paul, 1987.

Husserl, Edmund. *The Idea of Phenomenology*. Translated by William P. Alston and George Nakhnikian. The Hague: Nijhoff, 1974.

Inciarte, Fernando. *First Principles, Substance and Action: Studies in Aristotle and Aristotelianism*. Edited by Lourdes Flamarique. Hildesheim: Olms, 2005.

Jaeger, Werner. *Theology of the Early Greek Philosophers*. New York: Oxford University Press, 1947.

Jaffa, Harry Victor. *Thomism and Aristotelianism*. Chicago: University of Chicago Press, 1952.

James, William. *The Will to Believe: And Other Essays in Popular Philosophy and Human Immortality*. New York: Smith, 1960.

Jaspers, Karl. *The Perennial Scope of Philosophy*. Translated by Ralph Manheim. New York: Philosophical Library, 1949.

———. *Philosophical Faith and Revelation*. Translated by E. B. Ashton. New York: Harper & Row, 1967.

———. *Way to Wisdom: An Introduction to Philosophy*. Translated by Ralph Manheim. New Haven: Yale University Press, 1954.

John of the Cross, Saint. *The Collected Works of St. John of the Cross*. Translated by Kieran Kavanaugh and Otilio Rodriguez. Rev. ed. Washington, DC: ICS, 1991.

———. *The Collected Works of St. John of the Cross*. Vol. 2, *The Dark Night of the Soul, Spiritual Canticle of the Soul and the Bridegroom Christ, The Living Flame of Love*. Translated by David Lewis. Cosimo Classics. New York: Cosimo, 2007.

———. *The Complete Works of St. John of the Cross*. Translated by D. Lewis. London: Longman, Green, 1864.

———. *The Mystical Doctrine of St. John of the Cross*. Edited by R. H. J. Steuart. New York: Continuum, 2002.

John Paul II, Pope. *Salvifici Doloris*. Vatican City: Libreria Editrice Vaticana, 1984.

Jones, Rachel K., and Jenna Jerman. "Abortion Incidence and Service Availability in the United States, 2014." *Perspectives on Sexual and Reproductive Health* 49 (2017) 17–27.

Journet, Charles. *Aquinas*. Edited by Anthony Kenny. New York: Doubleday, 1969.

———. *The Five Ways: St. Thomas Aquinas' Proofs of God's Existence*. Notre Dame: University of Notre Dame Press, 1980.

———. *The Meaning of Grace*. Glen Rock, NJ: Paulist, 1962.

Jouvenel, Bertrand de. *On Power: Its Nature and the History of Its Growth*. Translated by J. F. Huntington. Boston: Beacon, 1962.

Kant, Immanuel. *Critique of Pure Reason*. New York: Hackett, 1996.

Kasum, Jacqueline. *The War against Population: The Economics and Ideology of World Population*. San Francisco: Ignatius, 1987.

Kazantzakis, Nikos. *God's Pauper: Saint Francis of Assisi*. Translated by Peter A. Bien. Oxford: Cassirer, 1975.

———. *Journeying: Travels in Italy, Egypt, Sinai, Jerusalem and Cyprus*. Translated by Themi Vasils and Theodora Vasils. Boston: Little, Brown, 1975.

Kendall, Willmoore. *The Conservative Affirmation*. Chicago: Regnery, 1963.

Kengor, Paul. *God and Hillary Clinton: A Spiritual Life*. New York: HarperPerennial, 2007.

Kenner, Hugh. *Paradox in Chesterton*. New York: Sheed & Ward, 1947.

Keulman, Kenneth. *The Balance of Consciousness: Eric Voegelin's Political Theory*. University Park: Pennsylvania State University Press, 1990.

Khayyam, Omar. *The Rubaiyat of Omar Khayyam*. Translated by Edward Fitzgerald. Oxford: Oxford University Press, 2015.

Kierkegaard, Søren. *The Concept of Anxiety: A Simple Psychologically Orienting Deliberation on the Dogmatic Issue of Hereditary Sin*. Translated by Reidar Thomte. Princeton: Princeton University Press, 1980.

———. *Concluding Unscientific Postscript*. Translated by Alastair Hannay. Cambridge: Cambridge University Press, 2009.

———. *The Essential Kierkegaard*. Edited by Howard V. Hong and Edna H. Hong. Princeton: Princeton University Press, 2000.

———. *Fear and Trembling and Sickness Unto Death*. Translated by Walter Lowrie. Princeton: Princeton University Press, 1954.

———. *The Moment and Late Writings*. Translated by Howard V. Hong and Edna H. Hong. Princeton: Princeton University Press, 1998.

———. *The Parables of Kierkegaard*. Edited by Thomas Oden. Princeton: Princeton University Press, 1989.

———. *Philosophical Fragments, Johannes Climacus*. Translated by Howard V. Hong and Edna H. Hong. Princeton: Princeton University Press, 1985.

———. *The Sickness Unto Death: A Christian Psychological Exposition for Upbuilding and Awakening*. Translated by Howard V. Hong and Edna H. Hong. Princeton: Princeton University Press, 1983.

———. *The Soul of Kierkegaard: Selections from His Journals*. Edited by Alexander Dru. Mineola, NY: Dover, 2003.

———. *Works of Love*. Translated by Howard V. Hong and Edna H. Hong. New York: HarperCollins, 2009.

Kirk, G. S., et al, eds. *The Presocratic Philosophers: A Critical History with a Selection of Texts*. 2nd ed. New York: Cambridge University Press, 1983.

Kirk, Russell. *The Conservative Mind: From Burke to Eliot*. Washington, DC: Gateway, 2016.

———. *The Essential Russell Kirk: Selected Essays*. Edited by George A. Panichas. Wilmington: Intercollegiate Studies Institute, 2007.

———. "The Idea of Conservatism." In *The Essential Russell Kirk: Selected Essays*, edited by George A. Panichas, 4–49. Wilmington: Intercollegiate Studies Institute, 2007.

———. *The Politics of Prudence*. Wilmington: Intercollegiate Studies Institute, 2014.

Kisiel, Theodore. *The Genesis of Heidegger's "Being and Time."* Berkeley: University of California Press, 1993.

Klick, Jonathan, and Thomas Stratmann. "The Effect of Abortion Legalization on Sexual Behavior: Evidence from Sexually Transmitted Diseases." *Journal of Legal Studies* 32.2 (2003) 407–33.

Knox, Ronald. *Enthusiasm*. Oxford: Oxford University Press, 1950.

Koller, John M., and Patricia Joyce Koller, eds. *Sourcebook in Asian Philosophy*. Upper Saddle River, NJ: Prentice Hall, 1991.

Kreeft, Peter. *Everything You Wanted to Know about Heaven but Never Dreamed of Asking*. San Francisco: Ignatius, 1990.

Kretzmann, Norman, and Eleanore Stump, eds. *The Cambridge Companion to Aquinas*. New York: Cambridge University Press, 1993.

Leahy, David G. *Faith and Philosophy: The Historical Impact*. Burlington, VT: Ashgate, 2003.

———. *Novitas Mundi*. New York: New York University Press, 1980.

Lee, Eric Austin, and Samuel Kimbriel, eds. *The Resounding Soul: Reflections on the Metaphysics and Vivacity of the Human Person*. Eugene, OR: Cascade, 2015.

Leo XIII, Pope. *Rerum Novarum*. Vatican City: Libreria Editrice Vaticana, 1891.

Lepicier, Alexis Henri Marie. *The Unseen World: An Exposition of Catholic Theology in Reference to Modern Spiritism*. New York: Benzinger, 1929.

Leslie, Shane. *The End of a Chapter*. New York: Scribner's, 1916.

Letts, Emily. "Emily's Abortion." *YouTube,* June 7th, 2014. https://www.youtube.com/watch?v=Y4xiVUeecNQ.

Levinas, Emmanuel. *The Levinas Reader.* Edited by Seán Hand. Oxford: Blackwell, 1989.

Lewin, Tamar. "Rape and Incest: Just 1% of All Abortions." *The New York Times,* October 13th, 1989. https://www.nytimes.com/1989/10/13/us/rape-and-incest-just-1-of-all-abortions.html.

Lewis, C. S. *The Abolition of Man.* New York: Harper, 2001.

———. *The Complete C. S. Lewis Signature Classics: Mere Christianity, The Screwtape Letters, Miracles, The Great Divorce, The Problem of Pain, A Grief Observed, The Abolition of Man.* New York: HarperOne, 2001.

———. *Until We Have Faces: A Myth Retold.* New York: Harper, 1984.

———. *The Weight of Glory and Other Addresses.* New York: Harper, 2001.

Lewis, Wyndham, ed. *The Enemy: A Review of Art and Literature.* London: Cass, 1968.

Lonergan, Bernard. *Collected Works of Bernard Lonergan.* Vol. 1, *Grace and Freedom: Operative Grace in the Thought of St. Thomas Aquinas.* Edited by Frederick E. Crowe and Robert M. Doran. Toronto: University of Toronto Press, 2000.

———. *Verbum: Word and Idea in Aquinas.* Notre Dame: University of Notre Dame Press, 1967.

Lopez, Kathryn Jean. "Gosnell, Game Changer." *National Review,* January 30, 2017. https://www.nationalreview.com/2017/01/kermit-gosnell-serial-killer-abortionist-new-book-tells-story/.

Loseff, Lev. "Dostoevsky & 'Don Quixote.'" *New York Review of Books,* November 19, 1998. https://www.nybooks.com/articles/1998/11/19/dostoevsky-don-quixote/.

Lovejoy, Arthur. *The Great Chain of Being: A Study of the History of an Idea.* Cambridge: Harvard University Press, 1976.

Lowith, Karl. *Meaning in History: The Theological Implications of the Philosophy of History.* Chicago: University of Chicago Press, 1957.

Lubac, Henri de. *Catholicism: Christ and the Common Destiny of Man.* Translated by Lancelot C. Sheppard and Elizabeth Englund. San Francisco: Ignatius, 1988.

———. *The Drama of Atheistic Humanism.* Translated by Mark Sebanc. San Francisco: Ignatius, 1995.

———. *Theology in History.* Translated by Anne Englund Nash. San Francisco: Ignatius, 1996.

Lynch, John W. *A Woman Wrapped in Silence.* New York: Paulist, 1968.

Maistre, Joseph de. *St Petersburg Dialogues: Or Conversations on the Temporal Government of Providence.* Edited and translated by Richard A. Lebrun. Montreal: McGill-Queen's University Press, 1993.

Marcel, Gabriel. *Creative Fidelity.* Translated by Robert Rosthal. New York: Fordham University Press, 2002.

Marion, Jean Luc. *God Without Being.* Chicago: University of Chicago Press, 1995.

Maritain, Jacques. *Approaches to God.* Translated by Peter O'Reilly. New York: Harper, 1954.

———. *Art and Scholasticism and the Frontiers of Poetry.* Translated by Joseph W. Evans. Notre Dame: University of Notre Dame Press, 1974.

———. *The Degrees of Knowledge.* Translated by Gerald Phelan. New York: Scribner, 1959.

——. *Existence and the Existent.* Translated by Gerald Phelan. New York: Vintage, 1966.

——. *Freedom and the Modern World.* Translated by Richard O'Sullivan. London: Sheed & Ward, 1935.

——. *God and the Permission of Evil.* Translated by Joseph W. Evans. Milwaukee: Bruce, 1966.

——. *The Grace and Humanity of Jesus Christ.* Translated by Joseph W. Evans. New York: Herder & Herder, 1969.

——. *Moral Philosophy: An Historical Survey of the Great Systems.* New York: Scribner's, 1964.

——. *The Peasant of the Garonne: An Old Layman Questions Himself about the Present Time.* Translated by Michael Cuddihy and Elizabeth Hughes. Reprint, Eugene, OR: Wipf & Stock, 2013.

——. *The Preface to Metaphysics: Seven Lectures on Being.* London: Sheed & Ward, 1945.

——. *The Range of Reason.* Translated by Geoffrey Bles. New York: Scribner's, 1952.

——. *Ransoming the Time.* New York: Scribner's, 1941.

Martin, Jennifer Newsome. *Hans Urs von Balthasar and the Critical Appropriation of Russian Religious Thought.* Notre Dame: University of Notre Dame Press, 2015.

Mauriac, Francois. *The Inner Presence: Recollection of My Spiritual Life.* Indianapolis: Bobbs-Merrill, 1968.

McCabe, Herbert. *Faith Within Reason.* New York: Continuum, 2007.

McInerny, Ralph Matthew. *Aquinas Against the Averroists: On There Being Only One Intellect.* West Lafayette, IN: Purdue University Press, 1993.

——. *Aquinas and Analogy.* Washington, DC: Catholic University of America Press, 1996.

——. *The Logic of Analogy: An Interpretation of St. Thomas.* The Hague: Nijhoff, 1961.

McLuhan, Marshall, and Bruce R. Powers. *The Global Village: Transformation in World Life and Media in the 21st Century.* Communication and Society. Oxford: Oxford University Press, 1989.

Milbank, John, et al., eds. *Radical Orthodoxy: A New Theology.* London: Routledge, 1998.

Milton, John. *Paradise Lost.* Edited by Roy C. Flannagan. New York: Dover, 2005.

Moltmann, Jürgen. *Theology of Play.* Translated by Reinhard Ulrich. New York: Harper, 1972.

Montaigne, Michel de. *The Complete Essays.* Translated and edited by M. A. Screech. London: Penguin, 2003.

Mosher, Steven. "Too Many People? Not by a Long Shot!" *Population Research Institute Review* 7.2 (1997) 1–17.

Neruda, Pablo. *On the Blue Shore of Silence.* Translated by Alastair Reid. New York: Harper, 2003.

Newman, John Henry. *The Apologia Pro Vita Sua.* New York: Norton, 1968.

——. *An Essay in Aid of a Grammar of Assent.* New York: Doubleday, 1955.

——. *Meditations and Devotions.* London: Longmans, Green, 1933.

Nichols, Aidan. *The Word Has Been Abroad: A Guide through Balthasar's Aesthetics.* Edinburgh: T. & T. Clark, 1998.

Nietzsche, Friedrich. *The Antichrist.* Translated by H. L. Mencken. New York: Knopf, 1918.

———. *Basic Writings*. Translated by Walter Kaufmann. New York: Modern Library, 2000.

———. *The Essential Nietzsche: Beyond Good and Evil and The Genealogy of Morals.* New York: Quarto, 2017.

———. *Philosophy in the Tragic Age of the Greeks*. Translated by Marianne Cowan. Washington, DC: Regnery, 1998.

———. *Thus Spoke Zarathustra*. Translated by Walter Kaufmann. New York: Random House, 1995.

———. *Twilight of the Idols and the Anti-Christ: Or, How to Philosophize with a Hammer.* Translated by Reginald John Hollingdale. New York: Penguin, 1990.

———. *The Will to Power*. Translated by Walter Kaufmann and Reginald John Hollingdale. New York: Random House, 1967.

Nikolas, Katerina. "Outrage over Picture of Chinese Forced Abortion at Nine Months." *Digital Journal*, April 2nd, 2012. http://www.digitaljournal.com/article/322260.

North, Helen F. "The Concept of *Sophrosyne* in Greek Literary Criticism." *Classical Philosophy* 43.1 (1948) 1–17.

Nussbaum, Martha, and Richard Rorty, eds. *Essays on Aristotle's "De Anima."* Oxford: Clarendon, 1992.

O'Connor, Flannery. "A Fiction Writer and His Country." In *Mystery and Manners: Occasional Prose*, 29–35. New York: Farrar, Straus & Giroux, 1969.

———. *Mystery and Manners: Occasional Prose*. New York: Farrar, Straus & Giroux, 1969.

———. *A Prayer Journal*. Edited by W. A. Sessions. New York: Farrar, Straus & Giroux, 2013.

Oncale, Emily, and Robert Delaney. "Maternal Femininity and Paternal Masculinity: Recovering Authentic Gender in the Abortion Age." *Human Life Review* 45.2 (2019) 44–55.

O'Regan, Cyril. *The Anatomy of Misremembering*. New York: Herder, 2014.

———. *Theology and the Spaces Apocalyptic*. Milwaukee: Marquette University Press, 2009.

O'Rourke, Fran. "Creative Diffusion in Aquinas." In *Pseudo-Dionysius and the Metaphysics of Aquinas*, 225–74. Notre Dame: University of Notre Dame Press, 2005.

———. *Pseudo-Dionysius and the Metaphysics of Aquinas*. Notre Dame: University of Notre Dame Press, 2005.

Ortega y Gasset, Jose. *Meditations on Quixote*. Translated by Evelyn Rugg and Diego Marin. New York: Norton, 1963.

Owens, Joseph. "Aquinas on Infinite Regress." *Mind* 71 (1962) 244–46.

———. *The Doctrine of Being in the Aristotelian Metaphysics*. Toronto: Pontifical Institute of Mediaeval Studies, 1951.

———. "A Note on Aristotle, De Anima 3.4, 429b9." *Phoenix* 30.2 (1976) 107–18.

———. *St. Thomas and the Future of Metaphysics*. Milwaukee: Marquette University Press, 1957.

———. *St. Thomas Aquinas on the Existence of God*. Albany: State University of New York Press, 1980.

Parmenides. *Parmenides of Elea: A Text and Translation*. Edited by David Gallop. Toronto: University of Toronto Press, 1984.

Pascal, Blaise. *Pensées*. Translated by William Finlayson Trotter. New York: Dutton, 1958.

———. *The Provincial Letters; Pensées; Scientific Treatises*. Great Books of the Western World 33. Chicago: Encyclopaedia Britannica, 1952.

Pearce, Joseph. *Wisdom and Innocence: A Life of G. K. Chesterton*. San Francisco: Ignatius, 1997.

Pegis, Anton Charles. "Aquinas and the Natural Law: Some Notes toward a Reappraisal." Unpublished lecture, Wellesley College, 1965.

———. *At the Origins of the Thomistic Notion of Man*. New York: Macmillan, 1963.

———. *Introduction to St. Thomas Aquinas*. New York: Modern Library, 1948.

———. "Man as Nature and Spirit." *Doctor Communis* 4 (1951) 52–63.

———. "Necessity and Liberty: An Historical Note on St. Thomas Aquinas." *The New Scholasticism* 15 (1941) 18–45.

———. *The Problem of the Soul in the 13th Century*. Toronto: Pontifical Institute of Mediaeval Studies, 1934.

———. "Some Reflections on *Summa Contra Gentiles* II, 56." In *An Etienne Gilson Tribute*, edited by C. J. O'Neil, 169–88. Milwaukee: Marquette University Press, 1959.

———. "St. Anselm and the Argument in the Proslogion." *Mediaeval Studies* 28 (1966) 228–67.

———. *St. Thomas and Philosophy*. Milwaukee: Marquette University Press, 1964.

———. *St. Thomas and the Greeks*. Milwaukee: Marquette University Press, 1939.

———. "St. Thomas and the Meaning of Human Existence." In *Calgary Aquinas Studies*, edited by Anthony Parel, 49–64. Toronto: Pontifical Institute of Mediaeval Studies, 1978.

———. "St. Thomas and the Origin of Creation." In *Philosophy and the Modern Mind*, edited by F. X. Canfield, 49–65. Detroit: Sacred Heart Seminary, 1961.

———. "St. Thomas and the Unity of Man." In *Progress in Philosophy*, edited by J. A. McWilliams, 153–73. Milwaukee: Marquette University Press, 1955.

Péguy, Charles. *Basic Verities*. Translated by Ann Green and Julian Green. New York: Pantheon, 1943.

———. *God Speaks: Religious Poetry*. Translated by Julian Green. New York: Pantheon, 1945.

———. *Man and Saints*. Translated by Julian Green. New York: Pantheon, 1944.

———. *Notre Patrie*. Suresnes: Payen, 1905.

———. *The Portal of the Mystery of Hope*. Translated by David L. Schindler Jr. Grand Rapids: Eerdmans, 1996.

———. *Temporal and Eternal*. Translated by Alexandre Dru. Indianapolis: Liberty Fund, 2001.

Peters, Francis. E. *Greek Philosophical Terms: A Historical Lexicon*. New York: New York University Press, 1967.

Peterson, Sandra. "The Language Game in Plato's *Parmenides*." *Ancient Philosophy* 20.1 (2000) 19–51.

Pieper, Josef. *Happiness and Contemplation*. South Bend, IN: St. Augustine's Press, 1998.

———. *Leisure: The Basis of Culture; The Philosophical Act*. Translated by Alexander Dru. San Francisco: Ignatius, 2009.

Planned Parenthood. "2016–2017 Annual Report." https://www.plannedparenthood.org/
    uploads/filer_public/d4/50/d450c016-a6a9-4455-bf7f-711067db5ff7/20171229_
    ar16-17_p01_lowres.pdf.
Plato. *The Collected Dialogues of Plato, Including the Letters*. Edited by Edith Hamilton
    and Huntington Cairns. New York: Pantheon, 1961.
———. *Greater Hippias*. Translated by B. Jowett. In *The Collected Dialogues of Plato*,
    edited by Edith Hamilton and Huntington Cairns, 1534–59. Princeton: Princeton
    University Press, 1961.
———. *Plato: Complete Works*. Edited by John M. Cooper. Indianapolis: Hackett, 1997.
Possenti, Vittorio. *Nihilism and Metaphysics: The Third Voyage*. Translated by Daniel B.
    Gallagher. Albany: State University of New York Press, 2014.
Psailas, George. "Corfu's Constant Cemetery Gardener." *Deutsche Welle News*, February
    5th, 2016. https://www.dw.com/en/corfus-constant-cemetery-gardener/av-
    19228934.
Pseudo-Aristotle. *The Book of Causes: Liber de Causis*. Edited by Dennis J. Brand.
    Milwaukee: Marquette University Press, 1984.
Pseudo-Dionysius. *Pseudo-Dionysius: The Complete Works*. Translated by Colm
    Luibheid and Paul Rorem. New York: Paulist, 1987.
Pufendorf, Samuel von. *On the Duty of Man and Citizen according to Natural Law*.
    Cambridge: Cambridge University Press, 1991.
Rahner, Hugo. *Man at Play*. New York: Herder, 1967.
Ratzinger, Joseph. *On Conscience*. San Francisco: Ignatius, 2007.
Ratzinger, Joseph, et al. *Principles of Christian Morality*. San Francisco: Ignatius, 1986.
Regan, Tom, and Peter Singer, eds. *Animal Rights and Human Obligations*. Oxford:
    Oxford University Press, 1989.
Renard, Henri. *The Philosophy of God*. Milwaukee: Bruce, 1951.
Rilke, Rainier Maria. *The Book of Hours: Prayers to a Lowly God*. Translated by
    Annemarie Kidder. Evanston: Northwestern University Press, 2001.
———. *The Complete French Poems of Rainer Marie Rilke*. Translated by A. Poulin Jr.
    Saint Paul: Graywolf, 2002.
———. *Sonnets to Orpheus*. Translated by David Young. Middletown, CT: Wesleyan
    University Press, 1987.
Rosen, Stanley. *Plato's Symposium*. New Haven: Yale University Press, 1997.
Ross, Stephen David. *Metaphysical Aporia and Philosophical Heresy*. Albany: State
    University of New York Press, 1989.
Rousselot, Pierre. *The Intellectualism of St. Thomas*. Translated by James E. O'Mahoney.
    New York: Sheed & Ward, 1935.
Royce, Josiah. *Lectures on Modern Idealism*. New Haven: Yale University Press, 1964.
Russell, Bertrand. *Religion and Science*. Oxford: Oxford University Press, 1961.
———. "Science and Ethics." In *Religion and Science*, 223–43. Oxford: Oxford
    University Press, 1961.
Russman, T. A., ed. *Thomistic Papers V*. Houston: Center for Thomistic Studies, 1990.
Sandoz, Ellis. *Give Me Liberty: Studies in Constitutionalism and Philosophy*. South Bend,
    IN: St. Augustine's, 2013.
Santayana, George. *Egotism in German Philosophy*. London: Dent, 1916.
———. *The Essential Santayana: Selected Writings*. Edited by Martin A. Coleman.
    Bloomington: Indiana University Press, 2009.

———. *The Idea of Christ in the Gospels: Or God in Man, A Critical Essay.* New York: Scribner's, 1946.

———. *The Life of Reason.* Vol. 2, *Reason in Society.* Mineola, NY: Dover, 1983.

———. *Realms of Being.* New York: Scribner's, 1942.

———. *Soliloquies in England and Later Soliloquies.* Ann Arbor: University of Michigan, 1967.

———. *Winds of Doctrine, and Platonism and the Spiritual Life.* Gloucester, MA: Smith, 1971.

Sartre, Jean-Paul. *Being and Nothingness.* Translated by Hazel E. Barnes. New York: Washington Square, 1993.

———. "Being-for-Itself." In *Being and Nothingness,* translated by Hazel E. Barnes, 119–300. New York: Washington Square, 1993.

———. *Critique of Dialectical Reason.* Vol. 1, *Theory of Practical Ensembles.* Translated by Alan Sheridan-Smith. Edited by Jonathan Rée. London: Verso, 2004.

———. *Nausea.* Translated by Lloyd Alexander. New York: New Directions, 2007.

———. "The Pursuit of Being." In *Being and Nothingness,* translated by Hazel E. Barnes, 3–32. New York: Washington Square, 1993.

———. *Transcendence of the Ego.* Translated by Forrest Williams and Robert Kirkpatrick. New York: Noonday, 1962.

Savorana, Alberto. *The Life of Luigi Giussani.* Translated by Mariangela C. Sullivan and Christopher Bacich. Montreal: McGill-Queen's University Press, 2018.

Schelling, Friedrich William Joseph *Philosophical Inquiries into the Nature of Human Freedom.* Translated by James Gutman. LaSalle, IL: Open Court, 1989.

Schindler, David L. *Ordering Love: Liberal Societies and the Memory of God.* Grand Rapids: Eerdmans, 2011.

Schindler, D. C. "Love and Beauty, the 'Forgotten Transcendental,' in Thomas Aquinas." *Communio* 44.2 (Summer 2017). https://www.communio-icr.com/articles/view/love-and-beauty-the-forgotten-transcendental-in-thomas-aquinas.

———. *Plato's Critique of Impure Reason: On Goodness and Truth in The Republic.* Washington, DC: Catholic University of America Press, 2008.

Schlick, Moritz. *Philosophical Papers.* Vol. 2, *1925–1936.* Edited by Henk L. Mulder and Barbara F. B. van de Velde-Schlick. Translated by Peter Heath. Dordrecht: Reidel, 1979.

Schürmann, Heinz. "The Theo-logically/Eschatologically Oriented Values and Precepts." In *Principles of Christian Morality,* by Joseph Ratzinger et al., 27–33. San Francisco: Ignatius, 1986.

Sender, Raymond J. "Freedom and Constraint in Andre Gide." *New Mexico Quarterly* 3 (1950) 405–19.

Sertillanges, Antonin Gilbert. *Les sources de la croyance de Dieu.* Paris: Perrin, 1920.

Schaff, Philip. *Christ in Song.* New York: Randolph, 1869.

Shakespeare, William. *The Complete Works of William Shakespeare.* Ware, UK: Wordsworth Editions, 1996.

Sheck, Laurie. "Dostoyevsky's Empathy." *The Paris Review,* November 11th, 2016. https://www.theparisreview.org/blog/2016/11/11/dostoevskys-empathy/.

Sheehan, Thomas J. "On the Being and Conception of *Physis.*" *Man and World* 9.3 (1976) 219–21.

Shestov, Lev. *Athens and Jerusalem.* Translated by Bernard Martin. Athens: Ohio University Press, 1966.

———. *Dostoevsky, Tolstoy, and Nietzsche*. Translated by Spencer Roberts. Athens: Ohio University Press, 1969.

———. *Kierkegaard and the Existential Philosophy*. Translated by Elinor Hewitt. Athens: Ohio University Press, 1969.

Simon, Julian. "Population Growth's Effect upon Our Resources and Living Standards." In *The Ultimate Resource* 2, 311–512. Rev. ed. Princeton: Princeton University Press, 1996.

———. *The Ultimate Resource 2*. Rev. ed. Princeton: Princeton University Press, 1996.

Simpson, Christopher Ben. "Between God and Metaphysics: An Interview with William Desmond." *Radical Orthodoxy: Theology, Philosophy, Politics* 1 (2012) 357–73.

Singer, Peter. *Practical Ethics*. 2nd ed. Cambridge: Cambridge University Press, 1993.

Singh, Susheela, et al. "Abortion Worldwide 2017: Uneven Progress and Unequal Access." Guttmacher Institute, March 2018. https://www.guttmacher.org/report/abortion-worldwide-2017.

Sitwell, Edith. *Collected Poems*. London: Macmillan, 1957.

Solomon, David. "The Complexities of Natural Law." *First Things* 33 (1993) 42–43.

Solovyov, Vladimir. *Divine Sophia: The Wisdom Writings of Vladimir Solovyov*. Translated by Boris Jakim et al. Cornell Paperbacks. Ithaca: Cornell University Press, 2009.

———. *The Meaning of Love*. Translated by Thomas R. Beyer. Hudson, NY: Lindisfarne, 1985.

Sophocles. *The Three Theban Plays*. Translated by Robert Fagles. New York: Penguin, 1984.

Speck, Paula K. "The Making of a Novel in Unamuno." *South Atlantic Review* 47.4 (1982) 52–63.

Spencer, Herbert. *Social Statics: Or, the Conditions Essential to Human Happiness*. New York: Appleton, 1872.

Steptoe, Andrew. *The Mozart-Da Ponte Operas: The Cultural and Musical Background to Le Nozze di Figaro, Don Giovanni, and Così fan Tutte*. Oxford: Oxford University Press, 1988.

Strauss, Leo. *The City and Man*. Chicago: University of Chicago Press, 1978.

———. "Introduction to Political Philosophy: Aristotle. Sessions 10–16." Edited by Catherine Zuckert. Chicago: Estate of Leo Strauss, 1973.

———. *On Tyranny: Corrected and Expanded Edition, Including the Strauss-Kojève Correspondence*. Edited by Victor Gourevitch and Michael S. Roth. Chicago: University of Chicago Press, 2013.

Taylor, Alfred Edward. *The Faith of a Moralist: Gifford Lectures Delivered in the University of St. Andrews, 1926–1928*. London: Macmillan, 1931.

———. *The "Parmenides" of Plato*. New York: Oxford University Press, 1934.

———. *Plato*. New York: New York University Press, 1926.

———. *Plato: The Man and His Works*. London: Methuen, 1927.

———. *The Problem of Conduct: A Study in the Phenomenology of Ethics*. Toronto: University of Toronto Press, 1901.

Teresa of Avila, Saint. *The Collected Works of St. Teresa of Avila*. Vol. 1, *The Book of Her Life; Spiritual Testimonies; Soliloquies*. Translated by Kieran Kavanaugh and Otilio Rodriguez. Washington, DC: ICS, 1976.

———. *The Collected Works of St. Teresa of Avila*. Vol. 2, *The Way of Perfection; Meditations on the Song of Songs; The Interior Castle*. Translated by Kieran Kavanaugh and Otilio Rodriguez. Washington, DC: ICS, 1980.

Teresa of Calcutta, Saint Mother. "Whatever You Did unto One of the Least, You Did unto Me." An address at the National Prayer Breakfast, sponsored by the U.S. Senate and House of Representatives, February 3, 1994.

Tertullian. "Apology." In *Ante-Nicene Fathers, Vol. 3: Latin Christianity: Its Founder, Tertullian,* edited by A. Cleveland Coxe et al., 17–60. Buffalo: Christian Literature, 1885.

———. *Tertullian's Treatise on the Incarnation.* Edited and translated by Ernest Evans. London: SPCK, 1956.

Thomas Aquinas, Saint. *Commentary on Aristotle's Politics.* Translated by Richard J. Regan. Indianapolis: Hackett, 2007.

———. *Commentary on the De Anima.* Translated by Kenelm Foster and Silvester Humphries. New Haven: Yale University Press, 1951.

———. *Commentary on the Gospel of St. John.* Vol. 2. Translated by Fabian R. Larcher and James A. Weisheipl. Albany: Magi, 1998.

———. *Commentary on Aristotle's Physics.* Translated by John P. Rowen. Rev. ed. Notre Dame, IN: Dumb Ox, 1995.

———. *In Boethii de Trinitate.* Edited by B. Decker. Leiden: Brill, 1955.

———. "Prologus: Opuscula Theologica, II, no. 1129." In *In Duo Praecepta Caritatis et in Decem Legis Praecepta,* 245. Taurinen ed. Turin: Marietti, 1954.

———. *In Librum Beati Dionysii de Divinis Nominibus Expositio.* Edited by C. Pera and C. Mazzantini. Turin: Marietti, 1950.

———. *Meditations for Lent.* Translated by Philip Hughes. London: Sheed & Ward, 1937.

———. *On Being and Essence (De Ente et Essentia).* Translated by Armand Maurer. Toronto: Pontifical Institute of Mediaeval Studies, 1949.

———. *Opera Omnia; Leonine Edition.* Vol. 3, *Commentaria in Libros Aristoteles de Caelo et Mundo, de Generatione et Corruptione.* Rome: Ex Typographia Polyglotta, 1886.

———. *Praying in the Presence of Our Lord with St. Thomas Aquinas.* Edited by Mike Aquilina. Pittsburgh: Lambing, 2002.

———. *Summa Contra Gentiles.* Translated by James F. Anderson. Notre Dame: University of Notre Dame Press, 1992.

———. *A Summa of the Summa: The Essential Philosophical Passages of St. Thomas Aquinas' "Summa Theologica."* Edited by Peter Kreeft. San Francisco: Ignatius, 1990.

———. *Summa Theologiae.* Edited by Thomas Gilby. New York: Cambridge University Press, 1967.

———. *Summa Theologiae: A Concise Edition.* Edited by Timothy McDermott. Notre Dame: Ave Maria Press,1989.

———. *Summa Theologica.* Literally translated by Fathers of the English Dominican Province. 2nd and rev. ed. London: Burns, Oates & Washbourne, 1920.

———. *Tractatus De Spiritualibus Creaturis.* Edited by L. W. Keeler. Rome: Gregoriana University Press, 1938.

———. *Truth.* 3 vols. Chicago: Regnery, 1952.

Tolstaya, Katya. *Kaleidoscope: F. M. Dostoevsky and the Early Dialectical Theology.* Leiden: Brill, 2013.

Tolstoy, Leo. *My Confession; My Religion; The Gospel in Brief.* Complete Works of Lyof N. Tolstoi 8. New York: Crowell, 1899.

"Tolstoy's Grave." https://izi.travel/en/browse/1552fdf3-6450-4893-b4e7-d243a1f34b4f.

Torrell, Jean-Pierre. "Collationes in Decem Preceptis." *Revue des sciences philosophiques et théologiques* 69 (1985) 227–63.

Traherne, Thomas. *Centuries of Meditations.* Edited by Bertram Dobell. London: Dobell, 1908.

Ugobi-Onyemere, Mary Christine. *The Knowledge of the First Principles in Saint Thomas Aquinas.* Oxford: Lang, 2015.

Ulrich, Ferdinand. *Homo Abyssus: The Drama of the Question of Being.* Translated by D. C. Schindler. Washington, DC: Humanum Academic Press, 2018.

Unamuno, Miguel. *Our Lord Don Quixote: The Life of Don Quixote and Sancho with Related Essays.* Translated by Anthony Kerrigan. Princeton: Princeton University Press, 1967.

———. *Tragic Sense of Life.* Translated by J. E. Crawford Flitch. Mineola, NY: Dover, 1952.

Underhill, Evelyn. *Jacopone da Todi, Poet and Mystic 1228–1306: A Spiritual Biography.* London: Dent, 1919.

United States Conference of Catholic Bishops. "Greater Access to Contraception Does Not Reduce Abortions." http://www.usccb.org/issues-and-action/human-life-and-dignity/contraception/fact-sheets/greater-access-to-contraception-does-not-reduce-abortions.cfm.

van Goubergen, Martine. "Concerning Shestov's Conception of Ethics." *Studies in East European Thought* 48 (1996) 223–29.

van Tongeren, Paul. "Nietzsche's Revaluation of the Cardinal Virtues the Case of Sophrosyne." *Phronimon* 3.1 (2001) 128–49.

Vattimo, Gianni, and Pier Aldo Rovatti, eds. *Weak Thought.* Albany: State University of New York Press, 2012.

Velde, Rudi te. *Aquinas on God: The "Divine Science" of the Summa Theologiae.* Burlington, VT: Ashgate, 2006.

Voegelin, Eric. *Autobiographical Reflections.* Edited by Ellis Sandoz. Collected Works of Eric Voegelin 34. Baton Rouge: Louisiana State University Press, 1989.

———. "The Beginning and the Beyond." In *What Is History? And Other Late Unpublished Writings,* edited by Thomas A. Hollweck and Paul Caringella, 173–232. Collected Works of Eric Voegelin 28. Columbia: University of Missouri Press, 1990.

———. "Deformations of Faith." Lecture given at the seminar "Between Nothingness and Paradise: Faith." Center for Constructive Alternatives, Hillsdale College, Hillsdale, MI, 1977.

———. "The Gospel and Culture." In *Jesus and Man's Hope,* edited by Donald G. Miller and Dikran Y. Hadidian, 2:59–101. Pittsburgh: Pittsburgh Theological Seminary Press, 1971.

———. *Hitler and the Germans.* Translated and edited by Detlev Clemens and Brendan Purcell. Collected Works of Eric Voegelin 31. Columbia: University of Missouri Press, 1999.

———. *New Science of Politics.* Chicago: University of Chicago Press, 1987.

———. *Order and History.* Vol. 1, *Israel and Revelation.* Edited by Maurice P. Hogan. Collected Works of Eric Voegelin 14. Columbia: University of Missouri Press, 2001.

———. *Order and History.* Vol. 2, *The World of the Polis.* Edited by Athanasios Moulakis. Collected Works of Eric Voegelin 15. Columbia: University of Missouri Press, 2000.

———. *Order and History.* Vol. 3, *Plato and Aristotle.* Edited by Dante Germino. Collected Works of Eric Voegelin 16. Columbia: University of Missouri Press, 1999.

———. *Order and History.* Vol. 4, *The Ecumenic Age.* Baton Rouge: Louisiana State University Press, 1974.

———. *Published Essays, 1966–1985.* Edited by Ellis Sandoz. Collected Works of Eric Voegelin 12. Baton Rouge: Louisiana State University Press, 1990.

———. "The Republic." In *Order and History: Plato and Aristotle,* edited by Dante Germino, 3:46–134. Collected Works of Eric Voegelin 16. Columbia: University of Missouri Press, 1999.

———. *Science, Politics, Gnosticism.* Chicago: Regnery, 1968.

———. *What Is History? And Other Late Unpublished Writings.* Edited by Thomas A. Hollweck and Paul Caringella. Collected Works of Eric Voegelin 28. Columbia: University of Missouri Press, 1990.

von Speyr, Adrienne. *Confession.* San Francisco: Ignatius, 1985.

———. *The Cross: Word and Sacrament.* Translated by Graham Harrison. San Francisco: Ignatius, 2018.

Walsh, David. *After Ideology: Recovering the Spiritual Foundations of Freedom.* Washington, DC: Catholic University of America Press, 1995.

———. *Guarded by Mystery: Meaning in a Postmodern Age.* Washington, DC: Catholic University of America Press, 1999.

———. "Kant's 'Copernican Revolution' as Existential." In *The Modern Philosophical Revolution: The Luminosity of Existence,* 27–75. Cambridge: Cambridge University Press, 2008.

———. *The Modern Philosophical Revolution: The Luminosity of Existence.* Cambridge: Cambridge University Press, 2008.

———. "The Politics of Liberty." In *Guarded by Mystery: Meaning in a Postmodern Age,* 123–46. Washington, DC: Catholic University of America Press, 1999.

Watkin, Edward Ingram. *The Catholic Centre.* London: Sheed & Ward, 1945.

Waugh, Evelyn. *Brideshead Revisited.* New York: Back Bay, 2008.

Wax, Amy, and Larry Alexander. "Paying the Price for Breakdown of the Country's Bourgeois Culture." *Philadelphia Inquirer,* August 9th, 2017. https://www.philly.com/philly/opinion/commentary/paying-the-price-for-breakdown-of-the-countrys-bourgeois-culture-20170809.html.

Wells, H. G. *The Invisible Man.* Mineola, NY: Dover, 1992.

West, Perry. "What Mary Eberstadt Told Notre Dame about 'Humanae Vitae.'" *Catholic News Agency,* March 20th, 2018. https://www.catholicnewsagency.com/news/what-mary-eberstadt-told-notre-dame-about-humanae-vitae-52203.

Whitehead, Alfred North. *The Dialogues of Alfred North Whitehead.* Edited by Lucien Price. Boston: Godine, 2001.

Wilhelmsen, Frederick. *Christianity and Political Philosophy.* New York: Routledge, 2017.

———. *Citizen of Rome: Reflections from the Life of a Roman Catholic.* LaSalle, IL: Sherwood Sugden, 1978.

———. "The Natural Law, Religion and the Crisis of the Twentieth Century." *Modern Age* 10.2 (1966) 145–48.

Wilhelmsen, Frederick, and Willmoore Kendall. "Cicero and the Politics of the Public Orthodoxy." In *Christianity and Political Philosophy*, by Frederick Wilhelmsen, 25–59. New York: Routledge, 2017.

Williams, Charles. *The Figure of Beatrice*. Berkeley: Apocryphile, 2005.

Wippel, John F. *The Metaphysical Thought of Thomas Aquinas: From Finite Being to Uncreated Being*. Washington, DC: Catholic University of America Press, 2000.

———. "Truth in Thomas Aquinas (Part I-II)." *Review of Metaphysics* 43 (1990) 295–326.

Wittgenstein, Ludwig. *Culture and Value*. Translated by Peter Winch. Chicago: University of Chicago Press, 1980.

———. *Lecture on Ethics*. Edited by Edoardo Zamuner et al. Chichester, UK: Wiley, 2014.

———. *Philosophical Grammar*. Translated by Anthony Kenny. Oxford: Blackwell, 1974.

Wood, Ralph C. "Dostoevsky on Evil as a Perversion of Personhood: A Reading of Ivan Karamazov and the Grand Inquisitor." In *Dostoevsky's Polyphonic Talent*, edited by Joe E. Barnhart, 1–24. Lanham: University Press of America, 2005.

———. "Ivan Karamazov's Mistake." *First Things* (December 2002). https://www.firstthings.com/article/2002/12/ivan-karamazovs-mistake.

Wyers, Frances. *Miguel de Unamuno, the Contrary Self*. London: Tamesis, 1976.

Young, Sarah. *Dostoevsky's* The Idiot *and the Ethical Foundations of Narrative*. London: Anthem, 2004.

Zubiri, Xavier. *On Essence*. Translated by A. Robert Caponigri. Washington, DC: Catholic University Press of America, 1980.

Index

Schaff, Philip, 94
Sheck, Laurie, 47, 83
Shestov, Lev, xxix, 43, 68, 79, 293
Simon, Julian, 315–16
Simpson, Christopher Ben, 105
Singer, Peter, 297, 308, 310
Singh, Susheela, 307
socialism, 178, 180–81, 183–84, 195
Solovyov, Vladimir, 65, 174
Sophocles, 21, 23
sophrosyne, 164, 188
Speck Paula K, 138
Spencer, Herbert, 165
Steptoe, Andrew, 41
Strauss, Leo, 13, 19
subordinated ethic, xiii, xviii, xix–
    xxvii, xxix, xxx, xxxvi, 2,
    38–114, 119–20, 123, 130,
    137, 142, 160, 164, 171, 176,
    198, 209, 223, 236, 255, 259,
    270, 274–75, 278, 280, 285,
    289, 293, 295, 302, 306
suffering, xxx, xli, 13, 20, 33, 70, 76,
    80, 90, 141, 149, 151, 190–
    93, 199, 203, 265, 310
synderesis, xxxii, xxxiii

temporality, xix, xxii, xxxiii–xxxix,
    xl, xli, 1, 11, 16–17, 39,
    65–66, 98, 108, 138–39, 179,
    195, 199, 208, 210–12, 232,
    236, 241–42, 245, 251–52,
    254, 285, 287, 318
Teresa of Calcutta, Saint Mother,
    311
Tertullian, 297
Tolstaya, Katya, 127
Tolstoy, Leo, 28–29, 43, 53, 115, 203
Torrell, Jean-Pierre, 260
tradition, xii, xiv, xvii, xix, xxi, xxv,
    6, 18–19, 33, 36, 49, 66, 81,
    115–96, 223–24, 259, 280,
    282–86

Traherne, Thomas, 109, 181
transcendence, xiv, xxi, xxii, xxvii,
    xxx, xxxii, xxxviii, xli, 2, 10,
    13, 29, 30, 31, 34–35, 64,
    72, 77, 93, 95, 100, 103, 105,
    129, 150, 161, 163, 166, 168,
    170, 173, 177, 184, 189–200,
    207, 210–12, 216, 229,
    245–46, 253, 258, 262, 274,
    281–85, 287–89
trinitarian, 118, 120, 126

Ugobi-Onyemere, Mary Christine,
    49
Unamuno, Miguel, 15–20, 138, 342,
    344, 346
Underhill, Evelyn, 222

Van Goubergen, Martine, 68
Van Tongeren Paul, 184
Vattimo, Gianni, xxvii
Velde Rudi te, 48
virtue, xii, xiv, xxv, xxxiv, xli, 1, 3,
    6–8, 18, 40, 54, 68, 71, 81,
    84–85, 88, 90, 92, 133, 135,
    163–89, 210, 248, 255, 257,
    291, 295, 303
Voeglin, Eric, xxviii, xxxvii, 18, 171,
    177, 183, 292, 325, 344
Von Speyr, Adrienne, xxxvii

Walsh, David, xx, xxxviii, 116
Waugh, Evelyn, 29
Wax, Amy, 314
West, Perry, 317
Wilhelmsen, Frederick, xxi, 62,
    70–71, 77, 121, 165, 345
Wippel, John F, 200
Wittgenstein, Ludwig, xviii, 52–53,
    291–92
Wyers, Frances, 138

Young, Sarah, 22

www.ingramcontent.com/pod-product-compliance
Lightning Source LLC
Chambersburg PA
CBHW031935090426
42811CB00002B/189